CU00949987

# ARCHAEOLOGY IN
# GLOUCESTERSHIRE

*Frontispiece*
Nympsfield chambered tomb: view from the east after re-excavation prior
to restoration in 1974. (Photo: Alan Saville).

# ARCHAEOLOGY IN GLOUCESTERSHIRE

## FROM THE EARLIEST HUNTERS TO THE INDUSTRIAL AGE

Essays dedicated to Helen O'Neil and the late Elsie Clifford

Edited by

## Alan Saville

Jointly published by Cheltenham Art Gallery and Museums and the Bristol and Gloucestershire Archaeological Society.

Cheltenham

1984

First published 1984

Copyright © 1984 Cheltenham Art Gallery and Museums, the Bristol and Gloucestershire Archaeological Society, and the individual authors.

ISBN 0 905157 09 5

*Front cover*  The complete skeleton of an adult male inhumation placed at the entrance to the north chamber of the neolithic chambered tomb at Hazleton, excavated in 1981. (Photo: Alan Saville.)

*Rear cover*  Salvage excavation in progress in 1977 in an area of late Saxon and medieval features at North Street, Winchcombe. (Photo: Alan Saville.)

Typeset in Plantin by
Alan Sutton Publishing Limited
Designed by Alan Saville
Printed in Great Britain

# Contents

Prefaces                                                        7

Editor's introduction and acknowledgements                      9

List of contributors                                           12

Abbreviations                                                  15

PART ONE: TWO GLOUCESTERSHIRE ARCHAEOLOGISTS

Elsie M. Clifford: the person and the work                     19
  *Richard Reece*

Bibliography of the works of Mrs Elsie Margaret Clifford OBE FSA  26
  *Elizabeth Hall and Alan Saville*

Helen O'Neil: a personal appreciation                          31
  *Margaret U. Jones*

Bibliography of the works of Mrs Helen Evangeline O'Neil MBE FSA  38
  *Elizabeth Hall and Alan Saville*

PART TWO: THE PHYSICAL BACKGROUND TO
  GLOUCESTERSHIRE ARCHAEOLOGY

A summary of the geology and geomorphology of Gloucestershire   47
  *Gordon Margretts*

PART THREE: GLOUCESTERSHIRE PREHISTORY

Palaeolithic and mesolithic evidence from Gloucestershire       59
  *Alan Saville*

Neolithic Gloucestershire                                      80
  *Tim Darvill*

Bronze age Gloucestershire: artefacts and distributions        113
  *Ann Ellison*

The bronze age round barrows of Gloucestershire: a brief review     128
    *John Drinkwater and Alan Saville*

The iron age in Gloucestershire: a review of the evidence     140
    *Alan Saville*

## PART FOUR: ROMAN GLOUCESTERSHIRE

The Cotswolds: an essay on some aspects and problems of Roman
    rural settlement     181
    *Richard Reece*

Romano-British settlement in the Gloucestershire Thames Valley     191
    *David Miles*

The cities and large rural settlements of Roman Gloucestershire     212
    *Alan McWhirr*

## PART FIVE: GLOUCESTERSHIRE IN SAXON AND MEDIEVAL TIMES

Anglo-Saxon Gloucestershire     225
    *Carolyn Heighway*

Late Saxon and medieval pottery in Gloucestershire     248
    *Alan G. Vince*

The study of deserted villages in Gloucestershire     276
    *Mick Aston and Linda Viner*

Medieval urban archaeology in Gloucestershire     294
    *Roger Leech*

The medieval houses of rural Gloucestershire     304
    *Lionel F.J. Walrond*

## PART SIX: GLOUCESTERSHIRE IN THE INDUSTRIAL AGE

Industrial archaeology in Gloucestershire     317
    *David Viner*

Index of places     343

# Prefaces

It is with great pleasure that Cheltenham Art Gallery & Museums co-sponsor this invaluable work with the Bristol and Gloucestershire Archaeological Society. At the moment the Museums sadly lack an archaeologist on the curatorial staff, and it is to Alan Saville, the editor of this volume, that we turn for advice and help with regard to our very important collections on the archaeology of Gloucestershire and their display. This input on his part is, of course, over and above his already full programme of work, but it is a vital input and one that keeps archaeology very much alive within the Museums' service.

To celebrate the publication of this volume we have decided to base our major exhibition for 1984 around it, and hope that it will appeal to a wide audience. I would particularly echo Alan Saville's words in his introduction about the book – and the exhibition – being of use to those involved in historical education within the county. With the only professional museum education service in the county, we take our responsibilities in this area very seriously.

I would like to add my thanks to those of Alan Saville to all those who have helped in the preparation of this volume, but it is to him that a special debt is due for welding the wide-ranging texts together, and by this act filling a gap in the existing literature that has sadly existed for too long.

George Breeze
Director
Cheltenham Art Gallery & Museums
May 1984

New knowledge of the antiquity of what is today the county of Gloucestershire has come in abundance during recent years. Neolithic occupation and burial at Crickley Hill and Hazleton, substantial Romano-British settlement at Kingscote, and the earliest remains of St Oswald's Priory in Saxon Gloucester furnish just a few examples of this progress in knowledge by excavation, while equal progress has been achieved by the final publication of work at, for example, Roman Barnsley Park and Cirencester. It is, therefore, appropriate that new perspectives of Gloucestershire's past be essayed, by scholars at the forefront of research in all the periods of the historical continuum. And what better than to associate this survey, itself reflecting new and more traditional archaeological approaches, with two people who have contributed by excavation and publication so successfully and so enduringly to recovery of knowledge of this Cotswold region's past, Mrs Helen O'Neil and the late Mrs Elsie Clifford ? The Bristol and Gloucestershire Archaeological Society, in accordance with its permanent aim of supporting research and publication on the county's past, is pleased to join with the Cheltenham Art Gallery & Museums in the publication of this volume.

Peter Warren
Chairman of Council 1981–1984
The Bristol and Gloucestershire Archaeological Society
May 1984

In Memoriam

It is sad to have to record that Helen O'Neil died at Northleach on 23rd August 1984, when this volume was at press. The editor wishes to express his personal regrets, and those of the contributors and publishers, and hopes that the chapter about Mrs O'Neil will be regarded as a not inappropriate tribute.

# Editor's Introduction and Acknowledgements

The origin of this volume lies in a one-day symposium on 'The Archaeology of Gloucestershire' held at the College of St Paul and St Mary, The Park, Cheltenham, on the 8th September 1979 as part of the Prehistoric Society's Cotswold Conference. The intention, from the outset, was that the symposium proceedings should be published, and this was greatly encouraged by the success of the actual event. Since 1979 there have been numerous difficulties in translating this idea into a reality, but all the problems were finally resolved at the beginning of 1984 when Cheltenham Art Gallery and Museums and the Bristol and Gloucestershire Archaeological Society jointly undertook to sponsor the publication.

Twelve of the articles published here stem directly from the half-hour-long contributions given at, or prepared for, the symposium. These have all been extensively revised or completely re-written for this publication. The articles by Aston and Viner, Miles, and Walrond were written at the special request of the editor in order to fill obvious omissions in the coverage of the volume. The date at the end of each article indicates when the author's final typescript was submitted for publication.

Taken as a whole, the papers in this volume offer a representative overview of Gloucestershire archaeology as at the beginning of 1984, and thereby fill a notable gap in the existing literature, since there is no other survey of the archaeology of the modern county. The aim has been to offer a review of the present state of knowledge, which would be of use not only to archaeologists, but also to the interested general public, and in particular to those involved in historical education within the county, where the lack of a work of this kind has been particularly acute. Emphasis has been placed on making the accompanying bibliographies as comprehensive as possible, as an aid to further research. Naturally the individual papers differ in their approach and their scope. This is partly a reflection of the way in which archaeology has developed within the county; for example, iron age studies are well-established whereas this is not yet the case with the study of medieval villages. It is also a reflection of the depth of study which has been achieved, so that the neolithic and medieval pottery chapters have the benefit of arising directly from recent PhD theses, and thus include brand new research findings, while other contributions are necessarily restricted to a summary of material already published. Nevertheless, the coverage is extensive for almost every period and aspect of Gloucestershire archaeology, the only obvious exception being a wider consideration of Roman settlement, including the famous villas such as Chedworth and their mosaics. This omission is deliberate, in that the topic has recently received separate publication by one of the contributors to this volume (McWhirr, *Roman Gloucestershire*, 1981) and repetition seemed neither necessary nor desirable.

The message these papers collectively convey is that archaeology in Gloucestershire is flourishing, with many exciting developments of national importance taking place, which give this volume a significance far beyond that of a local survey. This is not to sound complacent about the state of archaeology in the county, however, since there are urgent problems concerning the preservation of archaeological sites and historic buildings, and with regard to the local organization of rescue archaeology. There is also one theme running throughout this volume, irrespective of period, which demands comment. This is the paucity of archaeological research which has taken place in Gloucestershire west of the River Severn; clearly a remedy for this situation must be found.

This volume, like the symposium which preceded it, is dedicated to Mrs Helen O'Neil and the late Mrs Elsie Clifford. The dedication was conceived as an acknowledgement by the current practitioners of archaeology in Gloucestershire of the enormous debt owed to these two women for their pioneering work within the county. This debt is made manifest by the bibliographies of their published works, and is given a personal dimension by the tributes from Margaret Jones and Richard Reece, which were specially prepared for this volume. I first met both Mrs Clifford and Mrs O'Neil in 1974, when I began work in the county, and it is a pleasure to be able to add my own thanks to these outstanding local archaeologists who, by the example of their work, have given me the motivation to see the present volume published.

My acknowledgements in an undertaking of this kind are necessarily legion, and I must apologize in advance for any that are overlooked. First and foremost, my grateful thanks are due to all my contributors, who have all been most co-operative and have shown great forbearance during the extended gestation of the volume. Secondly I must thank all those who had a direct hand in the preparation of the publication, especially Elizabeth Hall for her skilful typing and editorial help, Jonathan Hoyle and Marian Hoyle for their assistance with the illustrations, and Annette Carruthers for sharing many of the more tedious editorial chores. These thanks extend to all my colleagues at Cheltenham Museum, particularly the present Director, George Breeze, and his deputy, Steven Blake, and their respective predecessors David Addison and Mary Greensted, both for their help and for encouraging the happy and stimulating environment in which fruitful research can be pursued. For my own continual involvement in the practical archaeology of the county over the last ten years I must thank the Inspectorate of Ancient Monuments of the Department of the Environment and Western Archaeological Trust. For other assistance with this volume I am grateful to Mr R. Bryant, Professor G.E. Daniel, Miss C.I. Fell, Mrs M. Gardiner, Mr L. Jones, Mrs M.U. Jones, Mr W.T. Jones, Mr G. Kelsey, Dr R. Reece, and Mr R. Reed.

Finally, I am indebted to Cheltenham Art Gallery and Museums, especially the Director, George Breeze, and to the Bristol and Gloucestershire Archaeological Society, especially the Chairman, Professor Peter Warren, and the Hon. Treasurer, Gerard Leighton, for their support and confidence, which have allowed this book to be published. It remains to add that any shortcomings in the presentation are the sole responsibility of the editor.

Alan Saville
Cheltenham, April 1984

# List of Contributors

M.A. Aston BA FSA MIFA

Staff Tutor in Archaeology
University of Bristol
Department of Extra-Mural Studies
32 Tyndall's Park Road
Bristol BS8 1HR

T.C. Darvill BA PhD

Part-time Tutor in Archaeology
(University of Bristol
Department of Extra-Mural Studies)
209 Seymour Road
Gloucester GL1 5HR

J.H. Drinkwater LRSC
CertArch

Part-time Tutor in Archaeology
(University of Bristol
Department of Extra-Mural Studies)
44 Oakdale Court
Downend
Bristol BS16 6DU

A.B. Ellison BA PhD
FSA MIFA

Free-lance Archaeologist
c/o Western Archaeological Trust
City Museum and Art Gallery
Queens Road
Clifton
Bristol BS8 1RL

E.M. Hall BA

Archaeological Assistant
Western Archaeological Trust
Cheltenham Art Gallery and Museums
40 Clarence Street
Cheltenham GL50 3NX

C.M. Heighway BA FSA MIFA

Free-lance Archaeologist
6 Church Street
King's Stanley
Stroud
Glos GL10 3HW

M.U. Jones BA FSA

Director
Mucking Post-excavation
Thurrock Museum
Orsett Road
Grays
Essex RM17 5DX

R.H. Leech MA PhD FSA

Investigator
National Monuments Record
Royal Commission on Historical
    Monuments (England)
Green Lane
Southampton
Hants SO1 9FP

A.D. McWhirr BSc MA PhD FSA MIFA

Senior Lecturer
School of Humanities
Leicester Polytechnic/
Director of Excavations
Cirencester Excavation Committee
37 Dovedale Road
Stoneygate
Leicester LE2 2DN

G. Margretts MSc ARCS FGS

Principal Lecturer in Geology
Department of Geography and Geology
The College of St Paul and St Mary
The Park
Cheltenham GL50 2RH

D. Miles BA FSA

Deputy Director
Oxford Archaeological Unit
46 Hythe Bridge Street
Oxford OX1 2EP

R. Reece BSc DPhil FSA

Senior Lecturer in Roman Archaeology
Institute of Archaeology
University of London
31–34 Gordon Square
London WC1H OPY

A. Saville BA FSA MIFA

Archaeological Field Officer
Western Archaeological Trust
Cheltenham Art Gallery and Museums
40 Clarence Street
Cheltenham GL50 3NX

A.G. Vince BA PhD

Deputy Finds Officer
Department of Urban Archaeology
Museum of London
London Wall
London EC2Y 5HN

D.J. Viner BA FSA FMA

Museums Curator
Corinium Museum
Park Street
Cirencester
Glos GL7 2BX

L. Viner BA

Editorial Assistant
Cirencester Excavation Committee
Corinium Museum
Park Street
Cirencester
Glos GL7 2BX

L.F.J. Walrond FSA FMA

Curator
Stroud District (Cowle) Museum
Lansdown
Stroud
Glos GL5 1BB

# Abbreviations

*Organizations*

| | |
|---|---|
| CBA | Council for British Archaeology |
| CRAAGS | Committee for Rescue Archaeology in Avon, Gloucestershire, and Somerset (1973–1982) |
| DOE | Department of the Environment |
| GADARG | Gloucester and District Archaeological Research Group |
| GSIA | Gloucestershire Society for Industrial Archaeology |
| NMR | National Monuments Record |
| O.S. | Ordnance Survey |
| RCHM(E) | Royal Commission on Historical Monuments (England) |
| WAT | Western Archaeological Trust (formerly CRAAGS) |

*Dates*

Dates given in lower case (bc etc.) refer to uncorrected and uncalibrated radiocarbon years, those in upper case (BC etc.) refer to calendar years.

| | |
|---|---|
| bp, BP | before present (i.e. AD1950) |
| bc, BC | before Christ |
| ad, AD | *anno Domini* |

*Measurements*

| | |
|---|---|
| ha | hectare(s) |
| km | kilometre(s) |
| m | metre(s) |
| mm | millimetre(s) |

*Miscellaneous abbreviations used in the text*

| | |
|---|---|
| *c.* | *circa* |
| cf. | compare |
| MBE | Member of the Order of the British Empire |

| | |
|---|---|
| NGR | National Grid Reference |
| OBE | Officer of the Order of the British Empire |
| O.D. | Ordnance Datum (the standard sea-level of the Ordnance Survey) |
| pers. comm. | personal communication |
| TF | type fabric |

*References*

All bibliographic abbreviations follow the standard conventions adopted by the CBA, except in the following instances:

| | |
|---|---|
| Archaeol Rev | Archaeological Review (published annually on behalf of CBA Groups 12 and 13 by the University of Bristol Department of Extra-Mural Studies between 1966–1972) |
| BAR Brit Ser | British Archaeological Reports, British Series |
| BAR Int Ser | British Archaeological Reports, International Series |
| Glevensis | Annual Review of the Gloucester and District Archaeological Research Group |
| GSIAJ | Journal of the Gloucestershire Society for Industrial Archaeology |
| PCNFC | Proceedings of the Cotteswold Naturalists Field Club |
| PPS | Proceedings of the Prehistoric Society |
| TBGAS | Transactions of the Bristol and Gloucestershire Archaeological Society |

Other abbreviations used in the bibliographies:

| | |
|---|---|
| ed(s). | editor(s) |
| (rev) edn | (revised) edition |
| n.d. | not dated |
| Res Rep | Research Report |

# PART ONE:

# TWO GLOUCESTERSHIRE ARCHAEOLOGISTS

# Elsie M Clifford:
# The Person and the Work

## Richard Reece

I first met Mrs Clifford in June 1955 and my memories of her therefore only span the twenty-one years from then until her death in 1976. This misses out seventy of her ninety-one years, during which her archaeological activity stretched from observations made of gravel-digging during the First World War to the excavation of Bagendon. Mrs Clifford's father was a farmer and her husband owned and ran a successful garage; she therefore had the time and resources to devote herself to archaeology and remained proud of her amateur status. Her early discoveries in the Gloucester region brought her to the notice of the Cambridge faculty where she spent a year as a mature student (Daniel 1976). The links and friendships that she formed at Cambridge remained strong until her death, and the knowledge that she gained there was put to immediate use in a series of excavations in Gloucestershire. Bagendon was really the first site she touched that had not previously been excavated or assaulted, so that the series of long barrows – Notgrove, Nympsfield, Rodmarton – and the Roman villas – Hucclecote and Witcombe – were all campaigns of re-excavation, tidying up and re-interpretation, often in advance of consolidation or display by the Office of Works. But among these excavations of national importance there were a host of smaller digs and observations which ranged over all periods of the past and resulted in anything from a full article in 'B & G' to an entry on her card index or just a few words on her set of '6-inch' maps. There is no need to give the chronology of these events for they were written up with such speed that

*Figure 1*  Excavations at Notgrove long barrow, 1935. (Reprinted from the *Cheltenham Chronicle and Gloucestershire Graphic*, 7 September 1935.)

her bibliography gives an accurate picture of this aspect of her life, year by year.

Mrs Clifford was an important figure in the early days of the Prehistoric Society and she served on the Council of the Society of Antiquaries of London. Locally she had the distinction of being the first woman member of the Cotteswold Naturalists' Field Club in 1920, and their first woman President in 1936, then going on to become the first woman President of the Bristol and Gloucestershire Archaeological Society in 1949 (Ralph 1976). The award of an OBE in 1968 gave her much pleasure.

In Mrs Clifford the person and the work were inextricably combined and so far as I can see the public and the private were one. All this made for complete consistency, she practised a 'human' archaeology, and she led an archaeological life. In her last years she was very proud of having tidied up all her loose ends, published all her notes and minor sites, and disposed of all her material, notes, and maps. But this did not mean that she had retired from archaeology, it meant that she could sit back and enjoy the subject, and most of its practitioners, as they came across to her, through visits, letters, books, and gossip. She was under no illusions about her age, and, from time to time, would say that she did not particularly want to reach her ninetieth year, but this was always followed by a firm recognition that she would have to take things as they came. Each visit, usually in the holidays between each term, would terminate with my promise to come over and see her in the next holiday; to which her inevitable response was 'Well, I might not be here then'. The acceptable reply was that I would ring up, and if she *was* still there I would come over, if she wasn't I couldn't. A smile would always greet this matter-of-fact line, a wave of the hand, and then absorption in a pot plant which was ailing, or a seedling which needed water.

It is not impossible to get to know someone at the age of seventy and to remember them as an attractive and clear-minded person for twenty-one years, but it is very unusual. When Mrs Clifford and Dame Joan Evans (who perhaps also deserves mention in a volume of Gloucestershire archaeology, however acid she could be about diggers of post-holes) were both confined to their homes and no longer met, a certain rivalry grew up. Perhaps I felt a slightly malicious glee, when Dame Joan would intone devoutly 'Poor dear

*Figure 2*   Site tour at Bagendon, 1956. Mrs Clifford with Sir Mortimer Wheeler. (Photograph by Mr Leslie Jones.)

Elsie, I hear she really is wandering now', in saying with perfect truth, right up to the last time I saw her, 'Not at all, I saw her last week and she was as clear as anything; rather frail of course'. But parity had to be preserved, and when Mrs Clifford said with a sigh 'Poor Joan, I'm afraid she is rather sad now', it was true, and accepted, to say 'Well she was on very good form last week'. I do not just mean that she remained clear-minded, I mean something much more: her ways of thought were still flexible. Sometimes I would say something which surprised or slightly shocked her; then she would think about it and either change her mind aloud, working her way through her surprise, or she would sit silent for a little and then decide that she did not wish to change her view by saying perhaps, 'No, that's not for me'. But the great thing was that invariably she retained the agility to consider new ideas. She stuck to some very definite prejudices – 'That man has a card index where his heart ought to be' – but I can recall very few for whom I was not allowed to plead a cause.

A constant feature in my experience of the years from tea-time at Bagendon to the last time that I saw her was a particularly succulent bake of ginger-cake. This cake arouses memories in many archaeological minds: to quote only one, Professor Grimes remembers from his wartime digs at Bibury visits from Mrs Clifford, who scrutinized the site in detail, but felt that he needed sustenance and always left him not only with encouragement, but also with a slab of ginger-cake. Hospitality was a constant theme in her life, and a powerful means of remaining very closely in touch with the archaeological world after her days of actual digging were over. Who else would firmly invite the whole Ancient Monuments Board to sherry in the garden when they were on a summer tour in the area? This was not head-hunting, it was a straightforward welcome, and it was extended equally to Cambridge undergraduates in the area for their summer field trip, except that she recognized that they needed something more sustaining than just sherry. And their response and thanks conveyed by Brian Hope-Taylor in the form of a be-ribboned tin of cat-food for Tiny Sing, a large, indolent feline inside a shock of long, silky, black hair, delighted her more than any other gift of the year.

Her long life in archaeological circles meant that she moved with complete ease among the great names who flashed across the screen of my schoolboy-view of the digging world. She acted as a transformer, in the electrical sense, through whom Sir Mortimer Wheeler or Gordon Childe, Derek Allen, Stuart Piggott, Glyn Daniel, Molly Cotton, and a host of others were changed for the moment from international celebrities to human people who, if they did what was required of them for Gloucestershire, would be

*Figure 3*   Mrs Clifford's eightieth birthday party in 1966 at Charlton Kings,
Cheltenham, with Professor Glyn Daniel and Sir Mortimer Wheeler.
(Photograph by Cheltenham Newspaper Co. Ltd.; reproduced from a
print lent by Professor Daniel.)

rewarded with excellent meals over a weekend. For Wheeler at Bagendon the
lawnmower would be brought over from Witcombe, the baulks would be cut
and tended, and, on the morning of the visit, freshly-painted grid-pegs would
be set up at approved intervals in the Wheeler manner, only to be gathered in
for use the next year, or whenever he came again. For Childe, a morning's
digging – 'He always likes to get the feel of a site' – and then Mrs Clifford
disappeared into the toolshed to reappear in visiting clothes looking a little
apprehensive – 'I do wish he would let me drive, he really is dangerous' – to
be driven off to lunch at the De Navarros' at Broadway. For Dr Cotton it
would be a more professional, medical occasion, when the living-in
Scandinavian au pair took refuge in a fit of temporary derangement from the
perhaps rather dull life of house-keeping for an elderly lady. (That
experiment was not repeated, and local home help triumphed.)

Mrs Clifford did not eschew controversy, but, I think, preferred where
possible to make peace rather than war. That said, it would be wrong to

ignore the long-standing rift between her and the other archaeologist honoured in this volume, Helen O'Neil. I have the feeling that I got to know both ladies too late to get the full flavour of their disagreements, but I also feel that these were less the result of personal animosity than of a divergence in their attitudes towards archaeology. Perhaps Mrs Clifford's firm amateur status had provided room for disagreement in the past. This was a 'feud', though in my experience only smouldering, and it was neither helpful nor productive. But my meaning there is exact and not full of implications, for neither did it hinder. As a firm Bagendon worker I was not regarded as misbehaving in taking tea with Mrs O'Neil, and while coolness might prevail during mention of either party to the other, this was not a serious gaff.

Later on there was certainly a territorial feeling in the air when, for example, a Hillfort Committee was formed in Oxford to examine the problems of the Cotswold hillforts. My next visit for tea suggested to me a thunder-cloud positioned somewhere over Leckhampton or Crickley, and phrases were used concerning 'these bright young things who come and dig without knowing anything about the area'. Within a few years the diggers whom these bright young things brought along were being regaled at Little Witcombe House with sandwiches and the ubiquitous ginger-cake, and cordial relations had been established.

Bagendon remained a slight worry until her death. All her other work she regarded as re-excavation or recording, but Bagendon was her own project and she directed its excavation from the age of sixty-nine to seventy-one. Publication caused problems, but many people took over different aspects and the final book had the atmosphere of a Festschrift. That was not the end. People wrote articles about finds from the site, questioned the dating, and re-examined the pottery. She realized it was inevitable, but my first duty on many visits was to advise whether I thought she ought to 'do something' about the latest article. 'Doing something' at times raised the utterly impossible spectre of further excavation so that I hope that my suggestion of myself organizing further work on the site shifted some of the possible worries. She did not live to see the work, but I think she would have approved of what has been done, mainly by Steve Trow, a research student at the Institute of Archaeology. My only quarrel with his excellent studies on the Bagendon material is that he will refer to some authority called 'Clifford (1961)'. She wasn't 'Clifford', though I suppose in the future she must be, she was Mrs Clifford, a real person, who had a very great influence on the lives and careers of a whole generation of archaeologists, the youngest of whom turned up at Bagendon one day with the carefully rehearsed phrase: 'Mrs Clifford?' – 'Yes'. 'I'm Richard Reece and I want to dig'.

REFERENCES

Daniel, G.E. 1976. Mrs E.M. Clifford: obituary. *The Times*, 7 September 1976.

Ralph, E. 1976. The Society 1876–1976. In P. McGrath and J. Cannon (eds.), *Essays in Bristol and Gloucestershire history*, 1–49. Bristol. (Centenary volume of the Bristol and Gloucestershire Archaeological Society.)

**February 1984**

# Bibliography of the Works of
# Mrs Elsie Margaret Clifford OBE FSA

*Elizabeth Hall and Alan Saville*

### 1930

A prehistoric and Roman site at Barnwood near Gloucester. *TBGAS* 52, 201–254.

### 1933

An Anglian cross in Gloucestershire. *Antiq J* 13, 301–302.
The Roman villa, Hucclecote, near Gloucester. *TBGAS* 55, 323–376.

### 1934

An early Iron Age site at Barnwood, Gloucestershire. *TBGAS* 56, 227–230.
Finds at Barnwood, Gloucester. *TBGAS* 56, 231–235.
An early British fragment. *Antiq J* 14(1), 59–61.

### 1935

13th century pendant, Barnwood. *TBGAS* 57, 278–279.
Notes on some Roman villas in Gloucestershire. *PCNFC* 25(3), 237–256.
Notgrove long barrow. *PCNFC* 25(3), 302.
Palaeolithic hand-axe, Barnwood. *PCNFC* 25(3), 303.

## 1936

Notgrove long barrow, Gloucestershire. *Archaeologia* 86, 119–161.
Notes on the Neolithic period in the Cotteswolds. *PCNFC* 26(1), 33–49.
Jackbarrow. *PCNFC* 26(1), 101.
Excavations at Rodborough. *PCNFC* 26(1), 101.
Possible prehistoric site near Cross Hands. *PCNFC* 26(1), 101–102.
Mollusca from Barnwood gravels. *PCNFC* 26(1), 102.

## 1937

The earthworks at Rodborough, Amberley, and Minchinhampton, Gloucestershire. *TBGAS* 59, 287–307.
Jackbarrow, Duntisbourne Abbots. *TBGAS* 59, 334–337.
The Beaker folk in the Cotswolds. *PPS* 3, 159–163.
A palaeolith from Gloucestershire. *PPS* 3, 465–466.
Archaeological objects of special interest in Gloucestershire. *PCNFC* 26(2), 159–168.
Discovery of beaker at Prestbury. *PCNFC* 26(2), 206.
Nympsfield long barrow. *PCNFC* 26(2), 206.

## 1938

Roman altars in Gloucestershire. *TBGAS* 60, 297–307.
A beaker found at Prestbury, Gloucestershire. *TBGAS* 60, 348–349.
Human remains, Charlton Kings. *TBGAS* 60, 350–351.
Underground chambers, Miserden. *TBGAS* 60, 343–346.
The excavation of Nympsfield long barrow, Gloucestershire. *PPS* 4, 188–213.
The Soldier's Grave, Frocester, Gloucestershire. *PPS* 4, 214–217.
The Beaker phase in Cotswold. *PCNFC* 26(3), 256–264.
Witcombe Roman villa. *PCNFC* 26(3), 328.
An early British enamel. *Antiq J* 18, 75–76.

## 1939

Witcombe Roman villa. *PCNFC* 27(1), 54.
Rodmarton long barrow. *PCNFC* 27(1), 54.
Palaeolith from the Upper Thames. *Antiq J* 19, 193.
Roman fir-cone of terra-cotta. *Antiq J* 19, 194.
(With C.A. Simpson.) A possible neolithic trackway. *Geography* 24, 230–239.

## 1940

(With G.E. Daniel.) The Rodmarton and Avening portholes. *PPS* 6, 133–165.

## 1942

Working oxen at Cirencester. *TBGAS* 63, 168–171.

## 1943

Palaeolithic implements from Little Alne, Alcester, Warwickshire. *PPS* 9, 52–54.

## 1944

Graves found at Hailes, Gloucestershire. *TBGAS* 65, 187–198.

## 1947

Mosaic floor at Cirencester. *TBGAS* 67, 381–395.

## 1948

Archaeology (notes). *PCNFC* 30(1), 50.

## 1949

The Severn as a highway in prehistoric times. *TBGAS* 68, 5–13.
Archaeology (notes). *PCNFC* 30(2), 201.

## 1950

The Ivy Lodge round barrow. *TBGAS* 69, 59–77.
The Cotswold megalithic cultures: the grave goods and their background. In C. Fox and B. Dickens (eds.), *The early cultures of north-west Europe (H.M. Chadwick memorial studies)*, 23–40. Cambridge.

## 1954

The Roman villa at Witcombe, Gloucestershire. *TBGAS* 73, 5–69.
(With D.A.E. Garrod and H.S. Gracie.) Flint implements from Gloucestershire. (1. Introduction and descriptions of the gravels.) *Antiq J* 34, 178–187.

## 1955

Stamped tiles found in Gloucestershire. *J Roman Stud* 45, 68–72.

## 1957

(With D.R. Brothwell.) A Romano-British burial at South Cerney, Gloucestershire. *TBGAS* 76, 157–160.

## 1959

Fossil reptiles and other animals. *PCNFC* 33(3), 94–99.
Review of W.J. Wedlake, 'Excavations at Camerton, Somerset, 1926–1956'. *Antiquity* 33, 308–309.

## 1960

H.R. Cox (obituary). *PCNFC* 33(4), 232.
Miss C.A. Simpson (obituary). *PCNFC* 33(4), 235.

## 1961

The Hucclecote Roman villa. *TBGAS* 80, 42–49.
Quenington, Gloucestershire. *TBGAS* 80, 93–98.
*Bagendon, a Belgic Oppidum.* Cambridge.

## 1963

Burial at Kingscote, Gloucestershire. *TBGAS* 82, 205–207.
Hailes church. *TBGAS* 82, 208–209.
Palaeolithic implements from Little Alne, Alcester, Warwickshire (note). *PPS* 29, 429.

## 1964

Two finds of beaker pottery from Gloucestershire. *TBGAS* 83, 34–39.
Early iron age pottery from Rodborough Common and Duntisbourne Abbots, *TBGAS* 83, 145–146.

## 1965

The prehistory of Gloucestershire. (Report of the RAI Summer Meeting, Cheltenham, 1965.) *Archaeol J* 122, 175–177.

## 1966

Tumulus near Bownhill long barrow. *TBGAS* 85, 214–215.
Hetty Pegler's Tump. *Antiquity* 40, 129–132.

## 1967

Skeletons from Gloucester. *TBGAS* 86, 199.
Underground chambers, Miserden (note). *TBGAS* 86, 200.

## 1968–69

Professor H.L. Hawkins, D.Sc., F.R.S. (obituary). *PCNFC* 35(3), 151.

# Helen O'Neil: A Personal Appreciation

*Margaret U. Jones*

Her sister, the artist Amy Donovan, has said that 'archaeology came to Helen'. This happened following the retirement of their father, Lt.-Colonel C. Donovan, from the Indian Medical Service, when the family settled at Bourton-on-the-Water in a Cotswold stone farmhouse with an added Georgian-style façade. The name of their home – The Camp House – reflects its siting, straddling the west entrance of the iron age hillfort of Salmonsbury Camp (O'Neil 1977, fig. 3). Until both sisters moved to Northleach in 1983, The Camp House was to be the base for Helen's involvement in Gloucestershire archaeology throughout the next fifty years.

When, in 1931, a local committee was set up to organize the excavations at Salmonsbury Camp, Helen Donovan, as she then was, readily undertook to become the Hon. Secretary, being admirably qualified by living on the site (Dunning 1976, 77; O'Neil 1977, 11). This chance experience stimulated Helen's interest in archaeology, and though she went on to excavate and record in many other places, Salmonsbury and Bourton Vale always retained their importance, both in her life and in her work.

The dig at Salmonsbury also led to Helen's meeting with Bryan O'Neil of the Ancient Monuments Branch of what was then the Ministry of Works. Following a brief period when Helen was Honorary Curator of the Corinium Museum at Cirencester, she and Bryan were married in 1939. Although Bryan O'Neil was Inspector of Ancient Monuments for Wales he was based in London, and he and Helen lived conveniently near to Paddington Station in the now fashionable area of Little Venice.

In spite of the war Helen became increasingly involved with archaeology,

*Figure 1*  Salmonsbury Camp excavation, September 1933. Mrs O'Neil with the excavation director, the late Dr G.C. Dunning. (Photograph by Cheltenham Newspaper Co. Ltd.; Cheltenham Museum collection.)

which at this time was undergoing a major expansion as a result of the accelerated threats to all types of ancient sites (MOW 1949; Rahtz 1974, 55). It was during a wartime transfer to London that I first met Helen, who became a firm friend, and I was soon enjoying weekend escapes to her excavation at the Park Street Roman villa in Hertfordshire. This excavation became a minor classic in various ways, one of which was that it was one of the first 'official' rescue digs, with Helen blazing a controversial trail in claiming railway fares from Government funds! Another was that the resulting report on Park Street (1945) was a landmark with its many specialist contributions, including reconstruction drawings and pioneer work on building-mortars. The reprinting of this report in 1971 demonstrated its continuing importance. In addition to rescue excavation during the war years, Helen was also one of the first archaeologists to undertake 'official' watching-briefs in advance of the destruction of an archaeological site, as she did for example at Watling Street (1942).

Bryan O'Neil became Chief Inspector of Ancient Monuments in 1945, and after the war Helen was increasingly involved with the archaeological 'establishment', taking part in the busy round of lectures and excursions of the various societies, and attending conferences in Britain and abroad. She had been a member of the Royal Archaeological Institute since 1932, and was elected a fellow of the Society of Antiquaries of London in 1948. Some of the highlights of her archaeological life at this time were the immensely enjoyable digging holidays spent with Bryan in the Isles of Scilly. All this was sadly cut short by Bryan's premature death in 1954, leaving Helen to publish the report of their last Scillonian dig together, which appeared in 1964.

After Bryan's death Helen moved back permanently to Gloucestershire, sharing The Camp House with her sister Amy for the next three decades. Helen now became the local correspondent to both the Ordnance Survey and the Ancient Monuments Inspectorate, which entailed, amongst other tasks, annotating a set of '6-inch' maps with details of all archaeological discoveries and observations in the area – work from which the present County Sites and Monuments Records have evolved. After 1954 she assumed yet another role, that of archaeological consultant for the Ancient Monuments Inspectorate, which entailed undertaking rescue excavations and watching-briefs on a self-employed basis, remunerated by fees and expenses. As a freelance 'digger' she joined a select band of Ministry of Works' excavators – including Ernest Greenfield and Philip Rahtz – who were the precursors of the archaeological field officers of today (Rahtz 1974, 59). This activity explains, for example, how Helen came to dig at Ancaster in Lincolnshire (see Todd 1981).

*Figure 2* Prestbury Manor moated site excavation, May 1951. (Photograph by W.T. Jones; Cheltenham Museum collection.)

That Helen was constantly on call for her expert opinion is reflected in many of her notes, for example: 'a message was sent to ask me to visit the site' (1960, 166). She never had a car, and is fond of stressing that to understand the countryside one must travel slowly. In her article on the Jurassic Way she wrote of 'over thirty years wanderings on foot and push-bike along a stretch of some seventy miles of countryside' (1966). Later on the use of a moped enabled her to cope with her position as a veritable 'clearing-house' for archaeological information in north Gloucestershire. My own involvement in the dig at Rough Ground Farm, Lechlade (RCHM 1976, 73–75), came about because the site had been reported to Helen by local amateurs, and she submitted my name as a possible excavator.

She had joined both the Bristol and Gloucestershire Archaeological Society and the Cotteswold Naturalists' Field Club in 1933, and from 1955 to 1974 the journal of one or both of these societies carried an astonishing series of reports of her work annually, with a single gap in 1963! These reports were mostly of a practical nature, describing digs or new discoveries, though her contribution to Grinsell's barrow survey, published under their joint authorship in 1960, depended upon the patient accumulation of data Helen had undertaken year after year. The value of this accumulated local knowledge is also implicit in the special acknowledgement made to Helen in the foreword of the Gloucestershire volume published by the Royal Commission on Historical Monuments (RCHM 1976, xiv). Nor was her local knowledge restricted to archaeology, since geologists studying the Cotswold region were equally grateful for her observations (e.g. Richardson and Sandford 1960, 46).

In the background to her published work has been Helen's continuous involvement with local and national societies, sitting on committees, guiding excursions, and giving the occasional talk (she is a reluctant public speaker!). For many years she has been a member of the Cirencester Excavation Committee, and she was a stalwart of the Gloucester Roman Research Committee, becoming a founder member of the Gloucester and District Archaeological Research Group (GADARG) which replaced it. Helen became a Vice-President of the Cotteswold Naturalists' Field Club in 1970, and she was made an Honorary Member of that society in 1977. The Bristol and Gloucestershire Archaeological Society followed suit by making her an Honorary Member in 1984. Her services to archaeology were recognized nationally by the award of MBE in 1968.

Such events are merely the framework of another long and busy 'archaeological life' during which Helen has maintained her interest and involvement, despite the great changes which transformed archaeology from the pre-war

*Figure 3*    Site visit to Frocester Court Roman villa, *c*.1971. (Photograph by
             Mrs Mary Gardiner.)

pursuit of the leisured classes to an occupation which today attracts
widespread participation, and demands considerable professional expertise
from its practitioners.

Helen also managed to find time to cultivate other interests, such as natural
history (her father was an entomologist of repute), gardening (she set up a
Roman wellhead to make a flowerbed and her rockery was embellished with
stones from many digs), and antiques (she made a notable collection of
antique blue and white Spode, transfer-printed with 'Oriental Sports'
designs, reflecting her long love of India – she was born in Mandalay in
1893). Mementoes of her many travels decorated her rooms at The Camp
House; representations of elephants being special favourites. Roman pots
from her excavations were not hidden away in boxes, but were reconstructed
and placed on mantelpiece and dresser for everyday enjoyment.

Helen was usually her own illustrator and photographer, and proved an apt
pupil when my husband persuaded her that a Box Brownie was hardly
worthy of archaeological subjects. Even when climbing steep ladders – as on
the deep Roman defences at Gloucester – Helen made no concessions to
dress: blouse, skirt, and hat (plus jacket when cold) were *de rigueur*, with a

predilection for pink and for Indian silk scarves. Old shoes, saved up for digging, received ceremonial burial when the site was backfilled.

Helen is the first to admit that archaeology has enriched her life. Her enthusiasm and support (latterly by gifts of books no longer needed) has encouraged many, as all those who have 'been to tea' at The Camp House will testify. Above all she would agree that her archaeology has been fun – even when she was chased by a deranged workman wielding a fire-extinguisher at North Leigh Roman villa . . .

## REFERENCES

Dunning, G.C. 1976. Salmonsbury, Bourton-on-the-Water, Gloucestershire. In D.W. Harding (ed.), *Hillforts: later prehistoric earthworks in Britain and Ireland*, 75–118. London.

MOW (Ministry of Works). 1949. *War and archaeology in Britain*. London.

O'Neil, H.E. 1942. Watling Street, Cannon's Park, Middlesex. *Antiq J* 22, 220.

O'Neil, H.E. 1945. The Roman villa at Park Street, near St. Albans, Hertfordshire: report on the excavations of 1943–45. *Archaeol J* 102, 21–110.

O'Neil, H.E. 1960. Saxon burials in the Fosse Way at Bourton-on-the-Water, Gloucestershire, March 1958. *PCNFC* 33(4), 166–169.

O'Neil, H.E. 1964. Excavation of a Celtic Hermitage on St. Helens, Isles of Scilly, 1956–1958. *Archaeol J* 121, 40–69.

O'Neil, H.E. 1966. Archaeological observations on the Jurassic Way in northern Oxfordshire and the Cotswolds. *PCNFC* 35(1), 42–49.

O'Neil, H.E. 1977. Salmonsbury, Bourton-on-the-Water. Some aspects of archaeology in Bourton Vale. *TBGAS* 95, 11–23.

Rahtz, P.A. 1974. Rescue digging past and present. In P.A. Rahtz (ed.), *Rescue archaeology*, 53–72. Harmondsworth.

RCHM. 1976. *Iron Age and Romano-British monuments in the Gloucestershire Cotswolds*. London.

Richardson, L. and Sandford, K.S. 1960. Great Chessells gravel pit near Bourton-on-the-Water, Glos., and the occurrence of mammalian remains. *Proc Geol Assoc* 71, 40–46.

Todd, M. 1981. *The Roman town at Ancaster, Lincolnshire: the excavations of 1955–1971*. Exeter.

**March 1984**

# Bibliography of the Works of Mrs Helen Evangeline O'Neil MBE FSA

*Elizabeth Hall and Alan Saville*

### 1933 (as H.E. Donovan)

Excavations at Bourton-on-the-Water. *TBGAS* 55, 377, and plate I.

### 1934 (as H.E. Donovan)

Excavation of a Romano-British building at Bourton-on-the-Water, Gloucestershire, 1934. *TBGAS* 56, 99–128.

### 1935 (as H.E. Donovan)

Roman finds in Bourton-on-the-Water, Gloucestershire. *TBGAS* 57, 234–259.
A Roman oven at Bourton-on-the-Water, Gloucestershire. *TBGAS* 57, 260–265.
The Fosse Way. *TBGAS* 57, 280–281.
Archaeological notes. *PCNFC* 25(3), 302–303.

## 1936 (as H.E. Donovan)

(With G.C. Dunning.) Iron age pottery and saxon burials at Foxcote Manor, Andoversford, Gloucestershire. *TBGAS* 58, 157–170.
Archaeological notes. *PCNFC* 26(1), 105.

## 1937 (as H.E. Donovan)

Excavations, Prestbury Moat, near Cheltenham. *TBGAS* 59, 333–334.
Burial at Condicote, Gloucestershire. *TBGAS* 59, 334.
Skeleton at Great Rissington, Gloucestershire. *TBGAS* 59, 334.
Archaeological notes. *PCNFC* 26(2), 207.

## 1938 (as H.E. Donovan)

Adlestrop Hill barrow, Gloucestershire. *TBGAS* 60, 152–164.
(With F.M. Abell.) Foxcote finds. *PCNFC* 26(3), 242–244.
Archaeological notes. *PCNFC* 26(3), 328–329.

## 1939 (from this year onwards as H.E. O'Neil)

Reports on Roman remains, Gloucestershire. *TBGAS* 61, 107–131.

## 1941

Hoard of axes from Bourton-on-the-Water, Gloucestershire. *Antiq J* 21, 150–151.

## 1942

Watling Street, Cannon's Park, Middlesex. *Antiq J* 22, 220.

## 1945

The Roman Villa at Park Street, near St. Albans, Hertfordshire: Report on the excavations of 1943–45. *Archaeol J* 102, 21–110.

## 1949

Bronze and gilt buckle from Bourton-on-the-Water, Gloucestershire. *Antiq J* 29, 85–86.

## 1952

(With B.H. St. J. O'Neil.) The Roman conquest of the Cotswolds. *Archaeol J* 109, 23–38.
Whittington Court Roman Villa, Whittington, Gloucestershire. *TBGAS* 71, 13–87.
Spoonley Wood Roman Villa, Gloucestershire, May, 1952. *TBGAS* 71, 162–166.

## 1955

Woodchester Roman Villa. *TBGAS* 74, 172–175.
A Romano-British burial at Cutsdean, Gloucestershire, 1955. *TBGAS* 74, 176.

## 1956

Prestbury Moat, a manor house of the Bishops of Hereford in Gloucestershire. *TBGAS* 75, 5–34.

## 1957

Akeman Street, Quenington, Gloucestershire. *TBGAS* 76, 35–43.
Condicote earthwork, a henge monument, Gloucestershire. *TBGAS* 76, 141–146.

## 1958

(With J.M.C. Toynbee.) Sculptures from a Romano-British well in Gloucestershire. *J Roman Stud* 48, 49–55.

1–5, King's Square, Gloucester, 1958. *TBGAS* 77, 5–22.

A medieval site at Chalk Hill, Temple Guiting, Gloucestershire, 1957. *TBGAS* 77, 61–65.

A reputed underground passage at Coberley, Gloucestershire. *TBGAS* 77, 161–163.

## 1959

(With A.D. Saunders.) Wycomb Roman site, Andoversford. *TBGAS* 78, 161–162.

## 1960

(With L.V. Grinsell.) Gloucestershire barrows. *TBGAS* 79(1), 1–149.

Fifield long barrow I. *TBGAS* 79(2), 298–301.

Saxon burials in the Fosse Way at Bourton-on-the-Water, Gloucestershire, March 1958. *PCNFC* 33(4), 166–169.

## 1961

Commemorative plaque in Bourton Bridge at Bourton-on-the-Water. *TBGAS* 80, 173–174.

Some features of building-construction in a rural area of Roman Britain. In E.M. Jope (ed.), *Studies in building history: essays in recognition of the work of B.H. St. J. O'Neil*, 27–38. London.

## 1962

Friars' Orchard, Technical College, Gloucester, 1961. *TBGAS* 81, 10–40.

The Norman motte at Upper Slaughter, Gloucestershire. *PCNFC* 34(1–2), 32–36.

1964

Excavation of a Celtic Hermitage on St. Helens, Isles of Scilly, 1956–58. *Archaeol J* 121, 40–69.
The Fosse Way, Leygore Hill, Gloucestershire, 1964. *PCNFC* 34(3), 133–137.

1965

Excavations in the King's School Gardens, Gloucester, 1964. *TBGAS* 84, 15–27.
Some Byzantine churches and their frescoes in Serbia and Macedonia. *PCNFC* 34(4), 216–218.
A palaeolithic flint implement from Bourton-on-the-Water. *PCNFC* 34(4), 225–227.

1966

Sale's Lot long barrow, Withington, Gloucestershire, 1962–1965. *TBGAS* 85, 5–35.
(With J.S. Bunt.) A beaker from Leckhampton, Cheltenham, Gloucestershire, *TBGAS* 85, 216–217.
Archaeological observations on the Jurassic Way in northern Oxfordshire and the Cotswolds. *PCNFC* 35(1), 42–49.
A neolithic flint axe from Witney, Oxon. *Oxoniensia* 31, 162 and plate 6.

1967

Bevan's Quarry round barrow, Temple Guiting, Gloucestershire, 1964. *TBGAS* 86, 16–41.
Medieval ovens at Spoonley Farm, Winchcombe. *PCNFC* 35(2), 114–119.

1968

Review of C. Hart, 'Archaeology in Dean'. *Antiq J* 48, 124.
The Roman settlement on the Fosse Way at Bourton Bridge, Bourton-on-the-Water, Gloucestershire. *TBGAS* 87, 29–55.

Coney Warren on Elm Bank Farm, Cold Aston, Gloucestershire. *PCNFC* 35(3), 156–158.

A visit to Stonehenge. *PCNFC* 35(3), 163–164.

## 1969

Hailes Abbey, Gloucestershire. *PCNFC* 35(4), 229–231.

## 1970

South India revisited in 1969. *PCNFC* 36(1), 29–35.

## 1971

A hoard of Roman silver coins from Willersey, Gloucestershire, 1968. *TBGAS* 90, 120–123.

King's School Garden excavation: finds from the turf rampart. *TBGAS* 90, 221–223.

A Roman bathing establishment at The Grove, Ebrington, Gloucestershire. *TBGAS* 36(2), 87–93.

*The Roman villa at Park Street near St. Albans, Herts.* Hasprint No. 2, Hertfordshire Archaeol. Soc. Reprinted from *Archaeol J* 102 (1945) 21–110.

## 1972

Bourton Bridge Posting House, Bourton-on-the-Water. Part II – Pottery and finds. *TBGAS* 91, 92–116.

## 1973

The pottery. In P.E. Gascoigne, An Iron Age Pit at Wood House, Guiting Power. *TBGAS* 92, 205–206.

## 1974

Review of P.J. Fowler (ed.), 'Archaeology and the Landscape'. *TBGAS* 93, 189–190.

## 1975

A Romano-British settlement in Ballards Orchard, North Littleton, Worcestershire. *Vale of Evesham Hist Soc Research Papers* 5, 13–15.

## 1977

Salmonsbury, Bourton-on-the-Water. Some aspects of archaeology in Bourton Vale. *TBGAS* 95, 11–23.

Santhill, Romano-British settlement near Bourton-on-the-Water, Gloucestershire, 1960–1964. *PCNFC* 38(3), 28–30.

# PART TWO:

# THE PHYSICAL BACKGROUND
# TO GLOUCESTERSHIRE ARCHAEOLOGY

# A Summary of the Geology and Geomorphology of Gloucestershire

*Gordon Margretts*

## INTRODUCTION

Gloucestershire is a purely artificial unit, first mentioned under the name in the Anglo-Saxon period. Geological and topographical boundaries do not respect such historical divisions; on the contrary, physical boundaries normally influence human decisions in political and economic organization. Geologically, Gloucestershire holds an interestingly marginal position within the country. The great scenic variety in the county is directly the result of an accident of earth history. Few other parts of Britain can illustrate as well as Gloucestershire such variety of rocks and the strong influence that they and their structures have on landform and scenery.

The county may be divided geologically and topographically into three distinct regions, listed below from west to east.

1.  The older, harder, structurally more complex Palaeozoic rocks on which is developed the dissected plateau of the Forest of Dean.

2.  The central NE–SW-trending, broad Severn Vale, underlain by marls and sandstones of Triassic age to the west of the Severn and by clays of Liassic age to the east. Over these easterly-dipping Mesozoic rocks are strewn the more recent glacio-fluvial and fluvial-aeolian deposits produced under the influence of the colder and harsher climate of Pleistocene times.

3.  The predominantly limestone sequence of Jurassic age dipping gently towards the ESE. These rocks are responsible for the high ground of the

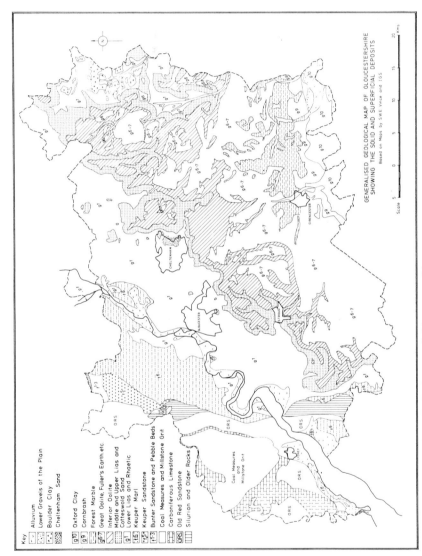

Key

□ Alluvium
□ Lower Gravels of the Plain
□ Boulder Clay
▨ Cheltenham Sand

g10 Oxford Clay
g9 Cornbrash
Forest Marble
g6-7 Great Oolite, Fuller's Earth etc
Inferior Oolite
Middle and Upper Lias and
Cotteswold Sand
g1 Lower Lias and Rhaetic
g6 Keuper Marl
t4,5 Keuper Sandstone
t1-3 Bunter Sandstone and Pebble Beds
Coal Measures and Millstone Grit
Carboniferous Limestone
ORS Old Red Sandstone
Silurian and Older Rocks

GENERALISED GEOLOGICAL MAP OF GLOUCESTERSHIRE
SHOWING THE SOLID AND SUPERFICIAL DEPOSITS
Based on Maps by S.W.E. Vince and IGS

Scale 5   0   5   10   15   20
                              Kms

*Figure 1*  Generalised geological map of Gloucestershire.

Cotswolds, forming a plateau which falls away to the Oxford clay plain to the east, and into which are carved the tributaries of the river Thames. Although there is a wide variety of rock ages and types within the county, they are all of a sedimentary nature, being the product of earth surface processes on pre-existing rocks with the help of biogenic activities in relatively shallow seas. These different lithologies and structures have been attacked by recent processes to produce changes in slope form and aspect which give uniqueness to the landscape. The variety of rocks is also largely responsible for the many soil types found, on which the mixed agricultural and forestry activities of the county are developed. Gloucestershire is well blessed with building-stone, aggregate, and clays for brickmaking, a fact which is underlined by many of the buildings in towns and established villages.

## THE STRUCTURAL BACKBONE

Very ancient earthmovements which date back to the Precambrian, more than 570 million years ago, besides overprints from the three main orogenies in Phanerozoic times, were responsible for the structural trends which underpin hill, plateau, valley, and vale.

The main N–S structure of the Malvern Hills lies outside the county, but the Malvernoid trend may be traced southwards along the eastern edge of the Forest of Dean coalfield. It is recognized in the May Hill inlier, an anticline with a NNW–SSE trend, which could represent an intersection of the Malvernoid trend with the NW–SE Charnian trend.

Across the Severn the Malvernoid trend is traceable southwards to Berkeley; then the fold trends diverge, the western anticline forms the Lower Severn axis on a NE–SW Caledonian trend, and the eastern one, the Bath axis, follows a slightly sinuous N–S Malvernoid direction (Kellaway and Welch 1948). It is along this general N–S anticlinal axis that the oldest rocks of the county are exposed at the surface; the Huntley Quarry Beds of supposed Precambrian age (Geological Survey Sheet 234; SO 709195) and the Cambrian-aged rocks south of Tites Point, east of the Berkeley Fault (Geological Survey Sheet 234).

This dominant N–S trend is again seen in the coal measure basin of the Forest of Dean to the west. The asymmetrical and heart-shaped structure (16km north to south, and 9km west to east) has small folds plunging towards the south on the northern rim, e.g. Wigpool syncline, and towards the north on the southern rim, e.g. Clanna anticline. Prominent N–S fault lines are also present, the Cannop Fault Belt being the best known (Geological Survey Sheet 233).

To the east, in the Cotswolds, the N–S fold trends are less pronounced, giving rise to open, broader anticlines and synclines. From west to east are recognized the Painswick Syncline, Birdlip Anticline, Cleeve Hill Syncline, and Vale of Moreton Anticline; the four major axes which control hill and valley surfaces and the shape of the Cotswold scarp edge. As expected, these landforms, which have been developing over millions of years, show anticlines matching the valleys and synclines matching the high ground. Numerous normal dip-faults cut the backslope of the Cotswold escarpment. These trend either WNW–ESE or N–S to produce block faults, which have allowed, after erosion, rocks of different lithology to rest against each other at the same topographical level on the surface. For example, the Fuller's Earth Clay ($g^6$) may be found on the same level as the Inferior Oolite ($g^5$) and the Great Oolite ($g^7$).


## THE GEOLOGY WEST OF THE SEVERN

The generalized distribution of the rocks within Gloucestershire is shown in Fig. 1. The Forest of Dean and Wye Valley region is a plateau, at approximately 215m above sea level, of ancient, hard rocks which belong mainly to the Upper Palaeozoic era. Throughout most of this area to the west of the Severn the strata represent the Devonian and Carboniferous systems, with sandstones and limestones, including dolomites, predominating. To the north of the Forest of Dean is an isolated hill which is conspicuous by the stand of pine trees on its summit. The Silurian rocks which form the May Hill inlier are Llandoverian sandstones, followed by Wenlock limestones, including reef structures seen to advantage at the disused Hobbs' Quarries at Longhope. These bioherms are covered with Ludlow shales. There was no break in sedimentation as the Silurian sea gave way to a series of coastal lakes, into which rivers poured material carried at speed from the highland to the north. Great thicknesses of sandstone, marl, and pebble beds were developed under continental conditions to produce the Old Red Sandstone facies of Devonian times.

Deposition continued into Carboniferous times, as the crust warped downwards to allow the sea to invade the area once again. Shallow marine sediments were formed under warm water conditions, judging by the type and number of shellfish present. Oolitic limestones as well as bioclastic limestones were deposited, some to be converted into dolomites as the land rose again, producing a rock which has been, and still is, extensively quarried for stone aggregate around the outer, raised rim of the coalfield. Hence the large quarry cut into the Carboniferous Limestone Series at Drybrook. It is within the Carboniferous Limestone Series, particularly the Crease Limestone, that fissure deposits of haematite occur. These iron deposits were worked up until the Second World War.

There is evidence of folding and erosion within the Carboniferous before the deposition of the Upper Coal Measures. This intra-system earthmovement and erosion is recognized by an unconformity which shows the Upper Coal Measures (d⁶) overstepping the Drybrook Sandstone group (d²). The area just to the north of Lydney illustrates this relationship.

The Upper Coal Measures comprise a sandstone-mudstone-shale sequence including thin coal seams. This is the product of cyclothemic sedimentation in the shallow marine and coastal conditions in which swamp forests grew. The coal, coupled with the iron deposits, Pennant sandstone used for building and ornamental purposes, and the Coal Measure clays used for brick-making, gave rise to a strong industrial base in the region. Today only a stoneworks survives.

The most impressive scenery in this western area is undoubtedly that associated with the narrow, incised river valley of the Wye. The valley between Symond's Yat and Chepstow exposes near-vertical cliffs of Quartz Conglomerate and associated sandstones of Devonian age, as well as the full range of rocks of the Carboniferous Limestone series. The river makes little allowance for the nature or structure of the rocks over which it runs. It is the one example where geology has little control over landform.

## THE GEOLOGY OF THE SEVERN VALE

The rocks which underlie the Severn Vale are soft, poorly cemented, and thus easily weathered. They are clays, marls, and sandstones, with thin limestone bands of Triassic and Lower Jurassic age. Three river sections at Wainlode (SO 845257), Garden Cliff, Westbury-on-Severn (SO 718128), and Hock (SO 728090) clearly illustrate the character of the rocks of the Vale.

The Garden Cliff site is a classic river section of Rhaetic rock (fg) and underlying Keuper Marls, now known as the Mercian muds. The succession is similar to that which is seen further up the Severn at Wainlode. The Triassic Mercian mudstones, which represent terrestrial deposits, formed as lake muds on land, after earthmovements had folded and raised the Palaeozoic basement. This happened during Permian times. No rocks of

Permian age have been found in Gloucestershire. The Rhaetic rocks were deposited over the Mercian mudstones. First to be seen is the famous 'Bone Bed' containing reptile remains, which is followed by black shales and eventually sandstone and limestone beds; the products of a shallow sea environment. Thus the Rhaetic rocks represent lagoonal conditions; a passage sequence between the continental deposits of Keuper age below, and the marine deposits of lower Jurassic age above. These river cliffs are capped by the more resistant Lower Lias Limestone beds. The ridge of Coombe Hill saw the development of an important line of communication between Gloucester and Tewkesbury, now represented by the A38 road, exploiting this more resistant Lower Lias Limestone outcrop. It produces the only raised, firm ground which was not subject to flooding in the Vale. Neither the Mercian mudstones to the west of it, nor the Lias clays to the east, although porous, will allow water to drain efficiently through them, thus producing overland flow and generally waterlogged ground.

The Hock Cliff river section, only 4km south of the Garden Cliff site, but on the east (left) bank of the Severn, shows the alternation of impure limestone and calcareous clay beds of Lower Lias age. Clay becomes the dominant rock type as the succession is traced vertically and eastwards towards the scarp-face of the Cotswolds. At Robins Wood Hill, an outlier to the south of Gloucester, the thick clay sequence has been quarried for the making of bricks. Similar works have been operative at Stonehouse and Cheltenham. Works in Cheltenham were on a large scale, producing materials, contrary to expectation, for the building of most of the original Spa Town. Very few buildings were faced with Cotswold limestone.

Another important deposit seen at Hock Cliff is the much more recently deposited river terrace material. It is a pebbly and friable sandstone. The pebbles and sand particles are mainly quartzitic, which makes these deposits ideal aggregates for making concrete. Large pits have been developed into shallow deposits at Twyning and Frampton on Severn for the extraction of such material. These deposits are most likely to be the result of outwashings from the glacial sheets which extended from the north-west into the Vale and even perhaps overrode the north Cotswolds to cover the Vale of Moreton. Similar material is found in isolated pockets across the floor of the Severn Vale. The nature of the material changes as the deposits are traced up against the scarp-edge of the Cotswolds. Here the material is better described as Head deposits; that is, the product of solifluxion, occurring when alternate freezing and thawing combine with the presence of ice or melt-water to allow mass downslope movement of shattered, local material over a frozen subsoil. Extensive deposits of this superficial material have been recognized in the entrance to the Stroud Valley and on the lower slopes of Bredon Hill. The material, unlike the water-smoothed surfaces of river-terrace particles, consists of unsorted, subangular fragments of local oolitic and Middle Lias Marlstone in what Tomlinson (1941) described as taele fans.

Besides the glacio-fluvial and solifluxion processes which were modifying the landscape and carrying superficial deposits into the Vale, there was yet a third major process at work during Pleistocene times. This was the wind, which scattered fine sand across the Vale to assist in the development of such deposits as the Cheltenham Sand. These accumulations underlie the older parts of Cheltenham, Bishops Cleeve, and smaller settlements to the north. It is recognized that such sandy deposits facilitate good drainage and are easier to cultivate than the dominant, heavier soils which are developed over the Lias Clay. These medium-grained, well-sorted, predominantly quartzose sands, dating from the Devensian glacial period, can be as much as 15·2m thick, as shown by a borehole at a building-site in Monson Avenue, Cheltenham (SO 922283). The sands are worked as an aggregate source, and are currently (1984) visible in extensive exposures at the Shurdington Sand Pit (SO 914178).


## THE GEOLOGY OF THE COTSWOLDS

The Middle Lias is characterized by a persistent and relatively hard Marlstone Rock Bed, which rarely exceeds 5m in thickness. It is a shelly, ferruginous limestone which weathers slowly by comparison with the clays below, and the clays or sands above, so that it is responsible for a pronounced platform known as the Cotswold sub-edge. It is clearly seen below Leckhampton Hill and Stinchcombe Hill.

Over most of the county the Upper Lias occurs as a narrow outcrop in the steeper parts of the Jurassic scarp. In the south the sediment is mainly sandy but gives way to clay as the formation is traced northwards to the Leckhampton Hill area. The Cotteswold Sands, as they are called, reappear in the far north near Chipping Campden. There is a close relationship between the fold axes and the facies type; the Sands occurring near the anticlinal axes suggesting that these structures were active during, and were influencing, sedimentation. The exposure of Upper Lias Clay below Sands and Inferior Oolite Limestone in the valleys of the north Cotswolds appears to have been an important factor influencing settlement sites. The majority of Cotswold villages are on the Upper Lias Clays or near their junction with the Sands.

The Inferior Oolite dominates the Cotswolds in areal extent. These rocks attain a maximum thickness of 90m on Cleeve Hill where the Cotswolds rise to 330m. There are many varieties of limestone recognized, some composed entirely of broken fossils while others are mainly formed of ooids. The type and abundance of the limestone particle, called allochem, and the nature of the cement, decides if the rock will be of value for building purposes. Although there are many types, they have all formed in warm, shallow seas where deposition was interrupted at frequent intervals by earthmovements.

An alternating sequence of clays and limestones completes the Jurassic succession. In the sequence the two rock-types of particular note are the Fuller's Earth Clay, which in the past has been used as a cleaning agent, and the Great Oolite, which in the north Cotswolds is developed as a fissile limestone and thus has been used as roofing 'slate' (Aston 1974).

The valleys of the Cotswold backslope are broad, open features, which are now dry in the upper reaches, or with only a very small meandering stream across their floors. The Windrush near Naunton (SP 129219) is a good example. It is recognized that running water was responsible for carving these valleys. One theory suggests that during glacial times the fissures and pore spaces in the limestones were filled with ice at depth, thus preventing the movement of water through the rocks. Yet thaw of ice and snow on the surface during the summer months would generate large runoff budgets which could cause large-scale erosion. Whatever the cause, these valleys, criss-crossed by dry-stone walls and bordered by stands and lines of beech trees, typify the Cotswold scene.

The scarp-edge is another area of the Cotswolds where water, sometimes in a frozen state, has been an important agent in bringing about landslip and rotation. This lubricant has weakened the cohesion of the underlying clays, so promoting downhill creep and camber of the Inferior Oolite. Floundered ground is shown surrounding large areas around Painswick Beacon (Geological Survey Sheet 234).

REFERENCES

Aston, M. 1974. *Stonesfield slate*. Oxford. (= Oxfordshire County Council Department of Museum Services Publication No. 5.)

Kellaway, G.A. and Welch, F.B.A. 1948. *British regional geology: Bristol and Gloucester District*. London.

Tomlinson, M.E. 1941. Pleistocene gravels of the Cotswold sub-edge plain from Mickleton to the Frome Valley. *Quarterly Journal Geological Society London* 96, 385–421.

OTHER SOURCES USED IN THE COMPILATION OF THIS ARTICLE

Beckinsale, P.R. 1970. Physical problems of the Cotswold rivers and valleys. *Cotteswold* 35, 194–205.

Dreghorn, W. 1967. *Geology explained in the Severn Vale and Cotswolds.* Newton Abbot.

Dreghorn, W. 1968. *Geology explained in the Forest of Dean and the Wye Valley.* Newton Abbot.

Dury, G.H. 1953. Meanders of the Coln Valley: a new interpretation. *Cotteswold* 31, 206–19.

Finberg, H.P.R. 1975. *The Gloucestershire Landscape.* London.

Macfadyen, W.A. 1970. *Geological Highlights of the West Country.* London.

Mudge, D.C. 1979. Stratigraphy and sedimentation of the Inferior Oolite of the Cotswolds. *Quarterly Journal Geological Society London* 135, 611–627.

Murray, J.W. and Hawkins, A.B. 1973. Geology and physical environment. In C. and A.M. Hadfield (eds.), *The Cotswolds, a new study,* 21–47. Newton Abbot.

Richardson, L. 1904. *A handbook to the geology of Cheltenham.* Cheltenham.

Trueman, A.E. 1949. *The Scenery of England and Wales.* Harmondsworth.

Walker, F. 1972. *The Bristol Region.* London.

Worssam, B.C. and Barrow, A.J.M. 1983. *Sheet SO92 Cheltenham. Geology with special emphasis on potential resources of sand and gravel.* Geological Survey.

**March 1984**

# PART THREE:
# GLOUCESTERSHIRE PREHISTORY

# Palaeolithic and Mesolithic Evidence from Gloucestershire

*Alan Saville*

## INTRODUCTION

The evidence for the earliest human occupation of Gloucestershire prior to the neolithic consists almost exclusively of finds of flint and stone implements which can on typological grounds be related to similar implements from stratigraphically- and chronometrically-dated deposits in other parts of England. The county is unfortunate in having no pre-neolithic archaeological deposits dated by radiocarbon determination, and virtually no pre-neolithic palaeoenvironmental data with cultural associations. Any account of early prehistory is thus extremely circumscribed, and this article can do little other than review the available artefactual material.

The earliest recognizable types of prehistoric implements to be found in the county belong to the handaxe category. These are bifacially-flaked artefacts, usually of flint, which appear to have had a multi-purpose use as knives, saws, and choppers in various domestic and hunting activities (Wymer 1982, 102–108). Handaxes come in many sizes and shapes, but the classic, basically triangular shape, with a broad butt and pointed tip, is the most common, and is the most distinctively Acheulian in character. The term Acheulian (after the French type-site of St Acheul) can conventionally be used to describe all types of lower palaeolithic handaxe, from the highly refined ficron with its elongated point and concave edges, through the heart-shaped cordates and the less pointed ovates, to the cleaver, which has a broad, straight, working edge. Handaxes are an extremely long-lived imple-

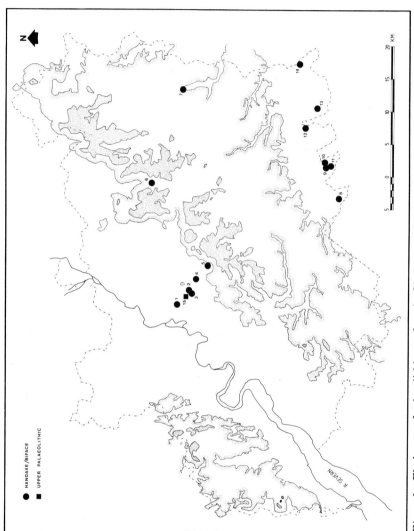

*Figure 1*    Findspots of palaeolithic artefacts in Gloucestershire. Land over 400 and 800 feet above O.D. stippled. (See Appendix 1 for key to findspots.)

ment type, however, and continued to be made through into the middle palaeolithic, though most distinctively in a modified *bout coupé* shape (Roe 1981, 183 ff.), described as Mousterian (after the French type-site of Le Moustier).

Lower palaeolithic occupation by handaxe-using people was certainly established in England by the Hoxnian interglacial stage, which commenced some 250,000 years ago, and middle palaeolithic occupation relates to the later Ipswichian interglacial and the early, warmer stages of the Devensian glaciation, perhaps persisting in parts of southern England as late as 50,000 BP. The dating of individual, unstratified finds of handaxes within this enormous 200,000-year period is a matter of guesswork, informed only by consideration of the typology and technology of each piece, set against what is known of these aspects from stratified finds and general developmental trends.

## THE LOWER AND MIDDLE PALAEOLITHIC (Fig. 1)

The first recorded find of a palaeolith in Gloucestershire was made in 1917 at the Upton Lane gravel pit at Barnwood, near Gloucester (Burkitt 1921; Clifford 1930, 210–211). This implement, a bifacially flaked handaxe, is somewhat inexplicit typologically, but appears to lie on the borderline between an Acheulian ovoid and a Mousterian *bout coupé*. The Barnwood gravels subsequently produced a further, very small handaxe-like implement (Clifford 1936), which is also difficult to categorize typologically.

Both implements came from the horizon described as Bed 1 in the former Lillies Field Pit at Upton Lane. A second former gravel pit at Barnwood, Forty Acre Field, produced artefacts from an apparently equivalent Bed 1, which, though not including any handaxes, have been accepted as of lower palaeolithic type (Clifford, Garrod and Gracie 1954; Roe 1968, 70). This horizon, an oolitic gravel of supposed local origin, has also produced a rich Pleistocene cold-stage fauna, including the remains of mammoth, woolly rhinoceros, horse, and musk ox. The homogeneity of this fauna remains in some doubt, as does its relationship to the associated artefacts (which may predate it), but on face value such a fauna is most likely to relate to a pre-Devensian cool period, or even to some less rigorous part of the early or mid-Devensian glaciation. A reference point for this may be supplied by the radiocarbon dating of a mammoth tusk from gravel at Little Rissington to 34500 ± 800 bp (Birm 466; Campbell 1977, Vol. 2, 23).

These early finds from Barnwood were made by chance during gravel extraction, and that they were recorded at all was due on the one hand to the relatively unmechanized methods of gravel-digging which then pertained, and on the other to the local presence of Mrs Clifford as an archaeological enthusiast. By the same token, however, the early date of the finds means that they were not recorded with the same attention to stratigraphic and palaeoenvironmental detail as would now be possible, and the Barnwood finds do pose problems of archaeological interpretation, particularly in view of the wealth of material of all later periods from the same location. For example, there are flint artefacts of micro-blade type in Gloucester Museum, recorded by Mrs Clifford as from Bed 1 in Forty Acre Field, which are clearly of a non-Acheulian, and probably post-palaeolithic, technology.

Barnwood remains important, even so, as the location at which a palaeolithic presence in the county was first identified, and the hope remains that unworked areas of gravel may be identified in the future which will allow clarification of the original discoveries. This hope is given some substance by the fact that other finds of palaeoliths have been made in the Barnwood area from gravel deposits which may be of a broadly similar nature. These comprise a handaxe found during sewer-trenching at Brockworth (Clifford 1937), a probable Acheulian biface from a gravel pit at Great Witcombe (Clifford, Garrod and Gracie 1954, 179), and a splendid ficron-type handaxe (Fig. 2) dug up from gravel beneath the garden of a house in Longlevens (Roe 1968, 70). The Brockworth handaxe is of particular interest in that typologically it possesses several of the features of the late Acheulian/Micoquian handaxes, best represented in Britain at Wolvercote, Oxfordshire (Roe 1981, 117–130 and pers. comm.). It must be admitted with some regret, however, that the last thirty years apparently have failed to reveal any new palaeolithic finds from this area, despite the increase in archaeological activity in and around Gloucester.

The other productive area for palaeoliths in Gloucestershire, and one which is continuing to produce new finds, is the Upper Thames Valley, where the gravel-spreads west of Lechlade have yielded seven handaxes, though not all have a detailed provenance. The first, again a potentially Mousterian implement, was discovered during gravel extraction at Lechlade in 1938 (Clifford 1939), with subsequent finds from Cerney Wick, South Cerney (Viner 1978), Fairford (Corinium Museum), Meysey Hampton (Fig. 3; Roe 1968, 70), Poole Keynes (Grinsell 1966), and South Cerney (Corinium Museum). The most recent find, of an ovate handaxe from South Cerney (Whitehead 1979), is perhaps the most important, since it is precisely provenanced to a gravel deposit which had an identifiable vertebrate fauna and correlations with Thames terrace deposits which have been radiocarbon-

*Figure 2* Handaxe from Longlevens, Gloucester. (Gloucester City Museum A3125.)
(Photo: A. Saville.)

dated to the mid-Devensian. This deposit therefore provides a *terminus ante quem* for the deposition of the handaxe at a date which is likely to precede 40,000 years bp. This in itself is not surprising, since it would be anticipated on typological grounds that such an Acheulian handaxe would be considerably older, but it is the first occasion on which any chronometric data have been associated, however indirectly, with a Gloucestershire palaeolith.

Peripheral to the Upper Thames handaxe distribution is the Acheulian cleaver which probably originated from the Santhill gravel pit near Bourton-on-the-Water (O'Neil 1965), from terrace gravels of the River Windrush, a Thames tributary. This remains an isolated find even when the handaxe distribution in adjacent parts of Oxfordshire is considered (Roe 1968).

To the south, in the Bristol region, are the prolific findspots along the lower reaches of the river Avon, some of them formerly in the pre-1974 county of Gloucestershire, in particular those from the Shirehampton area (Lacaille 1954). The hundreds of middle Acheulian flint and chert artefacts from this region represent one of the largest concentrations of lower palaeolithic finds outside southern and eastern England (Roe 1974 and 1981, 131–135).

That the handaxe finds in the modern county of Gloucestershire should all be concentrated in the Thames and Severn Valleys is a natural consequence of their post-depositional history, during which they became incorporated in river gravels, and of the opportunity for their rediscovery presented by modern working of these gravels for commercial reasons. None of the artefacts so far described is likely to represent *in situ* manufacture or activity, though the relatively fresh condition of some of the handaxes may indicate that they have not travelled far from their original resting-places. There are no a priori grounds for supposing that palaeolithic people did not roam freely throughout the county during phases of climatic improvement, but the severe erosion created during the later phases of the Pleistocene is likely to have obscured any archaeological indication of open settlement on the higher ground.

The only possible exceptions to the main pattern of lower palaeolithic distribution in the county are all either somewhat dubious typologically or of uncertain provenance. The implement from Brand Green, near Upleadon (Posnansky 1963, 389), made on a split quartzite pebble, cannot be regarded as a certain palaeolith because of its imprecise form, though Acheulian quartzite tools are common from the south Warwickshire and south Worcestershire region (Saville and Shotton 1976), and should be expected in the north of the county. The Elkstone find, originally described as a palaeolith (Anon. 1969; Smith 1973, 301–302), is a flake tool which cannot be given any

*Figure 3* Handaxe from Meysey Hampton. (Gloucester City Museum A3124.)
(Photo: A. Saville.)

definite typological attribution and need not be of palaeolithic date. This leaves the newly-recorded handaxe-like implement from Charlton Abbots (Saville forthcoming), which is typologically acceptable as an Acheulian artefact, but which has unfortunately imprecise details of provenance.

New and exciting finds, which extend the Gloucestershire lower and middle palaeolithic distribution into an altogether more predictable location, have been reported from Twyning in the far north of the county, where quartzite and flint handaxes and flakes are being correlated with the Avon No. 4 terrace on both sides of the Gloucestershire/Worcestershire border (Whitehead pers. comm.).

Typologically, the Gloucestershire handaxes include specimens of various kinds – cordate, cleaver, ficron, ovate, and *bout coupé* – and many of them are of small size. As indicated at the beginning of this paper, it would be wrong to suggest any precise dating or phasing based on typology for these isolated finds, which could fall almost anywhere within the known range of English handaxes from the Hoxnian through to the early Devensian. However, all the finds described above are, broadly speaking, attributable to the lower palaeolithic Acheulian or the middle palaeolithic Mousterian traditions, and there are no objects which can obviously be referred to the lower palaeolithic Clactonian (Roe 1981, 68–70). The picture which can be given, therefore, is of very sparse lower and middle palaeolithic activity in the county, restricted apparently to the major river valley systems, and likely to relate to the warmer episodes of the middle to late Pleistocene.

## THE UPPER PALAEOLITHIC

Artefacts attributable to the remainder of the Devensian glacial phase, which is the upper palaeolithic in archaeological terms, are almost non-existent within the county. The exception is again provided by the Barnwood gravels, where Clifford's Bed 3, a deposit stratigraphically overlying Bed 1 and from which it is separated by an archaeologically sterile Bed 2, has produced a fragmentary ivory point and a number of retouched and unretouched flakes, which Garrod regarded as of upper palaeolithic type (Clifford, Garrod and Gracie 1954). Campbell, in his recent reassessment of the British upper palaeolithic, has included 17 flint artefacts and the ivory point from Forty Acre Field gravel pit in the context of his earlier upper palaeolithic subdivision, which relates to the middle and early late Devensian phases (Campbell 1977, Vol. 2, 104–105 and fig. 98). The flint artefacts include two backed tools, one of which may be a tanged point, and three scrapers. As with the lower palaeolithic material from Barnwood, it is unfortunate that the occurrence of these later finds is so ill-defined. However, Campbell regards the assemblage as probably indicative of a small open-air encampment of the period near to the find-spot (1977, Vol. 1, 146), and his opinion has been followed by other writers (e.g. Morrison 1980, 87).

A further, possible, earlier upper palaeolithic artefact is the isolated find of an elongated retouched blade from a gravel pit at Eastington, near Stroud (Gardiner 1932), but this implement is not typologically distinctive enough to be accepted as definitely of this period. This is similarly the case with another implement from Eastington which was originally classed as of possible upper palaeolithic age (Burkitt 1938; Campbell 1977, Vol. 2, 104).

The later upper palaeolithic of the final stages of the Devensian glaciation, characterized by lithic tool-kits which feature a variety of backed blade implements, including the distinctive Creswellian point (Mellars 1974, 70–76), has left no apparent trace in Gloucestershire.

The paucity of upper palaeolithic finds in the county is not surprising in view of the great scarcity of contemporary material across virtually the whole of central England west of East Anglia, and indeed open sites of the period are generally extremely rare in Britain. The majority of known upper palaeolithic sites are in fact cave and rock shelter locations, where conditions for archaeological preservation have been enhanced. The distribution of such sites is naturally restricted to appropriate geological formations, such as the Mendip Hills in Somerset, where upper palaeolithic finds are prolific (Campbell 1970; Jacobi 1982), but they might also be expected to occur in the far west of Gloucestershire, along the Wye Valley, where on the other side of the river, in Herefordshire, the well-known site of King Arthur's Cave, near Whitchurch, has produced evidence for both earlier and later upper palaeolithic occupation (Campbell 1977, Vol. 2, 105 and 122–123). A claim to have discovered upper palaeolithic artefacts from just such a Gloucestershire Wye Valley cave-site near Symonds Yat has indeed been made (Rogers, Pinder and Russell 1981), but more detailed publication would be needed before this claim can be evaluated.

## THE MESOLITHIC (Fig. 4)

Archaeologically, it is not until the post-glacial period that the continuous human occupation of Gloucestershire can be said to begin. From this period the evidence is somewhat more prolific, and is easier to interpret, in that finds of mesolithic artefacts point directly to *in situ* habitation or activity. However,

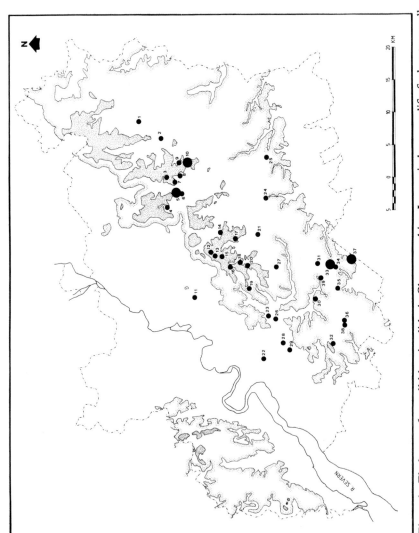

*Figure 4* Findspots of mesolithic microliths in Gloucestershire. Large circles = prolific findspots; small circles = up to 10 microliths. Land over 400 and 800 feet above O.D. stippled. (See Appendix 2 for key to findspots.)

recognizable mesolithic artefacts from Gloucestershire are known only as casual finds from fieldwalking, or by chance retrieval during the excavation of sites of later periods. It is assumed that the known mesolithic finds reflect the widespread presence of nomadic or semi-nomadic hunter-fisher-gatherer communities exploiting the abundant resources of the post-glacial environment. The distribution of mesolithic findspots (Fig. 4) shows clearly that the Cotswold upland was now inhabited. In fact, mesolithic people are likely to have colonized most areas and habitats within the county, but the conditions for archaeological recognition of their presence are more favourable on the Cotswolds, where the predominant arable landuse has left their flints on the surface, and where most rural archaeological excavations have taken place. Most distinctive among the mesolithic finds are the microliths, the small implements, with characteristic shaping and retouch, which usually formed the barbs and tips of wooden arrow-shafts or bone points.

The English mesolithic is currently subdivided chronologically and typologically into an earlier and later phase (Mellars 1974, 81–92), with microlithic industries dominated by broad, obliquely blunted points before the seventh millennium bc, and afterwards by small and narrow scalene triangles and other 'geometric' forms, which continue until the mesolithic is superseded by neolithic cultural traits. This rather crude subdivision is applicable to Gloucestershire insofar as, typologically speaking, there is as yet no conclusive evidence for earlier mesolithic occupation. Even the surface scatter from Tog Hill, a southern Cotswold site near Marshfield in Avon (Sykes and Whittle 1965), which has been claimed to represent early mesolithic ('Maglemosian') occupation (Gracie 1970, 9), is not wholly convincing, though its high proportion of 'non-geometric' forms does appear to present a typological contrast with the Gloucestershire assemblages. Occasional, isolated examples of the kind of relatively large (length 30mm or more), obliquely blunted point found at Tog Hill do occur among Cotswold surface finds, as at Naunton and Sevenhampton (Fig. 5, 39–40), but these cannot be accorded any certain typological dating by themselves. At the moment, therefore, it seems preferable to assume that mesolithic settlement in the county began relatively late in the post-glacial period, and to bear in mind the possibility that it may relate largely to the fifth and fourth millennia bc.

Significant large assemblages of mesolithic artefacts are so far known from four localities. At Cherington and Long Newnton there are prolific surface sites with artefacts spread across several fields, while the excavations of sites of later periods at Hazleton and Syreford have produced more discrete concentrations of finds. The Cherington (Witchell 1973) and Long Newnton

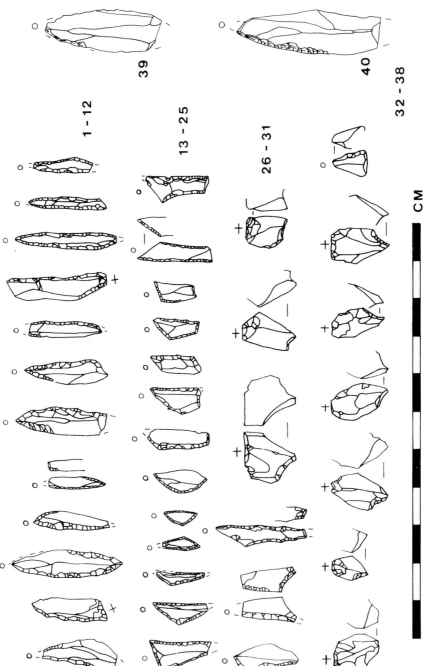

39

40

1 - 12

13 - 25

26 - 31

32 - 38

CM

*Fig 5* Mesolithic microliths and microburins from Syreford, Whittington (1–38), Naunton (39), and Puckham, Sevenhampton (40).

(Gracie 1942) assemblages are characterized by their microlithic components, which contain a significant proportion of later mesolithic 'geometric' forms. Other findspots from southern Gloucestershire which have produced several microliths each, such as Bagendon (Gracie 1961), Frocester Court (Price pers. comm.), Harcombe, Syde (Gander 1976), Hazelwood, Avening (Stroud Museum; Wymer 1977, 100), and Leonard Stanley (Gracie 1938) all appear to echo this pattern by the presence of at least one 'geometric' type in each case. The more numerous findspots with assemblages which are even less characterizable, other than as mesolithic, at least produce nothing which contradicts a later mesolithic attribution, for example Barnsley Park (Barfield 1981).

At Syreford, near Andoversford, Mr W.F. Cox has recovered a large flint assemblage during the course of his excavation of a late iron age/Romano-British site on a patch of gravel near the Cotswold scarp-edge (RCHM 1976, 125). This assemblage, which is almost exclusively mesolithic, includes over one hundred cores and commensurate débitage, but relatively few implements other than microliths; for example only eight scrapers. The manufacture of microliths on the spot is demonstrated by the presence of 14 microburins (Fig. 5, 29–38), alongside the 56 microliths. Only 28 of the latter are complete enough for classification and illustration (Fig. 5, 1–28), comprising an obliquely blunted point (1), edge-blunted points (2–9), narrow, double edge-blunted points (10–12), idiosyncratic forms (26–28), and 13 'geometrics': scalene triangles (13–17), a crescent (18), quadrangular forms (19–23), and micro-tranchets (24–25). The Syreford assemblage constitutes the most valid mesolithic flint industry recognized within the county so far, representing a manufacturing focus, which was probably also a settlement, of a kind now well known from the English mesolithic, if as yet poorly understood in terms of their precise nature (Mellars 1976).

A very similar microlithic component is present within the mixed flint assemblage recently recovered from beneath a neolithic Cotswold-Severn tomb at Hazleton (Saville 1983a and 1983b), where the distribution of microliths, concentrated in an area some 11m across beneath the west end of the long cairn, indicates a focus of mesolithic activity. The study of this assemblage has not been completed, but there are at least 55 microliths, of which 26 can be classified, comprising an obliquely blunted point, 3 edge-blunted points, 6 narrow, double-edge blunted (needle) points, and 16 'geometrics' (i.e. 12 scalene triangles, 3 crescents, and 1 micro-tranchet). The three-dimensional recording of all flint artefacts from this excavation does offer the opportunity of detailed spatial analysis, but the investigation of purely mesolithic activity is complicated by the admixture of late mesolithic and early neolithic flints, so that it may prove difficult to isolate anything other than the microlithic component.

Mesolithic findspots in the northern Cotswolds are rare, though this is likely to represent an imbalance in both the quantity and the quality of fieldwork undertaken. Thus the Royce collection from the Swell area contained, despite its large size, virtually no mesolithic flints (Gracie 1970, 7; Grinsell 1964) because it was highly selective in origin and biased towards later arrowhead types. By contrast, the casual, but extensive, fieldwork in the Sevenhampton area by Draper, during which all observed flints were collected, resulted in a collection which includes a proportion of distinctively mesolithic artefacts (Cheltenham Museum), as was the case with fieldwork in the Hazleton area in the vicinity of the chambered tomb (Saville in preparation). This point is emphasized by the most northerly Cotswold findspot available, which is firmly in the area covered by Royce, and results from recent intensive fieldwork. This location, the field known as Cow Common at Swell, produced a group of seven microliths, which was distinctive in including an edge-blunted point with inverse basal retouch (Saville 1979, 105 and fig. 12). While undue stress should not be placed on a single find, this microlith is of extreme interest as the first Gloucestershire example of a type now recognized as characteristic of certain later mesolithic assemblages in central England (Saville 1981a, 59–60). These assemblages give an indication of patterning which may reflect cultural or chronological variation within the later mesolithic of the region (Saville 1981b, 12–13), and perhaps carry an implication that in Gloucestershire there is a north/south diversity, though of a different nature to that suggested by previous writers (Gracie 1970, 9; Smith 1973, 76).

Away from the Cotswolds on the lower ground the distribution of mesolithic material is scanty, though this is more likely to reflect the masking effect of post-mesolithic alluvial and colluvial deposition than the prehistoric reality.

In the Severn Valley, Barnwood is again one of the best-known locations. The early observations produced characteristic microliths (Clifford, Garrod and Gracie 1954, 184), while in 1958 a mesolithic axe (Wymer 1977, 101) was apparently recovered from the Barnwood gravels, though the provenance is uncertain (Gloucester Museum records). This axe (Fig. 6), of classic tranchet form, is the only example of this tool-type, so well known in south-eastern England, to be found in the county, which accords with the generally sparse distribution of mesolithic axes in central England. The axe from Hampen, previously mentioned by Gracie (1970, 8; Wymer 1977, 103), must now be reclassified as a core.

*Figure 6* Mesolithic tranchet axe, thought to be from Barnwood, Gloucester. (Gloucester City Museum A3674.) (Photo: A. Saville.)

West of the Severn the artefacts from Tidenham claimed as mesolithic can only be regarded as of uncertain date in view of their inexplicit typology as originally illustrated (Scott-Garrett 1955, fig. 8), and their current unknown whereabouts. Undoubted mesolithic artefacts, including microliths, are present in Hereford Museum within the Ballard collection, which derives mainly from the Ledbury area but includes material from Dymock. Unfortunately it is not now possible to locate the exact provenance of any of the mesolithic items, which could come from either side of the county boundary, though a definite later mesolithic presence is attested for the general Ledbury area.

The limitations of the evidence for mesolithic occupation in Gloucestershire do not permit anything conclusive to be said of the role these communities played. However, the situation at Hazleton, where a mesolithic site was used for neolithic settlement, and later for the siting of a neolithic chambered tomb, may suggest that mesolithic people were in some way an influence on the landscape. As elsewhere in the country, the relationship between mesolithic and neolithic communities is inexplicit, but it could be that a clearing originally made by mesolithic people at Hazleton proved attractive to agriculturalists for their own settlement. If so, and remembering that many sites of later periods produce mesolithic finds, it may be the mesolithic inhabitants of the county who set in motion those anthropomorphically-determined ecological changes to the post-glacial landscape which underlie the present-day Gloucestershire countryside (cf. Smith 1973, 76–77).

## ACKNOWLEDGEMENTS

I am very grateful to the staffs of the museums at Cheltenham, Cirencester, Gloucester, Hereford, and Stroud for their help during the compilation of this article, and for permission to study and publish the objects in their collections. Thanks are also due to the following individuals for their assistance in various ways: Mr W.F. Cox, Dr T.C. Darvill, Mrs E.D. Gander, Dr P.J. Osbourne, Mr E.G. Price, Mr R. Randall, and Mr P.F. Whitehead. Finally I am indebted to Dr D.A. Roe for reading through this article in draft form, and for his many helpful comments which have considerably improved the final version. Any errors of fact or interpretation remain my own.

## APPENDIX 1: KEY TO PALAEOLITHIC FINDSPOTS PLOTTED ON FIG. 1

| *Handaxes/bifaces* | *N.G.R.* | *Publication/collection* |
|---|---|---|
| 1. Longlevens, Gloucester | SO 850 195 | Gloucester Museum A3125 |
| 2. Barnwood, Gloucester | *c.*SO 866 173 | Clifford 1936; Cambridge University Museum of Archaeology |
| 3. Barnwood, Gloucester | *c.*SO 866 173 | Burkitt 1921; Clifford 1930; Cambridge University Museum of Archaeology |
| 4. Brockworth | SO 889 165 | Clifford 1937; Cambridge University Museum of Archaeology |
| 5. Great Witcombe | *c.*SO 910 148 | Clifford *et al.* 1954; Cambridge University Museum of Archaeology |
| 6. Charlton Abbots | *c.*SP 034 242 | Saville forthcoming; Cheltenham Museum 1982:389 |
| 7. Santhill, Bourton-on-the-Water | SP 178 191 | O'Neil 1965; Ashmolean Museum, Oxford |
| 8. Poole Keynes | SU 012 946 | Grinsell 1966; Bristol City Museum |
| 9. South Cerney | SU 061 966 | Whitehead 1979; Private collection |
| 10. South Cerney | SU 068 968 | Viner 1978; Corinium Museum, Cirencester |
| 11. South Cerney | *c.*SU 06 96 | Corinium Museum, Cirencester |
| 12. Meysey Hampton | *c.*SU 120 998 | Gloucester Museum A3124 |
| 13. Fairford | *c.*SU 15 98 | Corinium Museum, Cirencester |
| 14. Lechlade | *c.*SP 217 007 | Clifford 1939; British Museum |
| *Upper palaeolithic* | | |
| 15. Barnwood, Gloucester | *c.*SO 866 173 | Campbell 1977; Clifford *et al.* 1954; Cambridge University Museum of Archaeology; Gloucester Museum |

## APPENDIX 2: KEY TO FINDSPOTS OF MESOLITHIC MICROLITHS PLOTTED ON FIG. 4

| *Location* (*No. of microliths in brackets*) | *N.G.R.* | *Publication/collection* |
|---|---|---|
| 1. Cow Common, Swell (7) | SP 135 263 | Saville 1979; Cheltenham Museum 1978:958:1 |
| 2. Naunton (1) | *c.*SP 110 230 | Cheltenham Museum 1978:345:1; present report Fig. 5, 39 |
| 3. Soundborough, Sevenhampton (1) | SP 050 219 | Cheltenham Museum 1979:1152 |
| 4. Puckham, Sevenhampton (2) | *c.*SP 002 222 | Cheltenham Museum 1978:336, 338; present report Fig. 5, 40 |
| 5. Syreford, Whittington (56+) | SP 0287 2025 | W.F. Cox collection (Cheltenham Museum); present report Fig. 5, 1–38 |

| Location (No. of microliths in brackets) | N.G.R. | Publication/collection |
|---|---|---|
| 6. Andoversford (1) | c.SP 025 197 | Cheltenham Museum, not accessioned |
| 7. Soundborough, Sevenhampton (1) | SP 0428 2075 | Cheltenham Museum 1976:249:5 |
| 8. Hampen, Shipton (1) | c.SP 052 198 | Cheltenham Museum 1978:355 |
| 9. Salperton, Hazleton (3) | c.SP 075 205 | Cheltenham Museum1978:342:1-3 |
| 10. Barrow Ground, Hazleton (55+) | SP 073 189 | Saville 1983b (Cheltenham Museum) |
| 11. Barnwood, Gloucester (2) | c.SP 865 179 | Clifford et al. 1954 (Gloucester Museum) |
| 12. Shab Hill, Cowley (1) | c.SO 935 152 | Cheltenham Museum 1978:344 |
| 13. Birdlip, Cowley (2) | SO 934 145 | Darvill 1984, fig. 23. |
| 14. Bubb's Hill, Elkstone (1) | c.SO 965 137 | Cheltenham Museum 1978:341 |
| 15. Blacklains, Brimpsfield (3) | c.SO 929 133 | Gloucester Museum A3061a |
| 16. Climperwell, Cranham (1) | c.SO 919 122 | Stroud Museum, not accessioned |
| 17. Harcombe, Syde (10) | c.SO 957 113 | Gander 1976; Private collection |
| 18. Whiteway, Miserden (2) | c.SO 920 105 | Gloucester Museum A3398 |
| 19. Longridge, Painswick (1) | c.SO 879 092 | Gloucester Museum A3409 |
| 20. Camp, Miserden (1) | c.SO 914 093 | Cheltenham Museum 1978:347 |
| 21. Duntisbourne Abbots (1) | SO 961 078 | Private collection |
| 22. Eastington Pit, Eastington (1) | c.SO 771 067 | Stroud Museum 46:26/8 |
| 23. Stroud (2) | SO 8365 0600 | Private collection |
| 24. Bagendon (4?) | c.SP 018 064 | Gracie 1961; (Corinium Museum, Cirencester) |
| 25. Barnsley Park, Barnsley (4) | SP 0810 0615 | Barfield 1981 |
| 26. Stroud (1) | SO 8339 0495 | Private collection |
| 27. Bournes Green, Bisley-with-Lypiatt (1) | SO 912 048 | Stroud Museum 73:69 |
| 28. Leonard Stanley (5) | c.SO 797 038 | Gracie 1938 |
| 29. Frocester Court, Frocester (5) | SO 785 029 | Private collection |
| 30. Hazel Wood, Avening (8) | c.ST 862 987 | Stroud Museum 46:2:277-283; 67:135 |
| 31. Field Barn, Cherington (1) | c.ST 916 983 | Stroud Museum 46:16/31 |
| 32. Symond's Hall Farm, Wotton-under-Edge (2) | c.ST 795 960 | Gloucester Museum 92/1969 |
| 33. Troublehouse Covert, Cherington (24+) | ST 916 961 | Witchell 1973; Private collection; Cheltenham Museum 1978:875:1 |
| 34. Troublehouse Covert, Cherington (1) | ST 9136 9567 | Cheltenham Museum 1978:874 |
| 35. Chavenage, Beverstone/Horsley (1) | c.ST 870 951 | Stroud Museum 44-6/1-20 |
| 36. Kingscote (1) | ST 830 942 | Cheltenham Museum 1978:945 |
| 37. Bowldridge Farm, Long Newnton (15) | c.ST 923 932 | Gracie 1942 |
| 38. Westonbirt with Lasborough (2) | ST 825 942 | Cheltenham Museum 1980:628, 729 |
| 39. Cherington (1) | ST 895 979 | Cheltenham Museum 1980:82 |

# REFERENCES

Anon. 1969. Note on a palaeolith from Elkstone. *Archaeol Rev* 4, 21.

Barfield, L.H. 1981. The flints. In G. Webster, The excavation of a Romano-British rural establishment at Barnsley Park, Gloucestershire, 1961–1979. *TBGAS* 99, 37–45.

Burkitt, M.C. 1921. A Gloucester palaeolith. *Antiq J* 1, 234.

Burkitt, M.C. 1938. Description of a flint implement from a digging in the gravel of the Eastington pit. *PCNFC* 26.3, 296–297.

Campbell, J.B. 1970. The upper palaeolithic period. In J.B. Campbell, D. Elkington, P.J. Fowler, and L.V. Grinsell, *The Mendip Hills in prehistoric and Roman times*, 5–11. Bristol.

Campbell, J.B. 1977. *The upper palaeolithic of the British Isles*. Oxford.

Clifford, E.M. 1930. A prehistoric and Roman site at Barnwood near Gloucester. *TBGAS* 52, 201–254.

Clifford, E.M. 1936. A palaeolith found near Gloucester. *Antiq J* 16, 91.

Clifford, E.M. 1937. A palaeolith from Gloucestershire. *PPS* 3, 465–466.

Clifford, E.M. 1939. Palaeolith from the Upper Thames. *Antiq J* 19, 193.

Clifford, E.M., Garrod, D.A.E., and Gracie, H.S. 1954. Flint implements from Gloucestershire. *Antiq J* 34, 178–187.

Darvill, T.C. 1984. *Birdlip Bypass project – first report: archaeological assessment and field survey*. Bristol. (Western Archaeological Trust.)

Gander, E.D. 1976. Possible mesolithic site at Harcombe, Syde. *Glevensis* 10, 12.

Gardiner, C.I. 1932. Recent discoveries in the Stroud Valley. *PCNFC* 24.3, 163–180.

Gracie, H.S. 1938. Surface flints from Leonard Stanley, Gloucestershire. *TBGAS* 60, 180–189.

Gracie, H.S. 1942. Surface flints from Long Newnton, Gloucestershire. *TBGAS* 63, 172–189.

Gracie, H.S. 1961. Flints. In E.M. Clifford, *Bagendon: a Belgic Oppidum*, 197–198. Cambridge.

Gracie, H.S. 1970. Mesolithic Gloucestershire. *TBGAS* 89, 5–10.

Grinsell, L.V. 1964. The Royce collection at Stow-on-the-Wold. *TBGAS* 83, 5–33.

Grinsell, L.V. 1966. A palaeolithic implement from Poole Keynes. *TBGAS* 85, 207–208.

Jacobi, R.M. 1982. Ice Age cave-dwellers 12000–9000 BC. In M.A. Aston and I.C.G. Burrow (eds.), *The archaeology of Somerset: a review to 1500 AD*, 10–13. Somerset County Council.

Lacaille, A.D. 1954. Palaeoliths from the lower reaches of the Bristol Avon. *Antiq J* 34, 1–27.

Mellars, P.A. 1974. The palaeolithic and mesolithic. In C. Renfrew (ed.), *British prehistory: a new outline*, 41–99. London.

Mellars, P.A. 1976. Settlement patterns and industrial variability in the British mesolithic. In G. de G. Sieveking, I.H. Longworth, and K.E. Wilson (eds.), *Problems in economic and social archaeology*, 375–399. London.

Morrison, A. 1980. *Early man in Britain and Ireland*. London.

O'Neil, H.E. 1965. A palaeolithic flint implement from Bourton-on-the-Water, *PCNFC* 34.4, 225–227.

Posnansky, M. 1963. The lower and middle palaeolithic industries of the English East Midlands. *PPS* 29, 357–394.

RCHM. 1976. *Iron Age and Romano-British monuments in the Gloucestershire Cotswolds*. London.

Roe, D.A. 1968. *A gazetteer of British lower and middle palaeolithic sites*. London. (=CBA Res Rep 8.)

Roe, D.A. 1974. Palaeolithic artefacts from the River Avon terraces near Bristol. *Proc Univ Bristol Spelaeological Soc* 13(3), 319–326.

Roe, D.A. 1981. *The lower and middle palaeolithic periods in Britain*. London.

Rogers, T., Pinder, A., and Russell, R.C. 1981. Cave art discovery in Britain. *The Illustrated London News*, January 1981, 32–34.

Saville, A. 1979. *Recent work at Cow Common bronze age cemetery, Gloucestershire*. Bristol. (=CRAAGS Occasional Paper 6.)

Saville, A. 1981a. Mesolithic industries in central England: an exploratory investigation using microlith typology. *Archaeol J* 138, 49–71.

Saville, A. 1981b. Honey Hill, Elkington: a Northamptonshire mesolithic site. *Northamptonshire Archaeol* 16, 1–13.

Saville, A. 1983a. Hazleton excavation project 1982. *Glevensis* 17, 14–19.

Saville, A. 1983b. A 5000-year-old tomb in the Cotswolds. *The Illustrated London News*, September 1983, 57–58.

Saville, A. Forthcoming. A palaeolith presumed to be from Charlton Abbots, Gloucestershire. *TBGAS*.

Saville, A. In preparation. The excavation of a Cotswold-Severn tomb at Hazleton, Gloucestershire, 1979–1982.

Saville, A. and Shotton, F.W. 1976. A palaeolithic implement from Hanley Castle, Worcestershire. *Trans Worcestershire Archaeol Soc* 5, 79–80.

Scott-Garrett, C. 1955. Tidenham Chase barrow. *TBGAS* 74, 15–35.

Smith, I.F. 1973. Prehistory. In C. and A.M. Hadfield (eds.), *The Cotswolds: a new study*, 76–84. Newton Abbot.

Sykes, C.M. and Whittle, S.L. 1965. A flint-chipping site on Tog Hill near Marshfield. *TBGAS* 84, 5–14.

Viner, D.J. 1978. A palaeolithic implement from Cerney Wick. *TBGAS* 96, 69–70.

Whitehead, P.F. 1979. An Acheulian handaxe from South Cerney, Gloucestershire. *TBGAS* 97, 117–118.

Witchell, A.N. 1973. Mesolithic evidence from Troublehouse, Cherington, Gloucestershire. *TBGAS* 92, 12–20.

Wymer, J.J. (ed.). 1977. *Gazetteer of mesolithic sites in England and Wales*. London. (= CBA Res Rep 20.)

Wymer, J.J. 1982. *The palaeolithic age*. London.


**March 1984**

# Neolithic Gloucestershire

## Tim Darvill

### INTRODUCTION

From shortly after 4000 bc fundamental changes in the lifestyle of those communities living in Britain came about. Dependence on gathering and hunting as a source of food was reduced, its place being taken by the cultivation of arable crops and the rearing of domesticated animals. Settlements became more permanent, the population expanded, and an economic and scientific revolution ensued, causing social changes of great magnitude. This was the period of the first farmers in Gloucestershire – traditionally termed the neolithic period – and it lasted for nearly 2000 years, until metal objects became common and society underwent another episode of change. It should not be imagined, however, that the neolithic period itself was uniform throughout. As will be shown in this paper, small-scale, isolated, farming groups changed through time to become part of a more complex society, in which a range of massive, stone-built monuments and enclosures provided the focus for ritual and settlement respectively. After about 600 years the pattern again changed. Many of the monuments were abandoned; there was a shift towards small dispersed settlements and localized adoption of more widespread traditions.

Of course, present county boundaries had no meaning to neolithic people, and our knowledge of their activities is based on the study of preserved monuments and artefacts from a wide area. Nevertheless, Gloucestershire is rich in neolithic remains. Appraisal of the evidence from within its bounds provides us with a neat, representative sample of neolithic society in the mid-west of England, not least because of the variety of habitats represented within the county by the Forest, the Vale, and the Cotswolds.

Mention must also be made of the fact that the diligent researches of Mrs Clifford and Mrs O'Neil from the 1930s onwards have furnished the present generation of archaeologists with a rich data-base through which to reconstruct the neolithic of Gloucestershire. In presenting this essay I would like to acknowledge my gratitude to both women for their work.

## HISTORICAL REVIEW

Interest in the neolithic of Gloucestershire has a long and distinguished history in which four main phases can be identified.

*To 1925.* The earliest explorations of neolithic monuments may have been during Roman times (O'Neil and Grinsell 1960, 54), but it was not until the late eighteenth and early nineteenth centuries that any serious studies of the origin, content, or structure of the monuments were undertaken. Long barrows, being one of the most conspicuous types of sites then known, were singled out for special attention, as shown by the work of Greenwell (1877), Rolleston (1876), Thurnam (1868), Witts (1883), and Sir Henry Dryden. Many other investigators, unnamed and unknown, left no records of their activities. Collections of stray finds, mostly recovered by farm labourers, began to be amassed at this time, as with the Royce collection from the Swell district of north Gloucestershire (Fig. 1; Grinsell 1964). The end of this first phase of study is marked by the publication of Crawford's invaluable study, *The long barrows of the Cotswolds* (1925), which summarized all the information on each site then known, and set the monuments as a group within their regional and chronological context.

*1925 – 1950.* This period of study saw the use of improved excavation techniques, and also the first investigations of neolithic sites other than barrows. From 1928 to 1930 excavations took place at Belas Knap (GLO 1), first under the direction of Hemp (1929) and later by Berry (1929 and 1930), in advance of restoration in 1930–1931 by the then Office of Works (Radford 1930). This was followed by Clifford's re-excavations at Notgrove (GLO 4) in 1934 (Clifford 1936a), Nympsfield (GLO 13) in 1937 (Clifford 1938a), and Rodmarton (GLO 16) in 1939 (Clifford and Daniel 1940). In the north Cotswolds, O'Neil investigated the Adlestrop barrow (GLO 44) from 1935 to 1938 (Donovan 1938). Supplementing the evidence from the barrows, the first traces of neolithic settlements were found at Barnwood (Clifford 1930), Salmonsbury (Dunning 1931 and 1976), and Bourton-on-the-Water (Dunning 1932). In 1950 Clifford published a review of 'The Cotswold megalithic culture' to elaborate two earlier papers synthesizing the available evidence (Clifford 1936b and 1937).

*1950 – 1970.* The 1950s and 1960s marked something of a hiatus for neolithic studies in Gloucestershire. The only excavations of specifically neolithic sites were both of a rescue nature: O'Neil (1966) at the Sale's Lot long barrow (GLO 94), and Arthur at Cam near Dursley (Smith 1968). Important publications from this period include Piggott's seminal work *The Neolithic cultures of the British Isles* (1954), which set the evidence known from the Cotswolds into a wider perspective; the definitive report on Grimes's meticulous war-time excavations at Burn Ground (GLO 60) and Saltway Barn (GLO 92), which included the first detailed treatment of the structural elements within Cotswold tombs (Grimes 1960); and Grinsell and O'Neil's gazetteer of barrows in Gloucestershire, compiled from research and fieldwork mostly undertaken in 1959 and 1960 (O'Neil and Grinsell 1960). The end of this phase is marked by the publication of Corcoran's study (1969) of the Cotswold long barrows, undertaken as part of a review of the megalithic tombs of western Britain.

*1970 – 1982.* The twelve years between 1970 and 1982 saw many new discoveries relating to the neolithic period in Gloucestershire. In 1971, research excavations designed to explore the iron age hillfort on Crickley Hill revealed the existence of extensive neolithic deposits. Work in succeeding seasons has provided detailed evidence from a large area of the hilltop, and at least four main phases of neolithic activity have been defined (Dixon 1969–1973 and 1979). In 1974 the Nympsfield long barrow was again re-excavated before being restored for public display (Saville 1979a). Rescue excavations took place at Condicote henge in 1977 (Saville 1983a), and from 1979 to 1982 the northern cairn at Hazleton (GLO 54) was completely excavated (Saville 1980a, 1981, 1982a and 1983b). The Hazleton project came about in response to the growing awareness of the damage caused to Cotswold barrows by ploughing (Saville 1980b). Trial trenching in 1980 and 1981 confirmed the existence of a causewayed enclosure on The Peak, near Birdlip (Darvill 1981 and 1982a). Other neolithic sites were discovered in the course of a number of excavations undertaken during the early 1970s (e.g. at Gloucester; Hurst 1972), and research work into the neolithic period generally has supplemented our understanding of the evidence, both locally and in its regional context (Darvill 1978, 1982b and 1983; Whittle 1977a). The constant trickle of neolithic artefacts recovered as stray finds, either by chance, or through fieldwork, continues much as it has since the late nineteenth century. Insights into the neolithic environment in the area have accrued over recent years through analysis of archaeological and non-archaeological deposits (Bell 1983; Brown 1982).

## ENVIRONMENT

Gloucestershire encompasses a range of environments. On the eastern side is the upland limestone plateau forming the Cotswold Hills, in the centre is the Severn Vale, with its clay floor only occasionally interrupted by spreads of alluvium and gravel, and to the west are the uplands of the Forest of Dean, with their much older rocks and essentially thin soils. Each of these three zones may have witnessed different exploitation in prehistory, and accordingly demand separate treatment for the reconstruction of the neolithic environment. Sadly, no relevant data are available from west Gloucestershire, and the evidence from the other two areas is pitifully slight.

Studies of pollen spectra derived from several peat deposits in the Severn Valley have been undertaken recently. Taken together, the results from the Ripple Brook site north of Tewkesbury and the Longney site south of Gloucester suggest that there was no major clearance of the woodland in the Vale until the end of the neolithic, or even the early bronze age (Brown 1982, 102). Small-scale clearances must have taken place, however, since current archaeological evidence suggests considerable settlement on many of the gravel areas in the Vale from earliest times.

Available evidence from the Cotswold uplands presents a rather different, and sometimes contradictory, picture. Although outside the county in west Oxfordshire, the soil profile discovered beneath the Ascott-under-Wychwood long barrow is the most intensively studied local sequence, and has relevance for the Cotswolds in general. The environmental record at Ascott stretches back to early post-glacial times. Molluscan remains suggest that at first the area had a light woodland cover, but that this gave way to more closed woodland in the fourth millennium bc, and was then cleared in the early third millennium bc. After a brief period as a settlement, the site became grassland until about 2800 bc, when the barrow was built (Evans 1971, 40). Although pollen rarely survives on calcareous soils, enough grains were found at Ascott to confirm the trends shown by the mollusca (Dimbleby and Evans 1974, 120).

At Nympsfield, molluscan samples were studied from a pre-mound feature, and from an orthostat socket (Spencer 1979, 83). Both samples were small and may reflect conditions only in the immediate vicinity of the features. Nonetheless, it is notable that no snail species which confine themselves to open-country environments were present in the pre-mound sample, and only a small number were recorded in the sample from the orthostat socket.

The late neolithic henge at Condicote appears to have been set within a wooded landscape (Bell 1983), but whether this should be seen as uncleared forest or regenerative growth in the late third or early second millennium bc is open to debate (cf. Whittle 1978).

Direct evidence of the tree species present in the neolithic woodland comes from the identification of carbonized wood found in sealed contexts within chambered tombs. Table 1 summarizes the evidence, although it cannot be used to gauge the relative frequency of individual species.

TABLE 1

*Tree species identified from charcoals recovered from excavated long barrows.*

|  | Nympsfield (Clifford 1938a; Saville 1979a) | Notgrove (Clifford 1936a) | Rodmarton (Clifford and Daniel 1940) | Sale's Lot (O'Neil 1966) |
|---|---|---|---|---|
| Ash (*Fraxinus excelsior*) | X | X | X | |
| Hazel (*Corylus avellana*) | X | X | X | nut shells |
| Hawthorn (*Crataegus oxyacantha*) | X | | X | |
| Beech (*Fagus sylvatica*) | X | | X | |
| Oak (*Quercus sp.*) | X | | X | |
| Yew (*Taxus baccata*) | X | | X | |
| Elm (*Ulmus sp.*) | X | | X | |
| Willow (*Salix sp.*) | | | X | |
| Pine (*Pinus sp.*) | X | | | |
| Gean / Cherry (*Prunus sp.*) | X | X | | |

Other details of the environment, such as the course and nature of the River Severn (which is shown on the maps in this paper by its present course) cannot be discussed because adequate data are simply not yet available. The neolithic climate is generally thought to have been a few degrees warmer, and slightly wetter, than that of today (Smith 1981; Taylor 1975).

## CHRONOLOGY

The most intractable difficulty experienced in reviewing the evidence for neolithic Gloucestershire is the absence of a sound chronological framework. The only radiocarbon dates available at the time of writing relate to the ditch fill of the henge at Condicote (Saville 1983a), and belong to the late neolithic/early bronze age transition. Even if more dates were available, however, only a fraction of the known evidence could be placed within any chronological framework.

One alternative is a relative chronology based on pottery typology. Seriation studies of well-provenanced assemblages (Darvill 1983, 53) broadly confirm the sequence suggested by Smith (1974, 106–120), and allow a three-fold division of the period to be proposed. Early neolithic assemblages are dominated by open, shouldered bowls. In the middle neolithic a greater variety of styles emerged, together with some regional variations; Gloucestershire neolithic pottery of this period displays Abingdon/Windmill Hill/Hembury affinities. Decoration became more common in the middle neolithic. The late neolithic is marked by the development of the Mortlake and Fengate styles out of the decorated middle neolithic wares, the appearance of grooved ware, which is seemingly unrelated to earlier types, and, at the end of the neolithic, the introduction of beaker-style pottery.

Even given these distinctions in pottery types it is often difficult to accurately assign evidence to one or other of the defined phases, and a certain amount of overlap has to be admitted. Nevertheless, the general outline of social change can be determined, especially as the occasional superimposition of one monument type over another gives additional clues to the order of events.

## THE EARLY NEOLITHIC (c.3500–2900 bc)

Little is known of the early neolithic in Gloucestershire. Traditional chronological distinctions between the mesolithic and the neolithic are hard to define in practice. Farming groups may well have co-existed with hunter-gatherers for several centuries. Indeed, the early farmers may have taken advantage of any small-scale clearances made by the hunters to improve grazing for use as crop cultivation plots. Both acculturation, through the interaction of coastal communities, and migration, from continental Europe, probably promoted the adoption of neolithic lifestyles in Britain.

Fig. 1 summarizes the evidence tentatively assigned to the early neolithic phase in Gloucestershire. Early type neolithic pottery, including open,

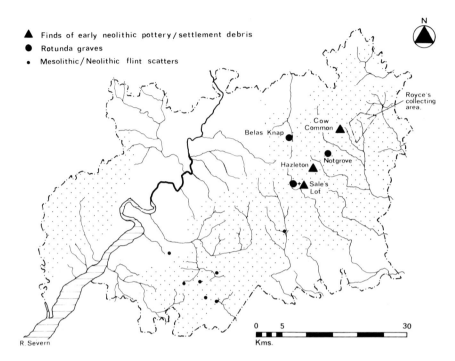

*Figure 1*   Distribution of early neolithic sites. Land over 120m above O.D. indicated
by stippling. Mesolithic/neolithic flint scatters after Wymer (1977).

carinated bowls, has been found in a midden-like deposit beneath the
Hazleton North barrow (Saville 1983b, 18), and similar vessels, illustrated
for the first time in Fig. 2, were found during the excavation of the Cow
Common long barrow (GLO 22) in 1867 (Greenwell 1877, 514). Another site
which may belong to this period is at Sale's Lot, where excavations in
1963–1965 revealed the post-holes of a structure in the disturbed forecourt of
a chambered tomb (O'Neil 1966). These were interpreted by the excavator as
the remains of a building post-dating use of the tomb, but re-examination of
the excavation records suggests that the building probably extends under the
unexcavated cairn, and would therefore pre-date the tomb (Darvill 1982b,
60).

Monuments which stratigraphically underlie, and therefore pre-date, long
barrows, may be assigned provisionally to the early neolithic. All are simple,
circular structures, known as rotunda graves. The most completely preserved
example was found in 1935 beneath the long barrow at Notgrove (Figs. 1 and

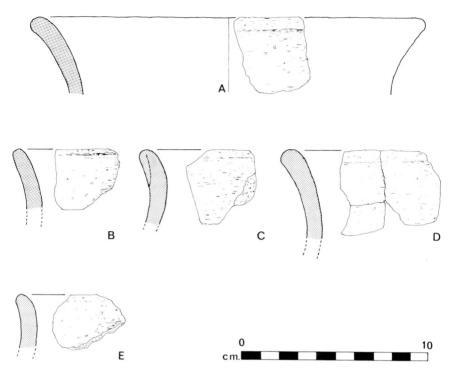

*Figure 2*   Early neolithic pottery from Cow Common long barrow (GLO 22), now in
the Ashmolean Museum, Oxford.

5). The rotunda cairn measured about 7m in diameter, and stood 0·76m high.
It was neatly built of local stone and at its centre was a slab-lined, sub-angular
cist. Within this cist were the remains of an adult male burial (Clifford 1936a,
125–128). Similar structures may be identified elsewhere. At Belas Knap the
'broken circle of stones' about 2·2m in diameter, surrounded by ashy soil and
lying on the old ground surface (Lawrence and Winterbotham 1866, 379), is
tantalizing evidence in the light of the Notgrove example, and grave 2 in the
badly disturbed, western end of the Sale's Lot cairn may be another instance
(O'Neil 1966, 19). In the latter case a few human teeth and a flint leaf-shaped
arrowhead were all that remained of the burial deposit.
    One other monument which might be placed in the early neolithic phase is
the so-called 'banana barrow' found sealed beneath the causewayed enclosure
on Crickley Hill. The monument comprised an enclosure, about 8m long,
bounded by a series of quarry pits, and, as the name suggests, was

banana-shaped in plan. Spoil from the pits was seemingly piled up in the central area, but was removed when the causewayed enclosure was built. The purpose of the structure is unclear (Dixon 1979, 143 and pers. comm.).

It is notable that the known early neolithic sites cluster in groups on the uplands. This may be a wholly artificial pattern created by the distribution of excavations; only further work will tell. One possibility which should be seriously entertained is that some of the many round barrows in Gloucester-shire represent early neolithic rotunda graves which never became covered by trapezoidal tombs of middle neolithic date. Potential examples of neolithic round barrows in the county are already known (Kinnes 1979, 70; O'Neil and Grinsell 1960, 97). Another possibility is that flint scatters containing both mesolithic and neolithic artefacts may point to early neolithic settlements (see Fig. 1 for some of these scatters).

## THE MIDDLE NEOLITHIC (*c*.2900–2400 bc)

Evidence relating to this phase of the neolithic (Fig. 3) is rather more abundant than for the early period. If the distributions of stray finds and monuments are taken together, it becomes clear that much of Gloucestershire was settled in the middle neolithic, although it should not be assumed that the disposition of activity types was homogeneous throughout the county. Discussion of the evidence is arranged under a series of thematic sub-headings.

### Settlements and Enclosures

Two types of settlement can at present be isolated; one enclosed, the other seemingly unenclosed. The latter can be dealt with quickly as only one instance can be cited: the Telephone Exchange site in Gloucester (Hurst 1972, 38). Here, a single pit, containing about one third of a neolithic bowl and several pieces of flint, was found cut into the natural sub-soil. The vessel has typological parallels among material from Windmill Hill, Wiltshire (Smith 1965, 52) and probably dates to the first half of the third millennium bc. Other settlements, similar to the one at Gloucester, undoubtedly remain to be discovered, but in view of the ephemeral nature of the evidence it is hardly surprising that more are not known. A detailed study of flint scatters may add new examples to this category of site.

Enclosures, causewayed camps, or interrupted ditch systems, as they are variously known, are widespread over England, and have been the subject of

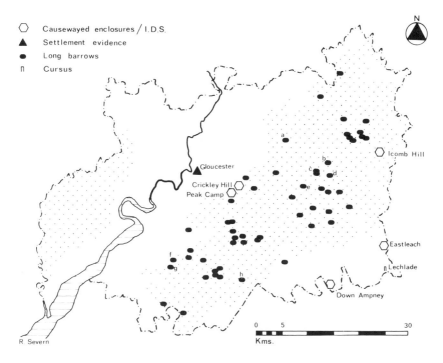

*Figure 3*  Distribution of middle neolithic sites. Land over 120m above O.D.
indicated by stippling. Sites: a – Belas Knap, GLO 1; b – Notgrove, GLO
4; c – Hazleton, GLO 33 and 54; d – Burn Ground, GLO 60; e – Sale's
Lot, GLO 94; f – Nympsfield, GLO 13; g – Hetty Pegler's Tump, GLO
14; h – Rodmarton, GLO 16.

much debate (Mercer 1980, 1–17; Whittle 1977b: both with earlier references). No consensus exists regarding their function, and it seems probable
that some variety of purpose underlies morphological similarities. Two
examples have been excavated in Gloucestershire, and a further three
examples have been identified from the distinctive segmented-ditch patterns
seen on aerial photographs.

At Crickley Hill, excavations have demonstrated that the neolithic enclosure underwent several episodes of refurbishment (Dixon 1979). The earliest
enclosure comprised a double line of causewayed ditches, each with a
stone-built rampart behind. There were at least four entrances, all provided
with wooden gates (Fig. 4). Both lines of ditches were deliberately filled, or
became filled, on several occasions. Each time they were re-dug. After this

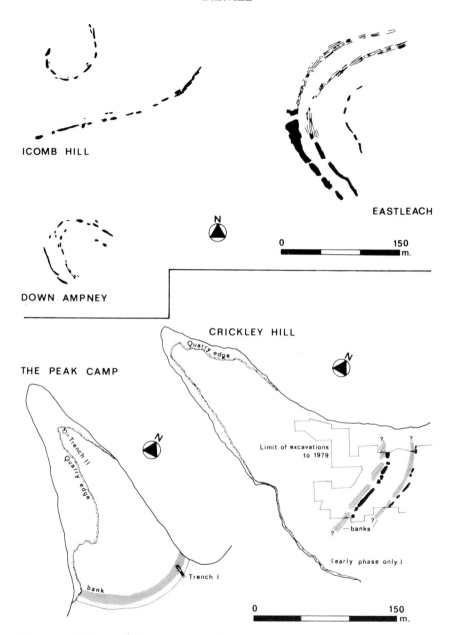

*Figure 4* Middle neolithic enclosures. (Sources: various.)

complex had finally been abandoned a much larger ditch was dug immediately outside, and parallel to, the inner ditch of the earlier enclosure. Unlike the earlier ditches, the new one was continuous except for two entrances. The rampart of this second enclosure appears to have been defensive, and in the interior the remains of roadways and houses suggest that by this time Crickley Hill was a fortified village.

Re-digging of the ditches was also a notable feature in the single section opened through the ramparts of the other excavated enclosure at The Peak, Birdlip (Fig. 4; Darvill 1981a and 1982a). The Peak Camp was probably another settlement, judging from the artefacts found, and is all the more interesting for being so close to Crickley Hill (Fig. 3). Very similar pottery, for example round-bottomed bowls with thickened rims, was in use at both sites, but the question of contemporaneity cannot be resolved until radiocarbon dates become available.

Among the enclosures recorded on aerial photographs, the example at Eastleach has three circuits of ditches, while both Down Ampney and Icomb Hill appear to have two circuits each (Fig. 4). The spread of sites across both the Cotswold uplands and the floor of the Thames Valley in eastern Gloucestershire is especially noteworthy (Darvill and Hingley forthcoming). Causewayed camps are often found to be situated on the interface between contrasting environments (Barker and Webley 1978), as with Crickley Hill and The Peak Camp, a circumstance which probably reflects the diverse subsistence strategies practised during the middle neolithic. Other enclosed settlements undoubtedly remain to be found; those hilltop sites yielding large quantities of neolithic flintwork, for example Uley Bury near Dursley (Saville and Ellison 1983, 1), must be high on the list of possibilities.

## Subsistence, Crafts and Material Culture

Direct evidence for neolithic subsistence practices comes from crop-processing equipment, animal bones, and carbonized cereal remains. Many fragments of flint blades with edge gloss, which probably formed part of composite sickles, have been found on the Cotswolds, and an example of a single-piece sickle is known from Barnwood (Clifford *et al.* 1954, fig. 4, 27). Querns have been found at Crickley Hill (Dixon pers. comm.), and among the stones of the Burn Ground long barrow (Grimes 1960, 74). Analysis of carbonized grain in soil samples from Crickley Hill attests the use of wheat and barley (Green pers. comm.), but only one cereal grain was recorded in samples taken from the ditch fill at The Peak Camp. Cattle are the dominant species among faunal assemblages from The Peak Camp and Crickley Hill.

Pig and sheep are recorded in lesser numbers on settlements, although at long barrows pig, cattle, and sheep are represented in more equal proportions. Table 2 summarizes the animal species known from the long barrows.

TABLE 2

*Animal bone finds in long barrows.*
(Data from O'Neil and Grinsell 1960, except where indicated).

| | Pig | Ox | Sheep/ goat | Horse | Dog (large) | Dog (small) | Cat | Deer | Fox | Bird |
|---|---|---|---|---|---|---|---|---|---|---|
| Avenis (GLO 75) | | X | X | | | | | | | |
| Burn Ground (GLO 60)* | X | X | X | | | | X | X | X | |
| Nympsfield (GLO 13)** | X | X | X | X | X | X | | X | | X |
| Notgrove (GLO 4) | X | X | X | X | X? | | | | | |
| Belas Knap (GLO 1) | X? | | | X | | | | X | | |
| Poles Wood S (GLO 2) | X | X | X | | | | | | | |
| Poles Wood E (GLO 24) | X | X | X | | | | | X | | |
| Hetty Pegler's Tump (GLO 14) | X | | | | | | | | | |
| Eyford Hill (GLO 3) | X | | X | | | X | | | | |
| Willersey (GLO 34) | | X | | | | | | | | |
| Bown Hill (GLO 20) | X | X | | | X | X | | | | |
| Randwick (GLO 10) | | | | | | | | | | X |
| Sale's Lot (GLO 94)*** | | | | | | | X | | X | |
| Total occurrences: | 9 | 8 | 7 | 4 | 4 | 1 | 2 | 4 | 2 | 2 |

\*    Grimes 1960
\*\*   O'Neil and Grinsell 1960; Saville 1979a
\*\*\*  O'Neil 1966

A great variety of crafts were undertaken at, or near, settlement sites. At Crickley Hill, flint-knapping floors on the hilltop show that flint nodules were converted into tools at the site (Burton 1980; Dixon 1979). Analysis of pottery fabrics from The Peak Camp shows that at least eighteen different combinations of local clays and tempering materials were used to produce a comprehensive range of vessels for domestic use. These included pots with good refractory properties for use in cooking, and porous vessels presumably for storage. The exploitation of local clays is also shown by pottery from long barrows, for example Nympsfield (Darvill 1979).

The range of tools, ornaments, and other objects available during the middle neolithic was considerable. Flint artefacts are well represented because of their high survival and recovery rates. Clifford (1950, 29) illustrates leaf-shaped arrowheads, while examples of other tools such as scrapers, borers, and knives will be found in many of the articles cited in the bibliography. Flint and stone axes occur widely as stray finds throughout the county (Evens *et al.* 1972; Tyler 1976). They demonstrate the wide geographical spread of neolithic activity in the landscape, as they were essential tools for farming and woodworking. Bone tools of various sorts are also known, principally from long barrows, and have been illustrated and discussed elsewhere, together with the beads, necklaces, pendants, and amulets that are found in similar contexts (Clifford 1950, figs. 5 and 7; Piggott 1954, 145–146). Pottery is known in a range of forms, although little from Gloucestershire has been published adequately. A pair of pottery spoons is known from the Cow Common long barrow, although the exact context is problematic (Greenwell 1877, 514; Leeds 1927; Piggott 1954, 75). Other artefact types, such as stone rubbers, haematite fragments, and stone mauls, are also recorded (Clifford 1950).

*Burials and Long Barrows*

Every society is faced with the problem of disposing of its dead, and during the middle neolithic a variety of practices were in common use. Some are poorly documented; for example the deposition of skulls and other human bones in the ditches of causewayed camps, as at Crickley Hill (Dixon pers. comm.). In contrast, burials in the long barrows (chambered tombs) are extremely well known and have come to characterize the neolithic of the area.

The long barrows of Gloucestershire and adjoining areas have been the subject of much discussion, and it is only possible to summarize the main points here. The barrows fall within the general family of Cotswold-Severn tombs (Corcoran 1969; Darvill 1982b), and can be differentiated from other chambered tombs in Britain on the basis of geographical location, shape, chamber plans, construction materials, structural details, and burial rites.

Modern Gloucestershire contains about sixty long barrows (Fig. 3). They are confined to the limestone uplands, mostly above the 120m contour; rarely on the tops of hills, but usually on false crests or ridges a little way from the summits. Many are situated with steep slopes on at least one side. There is a tendency for the long axes of the mounds to be aligned between SE-NW and NE-SW (Daniel 1950, 80), but so many exceptions could be cited that generalization is impossible. Sometimes two barrows occur together as a pair, for example at Eyford Hill (GLO 3 and 49), Upper Slaughter (O'Neil and Grinsell 1960, 15).

Fig. 5 shows the ground plans of a number of long barrows. The most noticeable element of each is the mound or cairn, which is either trapezoidal or rectangular in outline. All were carefully built from stone and soil derived

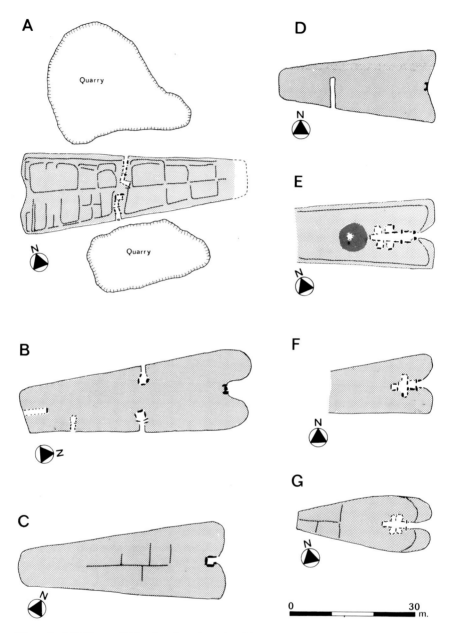

*Figure 5*  Middle neolithic chambered tombs. Sites: A – Hazleton North, GLO 54; B
– Belas Knap, GLO 1; C – Randwick, GLO 10; D – West Tump, GLO 8;
E – Notgrove, GLO 4; F – Nympsfield, GLO 13; G – Hetty Pegler's
Tump, GLO 14. (Sources: various.)

from the vicinity; in the case of Hazleton North from adjacent quarry pits (Saville 1983b). A faced, dry-stone wall circumscribed the cairn, and internal revetments were built in the course of heaping-up the cairn to stabilize the piled rubble and to facilitate construction. A forecourt was usually provided between two projecting horns at the wider, and putatively higher, end of the mound, perhaps to serve as a ritual focus.

There is considerable variety in cairn size. Smaller tombs, such as Nympsfield, are as little as 30m in length, while the largest example recorded in Gloucestershire, at Colnpen (GLO 69), is nearly 100m long.

Concealed within each cairn are one or more chambers. A passage of some sort gives access to the chambers from the exterior of the cairn. Large stones, or orthostats, were usually used to make the walls of both chambers and passages, the gaps between them being filled with dry-stone walling. Corbelling or large capstones were used to roof the passages and chambers.

Early attempts to classify excavated tombs made much of the position of the chambers; those tombs with laterally-placed chambers were firmly distinguished from those with terminal chambers (e.g. Thurnam 1868). Other features, such as the presence of a false portal in the forecourt wall of some laterally chambered tombs (e.g. Belas Knap), were also brought into the discussion as typology became pressed into service to provide a rudimentary chronological sequence, in which the terminally chambered types were seen as anterior to the laterally chambered types through a process of degeneration. The true entrance was replaced by a false entrance according to this line of argument (Daniel 1939, 164; Grimes 1939, 139). In more recent considerations of typology four groups are defined: cairns with simple box-like terminal chambers; cairns with transepted terminal chambers; cairns with chambers set laterally, with access from one or both sides of the cairn; and miscellaneous cairns (Corcoran 1969, 14). Kinnes (1975) has suggested, however, that the degree of partitioning within the chamber area, and the number of cellular chamber-units present, may be more important than their position in the cairn.

Human bones are found in the chambers, passageways, passage entrances, and occasionally in the forecourts. Inhumation was the usual burial rite, but some cremated bone has been found in most chambers which have been carefully excavated. With very few exceptions, burials are incomplete and disarticulated. The number of interments represented varies from about six individuals at Bown Hill (GLO 20) to about thirty-eight at Belas Knap (Piggott 1954, 140). Unless total excavation and careful recovery have been achieved, the number of burials reported are probably gross underestimates of the number originally present. Evidence for differential burial access by age and sex (Piggottt 1954, 140) may be less real in long barrows than is commonly thought, because of difficulties in ageing and sexing fragmentary skeletal material. One thing that can be said from present evidence is that the number of infant burials represented is too low to account for the mortality rate usual in primitive societies.

There is clearly an insufficient number of people represented by burials in long barrows to account for the total middle neolithic population of the region (Atkinson 1968), although just what qualifications entitled a person to such burial are unknown. On the other hand the possibility exists that chambers were periodically cleared out (Piggott 1973).

Grave-goods are few, and are limited to personal items such as pottery cups, beads, pendants, or other ornaments. In general, objects cannot be associated with specific individuals because of the jumbled nature of the burial deposits, while there are only enough grave-goods to have accompanied about one in seven of the interments. A rare exception was found in the entrance to the north chamber complex at Hazleton North, where an extended, male inhumation was accompanied by a large flint core under the right elbow and a quartzitic pebble hammerstone near the left hand (Saville 1982a, 15). Ritual activity undoubtedly accompanied burial ceremonies, and the tombs were probably also the scene of rites at other times. Whether complete bodies, or only collections of bones, were placed in the chambers is uncertain (Piggott 1962, 65), but sorting of the disarticulated remains did occur (Chesterman 1977), with skulls and long bones sometimes found in piles against the chamber walls (Saville 1983b, 14). Some bones, especially skulls and femora, seem to have been selectively removed, presumably for ritual use elsewhere (Smith 1965, 137). Excavations at Notgrove produced vivid evidence of the rites practised in the forecourt; a trough was found which contained unburnt human remains representing parts of several individuals, while other pits in the same area had contained fires (Clifford 1936a, 135–136).

The absence of radiocarbon dates from tombs in Gloucestershire hinders any assessment of their age or the duration of their use. On the basis of dates from other sites in the Cotswold-Severn area, however, it can be proposed that the trapezoidal tombs began to be built soon after 3000 bc. Ascott-under-Wychwood and Wayland's Smithy, both in Oxfordshire, were built after 2943±70 bc and 2820±130 bc respectively (Atkinson 1965, 132; Evans 1971, 40). To the west, Gwernvale in Powys, was built after 3100±75 bc (Britnell 1980, 147), and bone from one of the chambers at Pen-y-Wyrlod II, also in Powys, is dated 3020±80 bc (Savory 1980, 219). At all the sites where stratigraphy allows reconstruction of a sequence of events, the large trapezoidal tombs represent an elaboration of earlier traditions. Some trapezoidal tombs were built over earlier foci, some were new foundations (Corcoran 1972). Studies of the pottery found beneath, and inside, the various types of tomb, suggest that laterally chambered monuments were the earliest type to be built, and that terminal chambers and transepted chambers were later developments (Darvill 1982b, 15). All chambered tombs had long, useful lives, however, and there was undoubtedly considerable overlap in the currency of definable types.

It has been estimated that in the region of 15,700 man-hours would have been needed to build a large Cotswold-Severn tomb (Startin and Bradley 1981, 292). Exactly why middle neolithic Cotswold societies constructed such large monuments, with such small chambers and at such great cost in labour, is unknown, although many ideas have been put forward (Darvill 1982a; Renfrew 1983). One thing which does seem certain is that the monuments represented much more than repositories in which to curate bones; possibly they were in some senses symbolic devices, conveying information on group identity and the communal ownership of resources (Renfrew 1976). If so, the dead ancestors may have had a role to play by legitimizing inheritance or descent patterns. The tombs were as much for the living as they were for the dead (Fleming 1973).

Most tombs seem to have fallen into disuse by about 2400 bc, if not before. Burials ceased, and while some tombs remained open and simply fell into ruin, others were quite deliberately blocked up to prevent further access.

## Exchange

Middle neolithic communities were by no means isolated. Trackways undoubtedly formed local and long-distance networks, although their alignment and form are only known in exceptional cases (Coles et al. 1973). The possible trackway along the dip-slope of the Cotswolds described by Clifford and Simpson (1939) should be seen as a local trackway if accepted at all. Artefacts reflect the scale and orientation of inter-regional contact as they were demonstrably moved over great distances through various kinds of trade and exchange (Clark 1965; Hodder and Lane 1982; Renfrew 1975 and 1977).

Querns were imported into areas without suitable local stone; the example from Burn Ground probably originated in the Bristol-Somerset coalfield (Grimes 1960, 75). Flint of the type needed for toolmaking is not natural to Gloucestershire, and many tons must have been brought from areas to the south and east in prehistoric times, to judge from the quantities of waste debris still littering the landscape (Saville 1982b).

Ornaments were exchanged also. Shale beads, possibly from Kimmeridge in Dorset, are known from Notgrove (Clifford 1936a, 146) and Eyford Hill (GLO 3; Greenwell 1877, 514 and fig. 162). A shale pendant, also possibly from Kimmeridge, was found in a ditch within the enclosure on The Peak, Birdlip (Darvill 1982a, 23). The sea-shell pendant found at Nympsfield (Clifford 1938a, 191) is clearly of non-local origin.

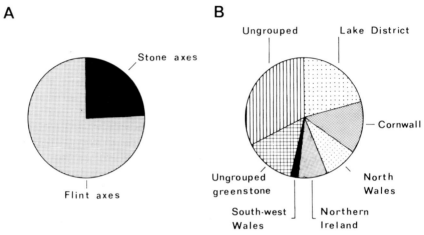

*Figure 6*    Pie diagrams showing (A) the relative frequency of flint and stone axes, and (B) the sources of stone axes. Compiled from data available up to October 1982.

Perhaps the best-documented objects which were commonly exchanged are axes and axe-like tools, such as wedges, adzes, and chisels (Clark 1965; Cummins 1974 and 1979). Sadly, it is necessary to consider all known examples together, even though some are not of middle neolithic date, because most are stray finds and lack contextual data which might otherwise allow chronological partitioning of the group. Stone axes have often been given special attention to the exclusion of flint axes, but in Gloucestershire all represent imports and therefore merit equal treatment. Fig. 6A shows, in pie-chart form, the proportions of flint and stone axes recorded from Gloucestershire, while Fig. 6B shows a breakdown of the sources contributing to the stone axe segment of Fig. 6A (data from Evens *et al.* 1972; Tyler 1976; and author's own research). As might be expected, flint axes were by far the most common imports, possibly because of the relative proximity of the sources in southern and eastern England. Stone axes from many parts of western Britain attest links over wide areas.

*Cursus Monument*

Another monument which tentatively can be assigned to this period is the cursus revealed by aerial photography at Lechlade (Smith 1972, 164). Little is known of its original length, but it is about 50m wide and consists of a pair of parallel ditches which originally had internal banks. Trial trenching in 1965 showed a line of post-holes along the inner edge of the ditch (Vatcher 1966). Nothing is known with certainty of the function of this kind of monument.

## THE LATE NEOLITHIC (*c.*2400–1900 bc)

The pattern of events in the later part of the third millennium bc is not easy to reconstruct from available evidence. It was once widely thought that social development was continuous throughout the third millennium bc, but it now seems that a hiatus can be recognized at about 2400 bc. Bradley and Hodder (1979, 96) note the cessation of monument-building and suggest a trend towards smaller social units. Whittle (1978) proposes social contraction on the basis of possible evidence for forest regeneration in several dated pollen sequences from northern and western Britain. The evidence currently available from Gloucestershire supports the notion of a hiatus, indeed it is suggestive of profound social change.

The fortified enclosure on Crickley Hill was razed before the currency of Peterborough pottery styles (Dixon pers. comm.). Its end was sudden and violent. In the ditch, and along both sides of the rampart, the excavators found many leaf-shaped arrowheads. Fire destroyed the gates, the houses, and the wooden fence topping the rampart. The site was clearly attacked and overrun (Dixon 1979, 147). At the nearby site of The Peak Camp, a similar, although less vivid, picture emerges. No evidence suggesting activity on the hilltop after the mid-third millennium bc was recovered.

Tombs in Gloucestershire, which were seemingly so important in middle neolithic times, were abandoned or deliberately blocked up. At Nympsfield, stones and soil were piled into the forecourt to prevent further access to the chambers. Pottery which was intermixed with this blocking comprised Ebbsfleet and Mortlake sub-styles of the Peterborough series (Clifford 1938a, 202; Saville 1979a, 64–65). Similar deposits were encountered during the excavation of other sites, including Notgrove (Clifford 1936a, 138), Burn Ground (Grimes 1960, 47), and Rodmarton (Clifford and Daniel 1940, 141). Absolute dates for these events are not available from Gloucestershire, but at Gwernvale in Powys, the tomb was probably sealed up shortly after 2440±70 bc (Britnell 1980, 147). By the end of the late neolithic, chambered tombs had probably become forgotten ruins. At Poles Wood South (GLO 2), a Peterborough-style vessel was found in what appears to be a secondary context, possibly accompanying some kind of burial dug into the cairn (Crawford 1925, 127). At Sale's Lot an adult male, accompanied by a fine, beaker-style vessel, was buried in a grave dug into the body of the mound (O'Neil 1966, 24). Beaker pottery has also been found in secondary contexts at Eyford Hill, Poles Wood South, and Notgrove (Clifford 1937, 161).

The society which emerged after this hiatus seems to have been less concerned with spectacular monuments. A return to simple, small-scale social groups, similar to those of the early neolithic, can be postulated. Certainly this would fit the expected patterns of social change after the collapse of relatively complex societies (cf. Renfrew 1978).

*Settlements*

Fig. 7 shows the distribution of known late neolithic sites in Gloucestershire. These fall into two groups on the basis of ceramic associations: those with late Peterborough-series pottery (i.e. Mortlake and Fengate wares), and those with grooved ware pottery. All are situated in valley bottoms, often on well-drained gravel-spreads, and usually near to permanent water-courses. No structural evidence has so far been recovered to indicate the size, shape, or nature of local late neolithic dwellings.

At Salmonsbury, late neolithic features were defined in several of the areas excavated. Nine pits were found sealed beneath the iron age rampart on site I, but only one sherd of Mortlake pottery was recovered (Dunning 1976, fig. 11, 1). Site VI contained several ditch segments which were thought to be of late neolithic date, and site V yielded another sherd of Peterborough ware. Worked flints were also found. Whether these remains represent a single occupation site, or parts of several, is uncertain.

North of Bourton-on-the-Water, a pit, revealed by gravel-extraction, contained a large sherd of Fengate ware, human bones, and animal remains (Dunning 1932), but unfortunately no further exploration of the site has taken place. At Barnwood a single sherd of Peterborough ware, and a large number of late neolithic flints, suggest the former existence of a settlement (Clifford 1930 and 1934). In Gloucester, sherds of Mortlake ware from disturbed contexts on the Telephone Exchange site are tantalizing evidence of a settlement near the River Severn (Hurst 1972, 38). Recently, a small cache of what may be late neolithic pottery was found on a building-site at Squire's Gate, Gloucester (Garrod pers. comm.). At the Cinema site in

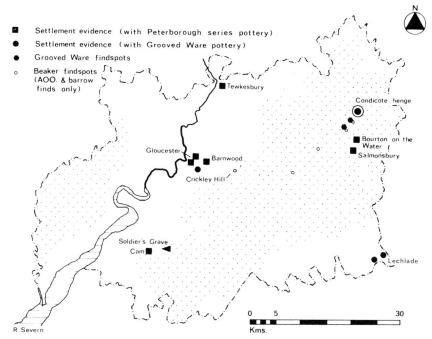

*Figure 7*   Distribution of late neolithic sites. Land over 120m above O.D. indicated
by stippling.

Tewkesbury, excavations revealed late neolithic pottery and a few neolithic
features cut into the natural subsoil (Miles and Fowler 1973, 18; Hannan
1972 and pers. comm.).

Perhaps the best known late neolithic settlement with Peterborough
pottery in the county is at Cam, near Dursley. Excavations in 1961 revealed
two circular pits containing pottery of Mortlake and Fengate traditions,
animal bones, daub, and a perforated stone mace-head manufactured from
local rock (Smith 1968).

Grooved ware, so-called because of its characteristic decoration, has only
been recorded from Gloucestershire in recent years. Apart from a possible
sherd in the Royce collection, thought to have come from one of the Swell
barrows (Grinsell 1964, 18), and the equally doubtful fragment found close to
Cow Common long barrow (Saville 1979b, 94), there are three recorded
instances of grooved ware in putatively domestic contexts.

At Lechlade, pits containing grooved ware were discovered in the course of
rescue excavations during the 1960s at two sites, The Loder's and Rough-

ground Farm (Jones 1977). At the former, sixty-one sherds, representing two vessels in the Woodlands sub-style, together with a broken flint knife, a point, a scraper, and animal bones, were found in an isolated pit about 1m across and 0·9m deep. At Roughground Farm several features can be assigned to grooved ware occupation of the site. Flint tools, débitage, and animal remains were present in the recorded pits, together with small quantities of grooved ware pottery (Darvill, work in progress). Grooved ware has also been found on a building site at Saintbridge on the eastern side of Gloucester. Rescue excavations located a hearth-pit, and at least three post-holes, in loose association with a single sherd of grooved ware pottery (Garrod pers. comm.).

*Subsistence, Crafts, and Material Culture*

Evidence for subsistence practices in the late neolithic is scant. Animal bones from the pits at Cam attest the presence of domesticated cattle (two breeds), sheep or goats, and pigs. Of these, pigs were numerically dominant, but the assemblage was so small that no realistic assessment of relative frequency is possible. Remains of red deer and wild boar were also present, forming a small proportion of the total (Smith 1968, 20). Faunal remains from The Loder's, Lechlade, included domestic cattle, pig, and sheep or goat, but again the assemblage was too small to give any indication of species representation. The combined evidence from several features containing grooved ware at Roughground Farm suggests that pig was the dominant species, followed by cattle, and lastly sheep or goat (Darvill, work in progress).

The presence of pits on nearly all recorded settlement sites may be taken as evidence for the storage of cereals, but no carbonized grain has been identified in the soil samples analysed.

A discarded piece of red deer metatarsus in the late neolithic pit at The Loder's shows that boneworking was undertaken in the vicinity, since the posterior face had clearly been removed by the groove-and-splinter technique.

Petrological studies of pottery from both Roughground Farm and The Loder's show that local clays and tempering materials were used, although the exact sources of each cannot at present be specified. Late neolithic pottery assemblages contain a more restricted range of forms and fabrics when compared with those of the middle neolithic. The thick walls and liberal use of tempering, so characteristic of late neolithic wares, suggest that pottery was less carefully made. Use of grog (crushed pot) as a tempering material became widespread in the later neolithic, possibly because its heat-conducting properties negated the need to produce a variety of wares each with different tempering and each suited to a different need. Decoration was commonly applied to pottery at this time.

Flintworking was normally carried out at settlement sites, to judge from the quantities of waste flakes found. In pit 785 at Roughground Farm a worked core, a hammerstone, and twenty-two detached flakes were found as a single deposit, representing the remains of a flintworking session. Flint-work in the late neolithic was generally more chunky, with less intricate pressure-flaking. Waste flakes tended to be broad and squat. New implement types became widely adopted, including the distinctive *petit tranchet* deriva-tive arrowheads (Clark 1934). Unperforated axes continued to be used, but perforated implements (of unknown function) such as mace-heads, axe-hammers, and battle-axes were circulating by the end of the period (Roe 1979). Some metal tools and ornaments may have been available by the end of the neolithic (Britton 1963).

*Burials*

Burials which can confidently be assigned to the late neolithic are few, although this may be a reflection of the fact that they are difficult to recognize because they lack good associations or distinctive grave-goods.

Near Bourton-on-the-Water, a human cranium was found in a putatively domestic pit containing Fengate-style pottery (Dunning 1932). Rather more formal, but again loosely associated with domestic activity, was a grave, containing the crouched inhumation of an adult female, which was found cutting late neolithic features at the Cinema site in Tewkesbury. No grave-goods were with the body but unabraded sherds of Mortlake ware were found in the grave-fill (Hannan pers. comm.).

Burials under round barrows were probably more common in late neolithic times than is often thought, and there may have been some continuity in this particular mode of burial throughout the neolithic (Kinnes 1979). The well-known late third millennium bc burial within a ring-ditch at Linch Hill Corner in Oxfordshire (Grimes 1960, 154) is persuasive evidence that similar sites may be represented among the numerous round barrows and ring-ditches of the Cotswolds and Severn Valley. At present, however, the only possible late neolithic round barrow which can be cited is The Soldier's Grave, Frocester. Here, between twenty-eight and forty-four individuals were interred in a boat-shaped cist beneath a large stone mound (Clifford 1938b).

Some burials found around the edge of middle neolithic long barrows (e.g. West Tump, GLO 8, Witts 1881, 204; Randwick, GLO 10, Witts 1884, 156) may be late neolithic in date.

### Exchange

Flint and stone axes, and flint for toolmaking, continued to be transported into the area, although little is known about the extent or orientation of exchange at this time. Perforated implements were sometimes made locally (cf. Smith 1968, 19), but more commonly were imported from Cornwall, Wales, Shropshire, the Lake District, and the Midlands. Pottery, too, may have been the subject of exchanges, as the flint-tempered Ebbsfleet vessels from Nympsfield (Darvill 1979, 78) and Burn Ground (Grimes 1960, 73) contrast with the locally-produced Peterborough wares (e.g. the fossil-shell-tempered wares from Cam), and could have been made in north Wiltshire.

The introduction of beaker pottery styles, metal objects, and metallurgy itself, in the closing centuries of the neolithic may have been accomplished by some immigration of people from the Continent (Darvill 1983). Population movements do not explain all the changes in the late neolithic and early bronze age, however, as many elements of second millennium bc society had late neolithic ancestry (Whittle 1981).

### Ceremonial Monuments

The most widespread type of ceremonial monument in late neolithic Britain was the so-called 'henge' (Wainwright 1969). Condicote henge is the only definite example known in Gloucestershire. Typologically it can be classed as a Group Ia henge, having a bank set between a double ditch, and, on present evidence, only one entrance. Despite watching-briefs by Mrs O'Neil (1957), and the excavation of part of the interior and a section through the inner ditch (Saville 1983a), little can be said of its purpose. Radiocarbon dates on charcoal from the ditch suggest that it was constructed before the eighteenth century bc.

A second henge, at Cutsdean, has tentatively been identified from aerial photographs (Saville 1980b, 27), but nothing is visible on the ground and further work is required before it can be cited as a definite example. Similarly, the possible hengi-form monuments on the Thames gravels between Kempsford and Lechlade require clarification through excavation before their authenticity as late neolithic monuments can be accepted (Smith 1972, 164).

Another ceremonial monument of the late neolithic, or even later date, is the long mound on Crickley Hill. This linear structure is 4m wide and 100m long. It was carefully built, apparently using topsoil brought onto the site from elsewhere. At the eastern end was a semi-circular paved area in which was a large post-hole, possibly the socket for a marker or totem (Dixon 1979, 147). At the western end was another paved area, in this case forming some kind of ritual focus (Dixon pers. comm.). The mound was built over the top of the razed neolithic settlement described above, and is superficially similar to the bank barrow at Maiden Castle, Dorset (Wheeler 1943).

Mention should also be made of the standing stones in the Cotswolds (Saville 1980b, 8 and 45) and the Forest of Dean (Hart 1967, 7). These are strictly speaking undated, but some examples in other parts of Britain have been shown by excavation to be of neolithic date (Wilson 1983).

## CONCLUSION

A relatively coherent picture of changing lifestyles during the neolithic period in Gloucestershire can be built up from the evidence which has accumulated over nearly 150 years of archaeological research. However, many problems remain. The need for detailed environmental reconstruction and a better chronological framework has been highlighted above, but in looking forward to the next phase of neolithic studies in the county several other questions merit brief comment.

The interpretation of archaeological distributions is always difficult, especially so when they are derived from piecemeal research. Objective, large-scale field-surveys are needed west of the River Severn and in the Severn Valley, to establish whether these areas were truly voids in early and middle neolithic settlement patterns. Similar work is needed on the Cotswolds to check present reconstructions of late neolithic settlement patterns. The formulation, and constant revision, of detailed problem-orientated research-designs to provide strategies for deploying the scarce resources available for rescue archaeology would undoubtedly promote the resolution of some distributional uncertainties. Research projects also have an important role to play in future work, firstly because they can be more selective about sites or areas to investigate, and secondly because they often permit the deployment of a greater range of techniques and methodologies.

Neolithic sites in Gloucestershire are a diminishing resource. The sheer antiquity of the evidence makes it fragile and vulnerable. Recent surveys have revealed the full extent of the modern damage to even the most robust neolithic monuments – the long barrows. Of the seventy recorded examples in Gloucestershire and Avon, over fifty per cent are currently affected by ploughing (Saville 1980b, 26–27). This problem clearly demands increased attention.

Finally, there is the question of explanation. It is one thing to describe the evidence available, much as has been attempted here, but it is quite another to seek insights into the causes of change, or the reasons for observed variation in the data. If nothing else, it is hoped that the above discussion has helped to set the stage for this next phase of research.

*Note*

Gloucestershire long barrows are referred to throughout this paper by their common or local names. The first mention of each long barrow is accompanied by its county reference number in parenthesis, following the system used by Corcoran (1969).

## ACKNOWLEDGMENTS

The preparation of this paper would have been impossible without the help of numerous individuals. I would particularly like to thank Philip Dixon, Patrick Garrod, Frank Green, Alan Hannan, Henry Hurst, Mark Maltby, Alan Saville, Andrew Sherratt, David Viner, and Malcolm Watkins for allowing me to use information from their excavations, research, or the collections in their care. I would also like to thank Leslie Grinsell, Alan Saville, Isobel Smith, and Jane Timby for their comments on earlier drafts of this paper, and for discussing problems of the neolithic period with me. All responsibility for any misinterpretations remains firmly with the author.

## REFERENCES

Atkinson, R.J.C. 1965. Wayland's Smithy. *Antiquity* 39, 126–133.

Atkinson, R.J.C. 1968. Old mortality: some aspects of burial and population in neolithic England. In J. Coles and D.D.A. Simpson (eds.), *Studies in ancient Europe*, 83–94. Leicester.

Barker, G. and Webley, D. 1978. Causewayed camps and early neolithic economies in central southern England. *PPS* 44, 161–186.

Bell, M. 1983. The land mollusca and other palaeoenvironmental evidence. In A. Saville, Excavations at Condicote henge monument, Gloucestershire, 1977. *TBGAS* 101, 39–45.

Berry, Sir J. 1929. Belas Knap long barrow, Gloucestershire: report of the excavations of 1929. *TBGAS* 51, 273–303.

Berry, Sir J. 1930. Belas Knap long barrow, Gloucestershire: report of the excavations of 1930. *TBGAS* 52, 123–150.

Bradley, R. and Hodder, I. 1979. British prehistory: an integrated view. *Man* 14, 93–104.

Britnell, W. 1980. Radiocarbon dates from the Gwernvale chambered tomb, Crickhowell, Powys. *Antiquity* 44, 147.

Britton, D. 1963. Traditions of metal-working in the later neolithic and early bronze age of Britain: Part 1. *PPS* 29, 258–325.

Brown, T. 1982. Human impact on the former floodplain woodlands of the Severn. In M. Bell and S. Limbrey (eds.), *Archaeological aspects of woodland ecology*, 93–104. Oxford. (=BAR Int Ser S146.)

Burton, J. 1980. Making sense of waste flakes: new methods for investigating the technology and economies behind chipped stone assemblages. *J Archaeol Sci* 7, 131–148.

Chesterman, J.T. 1977. Burial rites in a Cotswold long barrow. *Man* 12, 22–32.

Clark, J.G.D. 1934. Derivative forms of the *petit tranchet* in Britain. *Archaeol J* 91, 32–58.

Clark, J.G.D. 1965. Traffic in stone axe and adze blades. *Economic Hist Rev* 18, 1–28.

Clifford, E.M. 1930. A prehistoric and Roman site at Barnwood near Gloucester. *TBGAS* 52, 201–254.

Clifford, E.M. 1934. Finds at Barnwood, Gloucester. *TBGAS* 56, 231–232.

Clifford, E.M. 1936a. Notgrove Long Barrow, Gloucestershire. *Archaeologia* 86, 119–161.

Clifford, E.M. 1936b. Notes on the neolithic period in the Cotswolds. *PCNFC* 26, 33–49.

Clifford, E.M. 1937. The beaker folk of the Cotswolds. *PPS* 3, 159–165.

Clifford, E.M. 1938a. The Excavation of Nympsfield Long Barrow, Gloucestershire. *PPS* 4, 188–213.

Clifford, E.M. 1938b. The Soldier's Grave, Frocester, Gloucestershire. *PPS* 4, 214–217.

Clifford, E.M. 1950. The Cotswold megalithic culture: the grave goods and their background. In C. Fox and B. Dickens (eds.), *The early cultures of north-west Europe*, 23–40. Cambridge.

Clifford, E.M. and Daniel, G.E. 1940. The Rodmarton and Avening portholes. *PPS* 6, 133–165.

Clifford, E.M., Garrod, D.A., and Gracie, H.S. 1954. Flint implements from Gloucestershire. *Antiq J* 34, 178–187.

Clifford, E.M. and Simpson, C.A. 1939. A possible neolithic trackway. *Geography* 24, 230–239.

Coles, J., Hibbert, F.A., and Orme, B.J. 1973. Prehistoric roads and tracks in Somerset: 3: The Sweet Track. *PPS* 39, 256–293.

Corcoran, J.X.W.P. 1969. The Cotswold-Severn Group. In T.G.E. Powell (ed.), *Megalithic Enquiries in the West of Britain*, 13–104. Liverpool.

Corcoran, J.X.W.P. 1972. Multi-period construction and the origins of the chambered long cairn in western Britain and Ireland. In F. Lynch and C. Burgess (eds.), *Prehistoric Man in Wales and the West*, 31–63. Bath.

Crawford, O.G.S. 1925. *The Long Barrows of the Cotswolds*. Gloucester.

Cummins, W.A. 1974. The neolithic stone axe trade in Britain. *Antiquity* 48, 201–205.

Cummins, W.A. 1979. Neolithic stone axes: distribution and trade in England and Wales. In T.H. McK. Clough and W.A. Cummins (eds.), *Stone axe studies*, 5–12. London. (=CBA Res Rep 23.)

Daniel, G.E. 1939. The transepted gallery graves of western France. *PPS* 5, 143–165.

Daniel, G.E. 1950. *The Prehistoric Chamber Tombs of England and Wales*. Cambridge.

Darvill, T.C. 1978. Perspectives and problems in the study of Gloucestershire in the third and fourth millennia BC. *Glevensis* 12, 13–22.

Darvill, T.C. 1979. Petrological examination. In A. Saville, Further excavations at the Nympsfield chambered tomb, Gloucestershire, 1974. *PPS* 45, 77–78.

Darvill, T.C. 1981. Excavations at The Peak Camp, Cowley – an interim note. *Glevensis* 15, 52–56.

Darvill, T.C. 1982a. Excavations at The Peak Camp, Cowley, Gloucestershire – second interim report. *Glevensis* 16, 20–25.

Darvill, T.C. 1982b. *The Megalithic Chambered Tombs of the Cotswold-Severn Region*. Highworth. (=Vorda Research Series No. 5.)

Darvill, T.C. 1983. *The neolithic of Wales and the mid-west of England: a systemic analysis of social change through the application of action theory.* Unpublished PhD thesis, University of Southampton.

Darvill, T.C. and Hingley, R.C. Forthcoming. Interrupted ditch systems in the Upper Thames Valley.

Dimbleby, G.W. and Evans, J.G. 1974. Pollen and land-snail analysis of calcareous soils. *J Archaeol Sci* 1, 117–133.

Dixon, P.W. 1969–1973. *Crickley Hill: interim reports 1–5*. Cheltenham. (Duplicated reports.)

Dixon, P.W. 1979. A neolithic and iron age site on a hilltop in southern England. *Sci American* 241(5), 142–150.

Donovan, H.E. 1938. Adlestrop Hill barrow, Gloucestershire. *TBGAS* 60, 152–164.

Dunning, G.C. 1931. Salmonsbury Camp, Gloucestershire. *Antiquity* 5, 489–492.

Dunning, G.C. 1932. Bronze age settlements and a Saxon hut near Bourton-on-the-Water, Gloucestershire. *Antiq J* 12, 279–293.

Dunning, G.C. 1976. Salmonsbury, Bourton-on-the-Water, Gloucestershire. In

D.W. Harding (ed.), *Hillforts: later prehistoric earthworks in Britain and Ireland*, 75–118. London.

Evans, J.G. 1971. Habitat change on the calcareous soils of Britain: the impact of Neolithic man. In D.D.A. Simpson (ed.), *Economy and Settlement in Neolithic and Early Bronze Age Britain and Europe*, 27–73. Leicester.

Evens, E.D., Smith, I.F., and Wallis, F.S. 1972. The petrological identification of stone implements from south-western England. *PPS* 38, 235–275.

Fleming, A. 1973. Tombs for the living. *Man* 8, 177–193.

Greenwell, W. 1877. *British Barrows*. Oxford.

Grimes, W.F. 1939. The excavation of Ty-isaf Long Cairn, Brecknockshire. *PPS* 5, 119–142.

Grimes, W.F. 1960. *Excavations on defence sites 1939–1945, 1: mainly neolithic-bronze age*. London. (=Ministry of Works Archaeological Reports No. 3.)

Grinsell, L.V. 1964. The Royce collection at Stow-on-the-Wold. *TBGAS* 83, 5–23.

Hannan, A. 1972. Tewkesbury, Oldbury Road. *Archaeol Rev* 7, 34–35.

Hart, C. 1967. *Archaeology in Dean*. Gloucester.

Hemp, W.J. 1929. Belas Knap Long Barrow, Gloucestershire. *TBGAS* 51, 261–272.

Hodder, I. and Lane, P. 1982. A contextual examination of neolithic axe distribution in Britain. In J.E. Ericson and T.K. Earl (eds.), *Contexts for prehistoric exchange*, 213–235. London.

Hurst, H. 1972. Excavations at Gloucester 1968–1971: first interim report. *Antiq J* 52, 24–69.

Jones, M.U. 1977. Neolithic pottery found at Lechlade, Gloucestershire. *Oxoniensia* 41, 1–5.

Kinnes, I. 1975. Monumental function in British neolithic burial practices. *World Archaeol* 7, 16–29.

Kinnes, I. 1979. *Round barrows and ring-ditches in the British neolithic*. London. (=British Museum Occasional Paper No. 7.)

Lawrence, W.L. and Winterbotham, L. 1866. Examination of a chambered long barrow in Gloucestershire. *Proc Soc Antiq London* 3, 375–382.

Leeds, E.T. 1927. Neolithic spoons from Nether Swell, Gloucestershire. *Antiq J* 7, 61–62.

Mercer, R.J. 1980. *Hambledon Hill, a neolithic landscape*. Edinburgh.

Miles, D. and Fowler, P.J. 1972. *Tewkesbury, the archaeological implications of development*. Tewkesbury.

O'Neil, H.E. 1957. Condicote Earthwork, a henge monument, Gloucestershire. *TBGAS* 76, 141–146.

O'Neil, H.E. 1966. Sale's Lot long barrow, Withington, Gloucestershire, 1962–65. *TBGAS* 85, 5–35.

O'Neil, H.E. and Grinsell, L.V. 1960. Gloucestershire barrows. *TBGAS* 79(1), 1–149.

Piggott, S. 1954. *The neolithic cultures of the British Isles.* Cambridge.

Piggott, S. 1962. *The West Kennet Long Barrow: Excavations 1955–56.* London. (=Ministry of Works Archaeological Reports No. 4.)

Piggott, S. 1973. Problems in the interpretation of chambered tombs. In G.E. Daniel and P. Kjaerum (eds.), *Megalithic graves and ritual*, 9–15. Copenhagen. (=Papers presented at the III Atlantic Colloquium.)

Radford, C.A.R. 1930. Belas Knap Long Barrow, Gloucestershire: report on the work carried out during the winter 1930–1931. *TBGAS* 52, 295–299.

Renfrew, A.C. 1975. Trade as action at a distance: questions of integration and communication. In J.A. Sabloff and C.C. Lamberg-Karlovsky (eds.), *Ancient civilization and trade*, 3–59. Albuquerque, New Mexico.

Renfrew, A.C. 1976. Megaliths, territories and populations. In S.J. De Laet (ed.), *Acculturation and continuity in Atlantic Europe: papers of the IV Atlantic Colloquium*, 198–220. Brugge. (=Dissertationes Archaeologicae Gandenses 16.)

Renfrew, A.C. 1977. Alternative models for exchange and spatial distribution. In T. Earle and J.E. Ericson (eds.), *Exchange systems in prehistory*, 71–90. London.

Renfrew, A.C. 1978. Trajectory discontinuity and morphogenesis: the implications of catastrophe theory for archaeology. *American Antiquity* 43, 203–222.

Renfrew, A.C. 1983. The social archaeology of megalithic monuments. *Sci American* November 1983, 128–136.

Roe, F.E.S. 1979. Typology of stone implements with shaftholes. In T.H.McK. Clough and W.A. Cummins (eds.), *Stone axe studies*, 23–48. London. (=CBA Res Rep 23.)

Rolleston, G. 1876. On the people of the long barrow period. *J Roy Anthr Inst* 5, 120–173.

Saville, A. 1979a. Further excavations at Nympsfield chambered tomb, Gloucestershire, 1974. *PPS* 45, 53–91.

Saville, A. 1979b. *Recent Work at Cow Common Bronze Age Cemetery, Gloucestershire.* Bristol. (=CRAAGS Occasional Paper No. 6.)

Saville, A. 1980a. Hazleton excavation project 1979. *Glevensis* 14, 36–38.

Saville, A. 1980b. *Archaeological Sites in the Avon and Gloucestershire Cotswolds: an extensive survey of a rural archaeological resource with special reference to plough damage.* Bristol. (=CRAAGS Survey No. 5.)

Saville, A. 1981. Hazleton excavation project 1980. *Glevensis* 15, 57–59.

Saville, A. 1982a. Hazleton excavation project 1981. *Glevensis* 16, 13–16.

Saville, A. 1982b. Carrying cores to Gloucestershire: some thoughts on lithic resource exploitation. *Lithics* 3, 25–28.

Saville, A. 1983a. Excavations at Condicote henge monument, Gloucestershire, 1977. *TBGAS* 101, 21–47.

Saville, A. 1983b. Hazleton excavation project 1982. *Glevensis* 17, 14–19.

Saville, A. and Ellison, A. 1983. Excavations at Uley Bury hillfort, Gloucestershire, 1976. In A. Saville, *Uley Bury and Norbury hillforts*, 1–24. Bristol. (=Western Archaeological Trust Excavation Monograph No. 5.)

Savory, H.N. 1980. The neolithic in Wales. In J.A. Taylor (ed.), *Culture and environment in prehistoric Wales*, 207–231. Oxford. (=BAR Brit Ser 76.)

Smith, A.G. 1981. The neolithic. In I. Simmons and M. Tooley (eds.), *The Environment in British prehistory*, 125–209. London.

Smith, I.F. 1965. *Windmill Hill and Avebury: excavations by Alexander Keiller, 1925–1939*. Oxford.

Smith, I.F. 1968. Report on late neolithic pits at Cam, Gloucestershire. *TBGAS* 87, 14–28.

Smith, I.F. 1972. Ring ditches in eastern and central Gloucestershire. In P.J. Fowler (ed.), *Archaeology and the Landscape*, 157–167. London.

Smith, I.F. 1974. The neolithic. In C. Renfrew (ed.), *British prehistory: a new outline*, 100–128. London.

Spencer, P.J. 1979. Molluscs. In A. Saville, Further excavations at Nympsfield chambered tomb, Gloucestershire, 1974. *PPS* 45, 83–84.

Startin, B. and Bradley, R. 1981. Some notes on work organisation and society in prehistoric Wessex. In C.L.N. Ruggles and A.W.R. Whittle (eds.), *Astronomy and society in Britain during the period 4000 – 1500 BC*, 289–296. Oxford. (=BAR Brit Ser 88.)

Taylor, J.A. 1975. The role of climatic factors in environmental and cultural changes in prehistoric times. In J.G. Evans, S. Limbrey, and H. Cleere (eds.), *The effect of man on the landscape: the highland zone*, 6–19. London. (=CBA Res Rep 11.)

Thurnam, J. 1868. On ancient British barrows, especially those of Wiltshire and the adjoining counties: Part 1, long barrows. *Archaeologia* 42, 161–244.

Tyler, A. 1976. *Neolithic flint axes from the Cotswold hills*. Oxford.(=BAR Brit Ser 25.)

Vatcher, F. de M. 1966. Lechlade cursus. In Ministry of Public Building and Works, *Excavations Annual Report 1965*, 5. London.

Wainwright, G.J. 1969. A review of henge monuments in the light of recent research. *PPS* 35, 112–133.

Wheeler, R.E.M. 1943. *Maiden Castle, Dorset*. Oxford. (=Soc Antiq London Res Rep 12.)

Whittle, A.W.R. 1977a. *The earlier neolithic of southern England and its Continental background*. Oxford. (=BAR Int Ser S35.)

Whittle, A.W.R. 1977b. Earlier neolithic enclosures in north-west Europe. *PPS* 43, 329–348.

Whittle, A.W.R. 1978. Resources and population in the British Neolithic. *Antiquity* 52, 34–42.

Whittle, A.W.R. 1981. Late neolithic society in Britain, a re-alignment. In C.L.N. Ruggles and A.W.R. Whittle (eds.), *Astronomy and society in Britain during the period 4000 – 1500 BC*, 297–342. Oxford. (=BAR Brit Ser 88.)

Wilson, J.C. 1983. The standing stones of Anglesey: a discussion. *Bull Board Celtic Stud* 30, 363–389.

Witts, G.B. 1881. Description of the long barrow, called 'West Tump', in the parish of Brimpsfield, Gloucestershire. *TBGAS* 5, 201–211.

Witts, G.B. 1883. *Archaeological Handbook of the County of Gloucester*. Cheltenham.

Witts, G.B. 1884. Randwick Long Barrow. *PCNFC* 8, 156–160.

Wymer, J.J. (ed.). 1977. *Gazetteer of mesolithic sites in England and Wales*. London. (=CBA Res Rep 20.)

**February 1984**

# Bronze Age Gloucestershire: Artefacts and Distributions

## Ann Ellison

### INTRODUCTION

Although the material results of antiquarian and recent excavations in Gloucestershire cannot match the extensively studied corpora of ceramic and metal finds from the barrows and bronze age settlements of Wessex, the existence of a few remarkable and well-recorded early bronze age assemblages was demonstrated last century (notably by Canon Greenwell). Together with the recording in this century of a few, but surprisingly varied, finds of later bronze age metalwork and pottery, these assemblages have provided a fine and representative collection of most of the bronze age artefact types known from southern Britain. Amongst these, the Snowshill grave group (now in the British Museum), one of the definitive assemblages of the later stages of the so-called 'Wessex Culture', is of outstanding importance. Most pottery evidence in the county derives from burials but the growing settlement evidence, linked to a study of the known artefact distributions, provides the first clues to the interpretation of social and economic processes.

The following account is illustrated by two period distribution maps, one for the early bronze age (Fig. 1) and one showing later bronze age finds (Fig. 4). They have been compiled from an unpublished gazetteer of bronze age finds from Gloucestershire prepared by Dr Isobel Smith. The periodization of the earlier bronze age utilized in the survey is that presented by Burgess in his book *The Age of Stonehenge* (1980).

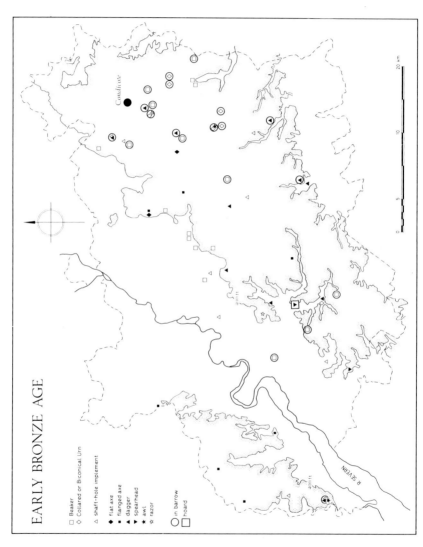

EARLY BRONZE AGE

□ Beaker
◇ Collared or Biconical Urn
△ shaft-hole implement

◆ flat axe
■ flanged axe
◀ dagger
▶ spearhead
★ awl
☆ razor

◯ in barrow
▢ hoard

Condicote

R. SEVERN

20 km

Figure 1  Gloucestershire: findspots of early bronze age pottery and metalwork.

EARLY BRONZE AGE: OVERTON AND BEDD BRANWEN
PERIODS (c.2000 – 1400 BC)

Following the appearance of early beaker pottery, which is represented in the county at the Crickley Hill enclosure (Dixon 1971, fig. 8, 15) and the Eyford Hill long barrow at Upper Slaughter (O'Neil and Grinsell 1960, 16 and 93), and the development of a series of types with distinct Dutch and German prototypes, comb decoration on pottery vessels began to spread throughout Britain. This gave rise to two main series of indigenous beaker styles which are found substantially in northern (N1 to N4) and southern (S1 to S4) Britain respectively (Clarke 1970). Clarke's scheme has been clarified and simplified by Case (1977), who divides the stages into early-, middle-, and late-style beakers. Middle-style beakers in Gloucestershire are represented by a fine northern/north Rhine vessel from Prestbury (Clifford 1938, 348), while the N2 beaker from Barnwood (Clifford 1930, fig. 7), a vessel from Leckhampton (O'Neil and Bunt 1966), and southern-style pots from Ivy Lodge, King's Stanley (Gardiner 1930, pl. 19) and Bourton-on-the-Water (Clifford 1937a, pl. 11, A) belong to the late style.

Finger-nail and finger-tip decorated beaker domestic wares have not so far been found in the county (but see Saville 1983), and most of the known beakers derive from sepulchral contexts: either within long and round barrows or from a series of typical flat graves. These latter are best represented by the male adult with an associated flint knife (Clifford 1930, fig. 8), found during gravel-digging at Barnwood, a second adult male associated with the beaker from Prestbury, and the crouched, unaccompanied skeleton of a tall youth found in a cist constructed from carboniferous limestone slabs at Beachley (Barnett 1964). The known beaker finds concentrate in the flood-plain of the Severn (Fig. 1). This reflects the distribution pattern observed in the neighbouring county of Oxfordshire and implies exploitation of the river gravels as well as the Cotswold uplands, where beaker sherds are widely dispersed in long and round barrows.

Copper metalwork is represented in Gloucestershire by a single find, the small, broad-butted, developed copper axe from Hawling (Needham pers. comm.), illustrated here for the first time (Fig. 2). The earliest phase of tin-bronze metalworking in Britain is demonstrated locally by the small hoard of two axes recently recovered from Oddington (Needham and Saville 1981). These belong to the southern British early bronze age Tradition 1 (Needham 1979), and form the earliest reliably provenanced hoard from lowland Britain (Fig. 3).

Low-flanged axes have been found at Awre (Hart 1967, 11), Bisley-with-

*Figure 2*  Copper axe from Hawling. (Photo: A Saville; Cheltenham Museum collection 1936:1.)

Lypiatt (Gardiner 1937), and Cleeve Hill, Southam (Dent 1877, 9 and plate). The Staunton axe (Hart 1967, 11 and pl. VIIb), possessing a crescentic blade and low stop-ridge, is possibly of Burgess and Cowen's Derryniggin type, and was probably contemporary with the hoard of two end-looped spearheads with kite-shaped blades from Rodborough Common (Fisher 1919), which also belongs to the Irish Inch Island/Derryniggin tradition (Burgess and Cowen 1972, 179). These finds compare with the well-known hoard from Westbury-on-Trym, just south of the county border, which contained types of the Arreton Tradition only (Britton 1963, fig. 18). The distribution of these early axes (Fig. 1), similar to that of beaker pottery, further indicates exploitation of all topographical zones during this period. Other early bronze age axeheads from the county are few in number, but include the finely-decorated example from Whittington which belongs to Megaw and Hardy type Ia$^2$ (Needham 1979, 267 and fig. 2.5), and is probably contemporary with the axe from Awre.

The prosperity of the northern Cotswolds in the earlier part of the early bronze age, evidenced by the Oddington axes, is reflected in the latest phase by the existence of one of the richest grave groups ever recorded outside the Wessex heartland. The assemblage from the Snowshill barrow (Greenwell

1890, 70–72) is a rich, Wessex 2 grave-group comprising a bronze dagger, spearhead, crutch-headed pin, and a fine polished stone battle-axe. The spearhead is tanged-and-collared and belongs to the Arreton Tradition of metal-working, while the dagger and battle-axe have both served as archaeological prototypes for widespread classes of artefacts of the later early bronze age in Britain. The bronze dagger, with its ogival blade displaying grooves and a thickened centre or mid-rib and an arched butt supporting three thick rivets, is prototypical of the Camerton-Snowshill dagger-series of the Wessex 2 period (ApSimon 1954; Gerloff 1975: Snowshill Type), while the long thin battle-axe, with semi-circular butt and raised ribs parallel to the hole, has provided the class name for Roe's eighth group of battle-axes, belonging to her Stage V (Roe 1966, 212 and fig. 56), recently reclassified as the 'Developed' type (Roe 1979, 23). This implement was made from Group XII rock at Cwm Mawr in mid-Wales, where battle-axe manufacture was a speciality, and the axe-hammer from Cromhall (Evens, Smith and Wallis 1972, 262, no. 1245), now in the county of Avon, is also of this rock-type.

Other shaft-hole implements from the county include a battle-axe of Group XVIII rock (from north-east England) found at St Briavels (Saville and Roe forthcoming), sandstone adzes from Cutsdean and Hucclecote (Evens, Smith and Wallis 1972, 264, nos. 1471 and 1473), and three mace-heads. The importance of the Cotswolds in the later early bronze age is further demonstrated by the occurrence of a series of bronze daggers. These include two more of Camerton-Snowshill type, from Swell (Thomas 1979) and Colesbourne Park, and examples belonging to Gerloff's Plymstock-Totland Group from Bibury and from near Cirencester (Gerloff 1975, 169, no. 319 and 131, no. 212). The knife-dagger from the Soldiers' Tump barrow at Tidenham was associated with a bronze awl and a fragment of pottery belonging to a collared urn (Scott-Garrett 1955; Gerloff 1975, 162, no. 252).

The wide range of early bronze age ceramics with their varying styles of decoration, so well represented in Wessex, are not found at all in Gloucestershire, and the known examples of the ubiquitous collared urn category are few and relatively plain in character. This class of pottery has been exhaustively studied by Longworth who originally defined a primary series carrying early traits, which could be linked to late neolithic Peterborough ware (Longworth 1961), developed by the first phase of the Wessex culture, with the secondary series developing gradually during the early bronze age period. Traits defining the primary series include an internal moulding, whipped-cord decoration, internal decoration, and decoration extending below the shoulder. In Gloucestershire, two primary examples derive from Lower Slaughter (Dunning 1932, fig. 2, 4–5), while examples of the

*Figure 3*   The Oddington early bronze age axes. (Photo: A. Saville; Cheltenham
Museum collection 1980:2182–2183.)

secondary series from Farmington (O'Neil and Grinsell 1960, fig. 4) and
Burn Ground, Hampnett (Grimes 1960, fig. 42) belong to Longworth's
South-Eastern style (Longworth pers. comm.).

The collared urns mainly derive from round barrows where they had been
used as cinerary urns by the local early bronze age people. The society they
relate to was characterized by settlement units smaller and less stable than
those of the middle neolithic segmented social groups discussed by Darvill
(1982). The social status of high-ranking individuals or groups was probably
enhanced through the construction of henges or monumental megalithic
structures and was reflected in the variety of single burial rituals. Certainly,
the distribution of round barrows on the Cotswolds (Drinkwater and Saville,
this volume) does not reflect a pattern of small individual territories but
displays a concentration of barrows and prestige grave-goods around the only
known major communal structure of the region: the henge monument at
Condicote (Fig. 1; Saville 1983). Metalworking traditions and the major
pottery styles, such as beakers and collared urns, were very widely distributed and 'might symbolize different rights of access to status and resources'
(Bradley and Hodder 1979, 97). However, the development of small,
localized prestige-groups is indicated by the occurrence of discrete distribu-

tions of polished stone battle-axes and axe-hammers from specific sources. The absence of Bush Barrow-type daggers (Wessex 1 period) in Gloucester-shire suggests that a strongly stratified form of social organization did not develop here until the later early bronze age, and the late development of ranked organization north of the Wessex heartland may perhaps be correlated with the floruit of the battle-axe factories of the Midlands and of north-east England during the Wessex 2 period.

The hierarchical system appears to have developed throughout the early bronze age, leading in turn to increasing social stress and to major changes at the beginning of the middle bronze age. These changes were accompanied by the appearance of small-scale, pottery-type distributions towards the very end of the early bronze age, including the regional types of Wessex biconical urns defined by the present writer (Ellison 1975) and represented in Gloucestershire by the very fine urn from Cow Common (Swell 1 barrow). This bears multiple plastic cordons and arcaded, cord-impressed, triangle-motifs reminiscent of applied horseshoes (Greenwell and Rolleston 1877, 446–447). The vessel belongs to my Type A and was associated with a Class Ib tanged bronze razor of late early bronze age type (Butler and Smith 1956, 33). In a secondary position to the biconical urn at Swell I was a bucket urn of middle bronze age type. A tanged bronze razor similar to that from Cow Common was found recently on Haresfield Hill, Standish (Gloucester Museum records; S. Needham pers. comm.).

## MIDDLE BRONZE AGE: KNIGHTON HEATH PERIOD (c.1400 – 1000 BC)

Metalwork of the middle bronze age period in Gloucestershire comprises the usual range of tools and weapons, but ornament types are totally absent. This is particularly remarkable considering the very dense distribution of important Taunton-phase hoards of the 'Ornament Horizon' in Somerset and the cluster of such finds around Bath. In this respect the Gloucestershire middle bronze age bronzes are more similar to those in the Thames valley assemb-lages. The identifiable palstaves belong to Rowlands' Class 1 ('shield pattern') and Class 2 ('side-flanged') categories, both of which are found in the Thames Valley (Rowlands 1976). Class 1 palstaves are known from Tidenham (unpublished; National Museum of Wales), Newent (Hart 1967, 11), and South Cerney (Gingell n.d., 4), while another from South Cerney (Rowlands 1976, 305, no. 528) belongs to Class 2. The example from Tewkesbury (photograph in Cheltenham Museum) bears trident decoration and is of Class

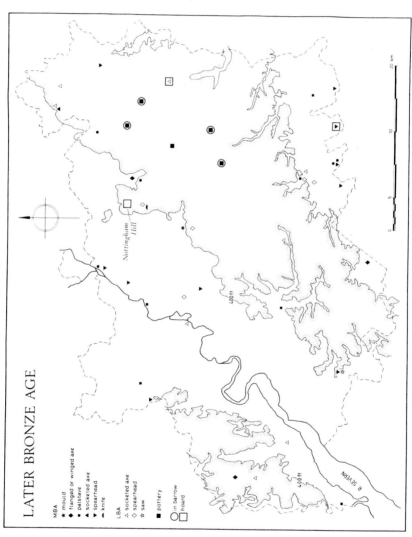

## LATER BRONZE AGE

MBA
★ mould
◆ flanged or winged axe
■ palstave
▲ socketed axe
▼ spearhead
🔪 knife

LBA
△ socketed axe
◇ spearhead
☆ saw
■ pottery
◯ in barrow
□ hoard

*Nottingham Hill*

400 ft

400 ft

R. SEVERN

0          5          10          20 km

*Figure 4*  Gloucestershire: findspots of middle and late bronze age pottery and metalwork.

5. The Taunton-Hademarschen axe from Weston Subedge (Rowlands 1976, 347, no. 1080) represents a type originally defined by Butler (1963). It is a late middle bronze age form similar to those of Montelius III and IV and belonging to a group of specialized craftsmen's tools: light axes, chisels, punches, and anvils that was current after 1300 BC.

The middle bronze age weapons from the county are side-looped and basal-looped spearheads. The eight side-looped examples are all of Rowlands' Group 2, with flame-shaped blade, lozenge-sectioned mid-rib, and 'string loops' which lack plates. This type displays a tight regional distribution in Berkshire, north Wiltshire and Gloucestershire (Rowlands 1976, 63). They include two examples comprising the only middle bronze age hoard in the county, from Down Ampney (Rowlands 1976, 236, no. 47). At Tormarton (now in Avon), the blade-points of two similar spearheads were found embedded in the lumbar vertebrae and pelvis of a human skeleton dated to 977 bc ± 90 (BM−542; *Radiocarbon* 13, 180). The identifiable examples of basal-looped spearheads, from Moreton-in-Marsh (Terry 1953; Rowlands 1976, 384) and South Cerney (Stroud Museum) are of Group 2: large, broad, leaf-bladed weapons with lozenge-sectioned mid-rib and loops possessing lozenge plates. This is a type common in the Cambridgeshire region and, once again, the Middle Thames valley. The kite-shaped spearhead from North Nibley (Gloucester City Museum) is the only weapon which can definitely be attributed to the early middle bronze age and its form is possibly Irish in origin. The distribution map (Fig. 4) demonstrates the Thames Valley connection well: most of the middle bronze age metalwork from the county derives from the headwaters of the Thames and through into the Severn valley.

Pottery and settlements of the middle bronze age are rarely represented in the county. Pointers to the existence of small homesteads at this time are provided by the finds of ditches and pits at Windmill Hill, Tewkesbury (Hannan 1976) and beneath the Roman villa at Hucclecote (Clifford 1933, 331–2 and fig. 23), while deposits of a possibly industrial nature at Sandy Lane, Charlton Kings, produced a small fragment of a clay mould for a socketed, ribbed spearhead (C.J. Young pers. comm.). Middle bronze age pottery has been recovered from several Gloucestershire locations, including simple bucket urns bearing finger-tip impressed cordons or impressed decoration from Swell 1 barrow (Greenwell and Rolleston 1877, 446–7) and from Hawling (Herdman 1933). The assemblage from Bevan's Quarry (Temple Guiting 8 bell barrow) comprised five secondary cremations in urns (O'Neil 1967). Nine different vessels were represented and the cremation burials included the bones of six adults and one child. The reconstructable vessels include biconical forms bearing finger-tip-impressed, applied cordons at the shoulder. Three vessels possessed internal rim bevels (urns 3, 4a and 5: O'Neil 1967, fig. 3) and the exterior of urn 3 was decorated all over with finger-nail rustication, a rare form of adornment for vessels of this date. These vessels can best be matched, as was the case with the contemporary bronzes, by the Upper Thames assemblages defined by the present writer (Ellison 1975), and best exemplified by the burial groups from Long Wittenham and Standlake in Oxfordshire. The specific biconical type is further represented in Gloucestershire by the upper portion of a slack biconical vessel, bearing two plain, applied cordons, found in a barrow at Lower Swell (Swell 11; Dunning 1935).

From extensive evidence throughout southern England it is known that by the middle bronze age a class of small homesteads formed the centres of numerous, localized, territorial units possessing field systems and practising intensive agriculture in the context of a complex pattern of developing ownership rights (Bradley and Hodder 1979; Ellison 1981). As already noted, hints of these small settlements are now recorded within Gloucestershire and some of the extant celtic field systems listed by the RCHM (1976) and Fowler (1978) must have their origins in the first or second millennium BC. The small-scale pottery distributions, such as the discrete Upper Thames/ Cotswolds assemblage described above, and the very specific, bronze ornament-type areas found a little further south, signify the symbolic representations of tight-knit social groups. Research elsewhere has suggested that a series of larger middle bronze age enclosures may have served to regulate a complex pattern of exchange networks, which in turn symbolized and reinforced the identity of small interlocking social groups within a crowded agricultural landscape (Ellison 1980). No such large enclosure has yet been identified in Gloucestershire, but the existence of one or more such sites must be strongly suspected. The concentration of metal finds near the headwaters of the Thames and in the Severn Valley (Fig. 4) might indicate the former existence of one or more such large sites in lowland situations within the county.

## LATE BRONZE AGE (c.1000 – 650 BC)

The beginning of the late bronze age in Gloucestershire is prefaced by an interesting series of imported bronzes belonging to the Penard phase. These include a median-winged axe with straight butt, possibly found near Sudeley (Clifford 1937b, 162–3; for the type see Burgess 1968, 5 and note 34), a

*Figure 5*  Socketed axe from Chipping Campden. (Photo: A. Saville; Cheltenham Museum collection 1944:56.)

recurved, single-edged knife with square-sectioned tang from Cleeve Hill, Southam (Cheltenham Museum), and the barbed-and-tanged bronze arrowhead from just over the Worcestershire border at Beckford (Oswald 1972, 14 and fig. 14, 1). The socketed, basal-looped, straight-based spearhead from Kempsford (information from Corinium Museum) is also a Penard type, while the saw from Brackenbury Ditches, North Nibley (Pritchard 1906) may be a little earlier in date.

Late bronze age metalwork is, in general, extremely rare within the county. However, many of the regional styles of socketed axe which were established are represented, and they are mapped in Fig. 4. These include three of Sompting type, two of 'Llanarth' type, and one faceted axe. Eight Ewart Park-phase socketed axes were found together at Bourton-on-the-Water (Dunning 1932; Green 1935), and another example, illustrated here for the first time (Fig. 5), came from Chipping Campden. Weapons are represented mainly by a series of peg-hole spearheads, one of which, from Cirencester (Ashmolean Museum) belongs to the Carps Tongue Tradition of metalworking. This meagre scatter of Gloucestershire late bronze age metalwork was amplified by the discovery in 1972 of an important hoard inside the hillfort on Nottingham Hill, near Cheltenham (Hall and Gingell

1974). This hoard, which may have been deposited in a wooden box, included weapons (slashing swords of Ewart Park type and a scabbard chape) and an interesting series of tools and waste. The occurrence of a tanged chisel, awl, and perforated whetstone in association with bronze wire, a casting jet, and a varied series of rivets, may suggest the presence of a metalworking tool-kit.

However, the major importance of this hoard is twofold. Not only has it doubled the number of late bronze age metal finds from the county; it was also found within the ramparts of a substantial iron age hillfort. Numerous other finds of middle or late bronze age metalwork have been found within, or very near to, other Gloucestershire hillforts and, when the earlier iron age pottery of the county becomes better understood, it may well be possible to demonstrate that some of the Cotswold hillforts were constructed within the bronze age period.

## ACKNOWLEDGEMENTS

I am very grateful to Dr Isobel Smith for allowing me to consult her detailed notes and gazetteer relating to the bronze age of Gloucestershire and to Dr Ian Longworth for providing details of the collared urns and their typology. Discussion of the Gloucestershire bronzes has benefited greatly from the advice of Dr Stuart Needham. Alan Saville provided the photographs which accompany this article, and helped in other ways with its preparation.

## REFERENCES

ApSimon, A.M. 1954. Dagger graves in the Wessex bronze age. *Bull Inst Archaeol Univ London* 10, 37–62.

Barnett, C. 1964. A beaker cist at Beachley. *Monmouthshire Antiq* 1.4, 112–116.

Bradley, R. and Hodder, I. 1979. British prehistory: an integrated view. *Man* 14, 93–104.

Britton, D. 1963. Traditions of metalworking in the later neolithic and early bronze age of Britain: part 1. *PPS* 29, 258–325.

Burgess, C.B. 1968. *Bronze age metalwork in northern England: c.1000–700 BC.* Newcastle.

Burgess, C.B. 1980. *The Age of Stonehenge.* London.

Burgess, C.B. and Cowen, J.D. 1972. The Ebnal hoard and early bronze age metal-working traditions. In C.B. Burgess and F. Lynch (eds.), *Prehistoric man in Wales and the west: essays in honour of Lily F. Chitty*, 167–181. Bath.

Butler, J.J. 1963. Bronze age connections across the North Sea. *Palaeohistoria* 9.

Butler, J.J. and Smith, I.F. 1956. Razors, urns and the British middle bronze age. *Bull Inst Archaeol Univ London* 12, 20–52.

Case, H.J. 1977. The beaker culture in Britain and Ireland. In R.J. Mercer (ed.), *Beakers in Britain and Europe*, 71–101. Oxford. (=BAR Int Ser 26.)

Clarke, D.L. 1970. *Beaker pottery of Great Britain and Ireland.* Cambridge.

Clifford, E.M. 1930. A prehistoric and Roman site at Barnwood near Gloucester. *TBGAS* 52, 201–254.

Clifford, E.M. 1933. The Roman villa, Hucclecote, near Gloucester. *TBGAS* 55, 323–376.

Clifford, E.M. 1937a. The Beaker folk in the Cotswolds. *PPS* 3, 159–163.

Clifford, E.M. 1937b. Archaeological objects of special interest in Gloucestershire. *PCNFC* 26, 159–168.

Clifford, E.M. 1938. A beaker found at Prestbury, Gloucestershire. *TBGAS* 60, 348–349.

Darvill, T.C. 1982. *The megalithic chambered tombs of the Cotswold-Severn region.* Highworth, Wiltshire. (=Vorda Res Ser 5.)

Dent, E. 1877. *Annals of Winchcombe and Sudeley.* London.

Dixon, P. 1971. *Crickley Hill: third report 1971.* Cheltenham. (Duplicated report.)

Dunning, G.C. 1932. Bronze age settlements and a Saxon hut near Bourton-on-the-Water, Gloucestershire. *Antiq J* 12, 279–293.

Dunning, G.C. 1935. Late bronze age urn from Lower Swell, Gloucestershire. *Antiq J* 15, 471–473.

Ellison, A.B. 1975. *Pottery and settlements of the later bronze age in southern England.* Unpublished PhD thesis, University of Cambridge.

Ellison, A.B. 1980. Settlements and regional exchange: a case study. In J. Barrett and R. Bradley (eds.), *Settlement and society in the British later bronze age*, 127–140. Oxford. (=BAR Brit Ser 83.)

Ellison, A.B. 1981. Towards a socioeconomic model for the middle bronze age in southern England. In I. Hodder, G. Isaac, and N. Hammond (eds.), *Pattern of the past: studies in honour of David Clarke*, 413–438. Cambridge.

Evens, E.D., Smith, I.F., and Wallis, F.S. 1972. The petrological identification of stone implements from south-western England. Fifth report of the sub-committee of the South-Western Federation of Museums and Art Galleries. *PPS* 38, 235–275.

Fisher, C.H. 1919. Two bronze spear-heads from Rodborough, near Stroud. *PCNFC* 13, 85–87.

Fowler, P.J. 1978. Pre-medieval fields in the Bristol region. In H.C. Bowen and P.J. Fowler (eds.), *Early land allotment in the British Isles*, 29–47. Oxford. (=BAR Brit Ser 48.)

Gardiner, C.I. 1930. The discovery of a beaker near Woodchester. *PCNFC* 24(1), 103–106.

Gardiner, C.I. 1937. Bronze celt from a field near Waterlane, SE of Bisley, Gloucestershire. *PCNFC* 26(2), 206.

Gerloff, S. 1975. *The early bronze age dagger in Great Britain and a reconsideration of the*

*Wessex culture.* Munich. (=Prähistorische Bronzefunde 6.2.)

Gingell, C.J. n.d. (but 1972.) *A penny for your past: archaeology and the Water Park* Cheltenham. (Duplicated report.)

Green, C. 1935. Some bronze implements from Gloucestershire. *Antiq J* 15, 196–198.

Greenwell, W. 1890. Recent researches in barrows in Yorkshire, Wiltshire, Berkshire, etc. *Archaeologia* 52, 1–72.

Greenwell, W. and Rolleston, G. 1877. *British barrows.* London.

Grimes, W.F. 1960. *Excavations on defence sites 1939–1945: 1. mainly Neolithic-Bronze Age.* London.

Hall, M. and Gingell, C. 1974. Nottingham Hill, Gloucestershire, 1972. *Antiquity* 48, 306–309.

Hannan, A. 1976. Holm Castle, Tewkesbury: excavations during 1975. *Glevensis* 10, 10–11.

Hart, C. 1967. *Archaeology in Dean.* Gloucester.

Herdman, D.W. 1933. Prehistoric vessel from Hawling. *TBGAS* 55, 381–382.

Longworth, I.H. 1961. The origins and development of the primary series in the collared urn tradition in England and Wales. *PPS* 27, 263–306.

Needham, S.P. 1979. The extent of foreign influence on early bronze age axe development in southern Britain. In M. Ryan (ed.), *The origins of metallurgy in Atlantic Europe: proceedings of the fifth Atlantic colloquium*, 265–293. Dublin.

Needham, S.P. and Saville, A. 1981. Two early bronze age flat bronze axeheads from Oddington. *TBGAS* 99, 15–19.

O'Neil, H.E. 1967. Bevan's Quarry round barrow, Temple Guiting, 1964. *TBGAS* 86, 16–41.

O'Neil, H.E. and Bunt, J.S. 1966. A beaker from Leckhampton, Cheltenham, Glos. *TBGAS* 85, 216–217.

O'Neil, H.E. and Grinsell, L. 1960. Gloucestershire Barrows. *TBGAS* 79(1), 1–149.

Oswald, A. 1972. Excavations at Beckford. *Trans Worcestershire Archaeol Soc* 3, 7–54.

Pritchard, J.E. 1906. Bristol Archaeological Notes for 1905: prehistoric. *TBGAS* 29, 281–282.

RCHM 1976. *Iron age and Romano-British monuments in the Gloucestershire Cotswolds.* London.

Roe, F. 1966. The battle-axe series in Britain. *PPS* 32, 199–245.

Roe, F. 1979. Typology of stone implements with shaftholes. In T.H.McK. Clough and W.A. Cummins (eds.), *Stone axe studies*, 23–48. London. (=CBA Res Rep 23.)

Rowlands, M.J. 1976. *The organisation of middle bronze age metalworking in southern Britain.* Oxford. (=BAR Brit Ser 31.)

Saville, A. 1983. Excavations at Condicote henge monument, Gloucestershire, 1977. *TBGAS* 101, 21–47.

Saville, A. and Roe, F.E.S. Forthcoming. A stone battle-axe from Wotton-under-Edge, and a review of battle-axe and mace-head finds from Gloucestershire. *TBGAS*.

Scott-Garrett, C. 1955. Tidenham Chase Barrow. *TBGAS* 74, 15–35.

Terry, W.N. 1953. A bronze spear-head from Moreton-in-Marsh. *TBGAS* 72, 150–151.

Thomas, N. 1979. A fragmentary bronze blade from Swell 7 round barrow, Cow Common, Gloucestershire. In A. Saville, *Recent work at Cow Common bronze age cemetery, Gloucestershire*, 111–112. Bristol. (=CRAAGS Occasional Paper 6.)

**February 1984.**

# The Bronze Age Round Barrows of Gloucestershire: A Brief Review

*John Drinkwater and Alan Saville*

## INTRODUCTION

The earliest specific catalogue of round barrows in the county was incorporated by Witts in his *Archaeological Handbook of Gloucestershire* (Witts 1883).
This account was of limited scope and uneven quality, in that it listed only
126 barrows and included sites of a doubtful nature, suggesting that Witts
had not personally verified all the inclusions. Eighty years of discovery and
destruction were to pass before the publication in 1960 of *Gloucestershire
Barrows*, the major reference catalogue for all barrow sites in Gloucestershire
(O'Neil and Grinsell 1960). In this account the location and dimensions of all
round barrows were given, together with any relevant information derived
from excavation. During the two decades since the 1960 publication an
increasing concern over the destruction of field monuments in rural areas has
initiated two field surveys in the county. The first, published in 1972, was a
reappraisal of the physical condition of all barrows, and their classification in
terms of current landuse (ploughed, under grass, tree-covered, etc.) and
surviving height above ground surface. On the basis of this survey recom-
mendations were made regarding sites suitable for conservation or excavation
(Drinkwater 1972). This account, which considered the problems of barrow
survival in generic terms, was partly superseded in 1980 by the publication of
an up-to-date gazetteer of all the archaeological sites of the Cotswold region,
which included a fresh assessment of the current state of preservation of the
round barrows (Saville 1980).

The approximately 340 round barrow sites listed for the modern county of Gloucestershire by O'Neil and Grinsell included all existing and destroyed sites and other possible barrow locations which had been recorded prior to 1960. More recently, surveys using aerial photography have shown a relatively high concentration of ring-ditch sites on the gravels of the Upper Thames Valley in Gloucestershire, which appears to represent at the minimum an additional sixty possible round barrows (Smith 1972, 166). It is not feasible to make any final determination of the total number of barrows formerly in existence in the county, since the detection of sites is highly dependent on the nature of the terrain, its agricultural usage, and the composition of the original barrow mound. Earthen barrows are easily spread by the plough and, if constructed without a surrounding quarry-ditch, leave no visible traces either on the ground or from the air. Similarly, cairns degenerate into the 'stony patches' often recorded by earlier field surveyors, and in time become indistinguishable from the natural limestone brash turned up by the plough. The numerous quarry-scoops found on the Cotswolds testify to the former practice of local stone extraction for dry-stone walling and road mending. The differentiation of the accompanying spoil-heaps from possible round barrows presents a particular problem which may in some cases be resolved by consulting tithe-map field-names or other local records.

## DISTRIBUTION

The distribution of barrows in the county is best considered by separate examination of the four geological and topographic areas into which Gloucestershire is naturally divided, namely, the gravels and hinterland of the Upper Thames, the Cotswold escarpment, the Severn Valley, and the Forest of Dean. The accompanying map (Fig. 1) depicts only the more reliably attested round barrows, and omits all ring-ditch sites.

### The Gravels and Hinterland of the Upper Thames

Aerial-photographic surveys of this area have revealed numerous circular crop-marks, commonly called ring-ditches (Leech 1977; Smith 1972). Excavation has shown that some of these features are likely to be the last detectable vestiges of round barrows, the filled-in ditch showing as a circular soil- or crop-mark. Only a few barrows survive in this area as visible field monuments and it must be left to aerial photography to locate the levelled sites, and to excavation to confirm their nature.

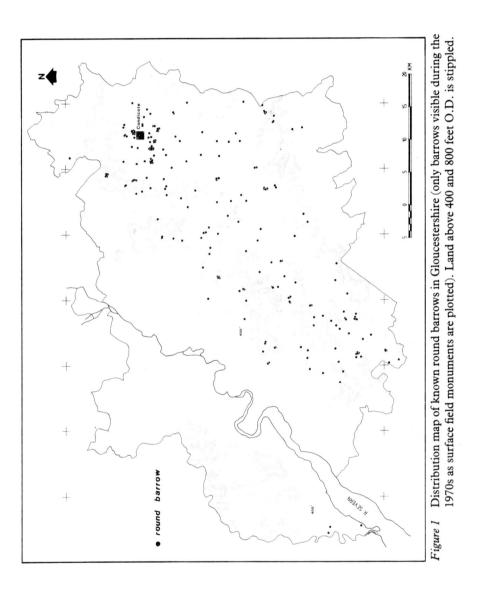

*Figure 1*   Distribution map of known round barrows in Gloucestershire (only barrows visible during the 1970s as surface field monuments are plotted). Land above 400 and 800 feet O.D. is stippled.

In terms of concentration the highest density of ring-ditch sites is around Lechlade, with two major groups of 15–30 sites each and numerous individual occurrences (Smith 1972, 158). Non-proven sites were regarded with caution by O'Neil and Grinsell, who included only two aerially-observed sites from this area in their 1960 survey (both at Lechlade: O'Neil and Grinsell 1960, 120). It is now possible to be more confident that at least a proportion (estimated at forty per cent by Smith 1972, 166) of crop-mark ring-ditches in the county do represent the sites of former bronze age barrows.

*The Cotswold Escarpment*

The most recent survey listed 215 sites on the Gloucestershire Cotswolds where some field evidence for the presence of a round barrow could be seen (Saville 1980). Many of the sites recorded by O'Neil and Grinsell for this area in the 1960 survey are omitted from the present reckoning, being either totally destroyed or in the final stages of eradication.

*Figure 2*   Sezincote 1 round barrow as it appeared after ploughing in January 1976. (Photo: A. Saville.)

The majority of the surviving barrows exist as isolated, or occasionally paired, mounds. Only one substantial Wessex-style barrow cemetery, at Hull Plantations, Longborough (O'Neil and Grinsell 1960, fig. 5), remains in an unploughed condition and this is covered and obscured by trees. It is certain that both linear and nucleated cemeteries were formerly more prevalent on the Cotswolds. Aerial photography, in spite of its limitation of being unable to detect low profile, ditchless barrows, has shown that some isolated mounds, such as Notgrove 1, are the sole survivors of larger groups, the other members of which have been removed by ploughing (Smith 1972).

The Cotswolds contain a sufficient concentration of round barrows to allow a study of siting and density. A number of sites exist where round barrows are positioned in close proximity to a long barrow (Drinkwater 1972, 144–148). The significance of such occurrences in terms of indicating 'continuity' must be treated with extreme caution (Saville 1979, 115). Although there is a preference for the round barrows in these groupings to be sited close to the eastern end of their respective long barrows, this is by no means a consistent feature. Only with the Burn Ground barrow cemetery at Hampnett has the interrelationship of the constituent members been fully defined by excavation (Grimes 1960). At this location six round barrows were found to be in an arc encircling the forecourt area of the long barrow. Two other sites, Hampnett I and Cherington I, have round barrows sited in a similarly significant position (Drinkwater 1972, 149–151). With both these sites, and in the remainder of the barrow groups of this class of cemetery, the attendant round barrows no longer exist as viable field monuments, due to severe depredation by ploughing, and it is not possible to define clearly the interrelationship of the constituent members.

For the majority of round barrows no consistent position for siting can be demonstrated. Predominantly, barrows are situated on the higher ground but not preferentially in a false crest or other prominent siting position. A few barrows, such as the Four Barrow Field group (Temple Guiting 1–6; O'Neil and Grinsell 1960, 134), formerly a fine linear crest-sited cemetery, were deliberately located in a conspicuous position, as is also the case with the small number of round barrows with a scarp-edge siting, e.g. Saintbury 1 (O'Neil and Grinsell 1960, 128) and Uley 1 (Saville 1980, 12). However, most barrows lie inconspicuously on the middle and lower slopes of the wolds, a situation typified by the Sezincote 1–2 barrows (O'Neil and Grinsell 1960, 129), sited well below the crest of the hill in a position not particularly obvious from any direction. Sites such as Snowshill 1–5 and Swell 11 (O'Neil and Grinsell 1960, 129–132) lie on, or near to the base of a valley surrounded or overlooked by higher ground.

The overall Cotswold distribution of round barrows does show a degree of patterning which is likely to reflect the socio-political organization of the region, though it is difficult to comment further on this in the absence of chronological markers and of positive evidence for settlement. Certainly the

*Figure 3*  Wyck Rissington 1 round barrow in April 1976. Note the injudicious siting
of the telegraph pole and the O.S. grid marker. (Photo: A. Saville.)

concentration in the north Cotswolds which centres around the parish of
Swell must be related in some way to the presence of the only known
Gloucestershire henge monument at Condicote (Fig. 1), dated by radiocarbon determination to the eighteenth century bc or later (Saville 1983: 1770 ±
80 bc and 1720 ± 100 bc). Other, less marked concentrations in the south of
the county suggest the possible former existence of a similar ceremonial
monument in the area from Bisley to Kingscote. These two areas, centred on
Swell and Avening, are precisely those where concentrations of neolithic long
barrows have been noted since Crawford first discussed their Cotswold
distribution (1925, 5–7), with the implication, *ceteris paribus,* of continued
foci, possibly of settlement and/or ceremonial observance, for over a millennium (Saville 1979, 115).

## The Forest of Dean

Only one barrow of confirmed bronze age date exists in Gloucestershire west
of the Severn. This site, the Soldiers' Tump, Tidenham, was fully excavated
in 1951–52 (Scott-Garrett 1955). A further two probable round barrows are
situated in the same parish (Ellison 1977, 5; O'Neil and Grinsell 1960, 135).
Place-name evidence suggests that other barrow sites may have existed in the

area, but the wooded nature of the higher ground, together with the extensive ancient industrial workings, cause difficulties in the detection and interpretation of sites.

## The Severn Valley

At present the landuse of the Severn Valley is predominantly pastoral. Few barrows survive as upstanding monuments and air-photographic survey, which has concentrated on the eastern side of the county, has not appreciably contributed to the known range of sites (Smith 1972).

The problem of regarding all ring-ditch sites as actual barrows is exemplified by Atkinson's excavation of the Netherhills Barrow group, Frampton on Severn, where only one of the five circles appeared to give positive evidence of a bronze age funerary function (O'Neil and Grinsell 1960, 114). Nevertheless, the evidence from this one barrow does indicate the potential of ring-ditch sites in the Severn Valley for any consideration of bronze age settlement in Gloucestershire, and makes the non-publication of this 1948 excavation all the more unfortunate.

## TYPOLOGY AND CHRONOLOGY

'It is regrettable that the number of barrows so far excavated with satisfactorily recorded results is insufficient for adequate statistical analysis' (O'Neil and Grinsell 1960, 12). Over twenty years have passed since Grinsell made this statement but it still, unfortunately, holds true. During these past two decades two round barrows have undergone excavation but we still have only one site from which a radiocarbon determination is available (see below). In the absence of a firm chronological basis, and given our inability to typologically classify round barrows from their external appearance, all analysis must be of a qualitative rather than quantitative nature.

The problem is further confounded by the absence of firm dating evidence and, therefore, of a definite chronological sequence, for the local long barrows. This causes a difficulty in defining the relationship and degree of chronological overlap, if any, between so-called 'late' long barrows and those 'early' round barrows such as the Soldier's Grave (Frocester II; Clifford 1938) and Dry Heathfield (Coberley 1a; O'Neil and Grinsell 1960, 97), which exhibited 'neolithic' features in the nature of their funerary deposits and structure. A similarity in certain structural features embodying comparable stone-building techniques is an insufficient criterion to demonstrate continuity in its true sense of an unbroken, uninterrupted tradition. When such techniques are found, even in cemeteries of closely associated long and round barrows, such as at Burn Ground, Hampnett (Grimes 1960, 102), they may represent no more than an instinctive response to the problems of building with stone, rather than providing evidence that the Cotswolds were a cultural backwater in which neolithic culture and its long barrow burial tradition survived into the early centuries of the second millennium BC.

We would have a better understanding of this 'transition' period if it were possible to assess the impact and extent of the beaker phase, especially with regard to the local funerary practices. Unfortunately beakers directly associated with burials, in either primary or secondary contexts, are rare in the county. The only primary beaker inhumation in a round barrow was obtained, after disturbance, from the Ivy Lodge barrow (King's Stanley 1; Clifford 1950), where a 'type A' beaker may have accompanied an inhumation in a slab-lined grave. The pottery accompanying the inhumation burials in the stone-lined boat-shaped burial pit beneath the Soldier's Grave round barrow has been regarded as a mixture of neolithic and beaker wares (O'Neil and Grinsell 1960, 98). Apart from these two sites, beakers have been recovered from flat graves and as secondary deposits in long barrows and round barrows (O'Neil and Grinsell 1960, 14–16). The most recent relevant discovery was of a secondary beaker burial in the enigmatic long barrow at Sale's Lot, Withington (O'Neil 1966).

Local geology has a strong influence on both the internal and external structure of round barrows. In areas where the soil layer is thin and the underlying 'natural' is hard rock, barrows seldom seem to have surrounding ditches. Neither aerial photography nor excavation have shown ditched barrows to be common on the Cotswolds, in contrast to the indications provided by the aerial surveys of the gravels of the Upper Thames.

On the Cotswolds the occurrence, survival, and detection of earthen barrows pose particular problems. The presence of this variety of barrow is well attested by excavation; Chedworth 2 for example was entirely composed of 'brown loamy soil' (Grimes 1960, 134). The recently excavated Swell 8 round barrow did not appear to have much stone incorporated in its composition, but ploughing had removed virtually all traces of the mound before excavation (Saville 1979). It is the potential for survival of the earthen barrow under arable conditions which causes concern. Any of the small, scraped-up mounds, such as those revealed as satellites to the larger barrows in the Snail Down cemetery, Wiltshire (Thomas and Thomas 1955), would by now have gone without trace if they were present on the Cotswolds. Otherwise, most of the surviving barrows on the escarpment appear, from field surveys, to be cairns, in that stone is a major constructional element,

*Figure 4*   North Cerney 2 round barrow in December 1976. Note the 'false berm'
effect (cf. O'Neil and Grinsell 1960, 126) created by ploughing up to the
modern barrier, which is well within the original extent of the burial
mound. (Photo: A. Saville.)

either for the whole of the mound, or as a capping over a composite turf
and/or earth core.

The problem of attempting to categorize round barrows by their external
features is illustrated by the apparent paucity, on the Cotswolds, of the bell,
disc, and other 'fancy' barrow types known from the Wessex region (Ashbee
1960, 24–29). However, Temple Guiting 8, when excavated in 1964, was
found to be a conventional bell barrow complete with berm and rock-cut
ditch (see below). The typological features of the barrow construction had
been completely obscured by ploughing, and it must therefore be probable
that other Wessex-type mounds are present in the county, but will only be
distinguished by geophysical survey and/or excavation. Such was presumably
the case with Snowshill 5 (O'Neil and Grinsell 1960, 130), presumed to be the
origin of the famous 'Wessex Culture' grave-group published by Greenwell
(1890), but no details of the external form of the barrow are recorded.

Prior to 1940 most of the information on barrow structure (and funerary
ritual) was derived from antiquarian delvings or casual observations made
during destruction. With a precursor in Clifford's excavation of the Soldier's
Grave at Frocester (Clifford 1938), the era of systematic, 'scientific' round

barrow excavation commenced with Grimes's 'total excavation' technique, which he employed in 1940 on the Chedworth 1–2 and Hampnett 1–6 sites (Grimes 1960). Although some of these barrows were in the final stages of destruction a considerable amount of detail regarding constructional and burial practices was recovered. The results of these, and all other pre-1960 barrow excavations, were summarized and analysed in the relevant sections of *Gloucestershire Barrows* (O'Neil and Grinsell 1960, 24–29, 35–38). Since this publication only two Gloucestershire round barrows have been excavated, namely Bevan's Quarry (Temple Guiting 8; O'Neil 1967) and Swell 8 (Saville 1979), both of which have made a significant contribution to our appreciation of the nature and excavation potential of the local bronze age round barrows.

Excavation revealed the apparently amorphous Bevan's Quarry site to be a bell barrow encircled by a deep, rock-cut ditch. Subsequent to the primary deposition of an unaccompanied cremation in a small, centrally situated pit, a complex sequence of constructional phases ensued, during which five satellite and five secondary cremation burials were incorporated in the mound. As previously stated one of the more important results of this excavation was the confirmation of a 'Wessex' style barrow on the Cotswolds.

The Swell 8 round barrow was a member of the Cow Common barrow cemetery 6km due west of Stow-on-the-Wold. It was chosen for excavation 'to assess the problems and potential of excavating plough-damaged barrows on the Cotswolds' (Saville 1979, 1). Prior to excavation in 1974 the barrow was visible only as a slight, non-stony, circular rise in the ploughed field close to the long barrow Swell I. Excavation revealed that the annual ploughing had removed the original mound down to the remnants of the bronze age pre-barrow soil. With this advanced state of destruction the nature of the mound could not be defined with certainty. Very few stones were present in the plough-soil and it is possible that the mound was not of solid cairn construction but was earthen or of a composite nature embodying a cairn ring. The barrow was ditchless and covered an apparently unaccompanied cremation in a shallow pit, a circumstance which finds parallels in other Cotswold round barrows (Saville 1979, 114). Burnt timbers which overlay the burial provided radiocarbon determinations of 1480 ± 80 bc and 1440 ± 80 bc, thus giving an approximate *terminus post quem* which suggests that Swell 8 is not earlier than the mid-fifteenth century bc, and could be somewhat later. These remain the only radiocarbon determinations available for a Cotswold round barrow.

The enigmatic ring-ditch at Bourton-on-the-Water, which was observed during its destruction in 1972 (O'Neil 1977, 15–17), produced no dating

*Figure 5*   Barrow Clump, Elkstone 1 round barrow in January 1977. A well-
preserved Cotswold round cairn, despite its situation within an arable
field. (Photo: A. Saville.)

evidence and no finds other than two dog burials from an off-centre pit. The
status of this site as a bronze age funerary monument is, therefore, in doubt.


CONCLUSIONS

This brief review of the current state of knowledge about Gloucestershire
round barrows will have served to emphasize how little archaeological
research has been undertaken on this class of monument within the county in
recent years. Further fieldwork and aerial photography will increase the
number of barrows known, and detailed analysis of distributions and
topographic locations could be helpful. The basic questions relating to the
chronology and cultural attribution of the round barrows, however, will only
be resolved by fresh excavation. This desirability of excavation on academic
grounds is enhanced by the need to respond to the continuing destruction,
particularly by arable cultivation and gravel-extraction, of archaeological sites
throughout the county. Thus there are pressing arguments for the adoption
of a new, carefully formulated campaign of excavations to allow the round
barrows to contribute more fully towards our understanding of the still
shadowy bronze age phase in Gloucestershire (cf. Saville 1979, 116; 1980,
28). By the same token there is an equally pressing need for renewed efforts

to ensure the continued preservation of those round barrows in the county which survive as important field monuments.

## REFERENCES

Ashbee, P. 1960. *The bronze age round barrow in Britain.* London.

Clifford, E.M. 1938. The Soldier's Grave, Frocester, Gloucestershire. *PPS* 4, 214–217.

Clifford, E.M. 1950. The Ivy Lodge round barrow. *TBGAS* 69, 59–77.

Crawford, O.G.S. 1925. *The long barrows of the Cotswolds.* Gloucester.

Drinkwater, J. 1972. Barrows in Gloucestershire: patterns of destruction. In P.J. Fowler (ed.), *Archaeology and the landscape,* 129–155. London.

Ellison, A. 1977. *A survey of the archaeological implications of forestry in the Forest of Dean.* Bristol. (CRAAGS duplicated typescript.)

Greenwell, W. 1890. Recent researches in barrows in Yorkshire, Wiltshire, Berkshire, etc. *Archaeologia* 52, 1–72.

Grimes, W.F. 1960. *Excavations on defence sites, 1939–1945.* London.

Leech, R. 1977. *The Upper Thames Valley in Gloucestershire: an archaeological survey of the river gravels.* Bristol. (=CRAAGS Survey 4.)

O'Neil, H.E. 1966. Sale's Lot long barrow, Withington, Gloucestershire, 1962–1965. *TBGAS* 85, 5–35.

O'Neil, H.E. 1967. Bevan's Quarry round barrow, Temple Guiting, 1964. *TBGAS* 86, 16–41.

O'Neil, H.E. 1977. Salmonsbury, Bourton-on-the-Water. Some aspects of archaeology in Bourton Vale. *TBGAS* 95, 11–23.

O'Neil, H.E. and Grinsell, L.V. 1960. Gloucestershire barrows. *TBGAS* 79, 1–149.

Saville, A. 1979. *Recent work at Cow Common bronze age cemetery, Gloucestershire.* Bristol. (=CRAAGS Occasional Paper 6.)

Saville, A. 1980. *Archaeological sites in the Avon and Gloucestershire Cotswolds.* Bristol. (=CRAAGS Survey 5.)

Saville, A. 1983. Excavations at Condicote henge monument, Gloucestershire, 1977. *TBGAS* 101, 21–47.

Scott-Garrett, C. 1955. Tidenham Chase barrow. *TBGAS* 74, 15–35.

Smith, I.F. 1972. Ring-ditches in eastern and central Gloucestershire. In P.J. Fowler (ed.), *Archaeology and the landscape,* 157–167. London.

Thomas, N. and Thomas, C. 1955. Excavations at Snail Down, Everleigh, 1953–1955: an interim report. *Wiltshire Archaeol Natur Hist Mag* 56, 127–148.

Witts, G.B. 1883. *Archaeological handbook of the county of Gloucester.* Cheltenham.

**January 1984**

# The Iron Age in Gloucestershire: A Review of the Evidence

## Alan Saville

INTRODUCTION

In comparison with the previous prehistoric phases, the iron age in Gloucestershire is prolific in archaeological material available for study, both in terms
of sites and artefacts. However, large-scale, modern excavation has taken
place at only two locations, Claydon Pike and Crickley Hill. At both sites
work is still in progress and the available publications are only of an interim
nature. Other excavations of iron age sites in the county have been relatively
small-scale and of varying standard, and virtually all of the archaeological
evidence available comes from the east of the county, so that the area west of
the River Severn remains *terra incognita* in this period.

These reservations help to explain why it is not yet possible to integrate
fully the evidence from settlements and artefacts into a coherent sequence of
development throughout the iron age. Nevertheless, a start can be made
using the published excavation reports, the unpublished material in museum
collections, the visible field remains of the surviving earthworks, and the
crop-marks recorded by aerial photography, together with previous reviews
of the available evidence. Of the latter, the key-works appeared in 1961 as
part of Clifford's seminal publication of her excavation at Bagendon (Allen
1961a; Cotton 1961; Hawkes 1961). Since then the outstanding contribution
has been the survey of the east of the county by the Royal Commission on
Historical Monuments (RCHM 1976), to which can be added the discussions
by Marshall (1978a and 1978b), and other reviews of more limited focus (e.g.

Champion 1976; Grinsell 1970; Painter 1966; Smith 1973). Equally important has been the re-evaluation of the nature of the local iron age pottery manufacture and distribution, first undertaken by Peacock (1968), and now being continued by Morris (1981a).

The objective of the present article is to give a thematic review of the various major categories of evidence available for the iron age in Gloucestershire, and thus a summary of the present state of knowledge. To achieve this some chronological subdivision is clearly desirable, despite the inherent difficulties caused by the small number of radiocarbon dates (Appendix 1). All conventional subdivisions of the iron age are of a tripartite nature, referring back to the former Hallstatt, La Tène, and Belgic horizons, as did the related 'ABC' nomenclature (Hawkes 1959). Such terminology is now far more confusing than useful, but it is still helpful to consider the period in three phases, which here will be termed simply early, middle, and late. Strictly speaking, the iron age begins with the introduction of iron objects and iron metallurgy into the existing bronze-using society, but in practice it is necessary to use other near-definitive attributes, such as the construction of the hilltop enclosures known as hillforts, to mark the advent of the iron age archaeologically. The early phase, using the radiocarbon determinations from Crickley Hill and by analogy with developments in adjacent areas, can be said to encompass approximately the period 700–400 bc, possibly with an even earlier starting date. The late phase relates to the period immediately before and during the successful Roman invasion of England in the first century AD, and perhaps can be extended back to as early as 100 BC on the basis of imported Roman pottery and related ceramics, the imported and local coinage, and distinctive types of metal brooch. The middle phase is thus the period between the two, i.e. c.400–100 bc/BC or later, which leaves the chronological scheme deliberately vague, providing only a means of ordering the evidence in a relative fashion in the light of the present ambiguities.

In view of the dedication of the volume in which this article appears, it is particularly appropriate to note that iron age studies in Gloucestershire not only owe a considerable debt to Mrs Clifford's work at Bagendon, but also to Mrs O'Neil's involvement in the investigations at Salmonsbury Camp (O'Neil 1977); the work of both women remains of importance for the iron age (cf. Dunning 1976, 118), as it does for so many other periods of Gloucestershire archaeology.

## HILLFORTS

Pride of place in any consideration of the Gloucestershire iron age must be

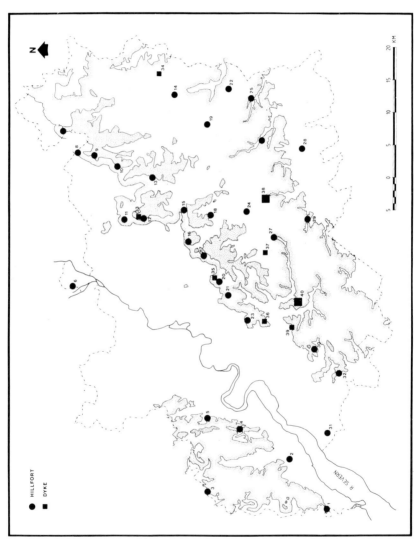

*Figure 1* Iron age Gloucestershire: location map of hillforts and dykes. (For key to numbers see Appendix 2.) Land over 400 and 800 feet above O.D. stippled.

given to the hillforts, of which the county has a superb series. The thirty-two forts marked on the map (Fig. 1 and Appendix 2) are concentrated mainly on the Cotswold Hills, including a clustering along the scarp-edge, with its obvious natural advantages for the strategic location of defensive sites, from Willersey in the north down to Brackenbury Ditches in the south. There are two hillforts at opposite ends of the Severn Valley, at Towbury Hill, Twyning, in the north, and at Bevington Camp, Ham and Stone, in the south, and a single fort, Ranbury Ring, Ampney St Peter, in the Upper Thames Valley. West of the Severn a group of five sites lies on the periphery of the Forest of Dean upland. Recent assessment of the field evidence for the Cotswold hillforts has led to a major re-evaluation, with many of the formerly accepted sites now discredited (RCHM 1976, xxix-xxxiv), but it seems likely that a similarly detailed scrutiny in the west of the county would have the opposite effect of increasing the number of recognized hillforts.

Excavation has taken place at nine of the Gloucestershire hillforts, at Crickley Hill, Leckhampton Hill, Nottingham Hill, Shenberrow, and Uley Bury along the scarp-edge, at The Ditches (North Cerney), Norbury (Northleach), and Salmonsbury across the Cotswold dip-slope, and at Lydney on the other side of the Severn.

These excavations fall into two quite distinct phases. In the 1920s and 1930s research excavations took place at Leckhampton, Lydney, Salmonsbury, and Shenberrow. Although limited in scale, all of these excavations were of high standard for their time, and have been published in final form, with Salmonsbury in particular being of fundamental importance to any study of the period. To these sites must be added that of Bredon Hill, now just outside the county, excavated between 1935–1937 (Hencken 1938). The second phase began in 1969 when research excavation was initiated at both Crickley Hill and Leckhampton Hill by the Committee for Research into the Iron Age in the North West Cotswolds. At Leckhampton the few short seasons of excavation were designed to re-examine some of the areas first exposed in the 1920s, but at Crickley the objective has become the total excavation of the hillfort interior. Work has continued annually at Crickley since 1969, and, now under the aegis of the Crickley Hill Trust, is programmed to extend into the 1990s. More recently, in 1982, a new and independent research project was started at The Ditches to examine this heavily ploughed site in the light of new evidence from the adjacent site of Bagendon. The other excavated hillforts, Norbury, Nottingham Hill, and Uley Bury, were the sites of small-scale rescue excavations during the 1970s.

Only at Crickley, where a single rampart and ditch delimit what is now a promontory enclosure of some $9\frac{1}{2}$ acres (3·8ha), can the excavations be described as extensive, and it is here that the details of rampart construction, ditch excavation, entrance elaboration, and interior occupation are best known (Dixon 1969–1973, 1972, 1973, and 1976). The earliest rampart was timber-laced with dry-stone facings, separated by a berm from the flat-bottomed external ditch. This rampart, which had a single entrance with front and rear gates, was destroyed by fire leaving a characteristic burnt remnant, in part reduced to quicklime and slaked. The defences were reconstructed on a larger scale, using the burnt rampart as a core. The entrance was rebuilt with flanking, dry-stone revetted bastions, and elaborated by the addition of an outer protective hornwork with its own ditch. Considerable modification of the original ditch took place, presumably both to increase the defensiveness and to provide material for the rebuilding of the ramparts. This rampart was also eventually destroyed by fire. The suggested reconstructions of these defences by their excavator (Dixon 1972, fig.1; Dixon and Borne 1977, figs. 2–3) provide a powerful impression of the strength of such fortifications when they were in use, contrasting with the picture of gentle landscaping gained from viewing these and many other local hillfort defences in their present, ruinous state. In particular it is the former presence of vertical dry-stone revetments which is obscured without excavation, though these should be expected as standard at hillforts in the Cotswolds, where dry-stone building using the local limestone had been traditional since the neolithic period.

At Leckhampton Hill a single rampart and ditch form another scarp-edge promontory enclosure, in this case of some 7 acres (2·8ha). Excavations, in the 1920s (Burrow et al. 1925) and more recently (Champion 1971 and 1976), concentrated on the hillfort entrance, which has been shown to be of relatively simple type, but with flanking, semi-circular 'guard-chambers' set into the rampart terminals. The rampart here was similar to the first-phase rampart at Crickley, and was also eventually burnt, but was not rebuilt.

At Shenberrow the small bivallate enclosure of 2½ acres (1ha) had dry-stone facing to the inner bank at least (Fell 1961), and at Uley Bury the excavated rampart similarly had an outer face of dry-stone revetment. Uley Bury, a large enclosure of some 32 acres (13ha), also has two lines of defence, in this case created by terracing of the natural slope, with a proven rampart crowning the upper terrace (Saville and Ellison 1983, fig. 18). Salmonsbury, a bivallate, rectangular enclosure of 56 acres (22·7ha), atypically sited on a low-lying gravel platform between the Rivers Dikler and Windrush at Bourton-on-the-Water, has V-shaped ditches and a gravel core to the ramparts, which were faced with imported stone (Dunning 1976). Lydney, a univallate (or multivallate?) promontory-type enclosure of 5 acres (2ha), had an earthen bank of uncertain form (Wheeler 1932). Details of the defences at The Ditches, a bivallate enclosure of some 10 acres (4ha), are not yet available (Trow 1982), while the excavations at Norbury (Saville 1983a) and Nottingham Hill (Hall and Gingell 1974) did not involve the defences.

The typology of the Cotswold hillforts has conveniently been described by the RCHM (1976, xxv-xxvi and figure) and discussed with reference to chronology by Marshall (1978a). The major fixed-point for starting to consider the implications of typology is Crickley Hill, where the enclosure is shown by radiocarbon dates to be early, perhaps with a range from 700–500 bc. Superficially resembling Crickley are a series of other, relatively small, univallate enclosures like Beckbury, Leckhampton, and Windrush, or small, bivallate enclosures like Cleeve Cloud and Shenberrow, which can also be suggested as potentially early, a dating apparently confirmed by the ceramic evidence from Shenberrow (Fell 1961) and possibly from Cleeve Cloud (see below). This model has been expanded by Marshall, following Cotton (1961, 25) and Fell (1961, 34), with reference to two small, univallate, Cotswold hillforts just across the Oxfordshire border, at Chastleton (Leeds 1931) and Lyneham (Bayne 1957), where pottery of early type, comparable to that at Crickley Hill, has been found. The typological argument continues with the suggestion that subsequent middle iron age hillforts in the region exhibit trends towards multivallation, large-scale defences, and general complexity, supported to some extent by the evidence from Salmonsbury with its middle and late iron age pottery, and by Uley Bury, where the pottery and a single radiocarbon date point to construction and use around 300 bc. The overall size of area enclosed is not necessarily seen as relevant to dating, since one of the largest, the 80-acre (32ha) Norbury Camp (Northleach), has often been regarded as early on typological grounds (Cotton 1961, 25; Wainwright 1967, 56).

However, it would be premature to regard such suggestions as anything more than possibilities, in the absence of further, more extensive excavations and additional radiocarbon dates. One of the few statements which can be made at the moment is that Salmonsbury is the only 'hillfort' with published evidence for continuity of use through the middle and late iron age and into the Roman period, and that this site is anyway atypical in its form, siting, and proximity to an eventual small Roman town. The Roman use of the Lydney site seems likely to represent re-occupation after abandonment during the middle iron age. Roman remains from the 1976 excavations at Uley Bury were extremely sparse considering the adjacent temple complex (Ellison 1980), and at Norbury (Northleach) the known Roman activity suggests re-use of the site in the second century AD. A picture of late iron age and

Roman occupation may be emerging at The Ditches (Trow 1982), but clarification must await further work, especially as the recent find of a currency bar hoard in the enclosure ditch (Trow pers. comm.) may well be an indicator of a middle iron age construction date. On the whole, the Gloucestershire evidence suggests that hillfort construction took place during the early and middle iron age, and that their use normally finished before the late iron age.

Seeking precursors for the hillforts is as tendentious in Gloucestershire as elsewhere, especially as the Crickley radiocarbon dates can no longer be seen as particularly early (e.g. Megaw and Simpson 1979, 364). The enormous 120 acre (48·6ha), bivallate promontory fort on Nottingham Hill has produced a late bronze age hoard from the interior (Hall and Gingell 1974), but the deposition of the hoard in this location could be entirely fortuitous, and the detailed publication of the settlement and ceramic evidence found during the 1972 excavation to recover the hoard is eagerly awaited. In complete contrast, the small (2½acre/1ha) univallate enclosure at Roel, Sudeley, has also been suggested as potentially early (Saville et al. 1983, 21), but no details are known. Other potential late bronze age enclosures recognized from aerial photographs are at Churcham (Spry and Wingham 1979) and Hawling (Saville 1979, 115). Excavation alone will clarify these instances, though even if some of the local enclosures can be 'moved back' into the bronze age the precise inspiration for hillfort-building within the socio-political development of celtic tribalism is likely to remain obscure (Cunliffe 1974, 305). It is always worth remembering that neolithic enclosures such as Crickley Hill and The Peak (Darvill, this volume), and the early bronze age enclosure at Condicote (Saville 1983b), would have existed as substantial earthworks in early iron age times.

Speculation on the origin of hillforts inevitably leads to the question of their function. Again Crickley provides the only reliable information, as the extensive excavation of the interior of this well-preserved site has allowed the reconstruction of dense internal settlement. Associated with the early rampart were a series of rectangular, timber-built structures, interpreted as large aisled-halls and small four-post huts or crop-stores (Dixon 1976, 173; Dixon and Borne 1977), with the halls erected in an organized layout on either side of the roadway leading into the fort from the entrance through the rampart. Subsequently a rather different type of settlement was associated with the re-vamped defences, comprising a large round-house and small round huts. In both cases it is difficult to interpret the excavated evidence in any other way than as denoting the existence of fortified villages.

Salmonsbury has also provided evidence for internal structures in the form of round huts, entirely of timber construction in the middle iron age, and with stone footings in the later phase (Dunning 1976, 82–85). The interior of Norbury (Northleach) contained at least three rectangular four-post structures in a planned setting (Saville 1983a). These were without dating evidence, but their resemblance to similar structures at Crickley may be significant. Underground pits of the kind normally interpreted as for grain-storage occurred at Salmonsbury, and a single example occurred at Shenberrow (Fell 1961, 23), thus forming a contrast with the apparent absence of pits at Crickley and Norbury. The evidence for a hut in the lee of the rampart at Shenberrow is equivocal (Fell 1961, 21). At Uley Bury, the palimpsest of internal crop-mark features (Hampton and Palmer 1977, fig. 1) is suggestive of a middle iron age round-house settlement of some density within the hillfort, a picture confirmed by the number and range of finds recovered during rescue excavation (Saville and Ellison 1983).

Thus the available data suggest that the Cotswold hillforts should be regarded as defended village-type settlements, if not in some cases virtually small enclosed towns. As such these settlements were presumably in some sense of higher status than other contemporary occupation sites, a distinction which must reflect the stratified organization of early to middle iron age society. An alternative hypothesis for the function of hillforts, particularly those of large size, is that they were stock enclosures (e.g. Wainwright 1967). Such an explanation would be difficult to prove without extensive excavation and the existing information for this type of enclosure within the county, at Northleach (Saville 1983a) and Nottingham Hill (Hall and Gingell 1974), is rather more indicative of settlement, though not yet conclusive.

Finally in this section, concern must be expressed over the current condition of the Cotswold hillforts in particular, which have suffered considerably from inappropriate landuse (Saville 1980, 29–30). The importance of these sites for the future understanding of the Gloucestershire iron age cannot be exaggerated, and their continued depredation, even though they are almost all scheduled ancient monuments, is deplorable.


## DYKES AND OTHER EARTHWORK SITES

The other major category of iron age field monuments known in Gloucestershire comprises linear and curvilinear stretches of banks and ditches which can be considered for convenience under the label of 'dykes'. A variety of different purposes are probably represented by the eight sites marked on the map (Fig. 1 and Appendix 2), even if these are all of iron age date, which is only established, and then only sketchily, at the two dyke complexes of Bagendon and Minchinhampton.

At Bagendon a series of at least nine separate dykes are recognized (RCHM 1976, 6–9), potentially delimiting an enormous area of some 500 acres (202ha) though the relationship between these earthworks is not easy to assess, particularly when, in the case of the so-called Scrubditch dyke, the ditch is internal to the supposed focus of enclosure. The dyke to the west of Cutham Lane was sectioned by Clifford (1961, 8–10), and found to comprise an externally revetted bank and a V-profile ditch. The core of this bank produced what were apparently wheel-thrown late iron age sherds, and the primary fill of the ditch contained a sherd of early Roman imported ware. These finds are usually regarded as dating this dyke to the beginning of the first century AD, and therefore as contemporary with the evidence for internal settlement and industrial activity. This industrial activity, principally comprising the working of iron, also included evidence for the minting of coins of the Dobunni, the celtic tribe whose coins have a distribution pattern centred on Gloucestershire (e.g. Cunliffe 1974, fig. 7:9). For this and other reasons (Clifford 1961, 1–2), Bagendon has been identified as a tribal capital or oppidum of the Dobunni, and is seen as the precursor in many ways of the early Roman fort and town at Cirencester. More recent excavations by Trow (1982) in the area adjacent to Clifford's trenches have demonstrated early Roman rather than iron age activity, and the precise dating of the Bagendon settlement is now very problematic. This is equally true of the status of Bagendon, since the identification as an oppidum, and particularly as a quasi-historical Dobunnic capital, must be regarded as premature. Indeed, the concrete archaeological data known from the Bagendon dyke complex are in inverse proportion to the amount of speculation about the site, and there is an urgent need for more excavation, aerial photography, and fieldwork to clarify the position. The cutting of a pipe-trench through the main Perrott's Brook Dyke (RCHM 1976, 8: dyke 'f') in 1983 was observed by Western Archaeological Trust, but no dating evidence was obtained, and none of the other dykes have been excavated. Limited exploration elsewhere at Bagendon has been equally unproductive (Gracie 1962).

The only other location in the county which is comparable to Bagendon is at Minchinhampton, where another dyke complex, even more difficult to regard as an enclosure or otherwise interpret from surface remains, straddles the Common (RCHM 1976, 81–84). The main stretch of dyke at Minchinhampton is known as The Bulwarks, and was sectioned by Clifford (1937), who recovered middle iron age pottery from both bank and ditch, and Roman pottery from the ditch only. The superficial similarity between

Bagendon and Minchinhampton has led to the incorporation of the latter site within the same pseudo-historical framework as the former, in which Minchinhampton becomes the stronghold of Caratacus of the Catuvellauni (Clifford 1961, 160–163), but this obviously goes far beyond the archaeological evidence.

None of the other dykes have been dated, although the one on Juniper Hill, Edgeworth, was sectioned by Clifford (1961, 159), but those most likely to be of iron age date are the cross-ridge dykes, where the earthworks cut off an area of high ground in the manner of a hillfort, as at Brockworth, Juniper Hill, King's Stanley, and Randwick (RCHM 1976, 22, 53, 70, and 97). The opportunity to examine the King's Stanley dyke was missed in 1976 when it was sectioned for a water-pipe trench. More enigmatic are the travelling earthwork on Cleeve Common (RCHM 1976, 107–109), regarded as potentially of iron age date in view of the spatial association with known settlements immediately to the north, and the bank and ditch at Icomb (see Appendix 2).

The former existence of dyke systems which have now been levelled by cultivation is suggested by crop-marks at Northleach (RCHM 1976, 90), while the three pit alignments revealed by aerial photography, at Condicote, Great Rissington, and Temple Guiting (RCHM 1976, 39, 60, and 117) may represent alternative methods of iron age spatial demarcation. In the Thames Valley, the palimpsest of crop-mark ditches (Leech 1977) is bound to incorporate iron age enclosures and boundary systems, but these cannot be disentangled from features of other periods without excavation.

Other earthwork sites likely to be of iron age date are few, but include the two small ringworks on the slopes of Cleeve Hill (RCHM 1976, 107), which could be farmstead or hut enclosures. The field-systems which survive in the county (Saville 1980, 21 and 33) may include examples of iron age date.

## NON-HILLFORT SETTLEMENTS

As discussed above, many if not all, of the Gloucestershire hillforts are likely to represent permanent settlement sites, but they will have been outnumbered throughout the iron age by a whole range of other settlements, with and without enclosures, comprising villages, smaller farmsteads, and isolated huts. The reason these settlements have in the past been archaeologically overshadowed by the hillforts is that they are so much more difficult to identify, being recognizable only as crop-marks on aerial photographs, or from the evidence of pits, post-holes, ditches, or simply pottery scatters, located by chance disturbance of the ground or during archaeological investigations of other features.

The vast numbers of crop-mark sites now known in the Upper Thames Valley (Leech 1977; RCHM 1976) must include a large proportion of iron age sites among or beneath the more readily identifiable Romano-British ones. In general these sites cannot be identified as iron age on the surface, partly because centuries of cultivation have destroyed the fragile early and middle iron age ceramics which would otherwise provide clues during fieldwalking. The sketchy information on iron age activity in this area, which has accumulated from sites like Roughground Farm, Lechlade (RCHM 1976, 73), is now being fleshed-out by the extensive excavations at Claydon Pike (Miles and Palmer n.d., 1983a, and 1983b). Three gravel 'islands' have been investigated, on each of which were clusters of middle iron age round-houses associated with drainage ditches and field boundaries. Over twenty round-houses have been defined, typically comprising the traces of a stake-built wall of some 8m diameter set inside a circular drainage gully. As the excavations at Claydon Pike proceed, and in particular as the well-preserved environmental remains from the site are processed, a full picture of a middle iron age domestic settlement and its economy will emerge. This will eventually be complemented by the picture from the similar settlement site of Beckford at the opposite end of the county, only four miles from Tewkesbury but over the boundary in Hereford and Worcester (Britnell 1974; Oswald 1970–1972), where extensive excavations took place in the 1960s and 1970s. Indeed, settlements of this type can be expected on gravel spreads throughout the county, as occasionally demonstrated by chance finds such as at Eastington, near Stroud, where a pit was recorded (Gardiner 1932), or at Frocester Court during excavation of the Roman villa (Price 1983, 141).

On the Cotswolds, part of a small middle iron age settlement has been excavated at Guiting Power (Saville 1979). Here the settlement was defined only by the presence of a cluster of underground 'storage' pits – though an adjacent unexcavated enclosure ditch was probably contemporary – since structural evidence in the form of post-holes had presumably been removed by ploughing. Such settlements are likely to represent farms, and are otherwise known on the Cotswolds by a few instances of distinctive crop-marks on aerial photographs, as at Northleach (Darvill and Hingley 1982) and Temple Guiting (RCHM 1976, 117–119), or by other finds of pits, as at Foxcote Manor (Donovan and Dunning 1936), King's Beeches (Gray and Brewer 1904), Oxenton (Powell 1933), and Wood House (Gascoigne 1973). Settlement activity of some kind is presumably indicated wherever even the most sketchy finds of iron age material have been located, for example at Copse Hill (Grinsell 1964) and Syreford (RCHM 1976, 125).

## POTTERY

The most abundant and archaeologically significant class of iron age artefact from the county is the pottery. A substantial body of this material is now available for study, and reassessment of the pioneering discussions contained in the Bagendon report (Cotton 1961; Hawkes 1961) is long overdue. The key to this reassessment will lie on the one hand in the publication of the large, new assemblages from Claydon Pike and Crickley Hill (and Beckford), and on the other in the correlation of the petrological information becoming available for assemblages inside and outside of the county. Attention should also be drawn to the potential for reanalysis of some older assemblages, for example that from Bagendon, but in particular the important assemblage from Salmonsbury, now in Cheltenham Museum, which contains far more material than appeared in the final excavation report (Dunning 1976), and demands quantitative treatment. There are also insights to be gained by re-examination of minor ceramic finds, and some of these are republished, or published for the first time, in this report (Figs. 2–3 and Appendix 3).

In brief, the three-phase sequence proposed for the Gloucestershire iron age can be characterized ceramically by the following details of form, decoration, and fabric (cf. Morris 1983, 18). In the early iron age, pottery is typified by the presence of angular 'situlate' and carinated forms, and of decoration by finger-tip impressions and geometric incised motifs, the latter sometimes with white infill. The early iron age pottery tends in the main to be made from clays found near to the sites on which it is found, and thus to have a very localized distribution. The middle iron age see the appearance of regionally distributed pottery, which becomes proportionally more and more important in assemblages during this phase, emanating from semi-specialist manufacturing centres, often outside the county. The forms are less angular than before, typically slack-profiled jars, and are decorated with stamped, linear-tooled, and incised, and sometimes burnished, linear and curvilinear motifs. Alongside the middle iron age pottery are found Droitwich briquet-age salt-containers, perhaps implying the import of salt into the county as part of the same distribution process bringing the non-local pottery, demonstrating the inter-regional exchange/trade networks in existence. By the late iron age the ceramic repertoire includes wheel-turned pottery of 'Belgic' type and imported Gallo-Belgic and early Roman wares. This crude overall framework can now be used to separate some of the ceramic assemblages from the county, and hence to offer insight into the phasing of the sites involved.

## Early Iron Age Pottery

For the early iron age, Crickley Hill and Shenberrow are the sites which have produced the definitive pottery assemblages. At Crickley the pottery can apparently be divided into two phases (Dixon 1976, 174). The earlier phase pottery, as yet only poorly characterized, but including angular forms with linear decoration, is replaced by pottery including carinated bowls, and with decoration by linear incision, frequently including chevron motifs and other incised ornament infilled with white paste. The correlation of different pottery assemblages with first the long-house settlement then the round-house settlement is a reminder that the simple 'early iron age' designation should be capable of further refinement and subdivision. Pottery decorated with finger-tip impressions is also present at Crickley (Dixon 1971, fig. 8,1), and provides a link with the assemblage from Shenberrow, where finger-tip and finger-nail impressions are the dominant decorative motifs, ocurring on vessels with distinct 'situlate' and carinated profiles, the decoration mainly located on the shoulder just below the rim, but also along the top of the rim (Fell 1961, figs. 6–7). Virtually all of the decorated pottery at Shenberrow came from a small area described as 'the dark occupation layer' in the lee of the inner rampart on the south-west corner of the fort, and it is worth emphasizing that the relationship between this deposit and the defences is not secure.

No other large and well-contexted assemblages of early iron age pottery have yet been found in Gloucestershire, and the asessment of potentially similar smaller groups can be extremely confusing. For example, only two decorated sherds appear to survive from the 1925 excavations at Leckhampton Hill, one with finger-nail impressions, the other with an apparent finger-tip impression and a shouldered profile (Burrow et al. 1925, plate 6, C; Marshall 1978c, fig. 4, 7–8). The original publication also includes a further sherd with finger-nail impressions, and a sherd with incised triangles infilled with diagonal cross-hatching (Burrow et al. 1925, plate 6, B and G). Marshall (1978c, 23), following the original report (Burrow et al. 1925, 105), regards the latter sherd as of possible Glastonbury-type, and therefore as appropriate to the later of two phases of occupation he postulates for Leckhampton, whereas Champion (1971, 15 and 1976, 187) interprets this same sherd as having the type of geometric decoration present on the pottery at Crickley. However, simply on the basis of the original illustration, this sherd could be compared with middle iron age pottery from the county (e.g. Guiting Power: Saville 1979, fig. 9, 38), as could the sherds with finger-impressed decoration (e.g. Uley Bury: Saville and Ellison 1983, fig. 9, 1, and fig. 10, 36). More significantly, six rims and twenty-one body sherds of the surviving total of forty iron age sherds from the 1925 excavation (Cheltenham Museum) have now been identified as of Peacock's Group $B_1$, Palaeozoic limestone-tempered fabric (Morris 1981b). Despite the arguments rehearsed by Champion (1976, 187–190),

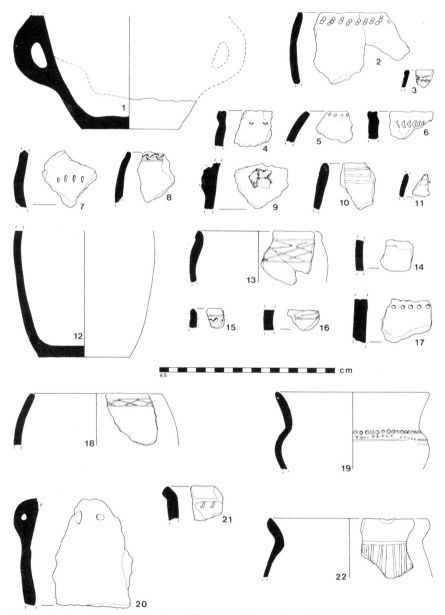

*Figure 2* Iron age pottery from Gloucestershire. 1–11 Oxenton; 12–17 King's Beeches; 18 Stables Quarry; 19 Syreford; 20 Birdlip; 21 Dumbleton; 22 Gloucester. (See Appendix 3.)

therefore, the date of fortification and occupation at Leckhampton must still be regarded as uncertain (cf. RCHM 1976, 77). This case study is salutary in emphasizing the extreme tenuousness of the evidence used to suggest early dates for some Gloucestershire sites.

At King's Beeches, an apparently open settlement below Cleeve Hill revealed during quarrying at the beginning of this century (Gray and Brewer 1904; RCHM 1976, 107), the early phase postulated on the basis of a single enigmatic sherd (Marshall 1978c, 17 and fig. 1, 10: drawn upside down?) should be regarded as dubious since the bulk of the pottery is firmly of middle iron age character (Fig. 2, 12–17 and Appendix 3). The same is true (Fig. 2, 1–11 and Appendix 3) of the unenclosed (?) hilltop settlement at Oxenton (RCHM 1976, 91), where Marshall sees a possible early phase on the basis of a single sherd (1978a, 9 and 1978c, fig. 3, 11; Powell 1933, fig. 1, 1), the whereabouts of which is now unknown. The supposed early phase at Salmonsbury (Cotton 1961, 23; Marshall 1978a, 9) rests on Dunning's original reference (1931, 489) to 'a few sherds of Hallstatt pottery' in a pre-rampart context, subsequently re-worded in the final report to 'a few sherds, some with finger-nail decoration' (1976, 78), and as such is too vague to substantiate. Equally unconvincing on present evidence are the suggestions of early pottery at Barnwood, Foxcote Manor, or Robinswood Hill (Cotton 1961, 23; Marshall 1978a, 9).

In fact, the only non-hillfort settlements which can be linked with the early phase are those at Ireley Farm and Sandy Lane, though in both cases the sites are very ill-defined. At Ireley Farm, Stanway (Appendix 3), the pottery includes classic late bronze age/early iron age angular forms with finger-tip and finger-nail decoration (Fig. 3, 31–33), while Sandy Lane, Cheltenham, produced pottery with incised, white-inlaid, geometric decoration (Purnell and Webb 1950, fig. 1) comparable with the Crickley material. In view of the intrinsic importance of the latter site it is to be regretted that the 1971 excavations remain unpublished (RCHM 1976, 23), as is the case with the possibly early pottery from Lechlade (RCHM 1976, 73). On purely typological grounds the 'situlate'-profiled jar from the Crypt Grammar school site at Gloucester (Dunning 1933, fig. 1), and the similarly-profiled jar with a row of finger-tip impressions from Ebworth, Cranham (Green 1942), are also of early iron age date, as possibly are the rim from Barnsley Park (Webster and Smith 1982, 137 and fig. 42, 204) and the sherd reported from Siddington (RCHM 1976, 102), though in each case the context of discovery is not particularly illuminating.

More significantly, two highly distinctive early iron age rim sherds (Fig. 3, 23–24) have recently come to light with a provenance to Cleeve Cloud hillfort, Southam (Appendix 3), offering the tantalizing possibility of an early date for this bivallate scarp-edge site (RCHM 1976, 106–107). Less distinctive, but with rim-top impressions of the kind paralleled at Shenberrow, is a tiny sherd (Fig. 3, 25) from the interior of the hillfort at Burhill, Buckland (Appendix 3).

Although the Gloucestershire early iron age pottery may be mostly of strictly local manufacture, it has clear parallels with contemporary ceramic styles and developments in adjacent areas of southern England, for example with Cunliffe's Long

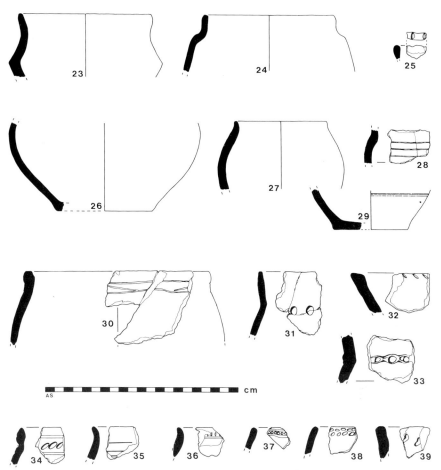

*Figure 3* Iron age pottery from Gloucestershire. 23–24 Cleeve Cloud; 25 Burhill;
26–29 Wood House; 30–33 Ireley Farm; 34–35 Churchdown; 36 Beckbury
(?); 37–39 unprovenanced. (See Appendix 3.)

Wittenham-Allen's Pit group (1974, 324) to the east in Oxfordshire, emphasizing the
continuity of inter-regional links already established in the bronze age (Ellison, this
volume).

## Middle Iron Age Pottery

Discussion of the middle iron age pottery in Gloucestershire is made easier by the
quantity of material available, but complicated by its obvious diversity, and by the

inadequate publication of the basic data. There are clearly grounds for a major subdivision based upon decorative styles and fabric types. Cotton (1961) recognized this subdivision by her 'Western Second B' and 'Western Third B' designations, which were in effect simply re-named as 'Salmonsbury-Broadway' phase and 'Bredon Hill-Danes Camp' phase by Marshall (1978a). The key feature in this subdivision is the presence of stamped and linear-tooled decoration as in Cunliffe's Croft Ambrey-Bredon Hill type (1974, 333), and its contrast with the linear and curvilinear style of incised decoration as in Cunliffe's Southcote-Blewburton Hill, Glastonbury-Blaise Castle, or Lydney-Llanmelin styles (1974, 332–333). The implication of this subdivision was formerly regarded as cultural, reflecting population groups of different regional or even ethnic origins, but Marshall (1978a), following Peacock (1968), is surely right in seeing the subdivision as more a reflection of regional ceramic distribution-patterns, which could indicate economically-defined trading boundaries. However, any such boundaries are unlikely to be hard-and-fast, and will in themselves perhaps indicate underlying socio-political divergence.

Amongst the middle iron age pottery of the county the subdivision referred to above suggests a dichotomy between the Salmonsbury, Guiting Power, Lydney, and Wood House (Gascoigne 1973; also Fig. 3, 26–29, and Appendix 3) assemblages on the one hand, and those from King's Beeches and Oxenton on the other (*pace* Marshall 1978a and 1978c: the newly published material in this report underlines the dominant position of stamped and linear-tooled decoration at the latter two sites; see Fig. 2 and Appendix 3). The range of decorated middle iron age pottery at Salmonsbury (from both Periods I and II: the phasing of this site is by no means precise) is very wide, and includes vessels with extensive curvilinear decoration (Dunning 1976, fig. 12) which are among the finest examples of this kind from southern England, making this assemblage an excellent index of the incised decorative style. The opposing stamped and linear-tooled style of decoration is less well defined by the assemblages within the county, and for more definitive examples of the repertoire one must look just to the north of the county at Bredon Hill (Hencken 1938), Dane's Camp (Painter 1966, 38–39; Thomas 1959), and Beckford (Oswald 1970–72), though none of these assemblages are adequately published, or further afield to sites like Croft Ambrey (Stanford 1974) and Midsummer Hill (Stanford 1981) in Herefordshire. However, the sherds illustrated here from King's Beeches, Oxenton, and Stables Quarry (Fig. 2) do give an indication of the nature of this decoration, with the designs usually restricted to a tight zone just below the rim.

Potentially undermining this dichotomy revealed by decorative styles, however, are two factors which have recently been highlighted by the work of Morris (1981a and 1983), involving firstly Droitwich briquetage and secondly pottery of 'Malvernian' fabrics. Briquetage fragments, resembling daub, are the remains of vessels which originally contained salt produced from the evaporation of brine. The natural salt springs at Droitwich were exploited for salt production in the middle iron age, and the briquetage vessels in use there are distinctive because of the particular characteristics of the local clay. These briquetage salt-containers were dispersed widely from the production centre, and have been shown by Morris' work to be present at virtually every Gloucestershire middle iron age site of any size, for example: Guiting Power (Morris 1981c), Lechlade (Morris 1983, 18), Oxenton (Morris 1982a), Salmonsbury (Morris 1982b), and Uley Bury (Morris 1983).

Petrological study of middle iron age pottery fabrics from the Gloucestershire/Herefordshire region, undertaken by Peacock (1968), identified distinctive inclusions which located the origin of some of the clays used, and hence almost certainly the respective pottery-manufacturing sites, in the general area of the Malvern Hills. Subsequent work by Morris has shown that two of Peacock's 'Malvernian' fabrics (A and $B_1$) are widely distributed in Gloucestershire, and are present at the sites listed below in the following proportions. The percentage figures indicate the approximate representation of these fabric types, expressed as the proportion by weight within the total assemblage, or within a sample therefrom.

| Assemblage | Source | Fabric A % | Fabric $B_1$ % |
|---|---|---|---|
| Claydon Pike | Morris 1981a | 0·1 | ? |
| Guiting Power | Morris 1981c | 1·5 | 15·4 |
| Ireley Farm | Morris 1981e | 4·6 | 2·5 |
| King's Beeches | Morris 1981d | 6·6 | 2·4 |
| Leckhampton | Morris 1981b | – | dominant |
| Oxenton | Morris 1982a | 16·5 | 44·2 |
| Salmonsbury | Morris 1982b | 3·0 | 8·6 |
| Uley Bury | Morris 1983 | – | 3·7 |

The above figures are presented here simply as a guide to the complex pattern of ceramic distribution and acquisition during the middle iron age. Future studies will need to relate the fabric types to the decorative motifs and vessel forms, particularly in the course of detailed quantitative and contextual analysis of the large pottery assemblages from newly excavated sites. The seriation studies of the Guiting Power (Morris 1981c) and Uley Bury (Morris 1983) assemblages are a pointer towards one of the productive lines of research. As a note of caution it is worth adding that the availability of any one pottery (fabric) type would be likely to fluctuate on a short time-scale, even from year to year. Since it will hardly be possible to refine the chronology of middle iron age sites to match such a time-scale, only very general trends will be observable. Nevertheless, one of the most exciting aspects of such study is the opportunity to compare the iron age Malvernian pottery distribution and the subsequent medieval pottery distribution from the same source. Since the circumstances of commercial pottery production and trading can be so much more closely defined in the medieval period (Vince 1977 and this volume), they can potentially be used, as more quantitative data become available, to offer insight into the nature of this 'industry' in the iron age.

West of the Severn it is only possible to refer to the ceramic assemblage from Lydney (Wheeler 1932), which Cunliffe has used to part-define his Lydney-Llanmelin style (1974, 43 and 333). The assemblage comprises slack-profiled jars with stamped, incised linear and curvilinear, and smoothed-line decoration, broadly comparable with the other middle iron age assemblages from the county, but perhaps, in decoration, showing more affinity with contemporary material from South Wales and Somerset.

It remains necessary in this discussion to list the other sites in the county, in addition to those already mentioned, which have produced middle iron age pottery, and these are tabulated below.

| Site Name | Reference |
|---|---|
| Amberley Camp, Minchinhampton | Dunning 1937, fig. 7, and earlier finds in Cheltenham Museum (1980:1017–1021). |
| Barnwood, Gloucester | Clifford 1930, fig. 11, 1 and 1934a, fig. 9. |
| Beckbury, Temple Guiting | Appendix 3. |
| Belas Knap, Sudeley | Berry 1929, 295–296 and figs. 20–21. |
| Birdlip, Cowley | Appendix 3. |
| Bishops Cleeve | Cheltenham Museum (1976:128:1–4). |
| Bourton-on-the-Water | Rawes 1980 and figure. |
| Burhill, Buckland | Appendix 3. |
| Churchdown, Gloucester | Hurst 1977, fig. 3, and Appendix 3. |
| Cirencester | Rigby 1982, 199. |
| Copse Hill, Upper Slaughter | Grinsell 1964, 11 and fig. 1. |
| Crypt Grammar School, Gloucester | Dunning 1933, fig. 2. |
| Dumbleton | Appendix 3. |
| Eastington | Gardiner 1932, figs. 2 and 3. |
| Foxcote Manor, Withington | Donovan and Dunning 1936, fig. 3. |
| Frampton on Severn | Cotton 1961, 27. |
| Friars' Orchard, Gloucester | Appendix 3. |
| Frocester Court, Frocester | Price 1983. |
| Hucclecote Villa, Gloucester | Clifford 1933, 334. |
| Ireley Farm, Hailes, Stanway | Clifford 1944, fig. 1, and Appendix 3. |
| King's Stanley | Rawes 1979 and figure. |
| Millhampost, Stanway | Marshall 1978a, 13–14. |
| Syreford, Whittington | Appendix 3. |
| Tewkesbury | Hannan 1974. |
| Willersey Hill Camp | Cheltenham Museum (1976:133:1–21). |

These findspots are all likely to represent the existence of middle iron age settlements of one kind or another, but the data available about each rarely go beyond the simple record of the pottery itself, and in some cases even the identification as middle iron age must remain in doubt. It is difficult to draw any conclusion other than the general one that settlement both on the Cotswolds and in the Severn Vale was obviously extensive. The same is also true for this period in the Upper Thames valley, where the Claydon Pike settlement at Lechlade is producing the largest middle iron age ceramic assemblage from the county, but assessment will have to await the eventual publication of the material. West of the Severn, apart from Lydney, remains an archaeological blank throughout the iron age.

The dating of this middle iron age pottery is extremely approximate. The only relevant radiocarbon determination from within the county is that from Uley Bury (Saville and Ellison 1983, 19), which may point towards a date after 300 bc at that site for the currency of pottery linked, albeit tenuously, to the linear-tooled and stamped ware styles. The presence of 'Malvernian' wares at Bagendon and Cirencester (Rigby 1982, 199) seems to imply the continuing dispersal and use of middle iron age type hand-made vessels well into the first century AD, although the absence of Droitwich briquetage at these sites (E. Morris pers. comm.) suggests a change of some kind in the regional ceramic distribution pattern, certainly by the Roman conquest, and . possibly before the end of the first century BC.

## Late Iron Age Pottery

The wheel-turned and wheel-thrown late iron age pottery of the county is well represented only at Bagendon and Salmonsbury. Dunning (1976, 100) has summarized the forms involved, among which necked bowls with low foot-rings, decorated with cordons and girth-grooves, and carinated, cordoned bowls or cups are the leading types. At both sites the conventional dating would ascribe the majority of this 'Belgic' pottery to the second quarter of the first century AD, though the view has been expressed that wheel-thrown pottery in the Cirencester region may not pre-date the arrival of the Roman army (Rigby 1982, 199). This highlights the problem of defining the late iron age phase, since ceramically it is currently so hard to document as a pre-Conquest entity. Nevertheless, to the east in Oxfordshire, although the dating is again uncertain, there do appear to be late first-century BC assemblages of wheel-turned vessels in shapes derived from Belgic prototypes (DeRoche 1978, 73).

Dunning (1976, 101) considered that while Bagendon and Salmonsbury shared some kiln products in common, they also had access to the products of separate, independent kilns. None of these kiln sites, which presumably would resemble those found at Hanborough, Oxfordshire (Harding 1972, fig. 9), have been located, and it is unclear what proportion, if any, of the 'Belgic' wares from Bagendon and Salmonsbury were produced locally within the county.

Apart from Bagendon and Salmonsbury, late iron age pottery has been found at Barnwood (Clifford 1930), Cirencester (Rigby 1982, 199), Frocester (Price 1983), and Rodborough (Clifford 1964, 145; Dunning 1937, figs. 8–9), and has been recorded from Duntisbourne Abbots but without any precise provenance (Clifford 1964, 145–146). However, detailed study of the assemblages from any of the larger, early Roman sites in the county is likely to reveal material comparable with that from Bagendon and Salmonsbury, as is the case at Wycomb (RCHM 1976, 125–126), reflecting a probable underlying continuity of settlement during the Conquest period. In this respect it is surprising that no late iron age ceramic phase has yet been recorded at Gloucester.

## BURIAL

Unlike the neolithic and bronze age periods in the county, the study of which tends to be dominated by the funerary remains, evidence for iron age burial is relatively scarce. Only one possible iron age barrow exists as a field monument. This is the round barrow inside a square-ditched enclosure on Leckhampton Hill, just outside the hillfort entrance. It was excavated in 1925 but without any conclusions about its date (Burrow et al. 1925, 100), and on balance the field evidence is probably more consistent with an interpretation as a bronze age round barrow surrounded by a post-medieval enclosure (O'Neil and Grinsell 1960, 121).

Otherwise, the limited evidence for iron age burial is mainly comprised of examples of casual disposal of the dead in disused 'storage' pits or ditches, as at Wood House (Gascoigne 1973) and Salmonsbury (Dunning 1976, 116 and plate IV). More careful inhumation in specially prepared graves and cists is possibly represented at Norbury (Saville 1983, 42) and Ireley Farm, Stanway (Clifford 1944). It is not clear if the middle iron age inhumation from Barnwood, accompanied by a reconstructable pot (Clifford 1930, 224–226), was placed in a pit or a more formal grave, and this is similarly the case with the burial from Crickley Hill, accompanied by a collection of iron objects (Staelens 1982, 27 and fig. 4). The suggestion of iron age cannibalism at Salmonsbury (Dunning 1976, 116–117) must remain an open question, as the evidence is susceptible to other, more mundane, interpretations.

Cremation burial of the late iron age, with the remains placed in pottery urns, may be attested at Bagendon (Clifford 1961, 155) and Barnwood (Clifford 1934, 232), but the original accounts are sketchy. This leaves the famous late iron age burial at Birdlip, where a female inhumation in a cist was accompanied by a splendid series of grave-goods, comprising, among other objects, two bronze bowls, a decorated bronze mirror, and a silver-gilt brooch (Staelens 1982, with earlier references; for an illustration of all the grave-goods see Harding 1974, plate 37). This 'rich' burial, probably part of a cemetery which has now been destroyed, offers a tantalizing glimpse of the aggrandized nature of part of late iron age society in the county.

## CURRENCY BARS AND COINAGE

During the middle iron age the practice of forming iron into standardized spit- and sword-shaped bars became common. These bars, known as currency bars, were probably a convenient unit of distribution and exchange for the raw material. Gloucestershire occupies a place of especial importance in the study of these objects, because the early discovery and announcement of a large hoard of currency bars at Salmonsbury was instrumental in making them well known (Allen 1967, 307). This hoard, of some 147 sword-shaped bars, was found in 1860, and a few other bars have since been located at Salmonsbury (Allen 1967, 328–329; Dunning 1976, fig. 25, 8). Until recently the only other currency bar known from within the county was the anomalous miniature example from Bagendon (Allen 1967, 332), though the presence of important finds of spit-shaped bars just outside the county at Meon Hill, Warwickshire, and at Bredon Hill and Malvern, Worcestershire (Allen 1967, 330–332) should be noted. However, there are now two spit-shaped bars from the hillfort at Uley Bury (Saville and Ellison 1983, fig. 14 and fiche B9), and a new hoard of currency bars from the enclosure ditch at The Ditches, North Cerney, excavated in 1983 (S. Trow pers. comm.). It is tempting to link the finds of currency bars in the Gloucestershire region with the potential for iron ore extraction in the Forest of Dean, but there is as yet no positive evidence for iron age exploitation of this resource.

The county is equally important for the study of late iron age coinage, lying as it does at the centre of the distribution of Dobunnic coins, which formed the basis for Allen's innovative examinations of celtic coinage in England, stimulated in large part by the finds at Bagendon (Allen 1961a, 75 and 1961b, 97). The iron age coins from Gloucestershire constitute a major class of evidence, normally without firm archaeological context, which it is impossible to review here. There continues to be a steady trickle of discoveries of coins of both common (Saville 1982) and uncommon (Saville 1983b, 37) types, and an up-to-date study of the iron age coins in the county is eagerly awaited. Suffice it to say that the inscribed coins bring us firmly into a proto-historical phase, offering for the first time in local prehistory the opportunity of identifying specific, named individuals. These personages, such as Bodvoc, must be seen as tribal chieftains in the celtic manner, ruling over loose confederations of social groups, mostly dispersed in farms and rural villages, but also, as perhaps at Bagendon, occupying larger settlements which had some of the characteristics of urban centres. The coins reflect the far-flung contacts which local iron age groups must have possessed, and these contacts are perhaps the explanation for the Italian bronze jug found at Tewkesbury (British Museum 1925, fig. 90) and the ?Spanish bronze statuette of a female figure from Aust, now in Avon (British Museum 1925, fig. 173).

With the often repeated, though perhaps apocryphal, account of the surrender of Bodvoc and the eastern Dobunni to Aulus Plautius in AD43 (e.g. Wacher 1974, 30), we move in archaeological terms from the iron age period to that of Roman Britain. It is always necessary to repeat that such historical conventions can have had little relevance to the day-to-day life of rural communities. The Romanization of iron age society in Gloucestershire began well before the invasion, and continued long after, as a gradual process. That this process was real enough, however, will be amply demonstrated by the current excavations at Claydon Pike, Lechlade, where the transformation from the middle iron age round-house settlement to its adjacent Roman successor with rectangular buildings is clearly emerging (Miles and Palmer n.d.).

## CONCLUSION

The above review has of necessity been restricted. Thus, for example, there has been no mention of the other, less prolific, categories of iron age artefacts known from the county, such as the carved and decorated bonework, bronze ornaments, iron implements, loom-weights, shale objects, glass beads, and quernstones (Dunning 1976, figs. 21–30; Saville and Ellison 1983, figs. 13 and 15), all of which help to fill out the picture of iron age life, nor indeed of the way in which these items were manufactured and distributed.

Neither has it been possible to offer any overview of the economy during the local iron age, since the evidence which is slowly becoming available (e.g. Levitan 1983; Wilson 1979) is as yet of a very partial nature and only permits very crude comparison to be made with other areas. A more theoretical discussion of the Cotswold iron age environment has been published by Marshall (1978b), who concluded that there was during this period a trend towards increased exploitation of the heavier soils.

Gloucestershire has produced relatively few examples of iron age art objects, though the Birdlip grave-group, with its superb brooch and mirror, is outstanding (Fox 1958; Staelens 1982). Other items are also mostly early finds, which tend to have very poorly documented provenances, such as the iron bowl ornamented with three bulls' heads from Lydney (Wheeler 1932, fig. 11, 9), the embossed bronze bands from Rodborough Common (British Museum 1925, fig. 169), and the La Tène I style brooch (Anon 1937) and enamelled strap-link (Clifford 1938; Fox 1958, 127 and plate 52d), both of which derive from the Sudeley Castle collection and may possibly have been found in the Winchcombe area.

As for spiritual aspects of iron age life, apart from the commonly held and presumably valid assumption that local 'native' Romano-British religious sculpture reflects the iron age substratum, nothing specific can be said, although the underlying iron age phase of the Romano-Celtic temple complex at Uley (Ellison 1980, 306) may, when this site is fully published, afford some new insights. The extraordinary decorated limestone 'cone' from Barnwood (Clifford 1934b; Fox 1958, 112) has been seen as a cult object, which would thus be an instance of the probable blend of art and ritual in late iron age society. However, the somewhat similar, though less extensively decorated, limestone pyramid from Salmonsbury (Dunning 1976, 112–114 and fig. 27) has a suspension loop suggestive of a more secular and prosaic function, perhaps as a loom-weight or measure, which could equally have been the case with the Barnwood 'cone'.

As will be apparent from this article, the state of iron age studies in the county is generally healthy, with further excavations to come at Crickley Hill, The Ditches, and Lechlade, continuing work on the fabric analysis of the local ceramics, and the imminent prospect of important publications emanating from these projects, and from the previous large-scale excavations at Beckford and West Hill, Uley. The publication of other excavations, some now long overdue, is awaited with concern, and the fuller publication of iron age material in local museums needs encouragement, perhaps with the objective of a comprehensive corpus. It will be obvious that more radiocarbon determinations are required, as is more extensive aerial photographic survey, particularly on the Cotswolds and in the Severn Valley, and much basic fieldwork is still required west of the River Severn. Otherwise, the greatest concern must be the fate of those sites where the archaeological potential is being removed, whether by such obvious destruction as quarrying, or by more insidious threats such as arable cultivation. The response to this situation needs constant review, as it will condition the data-base available for future studies of the iron age in Gloucestershire.

## ACKNOWLEDGEMENTS

I am indebted to the Directors and staffs of the Birmingham, Cheltenham, and Gloucester Museums and the former Tewkesbury Archaeological Centre for the opportunity to study and publish material from their collections. Other help during the preparation of this article was kindly given by Mr E.R. Cochrane, Elizabeth Hall, Elaine Morris, and Mrs H.E. O'Neil.

## APPENDIX 1: GLOUCESTERSHIRE IRON AGE RADIOCARBON DATES

*Crickley Hill*

640 ± 60 bc (HAR–392)    Charcoal, brushwood from lowest tier of Period 2 rampart lacing.

570 ± 90 bc (HAR–391)    Charcoal from oak gatepost (posthole 10), final entrance, Period 3B.

400 ± 80 bc (HAR–394)    Charcoal from rampart lacing, Period 2.

360 ± 70 bc (HAR–393)    Charcoal from rampart lacing, Period 2.

*Holm Castle, Tewkesbury*

360 ± 70 bc (HAR–1192)   Carbonized grain from occupation with fragmentary potsherds.

*Uley Bury*

300 ± 80 bc (HAR–2289)   Charcoal, early phase of rampart construction (Trench 1, layer 11).

## APPENDIX 2: KEY TO HILLFORTS AND DYKES MARKED ON FIG. 1

As noted in this article, considerable re-evaluation of the Cotswold hillforts was undertaken by the RCHM in 1976. The result was that many earthworks accepted as iron age by previous generations of scholars, culminating in the entries on the Ordnance Survey's *Map of Southern Britain in the Iron Age* (1962), are no longer regarded as genuine. For Fig. 1 the RCHM's survey has been taken as definitive, with the following exceptions:

i)   Icomb Hill is regarded here as a dyke, not a hillfort, in view of the inconclusive evidence for a complete enclosure (Saville 1978).

ii)  High Brotheridge, Cranham, is accepted here as a hillfort rather than a dyke, since the field evidence is potentially indicative of a formerly complete enclosure, and has not been tested by any excavation. The envisaged enclosure would complete a relatively small circuit to extend the definite stretch of bank and ditch as shown by the RCHM (1976, 41), rather than forming part of the large earthwork complex postulated by Harding (1977).

iii) Ring Hill, Haresfield, is thought to be too insubstantial, when examined in the field, to be the remains of an iron age hillfort.

iv)  Charlton Kings dyke is excluded here as there is no convincing reason why this short, enigmatic earthwork should be regarded as of iron age date or type.

Hillforts shown on Fig. 1 in the west of the county are those marked on the Ordnance Survey Map.

*Hillforts*

1. Spital Mead, Lancaut, Tidenham
2. Lydney Park, Lydney
3. Symonds Yat, English Bicknor
4. Soudley Camp, Lower Soudley, Ruspidge
5. Welshbury, Blaisdon
6. Towbury Hill, Twyning
7. Willersey Hill, Willersey
8. Burhill, Buckland
9. Shenberrow, Stanton
10. Beckbury Camp, Temple Guiting
11. Nottingham Hill, Gotherington
12. Cleeve Cloud, Southam
13. Roel, Sudeley
14. Salmonsbury Camp, Bourton-on-the-Water
15. The Castles, Dowdeswell
16. Leckhampton Hill, Leckhampton
17. Crickley Hill, Coberley
18. Norbury Camp, Colesbourne
19. Norbury Camp, Northleach-with-Eastington
20. High Brotheridge, Cranham
21. Painswick Beacon (Kimsbury), Painswick
22. Windrush Camp, Windrush
23. The Bulwarks, Haresfield
24. The Ditches, Woodmancote, North Cerney
25. Dean Camp, Coln St Aldwyns
26. Ablington Camp, Bibury
27. Pinbury, Duntisbourne Rouse
28. Ranbury Ring, Ampney St Peter
29. Trewsbury, Coates
30. Uley Bury, Uley
31. Bevington Camp, Ham and Stone
32. Brackenbury Ditches, North Nibley

*Dykes*

33. Cleeve Common, Southam
34. Icomb Hill, Icomb
35. Brockworth
36. Randwick
37. Juniper Hill, Edgeworth
38. Bagendon
39. Pen Hill, King's Stanley
40. Minchinhampton

APPENDIX 3: KEY TO THE POTTERY ILLUSTRATED IN FIGS. 2–3, WITH A DESCRIPTION OF THE PROVENANCES

*Oxenton* (Fig. 2, 1–11)

The Oxenton site (SO 973 313) has been variously known as The Knolls, Woolstone Camp, or Oxenton Hill Camp, and was formerly regarded as a hillfort (e.g. Witts 1883, 40), but is now considered to be an unenclosed hilltop settlement insofar as can be determined from the surviving surface evidence (RCHM 1976, xxix and 91). The only recorded excavation is that by Powell (1933, with a text figure of four rim sherds), who examined a mound on the east edge of the hilltop in 1932. This mound is likely to have been a dump from modern quarrying of the settlement rather than a contemporary feature. The sherds published by Powell currently cannot be traced, as is also the case with the decorated sherds from this site illustrated by Hencken (1938, fig. 22) and reproduced by Marshall (1978c, fig. 3).

However, previous excavations at Oxenton seem to be indicated by a collection in Cheltenham Museum of material, which, besides pottery and briquetage, includes two human skulls, a bone pin, and a bone point (Marshall 1978c, fig. 3, 23). This material was presented to the Museum in or before 1907 by Mr. W. Turner, in 1908 by Lt.-Col. J. Blyth and Major J.G.N. Clift, and in 1914 by Mr. E.C. Daubeney, and, apart from references to 'a pit dwelling in the camp' (which may again be a quarry feature), the circumstances of discovery are not recorded. This collection was studied by Marshall (1978c) but some of the decorated sherds he attributes to Cheltenham Museum (fig. 3, nos 11, 14, and 20–22) can no longer be found amongst the Oxenton assemblage; of those that are present (fig. 3, 3 and 16) it should be noted that both these sherds have a limestone and fossil shell temper, but that the decoration on them is quite dissimilar, on fig. 3, 3 being formed by burnished lines, and on fig. 3, 16 by incisions. It is also probable that two of the sherds illustrated by Marshall (1978, fig. 3, 18–19) are of Roman date, as are a few other sherds in the collection. The present report illustrates the remaining five, previously unpublished, decorated iron age sherds from Oxenton in the Cheltenham collection, together with a body sherd with a broken lug and a large base sherd which retains a perforated handle.

In addition to the Oxenton material at Cheltenham, Birmingham City Museum has a collection of nine sherds from this site, again without details of their discovery. It was this material which was studied by Peacock (1968, 427). The four decorated rim sherds at Birmingham are illustrated here, including one rim (no. 2), the larger fragment of which appears to be the same as that figured by Hencken (1938, fig. 22, 7) and Marshall (1978c, fig. 3, 20), despite the fact that both these authorities describe the fabric as red in colour when it is actually black.

A further plain rim sherd recovered from the site as a surface find in the 1970s was in the collection of the former Tewkesbury Archaeological Centre.

1.  Base sherd from a handled jar. Base diameter 105mm. Clay pellet fabric (Morris 1982a). (Cheltenham Museum 1917:87a:23.)

2.  Two joining rim sherds from a barrel-jar. Decorated just below the rim with a horizontal motif of oblique figure-of-eight stamped impressions. Two of the impressions have been doubled-stamped. (Birmingham Museum, unaccessioned.)

3.  Rim sherd. Unenclosed stamped decoration with a motif of pairs of lenticular impressions arranged as continuous, on-edge, left-pointing chevrons. The impressions appear to be produced by the tips of a chevron stamp. Sandy-tempered fabric (Morris 1982a). (Cheltenham Museum 1976:131:14.)

4.  Rim sherd. Decorated on the constriction below the rim eversion with a horizontal row of stamped, downward-pointing chevrons of small size. (Birmingham Museum 214:71.)

5.  Rim sherd. Decorated immediately below the rim with a horizontal row of small, irregular impressions of chevron type. (Birmingham Museum 213:71.)

6.  Rim sherd. The top of the rim is indented, as is no. 4, and has a pronounced internal bevel. The decoration, situated on the external constriction below the rim, comprises a horizontal row of left-pointing, stamped chevrons (Birmingham Museum 212:71.)

7.  Wall sherd. Decorated on the shoulder with a horizontal zone of upright wedge-shaped stamps. Fossil-shell-tempered fabric (Morris 1982a). (Cheltenham Museum 1914:87a:6.)

8.  Rim sherd. Tooled horizontal line parallel to the rim, with a continuous, curvilinear stamped motif above, possibly executed as a row of individual inverted U-shaped stamps, but this is not certain. There is possibly a second horizontal tooled line above the curvilinear motif, immediately below the rim, but the sherd is too fragmentary for this to be established. Limestone with fossil-shell-tempered fabric (Morris 1982a). (Cheltenham Museum 1914:87a:5.)

9.  Wall sherd, with the stub of a broken-off handle or lug. Palaeozoic limestone B$_1$ fabric (Morris 1982a). (Cheltenham Museum 1976:131:27.)

10. Rim sherd. Decorated just below the rim with three horizontal lines of tooling, not quite parallel. The upcast clay from the tooling has been smoothed down by semi-burnishing. Malvernian A fabric (Morris 1982a). (Cheltenham Museum 1914:87a:3.)

11. Wall sherd. Decorated with three parallel tooled lines. Palaeozoic limestone B$_1$ fabric (Morris 1982a). (Cheltenham Museum 1976:131:26.)

*King's Beeches* (Fig. 2, 12–17)

The apparently unenclosed settlement site at King's Beeches, Southam (SO 9827 2670), was discovered in 1903 when pits and other traces were noted during quarrying (Gray and Brewer 1904; RCHM 1976, 107).

Some of the pottery has been illustrated by Donovan and Dunning (1936, fig. 4, 2–3) and by Marshall (1978c, fig. 1). The two sherds sliced by Peacock (1968, 427) which are definitely from this site are those illustrated by Donovan and Dunning (1936, fig. 4, 2: Palaeozoic limestone B$_1$; fig. 4, 3 (upside down) Malvernian A). All the known extant material from this site, purchased from G.W.S. Brewer, is in Cheltenham Museum. It includes, besides pottery, two triangular clay loom-weights and human and animal bones. There has obviously been some confusion between material from King's Beeches and the adjacent Stables Quarry site, and objects in the collection have been assigned to King's Beeches unless specifically described as from Stables Quarry. However, the sherds illustrated here, which were not studied by Marshall, are specifically recorded as from King's Beeches.

12. Base of barrel-jar with base diameter of 100mm. Fossil-shell-tempered fabric (Morris 1981d). (Cheltenham Museum 1976:132:6.)
13. Rim sherd from barrel-jar. Tooled decoration of cross-hatching between two parallel horizontal lines. Rim diameter c.130mm. Malvernian A fabric (Morris 1981d). (Cheltenham Museum 1976:132:3.)
14. Wall sherd. A single horizontal tooled line is present, but probably represents only part of the original motif. Micaceous fabric with fossil shell (identified by E. Morris). (Cheltenham Museum 1976:132:27.)
15. Rim sherd. Tooled horizontal line under the rim, with a motif of discrete, stamped, U-shaped impressions below. The stamp appears to be a downward-pointing sub-chevron type. Palaeozoic limestone $B_1$ fabric (Morris 1981d). (Cheltenham Museum 1976:132:4.)
16. Wall sherd. Tooled decoration probably comprising a motif of cross-hatching within parallel horizontal lines, but incompletely represented on this sherd. Fossil-shell-tempered fabric (identified by E. Morris). (Cheltenham Museum 1976:132:17.)
17. Wall sherd. Decorated with a horizontal band of circular stamped impressions. Malvernian A fabric (Morris 1981d). (Cheltenham Museum 1976:132:5.)

*Stables Quarry* (Fig. 2, 18)

Stables Quarry, Southam (SO 986 269), which was recorded at the same time as the adjacent King's Beeches (Gray and Brewer 1904, 55), appears to be another unenclosed settlement or a part of the same spread of iron age occupation below Cleeve Hill. As explained above, there has been some confusion between the pottery from Stables Quarry and King's Beeches, and there are now only two sherds which can definitely be assigned to this provenance, both in Cheltenham Museum. One was illustrated by Donovan and Dunning (1936, fig. 4, 1) and by Marshall (1978c, fig. 1, 14), and is the sherd which was sliced by Peacock (1968, 427) and shown to be of his $B_2$ fabric. Both the extant sherds are assumed to result from Gray and Brewer's investigations, but this is not documented. The sherd illustrated here, which has not previously been published, has an accompanying label which reads: 'from Stables Quarry, about ¼ mile distant from King's Beeches'.

18. Rim sherd from a barrel-jar. Decorated just below the rim with a band of shallow-tooled cross-hatching between two horizontal lines. Rim diameter c.140mm. Non-calcareous fabric (unidentified). (Cheltenham Museum 1976:125:1.)

*Syreford* (Fig. 2, 19)

A single decorated rim sherd in Cheltenham Museum, reconstructed from fragments, is provenanced to the gravel pits at Syreford, Whittington (*c*.SP 028 202), though the date and circumstances of discovery are not recorded. A second, undecorated, rim sherd, of oolitic limestone-tempered fabric, probably derives from the same location.

19. Rim from a globular vessel, with a deep, everted rim over a markedly convex shoulder. Decoration, at the junction of rim and shoulder, comprises a horizontal row of impressed circles, 4mm in diameter, executed with a hollow, cylindrical stamp. This row is echoed by an underlying row of smaller circular impressions, below which is a tooled horizontal line. The design has been carelessly executed, so that overlapping, duplication, and gaps occur. Rim diameter 170mm. Palaeozoic limestone $B_1$ fabric (Morris 1981f).

*Birdlip* (Fig. 2, 20)

A single sherd in Cheltenham Museum (*contra* Staelens 1982, 25), presented by a Miss Helps, is provenanced to The Knap, Birdlip, which is presumed to be somewhere in the vicinity of the present Knap House (SO 924 148) at Birdlip Hill on the boundary of the parishes of Cowley and Great Witcombe.

20. Large wall sherd with a horizontally perforated lug. Palaeozoic limestone $B_1$ fabric (identification by E. Morris). (Cheltenham Museum 1908:44.)

*Dumbleton* (Fig. 2, 21)

A single decorated rim sherd found during field-walking by Mr E.A. Price in 1975 at Lane Farm, Dumbleton (SP 0315 3695), was in the collections housed at the former Tewkesbury Archaeological Centre.

21. Rim sherd. The decoration, only partially intact, comprises a recurrent, impressed motif, running in a horizontal zone below the rim, which appears to be very close to the so-called 'duck-stamp' design, with the upper half of the 'S' absent. The fabric is limestone-tempered, but has not been positively identified.

*Gloucester* (Fig. 2, 22)

Friars' Orchard, Gloucester (SO 8308 1828). An inspection pit dug in 1963 into the garage, which forms part of the range of workshops at the rear of the Technical College, produced the rim sherd with burnished decoration which is illustrated here. This site is adjacent to Greyfriars, where the 'Boys' Trench' in the Crypt Grammar School grounds produced the sherds previously described by Dunning (1933, fig. 2). It should be noted that the burnished design on one of the previously published sherds (Dunning 1933, fig. 2, 1) is unlikely to be of pendant triangles, and in fact resembles that on the sherd illustrated here, as far as can be judged from the surviving fragment. The iron age pottery from Friars' Orchard is stratified below Romano-

British levels, and appears to be the only indication of some kind of pre-Roman activity in the vicinity.

22. Rim sherd. Decorated by burnished lines in a motif comprising irregular near-vertical lines below a horizontal line at the base of the everted rim. There may originally have been further horizontal lines above the one indicated, but the surface is too badly weathered for certainty. Rim diameter $c.170$mm. Fabric not determined, but has limestone temper. (Gloucester Museum 1398.)

*Cleeve Cloud* (Fig. 3, 23–24)

Cleeve Cloud, Cleeve Common, Southam (SO 985 255), is a bivallate hillfort on the edge of the Cotswold escarpment (RCHM 1976, 106–107). Two rim sherds are in Cheltenham Museum with an accompanying label which states: 'two pieces of British pottery from end of entrenchment on Cleeve Cloud'. Nothing else is known of the date or circumstances of discovery, though it seems probable that the sherds were recovered from the eroding edge of the defences where they are cut by former quarrying of the scarp-face.

23. Rim sherd, undecorated, from a jar with a pronounced carination. Rim diameter $c.140$mm. Fossil-shell-tempered fabric (unidentified). (Cheltenham Museum 1976:126:1.)
24. Rim sherd, undecorated, from a 'situlate'-profiled shouldered jar. Faint thumb impressions survive where the rim has been pushed in from the shoulder. Rim diameter $c.140$mm. Very micaceous fabric with rare oolitic limestone (identification by E. Morris). (Cheltenham Museum 1976:126:2.)

*Burhill* (Fig. 3, 25)

Burhill, Buckland (SP 084 363) is a univallate scarp-edge hillfort discovered by L.V. Grinsell in 1960 (RCHM 1976, 22). Small collections of abraded sherds from the ploughed surface of the hillfort interior are in Cheltenham and Gloucester Museums, and include the single decorated rim published here.

25. Rim sherd. The top of the rim is decorated with finger-tip and finger-nail indentations. Fossil-shell-tempered fabric (unidentified). (Cheltenham Museum 1978:915.)

*Wood House* (Fig. 3, 26–29)

Wood House, Guiting Power (SP 083 258) is the location of an iron age pit salvaged by Gascoigne (1973). The pottery from this pit was described by O'Neil (1973), but the four most distinctive sherds are republished here to facilitate inter-assemblage comparison, with a concordance with the numbering in O'Neil's text figure. The Wood House pottery remains in the possession of Mr E.R. Cochrane of Guiting Power.

26. Base from a globular jar with a burnished exterior. Base diameter 100mm. Limestone and fossil-shell-tempered fabric (unidentified). O'Neil text figure no. 8.
27. Rim from a barrel-jar. Rim diameter 100mm. Limestone and fossil-shell-tempered fabric (unidentified). O'Neil text figure no. 1.
28. Wall sherd, decorated with three parallel, horizontal, incised/tooled lines. Limestone tempered fabric (unidentified). O'Neil text figure no. 9a.
29. Base, of diameter 80mm. Decorated by a shallow, horizontal, grooved line, 36mm above the base. Fossil-shell-tempered fabric (unidentified). O'Neil text figure no. 9.

*Ireley Farm* (Fig. 3, 30–33)

Big Ewe Leasow field, Ireley Farm, Hailes, Stanway (SP 0422 3065) was the site of rescue excavations in early 1945 when two cist-graves were unearthed (Clifford 1944). These excavations produced a small pottery assemblage, which included at least one iron age rim sherd (Clifford 1944, fig. 1a; Cheltenham Museum 1979:34:6a) among material which is largely Roman. Subsequent salvage excavation and surface-recovery in the same field in *c*.1965 at *c*.SP 039 306 produced a further, substantial collection of pottery, now in Cheltenham Museum, which is mainly of iron age type, although there is almost no documentation with this material. The rim sherd with linear-tooled decoration (Anon 1967, 26), which was published by Peacock (1968) and is republished below, is very different to anything else in the collection, which is otherwise dominated by fossil-shell-tempered fabrics, and with its decorative range of finger-tip impressions, raised finger-impressed cordons, and finger-tip impressed rims seems exclusively of early iron age character. The finds at Ireley Farm appear to denote an extensive iron age settlement, probably part of the same settlement as represented by the finds at adjacent Millhampost (Marshall 1978a, 13; RCHM 1976, 110–111).

30. Rim sherd from barrel-jar. Decorated below the rim with a crudely executed tooled-design of two roughly parallel, horizontal lines with oblique lines between. Rim diameter 200mm. Published by Peacock (1968, fig. 4, 10; caption transposed) and identified as Malvernian A fabric. (Cheltenham Museum 1967:150.)
31. Rim sherd rejoined from three fragments. Decorated with a presumably continuous horizontal row of finger-tip impressions in the angle between neck and body. Fabric unclassified (Morris 1981e). (Cheltenham Museum 1978:873:2H-I and 3.)
32. Rim sherd, everted, with oblique finger-nail impressions along the outer edge of the rim. Fossil-shell-tempered fabric (Morris 1981e). (Cheltenham Museum 1978:873:2L.)
33. Body sherd with a horizontal raised cordon which has a continuous pattern of finger-tip impressions. Four other sherds with this decoration may derive from the same vessel. Fossil-shell-tempered fabric (Morris 1981e). (Cheltenham Museum 1978:873:1.)

*Churchdown* (Fig. 3, 34–35)

Evidence for an iron age settlement, in the form of a pottery scatter, charcoal, animal bones, and a pit or ditch, was noted by N. Webley and A.P. Garrod during building work in 1966 for a covered reservoir on Churchdown Hill, Churchdown, Gloucester (SO 882 188), and some subsequent archaeological excavation was undertaken (Hurst 1977). However, the character of this settlement, in particular whether or not it is a hillfort, is not conclusively established. There are now some 16 sherds from Churchdown in Gloucester Museum, including nine rim sherds, of which two are decorated, though a third example has been published (Hurst 1977, fig. 3, 1).

34. Rim sherd. The decoration consists of two horizontal, tooled lines enclosing a motif of ovoid, obliquely-set impressions, probably stamped. This sherd was sliced by Peacock (1968, fig. 3, 17: caption transposed), and shown to be of his Group B$_2$ fabric. (Hurst 1977, fig. 3, 3; Gloucester Museum 24324.)
35. Rim sherd. The burnished exterior has surviving decoration of three horizontal, parallel incised lines. The sherd was sliced by Peacock, but not included in his report (Hurst 1977, fig. 3, 2; Gloucester Museum 24323.)

*Beckbury(?)* (Fig. 3, 36)

Beckbury Camp is a univallate hillfort at Temple Guiting (SP 064 299), where no recorded excavations have taken place (RCHM 1976, 116–117). A decorated rim sherd was found on the surface in 1938 by the late Dr Malcolm of Evesham (Hencken 1938, 94). This is the sherd which Peacock examined (1968, 427) and recorded as of his Malvernian A fabric. This sherd cannot now be located, but information supplied by Mrs O'Neil indicates that the fabric was black, and that the decoration consisted of (?) stamped, circular impressions under and on top of the rim.

The sherd illustrated here was presented to Cheltenham Museum in 1977 by Mrs O'Neil, after she had found it among her possessions with an attached label reading 'perhaps found at Beckbury Camp'. The date and circumstances of the find are unknown, and the provenance is certainly inconclusive, but the sherd warrants publication as a further decorated iron age vessel likely to have come from north Gloucestershire.

36. Rim sherd. The decoration comprises a tooled horizontal line, above which is a row of short, vertically-disposed linear impressions. There may originally have been a second horizontal line above these impressions, but the sherd is too abraded to judge. Limestone-tempered fabric (unidentified). (Cheltenham Museum 1977:196.)

*Unknown Provenance* (Fig. 3, 37–39)

The publication, or republication, of these three sherds completes the publication of all the identifiable decorated iron age pottery from Gloucestershire in the Cheltenham Museum collection, apart from the Salmonsbury material, and will hopefully avoid further confusion in the future. It should especially be noted that nos. 37 and 38 were sliced by Peacock and included in his Cleeve Hill assemblage (1968, 427). However, unless these sherds have become detached from a provenance label since Peacock studied them, there is no museum record of their origin, though it seems highly probable that they did derive either from the Oxenton or the King's Beeches assemblages.

37.   Rim sherd. Decorated with a horizontal band of adjacent stamped circles set between two unevenly-horizontal tooled lines. Malvernian A fabric (identification by E. Morris). (Cheltenham Museum 1976:124:1.)
38.   Rim sherd. Decorated with two close-set horizontal bands of lightly stamped ovoid impressions. Malvernian A fabric (identification by E. Morris). (Cheltenham Museum 1976:124:2.)
39.   Rim sherd. Stamped decoration, just below the rim, of sub-chevrons pointing right. Malvernian A fabric (identification by E. Morris). (Cheltenham Museum 1976:124:3.)


REFERENCES

Allen, D. 1961a. A study of the Dobunnic coinage. In E.M. Clifford, *Bagendon: a Belgic oppidum*, 75–149. Cambridge.

Allen, D. 1961b. The origins of coinage in Britain: a reappraisal. In S.S. Frere (ed.), *Problems of the Iron Age in Southern Britain*, 97–308. London. (=Univ London Inst Archaeol Occasional Paper No. 11.)

Allen, D. 1967. Iron currency bars in Britain. *PPS* 33, 307–335.

Anon. 1937. Bronzes from Sudeley Castle. *Antiq J* 17, 446–448.

Anon. 1967. Note on an iron age sherd from Ireley Farm, Hailes. *Archaeol Rev* 2, 26.

Bayne, N. 1957. Excavations at Lyneham Camp, Lyneham, Oxon. *Oxoniensia* 22, 1–10.

Berry, Sir J. 1929. Belas Knap Long Barrow, Gloucestershire: report of the excavations of 1929. *TBGAS* 51, 273–303.

British Museum. 1925. *A guide to antiquities of the early iron age*. London (2nd edn).

Britnell, W. 1974. Beckford. *Current Archaeol* 45, 293–297.

Burrow, E.J., Paine, A.E.W., Knowles, W.H., and Gray, J.W. 1925. Excavations on Leckhampton Hill, Cheltenham, during the summer of 1925. *TBGAS* 47, 81–112.

Champion, S.T. 1971. Excavations on Leckhampton Hill, 1969–70. Interim Report. *TBGAS* 90, 5–21.

Champion, S.T. 1976. Leckhampton Hill, Gloucestershire, 1925 and 1970. In D.W. Harding (ed.), *Hillforts: later prehistoric earthworks in Britain and Ireland*, 177–190, and 430–435. London.

Clifford, E.M. 1930. A prehistoric and Roman site at Barnwood, near Gloucester. *TBGAS* 52, 201–254.

Clifford, E.M. 1933. The Roman villa, Hucclecote, near Gloucester. *TBGAS* 55, 323–376.

Clifford, E.M. 1934a. Finds at Barnwood, Gloucester. *TBGAS* 56, 231–232.

Clifford, E.M. 1934b. An early British fragment. *Antiq J* 14, 59–61.

Clifford, E.M. 1937. The earthworks at Rodborough, Amberley, and Minchinhampton, Gloucestershire. *TBGAS* 59, 287–307.

Clifford, E.M. 1938. An early British enamel. *Antiq J* 18, 75–76.

Clifford, E.M. 1944. Graves found at Hailes, Gloucestershire. *TBGAS* 65, 187–198.

Clifford, E.M. 1961. *Bagendon: a Belgic oppidum, excavations 1954–1956*. Cambridge.

Clifford, E.M. 1964. Early iron age pottery from Rodborough Common and Duntisbourne Abbots. *TBGAS* 83, 145–146.

Cotton, M.A. 1961. The pre-Belgic iron age cultures of Gloucestershire. In E.M. Clifford, *Bagendon: a Belgic oppidum*, 22–42. Cambridge.

Cunliffe, B. 1974. *Iron age communities in Britain*. London.

Darvill, T.C. and Hingley, R.C. 1982. A 'banjo' type enclosure at Northleach. *TBGAS* 100, 249–251.

DeRoche, C.D. 1978. The iron age pottery. In M. Parrington, *The excavation of an iron age settlement, bronze age ring-ditches and Roman features at Ashville Trading Estate, Abingdon (Oxfordshire) 1974–76*, 40–74. London. (=CBA Res Rep 28.)

Dixon, P.W. 1969–1973. *Crickley Hill: interim reports 1–5*. Cheltenham. (Duplicated reports.)

Dixon, P.W. 1971. *Crickley Hill: third report, 1971*. Cheltenham. (Duplicated report.)

Dixon, P.W. 1972. Crickley Hill 1969–71. *Antiquity* 46, 49–52.

Dixon, P.W. 1973. Longhouse and roundhouse at Crickley Hill. *Antiquity* 47, 56–59.

Dixon, P.W. 1976. Crickley Hill 1969–72. In D.W. Harding (ed.), *Hillforts: later prehistoric earthworks in Britain and Ireland*, 161–175, 424–429, and 507–508. London.

Dixon, P.W. and Borne, P. 1977. *Crickley Hill and Gloucestershire prehistory*. Gloucester.

Donovan, H.E. and Dunning, G.C. 1936. Iron age pottery and Saxon burials at Foxcote Manor, Andoversford, Gloucestershire. *TBGAS* 58, 157–170.

Dunning, G.C. 1931. Salmonsbury Camp, Gloucestershire. *Antiquity* 5, 489–492.

Dunning, G.C. 1933. Report on pottery found in the Crypt Grammar School grounds, Gloucester, during excavations made 1931–32. *TBGAS* 55, 227–291.

Dunning, G.C. 1937. Report on pottery from Amberley and Rodborough. In E.M. Clifford, The earthworks at Rodborough, Amberley, and Minchinhampton, Gloucestershire. *TBGAS* 59, 301–303.

Dunning, G.C. 1976. Salmonsbury, Bourton-on-the-Water, Gloucestershire. In D.W. Harding (ed.), *Hillforts: later prehistoric earthworks in Britain and Ireland*, 75–118, 373–401, and 488–494. London.

Ellison, A. 1980. Natives, Romans and Christians on West Hill, Uley: an interim report on the excavation of a ritual complex of the first millennium AD. In W.J. Rodwell (ed.), *Temples, churches and religion: recent research in Roman Britain*, 305–328. Oxford. (=BAR Brit Ser 77.)

Fell, C.I. 1961. Shenberrow Hill Camp, Stanton, Gloucestershire. *TBGAS* 80, 16–41.

Fox, Sir C. 1958. *Pattern and purpose: a survey of early Celtic art in Britain*. Cardiff.

Gardiner, C.I. 1932. Recent discoveries in the Stroud valley. *PCNFC* 24(3), 163–180.

Gascoigne, P.E. 1973. An iron age pit at Wood House, Guiting Power. *TBGAS* 92, 204–207.

Gracie, H.S. 1962. Note on excavations at Bagendon. In Ministry of Works, *Excavations Annual Report 1961*, 5. London.

Gray, J.W. and Brewer, G.W.S. 1904. Evidences of ancient occupation on Cleeve Hill. *PCNFC* 15(1), 49–67.

Green, C. 1942. An iron age cremation burial in the Cotswolds. *Antiq J* 22, 216–218.

Grinsell, L.V. 1964. The Royce collection at Stow-on-the-Wold. *TBGAS* 83, 5–23.

Grinsell, L.V. 1970. Introduction to the prehistoric remains. In D. Verey, *Gloucestershire: The Cotswolds*, 69–76. Harmondsworth.

Hall, M. and Gingell, C. 1974. Nottingham Hill, Gloucestershire, 1972. *Antiquity* 48, 306–309.

Hampton, J.N. and Palmer, R. 1977. Implications of aerial photography for archaeology. *Archaeol J* 134, 157–193.

Hannan, A. 1974. Sabrina Cinema site, Oldbury Road. *Glevensis* 8, 7.

Hannan, A. 1976. Holm Castle, Tewkesbury. *Glevensis* 10, 10–11.

Harding, D.W. 1972. *The Iron Age in the Upper Thames Basin*. Oxford.

Harding, D.W. 1974. *The Iron Age in lowland Britain*. London.

Harding, G.T. 1977. High Brotheridge: the account of a survey and speculations. *Glevensis* 11, 17–22.

Hawkes, C.F.C. 1959. The ABC of the British Iron Age. *Antiquity* 33, 170–181.

Hawkes, C.F.C. 1961. The Western Third C culture and the Belgic Dobunni. In E.M. Clifford, *Bagendon: a Belgic oppidum*, 43–67. Cambridge.

Hencken, T.C. 1938. The excavation of the iron age camp on Bredon Hill, Gloucestershire, 1935–1937. *Archaeol J* 95, 1–111.

Hurst, H. (ed.). 1977. The prehistoric occupation on Churchdown Hill. *TBGAS* 95, 5–10.

Leech, R. 1977. *The Upper Thames Valley in Gloucestershire and Wiltshire: an archaeological survey of the river gravels*. Bristol. (=CRAAGS Survey No. 4.)

Leeds, E.T. 1931. Chastleton Camp, Oxfordshire, a hillfort of the early iron age. *Antiq J* 11, 382–398.

Levitan, B. 1983. Animal bones from Uley Bury. In A. Saville, *Uley Bury and Norbury hillforts: rescue excavations at two Gloucestershire iron age sites*, fiche C6–D5. Bristol. (=WAT Excavation Monograph No. 5.)

Marshall, A.J. 1978a. The pre-Belgic iron age in the northern Cotswolds. *TBGAS* 96, 9–16.

Marshall, A.J. 1978b. Environment and agriculture during the iron age: statistical analysis of changing settlement ecology. *World Archaeol* 9, 347–356.

Marshall, A.J. 1978c. Material from Iron Age sites in the Northern Cotswolds. *TBGAS* 96, 17–26.

Megaw, J.V.S. and Simpson, D.D.A. 1979. *Introduction to British prehistory*. Leicester.

Miles, D. and Palmer, S. n.d. (but 1982). *Figures in a landscape: archaeological investigations at Claydon Pike, Fairford/Lechlade, Gloucestershire: interim report 1979–81*. Oxford. (=Oxford Archaeological Unit Interim Report.)

Miles, D. and Palmer, S. 1983a. Claydon Pike. *Current Archaeol* 86, 88–92.

Miles, D. and Palmer, S. 1983b. Claydon Pike, Fairford/Lechlade, Gloucestershire. *PPS* 49, 385–388.

Morris, E.L. 1981a. Ceramic exchange in western Britain: a preliminary view. In H. Howard and E.L. Morris (eds.), *Production and Distribution: a ceramic viewpoint*, 67–81. Oxford. (=BAR Int Ser 120.)

Morris, E.L. 1981b. Petrological report on the pottery from Leckhampton hillfort, 1925 excavations. Archive report, Cheltenham Museum.

Morris, E.L. 1981c. Petrological report for the ceramic material from Guiting Power, Gloucestershire. Archive report, Cheltenham Museum.

Morris, E.L. 1981d. Ceramic report on the collection from King's Beeches, Southam, Gloucestershire. Archive report, Cheltenham Museum.

Morris, E.L. 1981e. Ceramic report on the collection of iron age material found near Ireley Farm, Hailes, Gloucestershire. Archive report, Cheltenham Museum.

Morris, E.L. 1981f. Petrological report for the pottery found at Syreford, near Andoversford, Gloucestershire. Archive report, Cheltenham Museum.

Morris, E.L. 1982a. Petrological report on the ceramic material from The Knolls, Oxenton, Gloucestershire. Archive report, Cheltenham Museum.

Morris, E.L. 1982b. Petrological report on some ceramic material from Salmonsbury, Gloucestershire. Archive report, Cheltenham Museum.

Morris, E.L. 1983. Petrological report; fired clay; Droitwich briquetage containers; and seriation analysis. In A. Saville, *Uley Bury and Norbury hillforts*, 14–19. Bristol. (=WAT Excavation Monograph No. 5.)

O'Neil, H.E. 1973. The pottery. In P.E. Gascoigne, An iron age pit at Wood House, Guiting Power. *TBGAS* 92, 205–206.

O'Neil, H.E. 1977. Salmonsbury, Bourton-on-the-Water: some aspects of archaeology in Bourton Vale. *TBGAS* 95, 11–23.

O'Neil, H.E. and Grinsell, L.V. 1960. Gloucestershire barrows. *TBGAS* 79(1), 1–149.

Ordnance Survey. 1962. *Map of Southern Britain in the Iron Age*. Chessington.

Oswald, A. 1970–72. Excavations at Beckford. *Trans Worcestershire Archaeol Soc* 3, 7–54.

Painter, K.S. 1966. *The Severn Basin*. London.

Peacock, D.P.S. 1968. A petrological study of certain iron age pottery from western England. *PPS* 34, 414–427.

Powell, T.G.E. 1933. Oxenton Hill Camp. *TBGAS* 55, 383–384.

Price, E.G. 1983. Frocester. *Current Archaeol* 88, 139–145.

Purnell, F. and Webb, E.W. 1950. An iron age A site near Cheltenham. *TBGAS* 69, 197–199.

Rawes, B. 1979. An early iron age pot from King's Stanley. *Glevensis* 13, 40.

Rawes, B. 1980. Report on an iron age vessel from Bourton-on-the-Water. *Glevensis* 14, 24.

RCHM. 1976. *Iron age and Romano-British monuments in the Gloucestershire Cotswolds*. London.

Rigby, V. 1982. The coarse pottery. In J. Wacher and A. McWhirr, *Early Roman occupation at Cirencester*, 153–200. Cirencester. (=Cirencester Excavations I.)

Saville, A. 1978. Excavations at Icomb Hill, Gloucestershire, 1975. *TBGAS* 96, 27–31.

Saville, A. 1979. *Excavations at Guiting Power iron age site, Gloucestershire, 1974*. Bristol. (=CRAAGS Occasional Papers No. 7.)

Saville, A. 1980. *Archaeological Sites in the Avon and Gloucestershire Cotswolds: an extensive survey of a rural archaeological resource with special reference to plough damage*. Bristol. (=CRAAGS Survey No. 5.)

Saville, A. 1982. Iron age coin from Ebrington. *Glevensis* 16, 16.

Saville, A. 1983a. Excavations at Norbury Camp, Gloucestershire, 1977. In A. Saville, *Uley Bury and Norbury hillforts: rescue excavations at two Gloucestershire iron age sites*, 26–45. Bristol. (=WAT Excavation Monograph No. 5.)

Saville, A. 1983b. Excavations at Condicote Henge Monument, Gloucestershire, 1977. *TBGAS* 101, 21–47.

Saville, A. and Ellison, A. 1983. Excavations at Uley Bury hillfort, Gloucestershire, 1976. In A. Saville, *Uley Bury and Norbury hillforts: rescue excavations at two Gloucestershire iron age sites*, 1–24. Bristol. (=WAT Excavation Monograph No. 5.)

Saville, A., Thomas, J., Wardle, P. and Williams, D. 1983. Geophysical survey at Roel Camp, Sudeley, Gloucestershire. *Glevensis* 17, 21–25.

Smith, I.F. 1973. Prehistory. In C. and A.M. Hadfield (eds.), *The Cotswolds: a new study*, 76–84. Newton Abbot.

Spry, N. and Wingham, H. 1979. Churcham: Long Brook Camp. *Glevensis* 13, 30–31.

Staelens, Y.J.E. 1982. The Birdlip cemetery. *TBGAS* 100, 19–31.

Stanford, S.C. 1974. *Croft Ambrey*. Hereford.

Stanford, S.C. 1981. *Midsummer Hill, an iron age hillfort on the Malverns*. Hereford.

Thomas, N. 1959. The excavations at Conderton Camp, Bredon Hill, 1958–59. *PCNFC* 33(3), 100–106.

Trow, S.D. 1982. The Bagendon project 1981–1982: a brief interim report. *Glevensis* 16, 26–29.

Vince, A. 1977. The medieval and post-medieval ceramic industry of the Malvern region: the study of a ware and its distribution. In D.P.S. Peacock (ed.), *Pottery and early commerce: characterization and trade in Roman and later ceramics*, 257–305. London.

Wacher, J. 1974. *The towns of Roman Britain*. London.

Wainwright, G.J. 1967. The excavation of an iron age hillfort on Bathampton Down, Somerset. *TBGAS* 86, 42–59.

Webster, G. and Smith, L. 1982. The excavation of a Romano-British rural establishment at Barnsley Park, Gloucestershire, 1961–1979. Part II. *TBGAS* 100, 65–189.

Wheeler, R.E.M. and T.V. 1932. *Report on the excavation of the prehistoric, Roman, and post-Roman site in Lydney Park, Gloucestershire*. London. (=Soc Antiq London Res Rep 9.)

Wilson, R. 1979. The animal bones. In A. Saville, *Excavations at Guiting Power iron age site, Gloucestershire, 1974*, 141–144. Bristol. (=CRAAGS Occasional Papers No. 7.)

Witts, G.B. 1883. *Archaeological Handbook of the County of Gloucester*. Cheltenham.

**March 1984**

# PART FOUR:
# ROMAN GLOUCESTERSHIRE

# The Cotswolds: an Essay on Some Aspects and Problems of Roman Rural Settlement

## Richard Reece

I hope I will be forgiven for starting with some very obvious statements. They may be fundamental to most people's way of thinking, but I need to make them explicit to explain some of my attitudes which will follow. For instance, cows need longer grass on which to graze than do sheep. Given the way in which the Cotswolds dry up quickly in a long spell without rain, upland pasture with a minimal depth of soil can only be relied upon to feed sheep, and even then they will need plenty of space in which to feed. This to some extent confines cattle in the summer to good pasture in the valleys if a good pile of cheese and a good fat herd need to be stocked up for the winter. Pigs, on the other hand, though perhaps only good to eat, and for fat for cooking, will live off a very wide selection of foodstuff and pasture. Wheat and barley for bread and beer, and, in the form of straw and hay as feed for working animals, can apparently grow almost anywhere on the Cotswold upland, provided there is enough depth of soil to plough and the field is not on too great a slope for the ploughing.

Given such basic information, what more needs to be known whether in the iron age, the Roman period, or the Middle Ages (Reece 1983, 152)? All that can be added is perhaps some comment on the balance which each age requires between stock and arable, and the social structure which accompanies the husbandry. The High Middle Ages saw a swing to sheep, and wool was the Cotswold product. When William Marshall wrote his treatise on the rural economy of Gloucestershire in 1789 he was able to say that the Cotswold part of the county 'is, in the strict sense of the phrase, an ARABLE COUNTRY. Corn, turneps, and cultivated herbage, occupy, perhaps, nine tenths of its surface. Some little SHEEPWALK and COWDOWN still remain' (Marshall 1789, Vol. 2, 11). One very basic problem then is to sort out, from environmental evidence, those particular potentials of the land which were being used in the Roman period. But the use of 'Roman' here is very much out of place. It is most unlikely that the conquest by the Roman armies saw an overnight swing in the Cotswold farms from beef to wool, or from barley to beef. At the time of the Roman invasion one particular phase of Cotswold agriculture was in full swing, and no doubt that phase gave place to a different phase as market pressures altered and social usages changed. The plotting of these changes is a very valid exercise but the changes will not be forced into pre-determined periods, and cannot be expected to correspond to units measured in less than decades, if even that span of time means anything in the life of a farm.

If, when we narrow down our field of interest to one particular stretch of countryside, the chronological periods by which the external archaeological world supports itself seem invalid, what divisions of time are appropriate? I would select three periods of change which surround two periods of relative tranquillity; because of the subject I have chosen, they fall in the last centuries BC and the first millennium AD. The first period of transition in which I am interested follows the abandonment of the iron age hillforts, the growth of more open settlements, of which, as yet, we know very few, and the introduction of wheel-thrown pottery, together with the import of fine wares from the Continent. This series of changes, while not necessarily affecting the small, basic farmstead, seems to me to be a fascinating object for study, and I cannot help regretting the tendency for prehistorians to deal mainly with the earlier, rather than the later, iron age. This is almost as bad as prehistorians dealing with the iron age and Romanists dealing with Roman Britain, or the equally troublesome division between Roman Britain and Saxon England. In the archaeological world at large such divisions may be (or may not be) a necessary evil, but in the Cotswolds they can be seen to be totally artificial.

The reasons which provoke my interest in the fall of the hillforts and the spread of the material well-represented at Bagendon (Clifford 1961), what I shall call for brevity the Bagendon transition, are very simple and dictated by a Roman self-interest, for the pattern which was set down during this major period of change endured through the first two centuries of the Romanization of Britain. Thus, to understand the early Roman settlements on the Cotswolds we have to know the late iron age settlements, and, if possible, the

forces which formed them. After this, my first period of change, I see a
period of Cotswold consolidation which lasts until the third century AD. It is
no accident that many of the crop-marks well known from aerial photography
of the Upper Thames gravels (Leech 1977), and also visible on the Cotswold
dip-slope, are ascribed to the late iron age/early Romano-British period, for
they span these two stages, apparently developing throughout in an orderly
manner. While it is bound to be of interest to understand the workings of
such farmsteads, they must lie within the general Cotswold parameters of
what is possible and what is not, so that I would favour a concentration of
resources on the factors which led to the establishment of these sites and, if
possible, the factors which led to their demise. If we cannot answer these
questions exactly, then at least it is worth spending considerable effort in
trying to establish the landuse before the site started its own independent life,
and after it had expired.

If many of these curvilinear farmsteads failed to grow into the third and
fourth centuries AD then other types of farm emerged, the most prominent
being the stone-built rectangular farm-house, which, if it has enough of the
Romanizing luxuries and appointments, is known as a villa. If I sound
sceptical at such a definition it is because I wonder what would happen if a
programme of research were carried out on present Cotswold farmers in
which an estimate of social status were made from a survey of wealth, habits,
and contacts, and this estimate were then compared with a survey of the
appointments of the farm-house concentrating particularly on the state of the
roof (tiles), the age of the wall-paper (wall-paintings), and the presence or
absence of an efficient central heating system (hypocaust) and antique carpets
(mosaics).

The third century is taken as a great turning-point in the Roman Empire at
large (Reece 1981). It is the time when the great Italian villas collapsed, when
Mediterranean trade, as judged by shipwrecks, sank to an all-time low, when
the tax system was completely changed, and when, economically, the Empire
turned inside-out so that the provinces appeared to prosper at the expense of
the centre. In Britain the third century marked the rise of national pottery
industries, the virtual end of imports, and, for a short time, an insular
coinage which was demonstrably better than that produced in the central
Empire. In the Cotswolds the third century marked the appearance of the
well-established villa, in some cases certainly building on an earlier prosperity, in others being a totally new growth, and the apparent flourishing of
villages, such as Kingscote and Bourton-on-the-Water.

In the world at large these changes were so great that they marked the
transition from Ancient to Medieval History, from the Classical World to the

Christian World, and from the world centred on Rome to the world divided between Constantinople and north-west Europe. It seems to me quite possible that, although I have called the third century one of my periods of Cotswold change, and used it to divide the late iron age from later Roman Britain, it may be no more than a greatly accelerated process of change which was already inherent in the Romanization of Britain. Thus it may be that the events of the third century brought an unusual prosperity to Britain in general, and the Cotswolds in particular, so that the assimilation of some Roman traits by the generally conservative British population speeded up by a considerable factor. My feeling is that much of the affluence in the countryside was due to the abandonment of urbanism and urbanization, which had never really worked in Britain on the Mediterranean model, so that all settlements in the fourth century shared equally in surplus wealth and in the duties of markets and services which had formerly been centred on the larger towns. Administration, I suspect, remained by tradition in the former towns, now simply administrative villages (Reece 1980).

Rural settlement is, therefore, the key to my next period of Cotswold consolidation which, with a period of accelerated development – which might or might not properly be called my last period of change – lasted well into the medieval period as normally understood (Reece 1976). The basic point here cannot be in doubt even though there would not necessarily be agreement with all that I propose. Rural Britain in the fifth century, as in the seventh century, is almost unknown, but the way into this period of uncertainty, as well as the way out, depends on the continued working of the countryside in exactly the way in which I described it at the beginning. At present, perhaps mainly because late Roman Britain belongs to the Romanists and early Saxon England belongs to the medievalists, this basic continuity is hidden beneath an uncertain veneer of different material cultures. So much seems agreed. The problem is to decide whether the Roman villa of the fourth century, and the pagan and Christian Saxon cemeteries and early churches are representative of a totally different social order, or one very much the same in the two cases. I think we must be agreed on the basic agricultural Cotswold similarities; we can only differ on the social superstructure.

What is our picture of the Cotswolds in the fourth century? I have emphasized the villa and this is indeed the most obvious material landmark. In the fourth century it has that concentration of luxury appointments which the town-house formerly enjoyed. The major products of the mosaic industry go to the villas; they show some of the later examples of wall-painting; the pottery industries, formerly clustered round the towns, now place themselves conveniently to reach the villa and village market. This last fact, noted by

Young (1977) in his study of the Oxfordshire industry, has been a puzzle to several commentators who have tried to explain it as tax-avoidance, or a move forced on an unwilling industry by exhausted fuel supplies. It is much easier to reverse the reasoning and say that pottery industries would move, as they always had done, towards the best markets. Thus, in the fourth century, the best markets, demonstrated by the siting of the pottery industries, lay in the countryside rather than in the towns. Certainly the Oxfordshire industries must have made a lot of money out of the Cotswold villas and those nearer at hand in the Upper Thames Valley.

If we draw a circle around Cirencester of about a ten mile radius this will enclose a number of the known Cotswold villas (RCHM 1976). Perhaps twenty villas are well documented in the circle which contains over 300 square miles, and so some 200,000 acres. If we double the number of villas to allow for those highly resistant to discovery, this still leaves a ration of some 5,000 acres per villa. This is, of course, on the assumption that the villas controlled all the Cotswold land. Even in modern, mechanized terms this would represent an estate rather than a farm and would need a considerable work-force to run it. Taking the comments of Marshall again (1789, Vol 2, 28): 'The sizes of farms are mostly large: from 200 to 1000 acres each. There is one instance of a tenant occupying near 2000 acres. Five hundred acres may be considered as a middle-sized farm'. If we wish to run the Roman Cotswolds from villas they cannot be more than estate offices, combined with small farms, and we have to look for other farming establishments elsewhere.

We could look at the map of the Cotswolds in Samuel Rudder's *New History of Gloucestershire*, which gives a very sketchy impression of settlement in 1779. The possible eighteenth-century counterpart to the Cotswold villa is the stately home with park, which appears on the map as an enclosure cut off from the countryside at large; that is left to the villages. Roman villages available for study are difficult to find; the best example at the moment is Kingscote where two properties have been excavated out of an occupied area of some fifty acres or more (KAA n.d.; RCHM 1976, 70–73). The houses in the village look for all the world like farms or villas. So far there seems to be nothing in the highest luxury bracket, but if these buildings were found in the countryside at large they would instantly, and rightly, be labelled typical villas. The Kingscote Roman village is presumably a nucleated settlement of farms, whereas we are used to non-nucleated farmsteads (Reece forthcoming).

However, we then have to face the problem that the Kingscote village is not only one of a rare category, but it is an unsuccessful village. Are the two things connected? It seems quite possible that this village is available for excavation because it failed, and if that is true, then the reason we know so little about Roman villages on the Cotswolds at large, is that those villages were successful, and continued, and are hidden near the Cotswold villages of today. When one thinks of French villas it is the superb aerial photographs taken by Agache (1972, 1976 and 1978), on the land to the south of Amiens in the Somme valley, which come to mind. When talking about his distribution maps Agache is always very careful to point out that aerial photography only picks out the failed villas, and he has said many times that his photographs show a very biased sample of villas – those which failed as estate centres and are therefore in the middle of arable fields ready to be photographed. He suspects that the modern villages hide many estate centres, and in a few cases he can show villas peeping out from under villages; this leads him to the suggestion that in some cases the village developed beside the successful villa, and eventually over-ran it.

Perhaps we can go just one step further before we worry about explanations for how the villa economy of the Cotswolds turned into the manor-and-village which we can still see today. When apportioning the land to the villas we needed something else besides villas, and turned to villages. Is the change-over from Roman to medieval perhaps the change from isolated proprietors occupying villas in the middle of their estates to village-dwelling proprietors who differ from the rest of the village-dwellers by owning more of the surrounding land?

And, finally, what is the process by which the Roman rural settlement of the Cotswolds turned into the medieval rural settlement of the Cotswolds? Finberg (1959), in his study of Roman and Saxon Withington, gave his account by which a Roman villa estate passed in working order to a monastery. The boundaries of the estate, as he saw them, determined the boundaries of the settlement around the monastery which became the medieval village. He chose to populate the village in Roman times for very much the same reason that I have been forced into peopling Roman villages: there had to be somewhere for the workers. He saw the whole estate as owned by the villa-owner, and this involves some 5,000 acres or more, divided between two valley systems. I will not comment further on Finberg's work here because in 1979, with students from the Institute of Archaeology in London, I surveyed all the hedges in the parish of Withington, financed by the Research Fund of the Society of Antiquaries, and the results have not yet been written up. They will lead inevitably to a discussion of Finberg's work, but I can say now that his slim booklet of forty pages has had over the past twenty years an influence far beyond its size, and his main thesis seems set to prosper rather than to fade away. In his honour I shall therefore call this period of change the Withington transition.

The Finberg model of Cotswold change is very near to that with which I started; it concentrates on the working of a productive estate which could either produce a considerable surplus of agricultural produce, and hence a financial profit, or could be harnessed to feed and clothe a community. Whatever the area owned by the proprietor of the Withington villa, that person was making a profit from somewhere which paid for the wall-painting, the mosaics, the servants to stoke hypocausts and cut wood, and the household staff. The religious inhabitants of the Withington monastery owned land outside the village, but it was presumably their 'home-farm' which provided them with their daily needs. When the monastery died out the village became a valued possession of the Bishop of Worcester, which presumably means that, again, it was making a profit, and that profit was leaving the village for seigneurial coffers. What on earth is the problem; how can Finberg possibly be faulted; on what grounds can continuity possibly be questioned?

There are alternative models, and they ought to be examined if only to be explicitly discarded. What about the Saxon fire, pillage, rape, and plunder which so dismembered civilization that it took to the Welsh hills and died-off there? Fire and pillage should be detectable archaeologically, and the late Calvin Wells published skeletal evidence of what he saw as Anglo-Saxon rape (Hawkes and Wells 1975). This evidence has been violently attacked by bone specialists and other Anglo-Saxons, but I think the violence of their reaction to a perfectly well-argued case says more about the emotiveness of the subject than anything else. Plunder, in which valuable objects move to unexpected places and turn up in surprising contexts, though less exciting, should be more easily demonstrated. As yet, as we all know, the case falls through lack of evidence.

The late John Morris was at times, and perhaps with his tongue in his cheek, devoted to the idea of an outbreak of genuine socialism in fourth-century Britain. This is partly based on the letter of a young man sometime in the early fifth century, nostalgic for the green, rolling hills of his home while he writes from Sicily to his parents on their estate. Morris christened this 'the letter of the Sicilian Briton', though it has to be admitted that there could be other homelands for which the writer could feel longing other than the green and rolling Cotswold hills (Morris 1973). But there is other evidence in Morris's case. The point at issue, the young man writes, is whether those who have, stick to their possessions and perish, or throw in their lot with the humble, and survive. This is, of course, by far the most attractive model for the Withington transition, as we see the grasping landowners one by one realizing the folly of their ways, giving up the villas, so expensive to run and such bones of social contention, and moving quietly into the villages to take their place in an equal society, where all work as they are able and benefit from the estate according to their real needs.

This picture is consonant with the material facts, which are the disappearance of the status-symbol villa, and the establishment of an apparently equally materially-endowed society, but there are two major stumbling-blocks, both in the form of historically-attested 'bad barons'. What we see of the late Roman landowners through the law codes of Theodosius II and Justinian are not the rich trying to reform, but the rich and powerful extending their influence. The first people we hear of in the medieval village are the lords of the manor, whose influence over the village could be remarkably strong. Law may be an interesting connection here, for the late Roman peasants had little hope of any litigation on their own behalf. If they were to enter the lawcourts of Imperial authority they had to be under the protection of their local landowners, their patrons, to hold out any hope of success. The Imperial court presumably ceased in the fifth century in Britain, and law moved on to a more local basis. Could the court of the lord of the manor derive from the very simple transfer of power by which the *Honestiores,* the late Roman magnates, instead of assisting their client-serfs to justice, simply dispensed it to them instead?

The last model I want to hold up for inspection is really an amalgam of much that has gone before. It has already been voiced completely independently as a possibility by Agache (1978) for the Somme region, and by Down (1979) for the Chilgrove valley, near Chichester in Sussex, and both of these workers are basing their ideas on processes which they see happening around them now, just as we see it here on the Cotswolds. I have suggested that the late Roman proprietors are more often documented increasing their holdings than diminishing them. Applied to the Cotswolds this would mean the development of the estate at the expense of the farm, so that large areas could be easily worked under one policy and as part of one unit. Surely this has a topical ring? Agache (1978) notes in the Somme not only crop-marks of deserted villas, but scars and skeletons of the remnants of once flourishing farmsteads, now only a group of barns, or a country cottage. Down (1979) documents in the Sussex landscape the occupants of 'farmhouses', many of whom have nothing to do with agriculture, and others who are now no more than cogs in an agricultural machine. This concentration of resources was already apparent in the fourth century; the process need do no more than speed up, and run to completion, to lead to the early medieval landscape. Thus, when the late Roman proprietors have settled near the villages, or the villages have grown up around the most powerful landowners, and they have established their rights, and have built churches for their workers, how can they be distinguished from the lords of the manor?

REFERENCES

Agache, R. 1972. New aerial research in Picardy and Artois. *Antiquity* 46, 117–123.

Agache, R. 1976. Aerial reconnaissance in northern France. In D.R. Wilson (ed.), *Aerial reconnaissance for archaeology*, 70–80. London. (=CBA Res Rep 12.)

Agache, R. 1978. *La Somme pre-romaine et romaine d'après les prospections aériennes*. Amiens. (=Mémoires de la Société des Antiquaires de Picardie 24.)

Clifford, E.M. 1961. *Bagendon, a Belgic oppidum*. Cambridge.

Down, A. (ed.). 1979. *Chichester excavations 4: The Roman villas at Chilgrove and Upmarden*. Chichester.

Finberg, H.P.R. 1959. *Roman and Saxon Withington* (2nd edn). Leicester.

Hawkes, S.C. and Wells, C. 1975. Crime and punishment in an Anglo-Saxon cemetery. *Antiquity* 49, 118–122.

KAA (Kingscote Archaeological Association). n.d. (but 1978.) *Excavations: The Chessalls, Kingscote, 1975–7*. Stroud. (Privately printed.)

Leech, R. 1977. *The Upper Thames Valley in Gloucestershire and Wiltshire, an archaeological survey of the river gravels*. Bristol. (=CRAAGS Survey No. 4.)

Marshall, W. 1789. *The rural economy of Gloucestershire*. London. (Reprinted Gloucester 1979.)

Morris, J. 1973. *The Age of Arthur*. London.

RCHM. 1976. *Iron age and Romano-British monuments in the Gloucestershire Cotswolds*. London.

Reece, R. 1976. From Corinium to Cirencester – models and misconceptions. In A. McWhirr (ed.), *Studies in the archaeology and history of Cirencester*, 61–80. Oxford. (=BAR Brit Ser 30.)

Reece, R. 1980. Town and country: the end of Roman Britain. *World Archaeol* 12(1), 77–91.

Reece, R. 1981. The third century; crisis or change. In A. King and M. Henig (eds.), *The Roman West in the third century*, 27–38. Oxford. (=BAR Int Ser 109.)

Reece, R. 1983. The end of Roman Britain – revisited. *Scottish Archaeol Rev* 2(2), 149–153.

Reece, R. Forthcoming. Continuity on the Cotswolds: some problems of ownership, settlement, and hedge survey between Roman Britain and the Middle Ages. *Landscape Studies*.

Rudder, S. 1779. *New History of Gloucestershire*. (Reprinted Dursley, 1976.)

Young, C.J. 1977. *The Roman pottery industry of the Oxford region.* Oxford. (=BAR Brit Ser 43.)

**February 1984**

# Romano-British Settlement in the Gloucestershire Thames Valley

*David Miles*

## INTRODUCTION

Since the time of Samuel Lysons' activities in the late eighteenth century, Gloucestershire has been well known for the quality of its Romano-British villas. Unfortunately, well-known does not mean well-understood. The county has seen surprisingly few large-scale, scientifically-conducted excavations on Romano-British rural settlements; systematic fieldwork has been very limited and even aerial photographic cover has not been so thorough as in many other parts of the country. The obvious attractions of the Cotswolds have also detracted from work in other parts of the county. It was only in the late 1960s and early 1970s that the archaeological possibilities of the western claylands between Gloucester and Bristol were appreciated, as a result of the work of the M5 Excavation Committee (Fowler 1977). Fieldwalking and trial-trenching along the line of the motorway revealed a surprising density of Romano-British rural sites, but relatively little about their character and layout. The work did emphasize, however, the variety of non-villa settlements, the practical difficulties of excavating them, and the limited results that could be gained from small-scale, salvage operations against a background of general ignorance.

On the eastern side of the county the valley of the Thames has been even more neglected than the Berkeley Vale. But the opportunities for investigating the Romano-British countryside are in many ways greater: sites are easier to discover by fieldwalking arable land; the results from aerial photography in this particular area have been prolific; gravel-quarrying on a massive scale makes extensive excavation possible; and a high water-table provides good conditions for the preservation of environmental data.

## THE UPPER THAMES

The area under discussion runs from near Ewen, about 4km south-west of Cirencester, to the Gloucestershire-Oxfordshire boundary 3km east of Lechlade, a total distance of about 24km, during which the course of the river falls through about 19m. On its northern side the Thames is joined by three major tributaries: the Churn, opposite Cricklade, the Coln, south-west of Lechlade, and the Leach, south-east of Lechlade. The valley is characterized by a narrow floodplain flanked by low-lying, first-terrace gravel deposits. The second gravel terrace, 4 – 6m higher, plays an important role in the ancient settlement patterns of the Oxfordshire Thames Valley (Benson and Miles 1974), but in Gloucestershire it is much less extensive. Limited fringes of second-terrace gravel occur at Down Ampney, Fairford, Kempsford, Lechlade, and Marston Meysey, all noticeably the sites of present-day villages or small towns. To the north are patches of third- and fourth-terrace gravel, a fragmented belt of Oxford Clay, and beyond them the slopes of cornbrash.

Much of this area coincides with the Cotswold Water Park, an increasingly large series of man-made lakes formed by the extraction of sand and gravel from the valley floor. Quarrying has operated on a large scale since the late 1950s. A planning policy was formalized in 1969 with the publication of *The Cotswold Water Park* (Cotswold Water Park Joint Committee 1969). Although certain aspects of conservation and recreation were taken into account, the destruction of extensive archaeological deposits was not mentioned. *A Penny for Your Past* (Gingell n.d.) attempted to draw attention to the omission. Unfortunately it failed to stimulate any action; archaeology continued to be officially ignored. In a second planning report, *Plan for the River Thames, Lechlade to Cricklade* (Gloucestershire and Wiltshire County Councils 1971), only the existence of a small number of scheduled ancient monuments was noted. The lack of communication between archaeologists and local authorities responsible for the Water Park continued until the end of the 1970s. The publication both of an archaeological implications survey of the area (Leech 1977) and a major inventory by the Royal Commission on Historical Monuments (RCHM 1976) impressed archaeologists with the wealth of rapidly disappearing evidence, but apparently failed to impinge on the consciousness of those responsible for planning the development of the valley.

The archaeological surveys did, however, draw the attention of the Inspectorate of Ancient Monuments of the Department of the Environment to the problems and potential of the Water Park. Not only did the Inspectorate begin, in 1980, to support large-scale excavations, it also funded the establishment in 1982 of a County Sites and Monuments Record based at the Gloucestershire County Planning Department (Allden 1983). In 1983, under the umbrella of the Sites and Monuments Record, the Inspectorate funded a re-survey of the Water Park. These developments have had a major impact on the archaeological study of the Gloucestershire Thames Valley in the past four years.

## THE DISTRIBUTION OF ROMANO-BRITISH SETTLEMENT (Fig. 1)

The distribution map of Romano-British settlement is based on the information available to the author from aerial photography and fieldwalking at the time of writing. There are, needless to say, problems and biases with any map of this kind. In this case there are several obvious ones. Certain areas are not available for archaeological investigation, notably the 300ha of the Fairford airfield, the worked-out gravel pits around South Cerney and Lechlade, and, to a certain extent, areas covered by present-day villages and farms. Other limitations to fieldwork are provided by pasture (now much decreased) and alluvial deposits, which can mask sites. Two of the best-preserved settlements, recently found under pasture, were not previously located precisely because they did not produce clear crop-marks.

Most of the sites within the Water Park marked on the distribution map have been fieldwalked over the past two years and have produced evidence of Romano-British occupation in the form of pottery, building debris, coins, or other artefacts. Fieldwalking can, however, be deceptive. At Claydon Pike, the area of middle iron age settlement (Fig. 2) produced no contemporary pottery when fieldwalked and only two sherds when the topsoil was sampled by excavation. The adjacent Romano-British settlement was littered with vast quantities of Romano-British pottery and building debris but nothing was found, prior to excavation, to indicate the underlying and masked late iron age occupation.

The area which has been most closely studied is from Fairford eastwards to just beyond Lechlade. In this stretch of the valley, about 9km long and up to 4km wide, it is evident that Romano-British settlement was continuous. Fieldwalking has almost doubled the number of Romano-British settlements mapped as crop-marks in the 1977 survey (Leech 1977, maps 4 and 5). In the

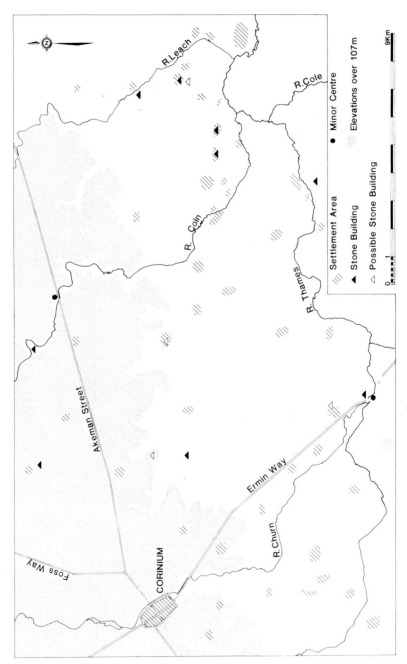

● Minor Centre

▒ Elevations over 107m

Settlement Area

▲ Stone Building

△ Possible Stone Building

0 ____ 9km

R.Leach

R.Cole

R.Coln

R.Thames

Akeman Street

Ermin Way

Foss Way

CORINIUM

R.Churn

*Figure 1* Romano-British settlement in the Gloucestershire Upper Thames Valley.

Water Park as a whole, aerial photography has added approximately sixty per cent more crop-mark information in the past seven years (R. Hingley pers. comm.).

Around Lechlade and Fairford the sites mainly cluster on the narrow first gravel terrace. In this favoured area settlements are found at intervals of 500m to 1km. At Claydon Pike and Whelford, eight separate settlement nucleii have been located in three square kilometres (SP 1799; 1899; 1999), which range in size from 1ha to 12ha. This landscape is a complex one and includes fields, paddocks, drainage ditches, roads and tracks, two cemeteries, a small rural shrine, and settlements of varying character with stone and timber buildings.

Elsewhere in the Water Park, settlement appears to be as complex and almost as concentrated. Crop-marks mainly indicate blocks of enclosures, often associated with trackways. The whole area was served by a network of trackways but few have so far been traced for more than 1km. At Claydon Pike one such trackway, regularly laid-out and partly metalled, was constructed at the end of the first century AD, but overlay a late iron age predecessor. The Roman trackway linked four settlements spaced over 3km; three further sites have been found along its projected route.

The area which is least well known is that immediately south and east of Cirencester. A number of settlements have been located within three kilometres of the town but the crop-mark evidence is not very informative and there has unfortunately been no extensive excavation.


## THE CHARACTER OF ROMANO-BRITISH SETTLEMENT

Romano-British settlements in the Gloucestershire Thames Valley provide a distinct contrast with those of the Cotswolds to the north. The limestone hills and their narrow, steeply-sloping valleys were incorporated into estates based on substantial villa houses. The Thames Valley, on the other hand, was densely colonized by peasant farmsteads, hamlets, and possibly villages. The only known villas comparable to those in the Cotswolds are on the higher slopes of the valley. At Driffield, 5km ESE of Cirencester, the main house (indicated by stone, tesserae, and tiles) sat within an enclosure of 0·4ha, surrounded by 5ha of further enclosures (RCHM 1976, 45 and plate 49). Another building about 1km to the north, in Ampney St Peter, was partially excavated by J.Y. Akerman c.1860 and may be the site of another villa (RCHM 1976, 3). Near Lechlade, Romano-British buildings of some substance were excavated on the second gravel terrace at Roughground Farm by

Margaret Jones from 1958 to 1965 (RCHM 1976, 73–75). There is some confusion about the site of another building recorded before 1742 'in a meadow near Lechlade' with a tessellated floor supported on brick pillars. Ordnance Survey records place a Roman building just south of the Rough-ground Farm site (RCHM 1976, 73), but this may be the 'subterranean building' found in the late eighteenth century. The 'meadow' location would more appropriately describe the site at Great Lemhill Farm, about 2km NNW of Roughground Farm. This site lies under water meadows, on the west bank of the River Churn and opposite the iron age and Romano-British settlement of Langford Downs, partially excavated by Williams (1946). It is difficult to assess the character of the Great Lemhill Farm site from surface evidence. Its location is similar to that of Shakenoak villa in the Oxfordshire Cotswolds (Brodribb *et al.* 1968) and while it is most likely to be a villa, a water-mill cannot be ruled out. Another interesting, though enigmatic, settlement complex exists at Ewen. Springs providing a major source of the Thames emerge here. Large quantities of Roman pottery, coins, metalwork, and building material have been found over about 1 – 2ha. The nature of the site is uncertain but a ritual complex may have existed in such a position.

   No other higher-status sites are known in the Gloucestershire Thames Valley. An area of particular interest, however, lies just beyond the Wiltshire county boundary where it extends north of the Thames near Cricklade. South of Latton a side road branches off Ermin Street and runs 600m to a settlement; surface evidence and crop-marks indicate a possible villa building and its enclosures. Five hundred metres south-east of this site there is an unusual system of radiating linear crop-marks (centred on SU 106949). It is possible that these may be related to the drainage system of the Thames and Severn Canal; however, there is said to be evidence from unpublished sections that they are, in fact, the ditches of Roman roads (Mike Stone pers. comm.). Certainly the area around them contains large quantities of Roman settlement debris, including traces of buildings. This may, therefore, be a small town site on the north bank of the Thames, opposite Cricklade.

## APPROACHES TO THE PAST IN THE UPPER THAMES VALLEY

The Gloucestershire Upper Thames Valley is a distinct micro-region which presents interesting possibilities for the study of Romano-British settlement. It has a complex, but essentially recoverable, settlement pattern; preservation is relatively good – some sites are unploughed or only infrequently ploughed; present-day occupation is not dense; and gravel pits, although massively destructive, provide an opportunity for large-scale excavation. Environmental evidence is also well preserved where the water-table is high, though new lakes and drainage schemes are causing waterlogged deposits to dry out.

There are obvious questions which need to be investigated. When and how was the area first colonized? To what extent was there continuity from the iron age? What was the economic basis of Roman settlement? How and why did Romano-British exploitation come to an end and to what extent was there continuity into the Anglo-Saxon period?

In order to begin to approach these problems a multi-disciplinary programme of fieldwork and excavation has been undertaken by the Oxford Archaeological Unit based on the site at Claydon Pike between Lechlade and Fairford. This has been complemented by the Gloucestershire Sites and Monuments Record survey of the Water Park and the post-excavation analysis of the Roughground Farm site by Tim Allen and Sarah Green of the Oxford Archaeological Unit in co-operation with Margaret Jones. It is not satisfactory to generalize about large-scale processes from particular excavations; nevertheless, this work suggests certain models of regional interaction which can be investigated further. Before discussing these it is necessary to outline the sequence of development at Claydon Pike and Roughground Farm.

## CLAYDON PIKE (Figs. 2–4)

It is possible to answer at least some of the questions which were posed earlier in the present discussion, though it should be emphasized that only limited analysis has been carried out of the data from the past five years of excavation: the chronology in particular is imprecise (Miles and Palmer n.d. and 1983).

1.   The area consists of islands and platforms of first-terrace gravel divided by marshland and relict watercourses. The watercourses were formed towards the end of the last period of glaciation. Only a very few flints and a fragment of a polished axe indicate earlier prehistoric activity. While the terrace may have been cleared of woodland gradually in the second and earlier first millennia bc the first permanent settlement dates to the middle iron age (c.220 bc). In the third century bc, drainage ditches were established across the open, first-terrace grasslands which demarcated paddocks for cattle and sheep. Clusters of round houses were integrated with the paddocks and were probably occupied by extended family groups of pastoralists.

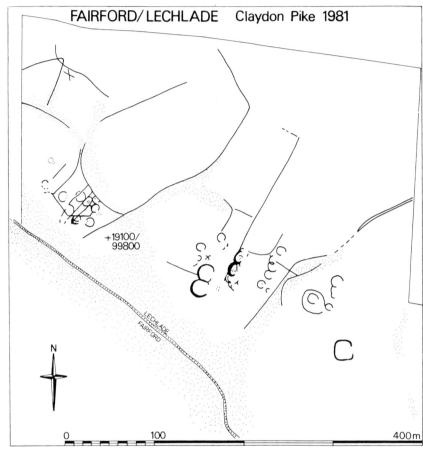

*Figure 2*  Claydon Pike, Lechlade: middle iron age settlement.

Textile equipment was common and, in the later phases of this settlement, salt (in briquetage containers) and fine pottery were obtained from the Droitwich/Malvern area 70km to the north-west. Carbonized cereal remains were retrieved from most features but in low densities, which suggest that they were the waste from food-preparation rather than crop-processing. Cereals may have been grown in small quantities or exchanged from arable farming communities nearby.

2.   A major shift of settlement took place in the late iron age, in the late first

century BC/early first century AD. A new, more nucleated settlement was established 200m south of the earlier one (Fig. 3). Although this has been traced over c.2·5ha the actual area of human occupation was limited. Most of the installations – paddocks and enclosures – served to control stock. There were several distinct zones: a trackway led into the site close to the area of habitation; beyond this were oval paddocks mostly about 20m across with ditches re-cut many times. The outer zone consisted of a block of rectangular enclosures bounded by a watercourse. The impression is of a highly organized, pastoral landscape managed at Claydon Pike by relatively few people. A Dobunnic Class M coin was found in an unstratified position.

3. A second major change occurred in the late first or early second century AD (Fig. 4), the more accurate dating of which awaits the study of stratified pottery groups. At this time a road was constructed in straight sections along the gravel terrace. A field system, covering at least 20ha, was also laid out, to be used predominantly for grazing. The late iron age or 'native' settlement at Claydon Pike probably continued until the later part of the first century AD. Elements of it, such as the trackway and outer boundary ditch, were retained, but most of the layout was ignored in the establishment of the new settlement. This was planned on a regular and systematic basis and, like the late iron age site, it showed elements of zoning. At the nucleus was an open space formed by a right angle in the road. To the east was an enclosed gravel platform on which were the most substantial buildings: an aisled house, a two-roomed timber structure of sleeper-beam construction, and an aisled barn. Entry to this enclosure was through an elaborate gateway fronting onto the central open space, down a metalled side-street and through another gateway. West of the central area was another platform on which stood lesser buildings; two, and possibly more, insubstantial cottages. Around these were a cluster of circular gullies 2 – 8m in diameter, probably stacking areas for animal fodder. South of the central area was a rectangular enclosure which is thought to have defined a shrine. It was fronted by a single ditch and a paved area, with double ditches on the other sides. The inside of the rear, south-east corner was cobbled and the centre was occupied by shallow pits containing charcoal and coal. Nearby a number of pits contained fragments of limestone pillars, capitals, and a very finely-wrought block of ashlar masonry. Beyond the occupation area were blocks of small paddocks, defined by ditches and possibly by hedged banks, and further out the fields already mentioned above. An interesting feature of this early Roman phase of occupation was the discovery of several fragments of military metalwork: a gilded vine-leaf, a bronze mount in the form of symbolic shield and vulva, and several bronze

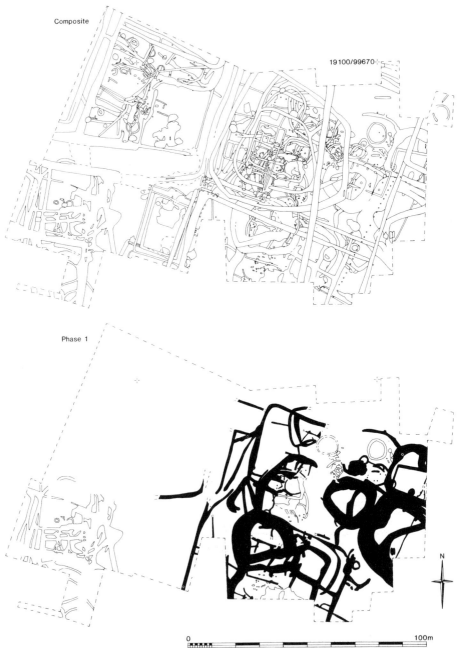

Composite

19100/99670

Phase 1

N

0                                                    100m

*Figure 3* Claydon Pike, Fairford: the nucleus of the settlement. Top: composite plan; bottom: Phase 1, late iron age.

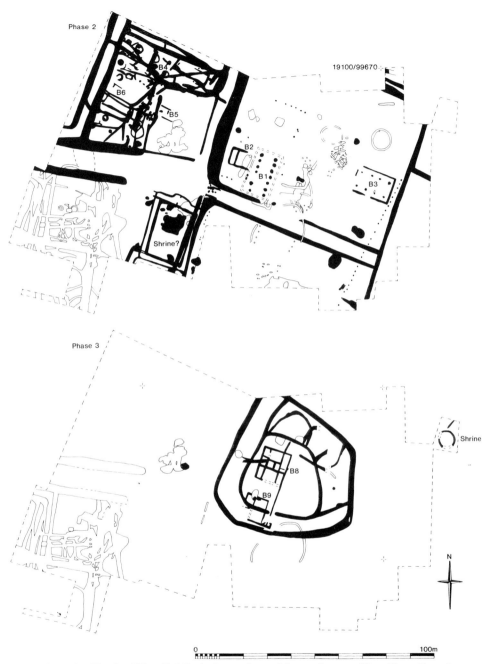

*Figure 4*  Claydon Pike, Fairford: the nucleus of the settlement. Top: Phase 2, early Romano-British; bottom: Phase 3, later Romano-British.

studs. Two intaglios – one showing an eagle mounted on an orb and thunder bolt, the other with clasped hands and cornucopias – may have had military owners. There were unusually large quantities of amphorae sherds, one of which was inscribed on the inside LEG II A, and also a silver republican coin minted in Rome in 12BC.

4.   In the later Romano-British period the character of the settlement changed quite distinctly. It retracted in size; the shrine was demolished but the eastern platform remained as the main area of occupation. The settlement could now be classed as a small farmstead or villa of the most modest kind (Fig. 4). The main house, Building 8, inside an oval walled-and-ditched enclosure, consisted of a block of eight rooms and two sunken chambers of uncertain function, whose floors were about 1m below the water table. South of Building 8 was an L-shaped building (Building 9) with three rooms, one of which had a hypocaust system. Attached to Building 9 was a small gatehouse which controlled access into the yard. Pastoralism was still predominant in the late Roman period but the economic basis was broadened. Rich cereal samples, in two corn-drying ovens, indicate that wheat and barley were being grown. Waterlogged samples also produced flax, which could have been utilized for oil and linen. Sixty metres east of the main house stood a circular shrine, built on broad stone foundations within a marshy area. A stone and gravel causeway linked the shrine with the road to the north. About three hundred mainly fourth-century coins were deposited as offerings inside the shrine. A model votive bronze axe and miniature bronze leaf were also found, and set in the centre of the paved floor was a small colour-coated beaker. A small cemetery lay 90m north-west of the farmhouse. The earliest inhumation was placed east-west inside a small ditched enclosure; a similar enclosure surrounded the second burial. Another nine burials clustered around these two, most orientated north-south, one of which had been decapitated and its skull placed by the feet. A second small group of burials, about six in number, was inserted into the demolished and partially-robbed foundations of Building 8.

5.   In the early fifth century the buildings at Claydon Pike all fell into disuse. The drainage ditches became blocked and the site flooded. Deposits of alluvium were laid over the Roman road and in the tops of most of the later ditches. The alluvium cannot be dated precisely; stratigraphically it appears to postdate the abandonment by a short period only. The alluvium implies, however, that bare soil was being eroded into the valley river system; this is most likely to happen when there is widespread arable cultivation, particular-

ly of winter wheat, on the valley slopes and when drainage ditches are present to carry the run-off. Lower down the Thames Valley such deposits have been dated to the late Saxon-early Norman period. At Claydon Pike there was little trace of post-Roman activity. A small gravel pit was dug into the site of the Roman building and produced two late Saxon silver coins, one of Alfred and another of King Baldred of Kent dating to AD 823–5. A fifteenth-century well and a fragment of wall were the only other post-Roman and pre-modern features. The area seems to have become a backwater of marshy pasture, grazed in summer by the flocks and herds of Fairford Manor. There is no evidence, however, that the land reverted to woodland. In the seventeenth century two farms were built north and south of Claydon Pike. For the first time in over a thousand years a system of drainage ditches and enclosures was re-established and the land re-occupied on a permanent basis.

## ROUGHGROUND FARM, LECHLADE (Fig. 5)

Only 2·5km to the north-west of Claydon Pike the history of settlement is very different. On the higher, second gravel terrace, occupation goes back at least to c.2000 bc, with pits producing Grooved Ware, a cursus, and hengiform features (Jones 1976; Leech 1977, map 5). Large-scale salvage excavation was carried out between 1958 and 1965 on the site of iron age and Romano-British settlement covering about 8ha at Roughground Farm (RCHM 1976, 73–75). I am grateful to Margaret Jones and Tim Allen for the information included here.

There seems to be a gap, spatially and chronologically, between the early iron age occupation and that of the Roman period. In the mid-first century a 'native' settlement was established. This included a sub-rectangular enclosure and outside it a cluster of pits, which were probably for grain storage. Larger, re-cut ditches, similar to those at Claydon Pike, may have bounded stock enclosures. To the south and east two side trackways led into an open space, east of the settlement area. The tracks could have functioned as droveways leading to pasture by the River Leach. While the dating evidence points to these tracks being in use in the second century AD, it is possible that their origins lie in the iron age. In the central open space a curious circular feature with a broad ditch was dated at least to the late third century AD. This may have been a central mound which provided a focal point rather like a market cross or other marker.

In the mid- to late second century the 'native' occupation area was built over. Masonry structures – Buildings I, IV, and probably II – were

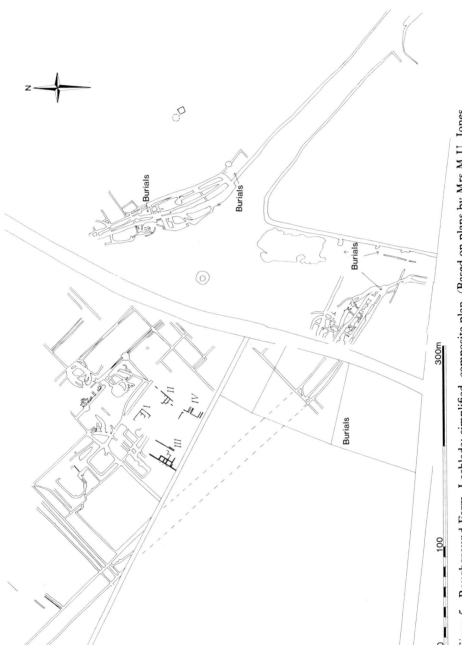

*Figure 5* Roughground Farm, Lechlade: simplified, composite plan. (Based on plans by Mrs M.U. Jones, and updated since RCHM 1976.)

Burials

Burials

Burials

Burials

N

0        100        300m

constructed. Buildings I and II produced painted plaster and tesserae; Building II had *opus signinum* floors. New trackways gave access to these buildings and a field system based on a rectangular unit of measurement was probably laid out at this time. Several ditched enclosures were tacked onto the droveway ditches in the later second century; one contained a four-post structure and another a corn-drying oven.

Building III was probably constructed in the early third century, with substantial stone foundations, mortar floors, and wall plaster with simple decoration in white, yellow, and red. It was soon rebuilt and more luxuriously appointed with at least three hypocausted rooms, mosaic and tessellated floors, and more decorative wall plaster. Opposite Building III, to the east, Building IV underwent various alterations into the fourth century. Unfortunately only part of a room and a yard flanked by a corridor were excavated. A fifth hypocausted building, possibly a bath house, may have stood to the north between Buildings I and II.

Burials were found in a number of locations, notably in enclosures and alongside the trackway ditches about 200m east, south, and south-east of the main building complex. These occurred singly or in groups of up to seven.

The site may have been abandoned in the last quarter of the fourth century. Only one of the 28 coins found was later than the House of Constantine – a siliqua of Honorius found among the extensive robbing of Building III.

## THE UPPER THAMES VALLEY AND THE PROCESS OF CHANGE

From the early iron age the Upper Thames Valley was increasingly densely occupied. The higher gravel terraces are characterized by communities practising mixed farming with a strong emphasis on cereal production (Jones 1981). On the Thames flood plain, excavations in Oxfordshire have investigated seasonally-occupied shielings which provided shelter for herders bringing their animals to the rich summer pasture (Lambrick and Robinson 1979).

In the Gloucestershire Upper Thames Valley the fragmented islands of first-terrace gravel provided a niche for pastoral communities to exploit the good grazing land. The appearance of the settlements of these communities in the third century bc coincided with an increasing population, so that the manpower was available to construct and maintain the necessary drainage system. This perhaps coincided with the peak of hillfort occupation, mainly on the limestone to the north. Unfortunately, little is known of the function of Cotswold hillforts. They may, however, have acted as communal focal-points in which produce could be stored and redistributed. Certainly the Claydon Pike herdsmen were in contact with a wider area, which provided them with cereals, salt, and stone.

The re-organization at Claydon Pike in the century before the Roman conquest is a typical manifestation of the changes which were taking place in celtic society at that time. These are well known: the growth of international trade, the development of new central places (oppida) and the decline of the hillforts, the appearance of a more systematically controlled landscape, and the use of wheel-thrown pottery and coinage.

Relatively few Roman sites in Gloucestershire have produced evidence of iron age occupation beneath them. However, this may be a reflection more of the limited scale of most excavations and of the 'Roman bias' of their excavators rather than of historical reality. In the Upper Thames Valley as a whole, continuity from the late iron age seems to be characteristic of 'native' settlements. It must be emphasized, of course, that the accurate dating of mid-first-century sites is difficult; in many contexts it is expecting too much of the evidence to require it to pinpoint or reflect a historical event like the Roman conquest. Nevertheless, there is clear evidence for dense 'native' occupation in the Thames Valley. What was the impact on these people of being absorbed into the new Roman province?

In many cases the answer, as far as the archaeological record is concerned, is very little. At excavated settlements in the Oxfordshire Thames Valley, such as Ashville, Abingdon (Parrington 1978), Barton Court Farm, Abingdon (Selkirk 1978), and Mount Farm, Dorchester (Lambrick 1979), Roman influence was only gradually absorbed: settlement organization changed little; Romanized pottery and coinage were introduced slowly; and the agricultural economic basis continued unchanged. So was this typical of the Gloucestershire Thames Valley? The area obviously had special characteristics: it was in close proximity to a major military and subsequently urban centre; it lay to the south of one of the greatest concentrations of rich estates in Britain; and it had specialized resources, namely its rich low-lying grazing land.

The fringes of the valley show signs of having developed rather like the Cotswolds. On the higher ground at Ampney St Peter, Driffield, and Lechlade, there are Romanized villa-type establishments. At Roughground Farm, masonry buildings appeared in the mid- to late second century AD and the site continued, apparently prosperously, into the late fourth century. On the lower land, however, the process was rather different. Most of the settlements known from aerial photography and fieldwork are 'native' in character and of low status. Iron age settlements probably continued to be occupied, while increasing population generated new post-conquest settlements and substantial infilling of the landscape.

Villas, and particularly large, well-appointed villas, are notable for their absence. This cannot be explained in terms of the richness of the land: Cotswold slopes and valleys are not more productive than the gravel terraces, clay slopes, and alluvial deposits of the Thames Valley. Instead we must envisage a situation where capital could not be accumulated in the Upper Thames Valley, so that the occupants were unable to invest in bricks and mortar, mosaics, and bathhouses.

The explanation for this may lie in the iron age background. The Thames Valley was extensively cleared of woodland at an early date and from the early iron age had a high level of population, with communities living in sites which reflect relatively little hierarchical development. This contrasts with the more widely scattered and often enclosed sites – the hillforts and banjo enclosures – of the Cotswolds. It has been suggested (Hingley 1983) that the two settlement zones had different socio-economic structures. In the more traditional, conservative, and clustered communities of the Thames Valley the forms of land-holding and inheritance might have inhibited the accumulation of wealth on the part of any single family or individual. On the Cotswolds a more entrepreneurial spirit, less inhibited by traditional restraints on land-holding, could have prevailed, as seems to have been the case among the assarting farmers of the Middle Ages.

Salway (1981) has suggested that the Cotswolds attracted large landowners and rich house-builders because they were an attractive area in which to live. No doubt, as today, there is an element of truth in this. However, other factors must be explained, such as the iron age settlement pattern and the availability of land on a large scale. The proximity of Corinium does not provide a simple explanation for the presence of rich houses; they do not cluster around the city to the south and east, and one of the largest clusters of all, around North Leigh in Oxfordshire, is well away from any major urban centre. Most of the villas are, however, conveniently close to main roads. Some of them are also situated on, or close by, rivers which, as well as an abundant water supply, may have provided relatively cheap transportation within their estates, if not on a wider basis. The development of the villas in the late third and fourth centuries may have depended less on the major towns than on the growth of local market centres, many of which were sited on roadways at the crossing points of rivers. Unfortunately, little investigation has been carried out of this important aspect of the late Romano-British economy.

The Claydon Pike excavations, one of the few examples of work on Romano-British rural settlements on a massive scale, have produced interesting evidence for the role of the Gloucestershire Thames lowlands in the early Roman Period. Unlike most other Upper Thames sites this one is re-organized on a substantial scale in the late first or early second century. The 'native' ranch is dispensed with and a new and regularly planned establishment is erected in its place. The roads which focus on this settlement linked it with other, less-Romanized, sites. Substantial buildings, including a hall dwelling and an aisled barn, lay in a courtyard behind an impressive gateway. Alongside the gateway was an enigmatic structure thought to be a shrine. Two further enclosures contained peasant cottages, wells, and many fodder stacks. All around these buildings were pens, paddocks, and pastoral fields. The settlement does not resemble a traditional villa; it is less comfortable than Roughground Farm in the second century, for example. Rather it appears to have been the centre of a ranching establishment, with occupants of differing status, literally on either side of the tracks. None of them, however, need have been the owner of the settlement and its land.

In some respects the settlement shows a surprising degree of Romanization, not only in the scale of re-development but also by the presence of early coins, large numbers of amphorae, and good quality bronzework. One or two fragments of military metalwork may be of little significance on a rural settlement, but at Claydon Pike the quantity of material is sufficiently large to suggest a military presence. The site has no strategic significance or military character. If the military were present, presumably in small numbers, then they probably served to police an agricultural centre where produce was collected from the surrounding countryside. This could have a number of implications for the area. It has been suggested (Miles and Palmer 1983, 88) that Claydon Pike could have been a local centre for collecting taxes in kind. Alternatively, retired veterans may have had this land allocated to them; it may have been legionary *prata* on which cattle and horses were reared, or part of an imperial estate. Crawford (1976) has shown that imperial property came in many guises, most of which are difficult to recognize from archaeological evidence when inscriptions are lacking.

The solution may partially lie in the investigation of neighbouring sites. Three kilometres to the east, further along the Roman roadway, another Romanized settlement has recently been found at Leaze Farm. This also produced fragments of military metalwork during fieldwalking. In contrast, the neighbouring settlement to the west, at Thornhill Farm, remained completely 'native' in character. The chronological details of this site are at present unknown but it is hoped that excavations will take place before its destruction over the next four years. These may clarify the role of the settlement in the late first and second centuries BC and its relationship with its more Romanized neighbour. If Claydon Pike functioned as a focal-point for a larger estate, potentially incorporating several hundred hectares, then the Thornhill Farm site may have been the home of the 'native' *coloni* who made up the labour force.

By the later third century Claydon Pike had undergone another major change in character. The substantial early Roman establishment had diminished in size and several large buildings, including the hall and shrine, were demolished. The modest farmhouse which occupied the site did not attain the standard of luxury of the nearby villa at Roughground Farm, Lechlade, nor even of the most modest Cotswold villas, such as Barnsley Park (Webster 1981; Webster and Smith 1982). The economy of the farmstead was less specialized than before. Further work on the environmental evidence from the area and the dating of neighbouring sites may make possible an assessment of the size of the farmstead's property. The modest nature of the house suggests that the property had been acquired by a non-residential landowner, possibly the occupant of one of the villas to the north; alternatively, if owner-occupied, the house must have been associated with only a small tract of land.

A historical model based on the Claydon Pike evidence can, therefore, be proposed. It is important to emphasize that this should not be accepted for the Gloucestershire Upper Thames Valley as a whole without being tested. All too often in British archaeology excavated settlements have been assumed to be typical. The archaeology of the Gloucestershire Water Park has been much neglected for most of the past twenty-five years. The opportunities exist, but only for a limited period, to follow up this work and investigate the Romano-British landscape with the care it deserves.

Low-lying land is cleared of woodland by the middle iron age. Permanent, scattered settlements exploit the rich grazing land but are dependent on labour-intensive drainage schemes. In the late iron age settlements are nucleated but the pastoral basis of the local economy continues. Settlements change little until the end of the first century when some more-Romanized centres like Claydon Pike and Leaze Farm are established on the first terrace, possibly under official Imperial control. Other 'native' sites do not change, though how long they were occupied is not known. At the same time more comfortable private farmsteads or villas begin to develop on the higher ground, at the centre of relatively large properties where iron age occupation was less intensive. By the later third century the official settlements on the first terrace have been broken-up and possibly sold-off. Many small farmsteads are found now in the valley lowlands. By the fifth century most of these sites are abandoned.

Meagre traces of early Saxon settlement, at Frilford and Lechlade, are on the higher gravel terraces or limestone slopes, more suitably located for mixed farming on naturally well-drained sites. The scale of abandonment of Romano-British settlements would make special pleading necessary in order to propose continuity of occupation on present-day village sites. Few Romano-British settlements are known to have existed under modern settlements because few modern settlements have been investigated. But with the density of Romano-British settlements that existed in the Thames Valley, it is to be expected that ancient and modern will sometimes coincide. The onus is therefore on those who would propose continuity to establish a stronger case than coincidence. In the Gloucestershire Water Park, catastrophe seems more prevalent than continuity in the fifth and sixth centuries AD. It would be misleading, however, to discount the low-lying settlements as historical failures. Between the third century bc and fourth century AD the celtic population thrived in a rich but difficult environment. Probably not until the seventeenth century AD was the area so successfully exploited again.

REFERENCES

Allden, A. 1983. The county sites and monuments record: a progress report May 1982–September 1983. *Glevensis* 17, 4–5.

Benson, D. and Miles, D. 1974. *The Upper Thames Valley: an archaeological survey of the river gravels.* Oxford.

Brodribb, A.C.C., Hands, A.R., and Walker, D.R. 1968. *Excavations at Shakenoak Farm, near Wilcote, Oxfordshire. Part I: sites A and D.* Oxford. (Privately printed.)

Crawford, D.J. 1976. Imperial estates. In M.I. Finley (ed.), *Studies in Roman property*, 35–70.

Fowler, P.J. 1977. Archaeology and the M5 motorway, Gloucestershire, 1969–1975: a summary and assessment. *TBGAS* 95, 40–46.

Gingell, C.J. n.d. (but 1972). *A penny for your past: archaeology and the Water Park.* Cheltenham. (Duplicated report.)

Hingley, R. 1983. *Iron age and Romano-British society in the Upper Thames Valley: an analysis of settlement data in terms of modes of production.* Unpublished PhD thesis, University of Southampton.

Jones, M. 1981. The development of crop husbandry. In M. Jones and G. Dimbleby (eds.), *The environment of man: the iron age to the Anglo-Saxon period*, 95–127. Oxford. (=BAR Brit Ser 87.)

Jones, M.U. 1976. Neolithic pottery found at Lechlade, Glos. *Oxoniensia* 41, 1–5.

Lambrick, G. 1979. Mount Farm, Berinsfield. *CBA Group 9 Newsletter* 9, 113–115.

Lambrick, G. and Robinson, M. 1979. *Iron age and Roman riverside settlements at Farmoor, Oxfordshire*. London. (=CBA Res Rep 32.)

Leech, R. 1977. *The Upper Thames Valley in Gloucestershire and Wiltshire: an archaeological survey of the river gravels*. Bristol. (=CRAAGS Survey No. 4.)

Miles, D. and Palmer, S. n.d. (but 1982). *Figures in a landscape: archaeological investigations at Claydon Pike, Fairford/Lechlade, Gloucestershire: interim report 1979–81*. Oxford. (Oxford Archaeological Unit.)

Miles, D. and Palmer, S. 1983. Claydon Pike. *Current Archaeol* 86, 88–92.

Parrington, M. 1978. *The excavation of an iron age settlement, bronze age ring-ditches and Roman features at Ashville Trading Estate, Abingdon (Oxfordshire) 1974–76*. London. (=CBA Res Rep 28.)

RCHM. 1976. *Iron age and Romano-British monuments in the Gloucestershire Cotswolds*. London.

Salway, P. 1981. *Roman Britain*. Oxford.

Selkirk, A. 1978. After Little Woodbury: village and farm in iron age Oxfordshire. *Current Archaeol* 63, 106–113.

Webster, G. 1981. The excavation of a Romano-British rural establishment at Barnsley Park, Gloucestershire, 1961–1979: part I. *TBGAS* 99, 21–77.

Webster, G. and Smith, L. 1982. The excavation of a Romano-British rural establishment at Barnsley Park, Gloucestershire, 1961–1979: part II. *TBGAS* 100, 65–189.

Williams, A. 1946. Excavations at Langford Downs, Oxon (near Lechlade), in 1943. *Oxoniensia* 11/12, 44–64.

**March 1984**

# The Cities and Large Rural Settlements of Roman Gloucestershire

## Alan McWhirr

### THE CITIES

An urbanizing policy was high on the list of priorities when a new province was annexed to the Roman Empire, and consequently urban centres were created in newly-conquered territories as soon as was practical. In the territory of the Dobunni two such centres (Figs. 1 and 2) were deliberately planted during the last quarter of the first century AD on land formerly occupied by detachments of the Roman army and therefore under Roman control. On the banks of the River Severn a *colonia* was founded utilizing the defences of the vacated legionary fortress which had occupied the site previously (Hurst 1976, 71). The date of the foundation of Glevum is suggested by the inscription on a tombstone found in Rome which is thought to record the birthplace of a member of the sixth legion as NER GLEVI, which is usually taken to be an abbreviation for *colonia Nervia Glevensium*, and therefore dates the founding of the *colonia* to the reign of Nerva, AD 96–98.

Some 26km south-east of the fortress at Gloucester and connected to it by Ermin Street, was a small auxiliary fort which was later to become the site for the chief administrative centre of the Dobunni (Wacher and McWhirr 1982). There are no inscriptions to indicate when Cirencester was founded but excavations have shown that the civic centre – the forum and basilica – was under construction during the Flavian period (AD 69–96), and this is usually taken to mark the beginnings of the city. It would appear, therefore, as though the cities of Gloucester and Cirencester were being built at about the same time.

Evidence for the early town at Cirencester is very sparse. Less than ten per cent of the Roman town has been archaeologically investigated and an even smaller percentage excavated to the lowest levels, so that knowledge of the early town is based on an extremely small sample. Likewise, there are sizeable gaps in our understanding of the later town. The site of the public baths is unknown and not one temple has been found. A possible theatre stood just inside the town's defences by the Gloucester Gate and the amphitheatre has survived to the south-west of the Bath Gate. It was situated well away from the town centre and outside the area that was later to be defended. Disused stone quarries were chosen for the site of this enormous structure, consisting of two earthen banks, in an area where a considerable amount of earth-moving had already taken place and where much quarry waste lay around to be used eventually in the seating-banks of the amphitheatre. The seating of the amphitheatre could have accommodated in the region of six thousand people.

Houses and shops at Cirencester were built in timber to begin with, but gradually during the second century they were replaced in stone. A number were provided with mosaics at this time and had painted walls.

The first buildings erected in the *colonia* at Gloucester closely resembled the earlier legionary barracks, the difference being one of internal arrangement and the inclusion of the verandah (Hurst 1972, 39). The military appearance of these *colonia* buildings may be due to army engineers helping with the initial construction of the city, and perhaps the stone bearing the inscription CO(H...) I(...) reflects this (Hurst 1976, 71).

During the second century some of these barrack-like buildings were replaced by stone structures, one of which was excavated on the site of the Telephone Exchange and was reminiscent of peristyled houses of the Mediterranean. Later in the century several houses in the same *insula* were built and others altered. The excavations at Berkeley Street have shown that during the second century the number of buildings per plot was gradually being reduced and this reduction in the density of building is, Hurst suggests, a general feature of the *colonia* at this time (Hurst 1976, 78). It may indicate a movement of people into the *territorium* although the buildings into which they moved are not apparent.

Unlike Gloucester, Cirencester remained undefended until the end of the second century, unless a hitherto unsuspected circuit of the town's defences is waiting to be discovered. At Gloucester, use was made of the legionary defences in the *colonia*, the earth bank of the fortress being reinforced by the

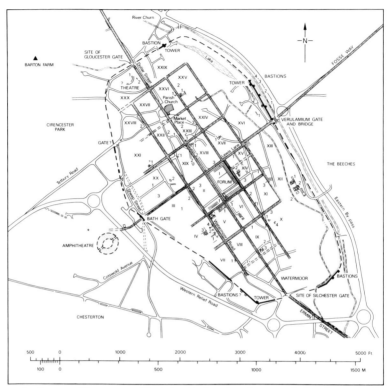

*Figure 1*  Roman Cirencester (Corinium), showing features dating from the first to the fifth centuries AD.

addition of a narrow stone wall, perhaps at the time the *colonia* was founded. The subsequent history of the defences at Gloucester is, as is the case at Cirencester, proving to be more complicated than hitherto believed (Heighway *et al.* 1983).

At Cirencester an earthen rampart with associated ditches was built with a number of contemporary internal stone towers and with at least two stone gates, the Verulamium and Bath Gates. A stone wall was added to the front of the rampart during the second quarter of the third century after which a number of modifications took place, including the rebuilding of various stretches of the wall in a broader gauge, and the addition of external bastions.

Two recent series of excavations at Cirencester deserve special mention. The first was on the site of a late Roman cemetery outside the Bath Gate, where the excavations produced 453 skeletons and three cremations, which have told us a great deal about burial practices at Corinium and much about the people who lived in the town (McWhirr *et al*. 1982). The second concerns the excavations in *insula* XII where two houses showing a distinctly rural character were found (McWhirr 1978). They appear to have been built in the fourth century on land which previously had been unoccupied. In particular, building XII,2 had the plan of a winged corridor villa, associated with a group of barn-like out-buildings (McWhirr 1981, 55–56). From unstratified levels above this building came an iron coulter and four bone tablets as used in tablet weaving (McWhirr 1981, 57 and 102). There seems little doubt that this building was concerned with farming. Whether the aisled building further south was part of the same complex could not be established. It may have been a smithy belonging to the farm, or the building may represent another farm with smithing facilities, storage, and living accommodation all under one roof.

Because of the close proximity of the two Roman towns at Gloucester and Cirencester they have frequently been compared with each other. Nearly forty years ago Professor Sir Ian Richmond in his masterly survey of the four *coloniae* of Roman Britain wrote:–

"It has already been observed that the capital of the Dobunni, out of whose territory the *colonia* was carved, lay only seventeen miles away across the Cotswolds. Of all the Romano-British tribal capitals Corinium Dobunnorum was quite the most successful. It was not only the largest, 240 acres in size, but it was plainly the wealthiest and most sumptuous. The art of its mosaic pavements and the architecture of its public buildings would not disgrace any of the western provinces, and it seems to have become in the fourth century the capital of Britannia Prima. It is plain that this native capital not merely eclipsed the *colonia Nervia* but drew away from it the enterprise and trade that might have produced from the same beginnings another Lincoln. The proximity of the two centres was manifestly unfortunate, but blame for this must not fall upon the founders of Glevum. The potentialities of Corinium can hardly have been fully apparent when the *colonia* was founded" (Richmond 1946, 73).

Other writers have echoed Richmond's comments since they were written (e.g. Wacher 1974, 155) and so it is perhaps time to re-examine some of the points of comparison between the two towns. The difference in the size of Cirencester and Gloucester is probably the most obvious feature that has invited comparison. The area within the walls of Gloucester is just over 43 acres (17·3ha), whereas Cirencester is 240 acres (96ha), which is nearly SIX times greater than the *colonia*, and surely it is this great difference that has

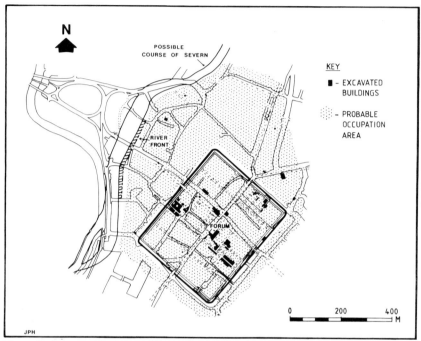

*Figure 2*   Roman Gloucester (Glevum), showing features dating to *c.*150 AD. (After Heighway 1981.)

caused people to look at the two towns and compare one with the other. However, it is now possible to suggest that these figures do not in fact reflect accurately the size of the settlements as they do not take into account suburbs, nor the extent to which the walled area was developed.

At Gloucester the re-use of the legionary defences for the *colonia* and the continuous use of this circuit for the next 300 years meant that if the town needed to expand it had to develop suburbs, which is precisely what happened. At Cirencester, on the other hand, expansion of the town was not restricted until the first defences were constructed towards the end of the second century and so the area which was then enclosed was one which had evolved over a period of a hundred years. If the first defences at Gloucester had been built at the same time as those at Cirencester, then a much greater area would have been enclosed to encompass all the inhabited area within the circuit of the defences.

Plans of Gloucester are now beginning to take into account buildings outside the walls and recent plans suggest that something like 100 acres

(40ha) were covered by the walled area and suburbs (Heighway 1981, map 17). One area which was likely to have been extensively developed lay between the walled area and the River Severn, alongside which was a Roman quay (Fig. 1). Extra-mural settlement has also been found on other sides of the *colonia*, but as yet neither the extent of the building nor the continuity of occupation are clearly established.

Now let us examine the 240 acres (96ha) of Corinium. This figure must be considered as a maximum as no extensive suburbs have been found, although perhaps something should be added to include the amphitheatre and building west of the town. As to the 240 acres within the town walls, there is some evidence to suggest that not all were fully occupied with buildings, but as so little has been archaeologically examined one must be cautious and treat the comments which follow as a personal view based on very little evidence. However, when the Waterloo Car Park was built, an area of 2–3 acres (1ha) was disturbed and no masonry structures were seen, although timber buildings could have existed and been missed during these casual observations. Similarly, when a trench was dug across City Bank playing field, no stone buildings were noted and, along with other areas of the town, there are hints that not all land within the walls was fully developed. The fact that quite large open spaces were included within the circuit of the town defences can be demonstrated in *insula* XII, where two sizeable stone buildings were erected during the fourth (or possibly fifth?) century on vacant land. Although the excavation of these buildings was far from complete, there was no indication of earlier structures on that particular site. Insufficient area was cleared during the excavations to be able to determine whether this land had been used for market gardening or other similar horticultural purposes. On present evidence it looks as though this low-lying area of 3–4 acres (1–2ha) was unoccupied when the defences were built and it raises the question of how many other such areas existed when the town was ringed with its defences. If many similar areas are to be found, then the built-up part of the town would be considerably less than the usually quoted 240 acres (96ha) and perhaps only twice that of Glevum and its suburbs.

## THE LARGE RURAL SETTLEMENTS

There are no other settlements in Gloucestershire which can be called cities in the true classical sense of the word, but there are several which during their lifetime may have acquired a limited number of urban functions as Reece seems to be suggesting (this volume). These settlements include Bourton-on-

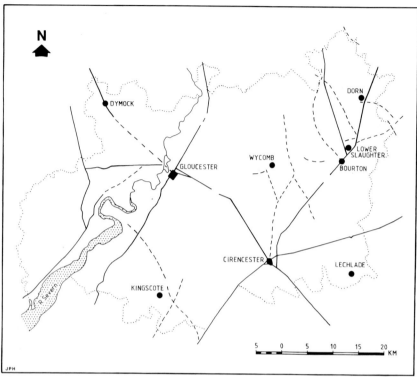

*Figure 3*  Roman Gloucestershire, showing cities and larger rural settlements. Major
roads are shown in solid line, minor or probable roads are dashed.

the-Water, Dorn, Dymock, Kingscote, Lechlade, Lower Slaughter, and
Wycomb (Fig. 3), and are perhaps best described as villages, as defined by
Rivet (1975, 114). He suggests that 'a village was mainly concerned with
agriculture whilst a town was involved with trade' and goes on to say of a
town that 'given a reasonable number of buildings, therefore, the criterion
might be the possession of a market building supplemented by other public
buildings such as temples, but temples on a scale which indicates that they
contributed to, rather than dominated, the life of the place'. There is no
example in those settlements listed above where we have a reasonable number
of buildings on which to make a judgement about its status, and much more
work will need to be done before this can be achieved.

At Bourton-on-the-Water, Roman buildings have been examined alongside
the Fosse Way and over the years Mrs O'Neil has managed to collect together
an impressive amount of information relating to the extent of the settlement

(RCHM 1976, 19–21). The exact function of the buildings found at Bourton is not clear. There may have been a posting house, stables, a bakehouse, and a wayside shrine beside the Fosse Way, as suggested by O'Neil (1968), but it is possible to interpret some of these buildings differently (McWhirr 1981, 65). More recently there have been investigations in a field south-east of Bourton Bridge and these have produced a puzzling series of buildings, including a number of apparently circular structures (Renfrew 1980). The Roman settlement at Bourton has all the appearances of haphazard development along what must have been one of the country's main arterial roads, as well as a spreading between the pre-Roman settlement of Salmonsbury and the Fosse. No doubt the road acted as a magnet to the local populace, who were not slow to see the benefits of building beside it.

Aerial reconnaissance has revealed that the Roman settlement at Dorn, just to the north of Moreton-in-Marsh, was defended with a ditch and possibly a wall (RCHM 1976, 12–13). The existence of a site at Dorn had been noted in the seventeenth century and small-scale excavations were conducted by Lt.-Col. R.K. Morcom between 1937 and 1939, which concentrated on uncovering one building (McWhirr 1981, 61). Dorn is the only large rural settlement which has so far produced any evidence for being defended, unless a ditch found at Wycomb is part of a defensive circuit. Another unusual feature about Dorn is the fact that it sits to one side of the Fosse Way, unlike Bourton or Dymock, which developed along both sides of a road. The shape and size of Dorn, ten acres (4ha), have often been taken to imply that there were some military associations with this site, but as yet there is nothing to substantiate this view.

At Dymock (McWhirr 1981, 67–70), stone and timber buildings have been found, ranging in date from the first to the third centuries, and aerial photography and excavations have revealed the line of a Roman road through the settlement, which has been delineated by a wide scatter of Roman material. A Dobunnic coin has been found at Dymock, which may indicate a pre-Roman origin to the settlement, and there is also some evidence for iron smelting. The settlement might be equated with Macatonion (or Magalonium) of the Ravenna Cosmography.

A large Roman settlement covering at least 75 acres (30ha) has been recognized in the parish of Kingscote and between 1975 and 1980 excavations were conducted on one of the buildings from within that area (KAA n.d.). Kingscote stands out among the larger rural settlements of Gloucestershire in a number of ways. First, it is perhaps the largest, the 75 acres being a conservative estimate of its size. Second, the quality of the archaeological material, be it wall plaster or bronze objects, is far superior to that from any other site, although this may be due to the lack of intensive excavation at other settlements. Sculpture is not yet well represented among the finds from Kingscote compared with pieces from Lower Slaughter or Wycomb, but the quality of the head of Minerva found in the eighteenth century is of the highest order.

The accumulating evidence from Kingscote suggests that it was a settlement of some standing, which may have acquired urban functions. It may also have been a local market centre and have provided services for that part of the *civitas*. The one building examined, which was perhaps the house and workshop of a craftsman, cannot be used to judge the overall character of the settlement and we must await further detailed fieldwork and/or excavation before we gain a reliable impression of the character of Kingscote.

Roman material has been found at Lower Slaughter (RCHM 1976, 79–80) extending over an area of at least 25 acres (10ha). Although not as extensive as the settlement at Kingscote it is nevertheless a sizeable and significant one among those being discussed. Ditches, pits, and wells are the main features recorded from the site. Two rectangular buildings have been noted, as well as a so-called corn drier. From close by one of these buildings has come part of a votive tablet and a nearby well contained eight votive objects, including two small altars, three plaques to Mars and to *genii cucullati*, and a number of other pieces of sculpture. It certainly looks as though there may have been a temple, or perhaps several, at Lower Slaughter, but whether these dominated the settlement or were its *raison d'être* cannot be determined on the available evidence. One would expect any sizeable Roman settlement to produce a fair amount of evidence relating to religious practices and what has been found at Lower Slaughter may be normal.

A number of the sites already discussed may have had their roots in the iron age. There is iron age pottery from Lower Slaughter, a Dobunnic coin from Dymock, and a number of other pieces which may indicate pre-Roman origins for some of the settlements. The evidence from Wycomb is even more persuasive. Here, several iron age brooches and at least three Dobunnic coins have been found, as well as a quantity of pre-Roman pottery, all of which point to a pre-Roman settlement of some significance. Aerial photography and nineteenth-century excavations have shown a series of roads/streets and a number of stone buildings, one of which may have been a temple. The 1864 plan produced by W.L. Lawrence shows a curving wall at least 20m long, although for most of its course it is shown as conjectural by being dotted, and so it is by no means certain that it ever existed for the full 20m (RCHM 1976, 125). This curving wall has been interpreted as part of a theatre, and if the length shown on the plan is genuine, then this would be a logical interpretation. If there was a theatre at Wycomb there must have been some special reason for it to have been built and the proximity of a temple possibly provides the answer, for they were often built to complement each other. A theatre-and-temple complex at the heart of a settlement must surely indicate that it was the focus of attention and perhaps the reason for its growth and development. There is an impressive list of votive objects from Wycomb, including two stone panels, one of which shows a *genius cucullatus*, two small stone idols, and a bronze statuette of Mars. One is reminded of the sites at Lydney (Wheeler 1932) and Uley (Ellison 1980), which were clearly rural shrines and which contained a temple, accommodation, and possibly shops for selling religious goods. Could the settlement at Wycomb be another? Claims have recently been made for Chedworth to be such a site (Webster 1983) and the evidence from Wycomb would seem to be equally convincing.

There are other places in the county where large Roman settlements once existed, although our knowledge of them is in most cases meagre. The work of the Oxford Archaeological Unit in the Lechlade area of the Upper Thames Valley has over the last few years added greatly to our knowledge of that region of the county (Miles this volume).

The relationship between Roman cities, towns, villages, or other settlements and the hundreds of farms which dotted the landscape has not been fully explored. However, although the data for such a study may not yet be available, attempts to understand this fundamental relationship must, in due course, be undertaken. The success or failure of large centres of population, whether we call them cities, towns, or villages, was after all dependent upon those who lived outside them. A city's markets could only survive if goods were provided by farmers and craftsmen, and religious shrines would serve no purpose if people did not frequent them; thus our understanding of these settlements must depend to a large extent on exploring further the relationship between town and country.

REFERENCES

Ellison, A. 1980. Natives, Romans and Christians on West Hill, Uley: an interim report on the excavation of a ritual complex of the first millennium AD. In W.J. Rodwell (ed.), *Temples, churches and religion: recent research in Roman Britain*, 305–328. Oxford. (=BAR Brit Ser 77.)

Heighway, C. 1981. Gloucester. In R. Leech, *Historic towns in Gloucestershire: archaeology and planning*, 39–44. Bristol. (=CRAAGS Survey No. 3.)

Heighway, C. *et al.* 1983. *The East and North Gates of Gloucester and associated sites:*

*excavations 1974–1981.* Bristol. (=Western Archaeological Trust Excavation Report No. 4.)

Hurst, H. 1972. Excavations at Gloucester 1968–1971: first interim report. *Antiq J* 52, 24–69.

Hurst, H. 1976. Gloucester (Glevum): a *colonia* in the West Country. In K. Branigan and P.J. Fowler (eds.), *The Roman West Country: classical culture and celtic society,* 63–80. Newton Abbot.

KAA (Kingscote Archaeological Association). n.d. (but 1978). *Excavations: The Chessalls, Kingscote, 1975–7.* Stroud. (Privately printed.)

McWhirr, A. 1978. Cirencester, 1973–1976: tenth interim report. *Antiq J* 58, 61–80.

McWhirr, A. 1981. *Roman Gloucestershire.* Gloucester.

McWhirr, A., Viner, L., and Wells, C. *Romano-British cemeteries at Cirencester.* Cirencester. (=Cirencester Excavations II.)

O'Neil, H.E. 1968. The Roman settlement on the Fosse Way at Bourton Bridge, Bourton-on-the-Water, Gloucestershire. *TBGAS* 87, 29–55.

RCHM. 1976. *Iron age and Romano-British monuments in the Gloucestershire Cotswolds.* London.

Renfrew, C. 1980. Bourton-on-the-Water: settlement area near Bourton Bridge. *Glevensis* 14, 23.

Richmond, I.A. 1946. The four *coloniae* of Roman Britain. *Archaeol J* 103, 57–84.

Rivet, A.L.F. 1975. Summing up: the classification of minor towns and related settlements. In W. Rodwell and T. Rowley, *The 'small towns' of Roman Britain,* 111–114. Oxford. (=BAR Brit Ser 15.)

Wacher, J. 1974. *The towns of Roman Britain.* London.

Wacher, J. and McWhirr, A. 1982. *Early Roman occupation at Cirencester.* Cirencester. (=Cirencester Excavations I.)

Webster, G. 1983. The function of Chedworth Roman 'villa'. *TBGAS* 101, 5–20.

Wheeler, R.E.M. and T.V. 1932. *Report on the excavation of the prehistoric, Roman, and post-Roman site in Lydney Park, Gloucestershire.* London. (=Soc Antiq London Res Rep 9.)

**April 1984**

# PART FIVE:

# GLOUCESTERSHIRE IN SAXON AND MEDIEVAL TIMES

# Anglo-Saxon
# Gloucestershire

*Carolyn Heighway*

## INTRODUCTION

Since Gloucestershire is the subject of this volume, it is worth a reminder that it was in the Anglo-Saxon period that the shire of Gloucester came into being. It is the last of a series of administrative territories which centred on the town. As early as the Roman period there would have been a territory administered by each of the Roman towns, and this territory in the case of Gloucester may have survived to the sixth century AD (Finberg 1957, 14–16). Gloucester was also the centre of a 'Kingdom' in 577 (Whitelock 1961).

The urban territories may have continued to exist as subdivisions of the wider area administered by the Anglo-Saxon tribe of the Hwicce. Their kingdom seems to have coincided with the medieval diocese of Worcester, and its principal town was also Worcester. Until the eighth century the Hwicce were a quasi-independent political group nominally under the overlordship of Mercia (Wilson 1969).

The creation of the shire of Gloucester, with the city of Gloucester as its metropolitan, apparently occurred relatively late in the 'shiring' process; in either *c.*1008 (Taylor 1957) or *c.*900–980 (Stenton 1971, 337). The shire of Winchcombe was created at the same time, although Finberg (1961, 228–230) recognizes that there was a territory administratively dependent on Winchcombe in the eighth century. By implication this would have been true of Gloucester also; without such sub-divisions it is hard to see how Offa managed his extensive kingdom so efficiently.

Winchcombeshire was absorbed into Gloucestershire *c.*1007–1017 (Finberg 1961, 234); the Forest of Dean was annexed to Gloucestershire before 1086 (Finberg 1961, 227). Thereafter there was little change until the nineteenth century, when anomalies in the northern borders were resolved (Darby 1954, 2). Thus the eleventh-century shire was still nearly intact in 1974 when the new county of Avon, with the City of Bristol, was separated from the historic county to the north.

The study of Anglo-Saxon Gloucestershire is fraught with difficulty, and the fifth and sixth centuries present particular problems. The written sources are almost non-existent and the archaeology seems to be nearly indistinguishable. The most intensive archaeological research will be necessary if the history of Anglo-Saxon Gloucestershire is to be amplified. That much remains to be done will be made apparent by the uncertainties expressed in the following account.

## SUB-ROMAN GLOUCESTERSHIRE

The withdrawal of Roman imperial protection from Britain had two consequences of significance for the archaeologist: the cessation of the coinage, and the collapse of the organized pottery industries. The result is the loss of the principal aids which provide the preceding Roman centuries with their confidently-dated framework.

The Anglo-Saxon immigrants took more than two hundred years to reach and conquer Gloucestershire and the West Country. In those two centuries there must have lingered a Romano-British culture which, due to this lack of dating evidence, we are unable to recognize. Many of the sites, both urban and rural, which are late Roman judged by their artefacts, may be fifth- or sixth-century. In the Roman towns, where archaeologists have been accustomed to excavate easily-recognizable stone buildings, there was in the late fourth to early fifth century a reversion to the use of timber, so that buildings have disappeared or perhaps in the past escaped attention. It is also true that the destruction rate of these particular deposits has, in past centuries, been exceedingly high. Finally, timber structures need lengthy and meticulous attention by the excavator, using the methods being applied, for example, at Wroxeter (Barker 1975); yet time is not a factor usually in evidence on urban sites. Even so, more attention has been given in recent years to the towns than to the countryside, where the evidence is even more sparse.

Many rural settlements in Gloucestershire must have continued in their native farming traditions throughout the Roman occupation. In the fourth century the agricultural scene was dominated by the great villas and their estates. Their prosperity may have been, as Reece suggests (this volume), at the expense of the towns; Gloucester may have been in decline well before the end of the fourth century. By the early fifth century the great country houses were also abandoned. They were ceasing to be Romanized and becoming more like native farms. At Frocester, for instance, the third-century villa was still in use early in the fifth century, but with badly patched floors, and with one of the rooms being used as a stable (Gracie 1970). Similar evidence comes from other large Romanized farmhouses (Branigan 1972). We should be careful how we interpret such evidence. The inability to maintain the great houses need not imply squalor and degradation. Timber buildings could be very splendid, and it is clear that the stone buildings had outlived their old function and were only outhouses. There is evidence at Frocester of timber buildings of the fifth century (Gracie and Price 1979, fig. 6) occupying the courtyard of the disused villa. The courtyard contained dozens of sherds of fifth-century grass-tempered pottery. The buildings, however slight their remains, could represent large buildings of high social status; whilst the dozens of sherds of grass-tempered pottery compare with a total of five sherds from all the excavations at Gloucester. Perhaps in the fifth century Frocester was at least as important as Gloucester, operating as a seasonal market centre. The decline of towns is no certain indication of a subsistence economy; the situation in Gloucestershire may have been similar to that in early medieval south-east Wales, where there were no towns, and rural sites were the centres of substantial estates, worked by a servile population. The surplus provided a small but powerful aristocracy with its wealth (Davies 1978, 59–64). If a similar political and economic situation prevailed in Gloucestershire, we can assume a similar wealth and surplus, the county being, then as always, rich farmland. I have a strong suspicion that the evidence provided by archaeology is, and is likely to remain, totally inadequate in assessing the social situation of the fifth and sixth centuries.

Many or most of the rural settlements were presumably taken over by the Anglo-Saxon settlers in the seventh century. If this occurred by conquest, as the battle of 577 seems to imply, then only the ownership changed, and the native population continued to farm as before. It was not to be expected that boundaries and the face of the countryside would greatly alter. Finberg's (1955) claim to see continuity from Roman to medieval boundaries in the parish of Withington has already been mentioned in this volume (by Reece), and Bassett (1977) has made a similar claim for other estates around Winchcombe. It is obvious, as Reece has said, that there was continuity from one culture to the other, but it will not be easy to prove in detail. At Frocester it is interesting, especially in view of Reece's comments about the third century, that medieval field boundaries on the whole respect Roman ones, and the real break with previous land boundaries occurred in the third century when the first villa was built (E. Price pers. comm.). Other sites which probably remained occupied throughout the fifth century are, as one might expect, the religious centres. The temple at Lydney, built after 367, was repaired several times and finally, after the building had decayed, surrounded with a bank, suggesting that the site retained its importance (Wheeler 1932). The Roman temple at Uley presents a particularly remarkable example of religious continuity. The site had been a ritual enclosure in the iron age before it became a Roman temple and later still a possible Christian church of the fifth century or later (Ellison 1980).

There is slightly more evidence from the two principal Roman towns. After all they had strong defences which could resist civil war; in the fourth century the walls of Gloucester and Cirencester were strengthened and provided with external towers for mounting ballistas. The towns may also have had a military force, if this can be inferred from the type II military buckles found in the towns and also on rural sites (Hawkes 1974; Hawkes and Dunning 1961; Hills 1978). At Cirencester, defences were repaired in the early part of the fifth century; the forum was used and kept clean until about 430. Wacher thinks, however, that the town was later abandoned, and that bodies lay in the streets, perhaps as a result of one of the plagues mentioned in fifth-century sources. The amphitheatre was in use in the fifth century. In it was a large timber building, and grass-tempered pottery was found. Perhaps a reduced population had taken refuge in this small and easily-defended area (Wacher 1976).

In fourth-century Gloucester it is clear that the Roman ideal of urban life was already declining. At the town centre public buildings were sub-divided for domestic and industrial use; some were used for metal-working. One building in front of the forum was burnt down, levelled over, and rebuilt in timber, with large sill-beams set on the ground. The timber produced a radiocarbon date of ad 430 (HAR-1652), while the associated coins suggest a construction date of c.370, but the usual cautions with regard to dating apply, and the early fifth-century date may be closer to the truth. Later this timber building was also demolished and the forum extended by the use of a large metalled area, sufficiently well made to suggest competent civic organization. The initiators of this fifth-century re-planning may have been still living in stone houses; stone buildings, probably private buildings, were constructed in parts of the town after 370 (Heighway and Garrod 1980).

Evidence of an urban economy in the fifth century is negligible. The scarcity of grass-tempered pottery in Gloucester has already been mentioned; other sites producing this ware are still emerging. The date-range of grass-tempered pottery is wide: fifth to eighth century (Appendix 1). Gloucester has also produced a few finds of sherds which have been identified as east Mediterranean Bii amphorae of the fifth and sixth centuries (Hurst 1976, 80). However, the identification of these, and of sherds from St Oswald's Priory, as 'Bii' is very doubtful (L. Alcock pers. comm.). There is, therefore, no certain evidence that Gloucester survived as a mercantile centre. It may, however, have had administrative significance; a function which served to maintain a small population. There are indications that it was occupied; its Roman name was known to the Anglo-Saxons who corrupted it to 'Gleawa(n)-ceastor' (Gelling 1978, 55). Street-sections, which are recorded whenever sewer lines are dug in Gloucester, might be expected to cast light on the post-Roman period, but the sections are ambiguous. The post-Roman centuries are represented by a loam layer 0·5m thick or less, containing bones and Roman pottery, but there is no reason to suppose this represents abandonment. The contrast between this layer and the Roman and some medieval street-sections is due to the fact that no street-metallings were laid from the fifth to the tenth century; this in turn may have lessened the likelihood of preservation of organic material (so distinctive a feature of later medieval street sections), which requires either waterlogging or the help of an impervious surface (Biek 1979).

Other reasons for assuming that the towns remained occupied are the two historical facts we possess for the two centuries: the conquest of the region by Anglo-Saxon forces in 577, when Gloucester, Cirencester, and Bath were captured (Whitelock 1961), and the founding of a minster at Gloucester c.679 (Finberg 1961, 153–166). Both events imply that the towns operated as administrative foci, and retained a memory of their Roman functions as centres for the region, even though they may have ceased to resemble towns in the Roman sense. If these assumptions are correct, then Cirencester was not deserted. Perhaps, as Wacher (1976) suggests, its only occupied area was the amphitheatre. However, there was at Cirencester a pre-tenth-century church of considerable size (Brown 1976, 41), presumably a minster, which is unlikely to have been founded in a place of empty ruins.

In the sixth century, the political situation can be defined by a plot of Saxon cemeteries (Fig. 1), which represents the advance of the pagan Saxon colonists for the two centuries before 700. They had reached the Cotswolds, where Cirencester had a Saxon cemetery before 550, presumably representing peaceful settlement (Brown 1976, 32), and they were moving up the

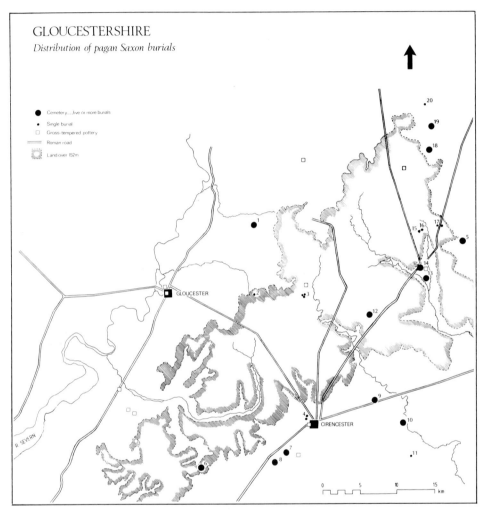

*Figure 1*   Gloucestershire: distribution of pagan Saxon burials, with a plot of 5th- to 8th-century grass-tempered pottery (see Appendix 1).

Saxon cemeteries: 1. Bishop's Cleeve, 2. Leckhampton, 3. Withington, 4. Barton, near Cirencester, 5. Oddington, 6. Chavenage, 7. Kemble I, 8. Kemble II, 9. Bibury, Ready Token, 10. Fairford, 11. Kempsford, 12. Burn Ground, Hampnett, 13. Salmonsbury, 14. Lower Slaughter, 15–16. Upper Swell I and II, 17. Broadwell, 18. Blockley, 19. Ebrington, 20. Hidcote Bartrim. For details of these sites see Meaney 1964.

(Drawn by Monica Anderson and Marian Hoyle.)

Thames valley and towards Cheltenham, where there was a late sixth-century cemetery at Bishop's Cleeve (Brown 1970). Yet around Gloucester is an archaeologically blank region with no artefacts except a few finds of grass-tempered pottery (Fig. 1). This blank must represent the area still controlled by the town, guarded presumably by troops, some mounted in the Roman manner, whose achievements have come down to us as the half-legendary tales of Arthur and Ambrosius. According to Gildas, one of the commanders of this district was called Aurelius (Morris 1978). The probable date of the great British victory at Badon, c.500, would fit into Gloucestershire history to explain why the Severn Valley was held against the Saxons for three-quarters of a century. In contrast to the Cotswolds, the Vale was uncolonized by Saxons, whether peaceably or otherwise, until the time of the battle of Dyrham in 577.

It seems extraordinary that two centuries should have left no sign of material culture, and we have to assume that we do not recognize it. Probably many of the materials used were perishable, of wood and leather, and other artefacts may have been identical (minus coins and pottery) to the culture of the fourth century. Pretty (1975), in her thesis on the Severn and Avon Valleys in the fifth and sixth centuries, has tried to indicate which 'late Roman' objects might also belong to these centuries.

The end of this Romano-British sub-culture is marked by the battle of 577. In 628 the region which is now Gloucestershire appears to have come under the rule of Penda's Mercia. Gloucestershire was part of the principality of the Hwicce, a sub-kingdom of Mercia. Penda's conquest of 628 may have been achieved with the help of Northumbria, for the rulers of the Hwicce seem to have had a Northumbrian origin (Finberg 1961, 167–180). The theme of Northumbrian influence occurs again in the course of the following centuries.


## MID-SAXON GLOUCESTERSHIRE

The advance of Christianity is a principal theme of the eighth to the tenth century. Some remnants of Roman Christianity may have survived. There are four stones marked with the Christian monograph at Chedworth (Richmond 1959, 22), and there is the famous word-square at Cirencester, although this may be Jewish rather than Christian (Atkinson 1957; Frend 1979, footnote 10). The tiles marked IHS mentioned by Taylor (1891, 121–122) are surely misreadings of magistrates' stamps and are not Christian at all. Late traditions of a sixth-century bishop are hardly reliable (Taylor 1891, 121–122), although the proximity to Gloucestershire of sub-Roman,

Christian Wales is a reminder that, whether or not Roman Christianity lingered on in Gloucestershire, re-conversion could have come about through Welsh missionaries even before the Anglo-Saxon intervention. The latter, when it came, was an aristocratic initiative, and was marked by the foundation of the religious communities known as minsters. By 670, or soon after, the rulers of the Hwicce were Christian (Plummer 1896; Finberg 1961, 171). The bishopric of Worcester was set up under Hwiccian princely patronage in about 679; Cedric, a Hwiccian under-king, founded a minster at Bath in 675 and one at Gloucester in 679–681. Offa of Mercia founded a minster at Winchcombe in 787 (Levison 1946, 249–259).

The evidence for the minster churches of Gloucestershire is much greater than for many regions of England. There is ample scope for detailed research into the Anglo-Saxon minsters of the area, using the full range of materials available: historical, archaeological, architectural, and topographical. To reap the full benefits from such a study, it would need to cover the whole of the medieval diocese of Worcester, thus including all the kingdom of the Hwicce.

Indeed, all parish churches and not just the minster churches would be worth considerable further study. Churches in Gloucestershire are quite often found to have occupied the site of a Roman building. This is a pointer, not so much to Christian continuity, as to the tenacity of settlement centres, particularly those of high status, from Roman times or even before. Nine or more parish churches in Gloucester are on or near a Roman building (Morris and Roxan 1980). At Rivenhall, Essex (Rodwell 1973), a building (? shrine) attached to a fifth-century Roman villa developed into a cemetery chapel nearby, and later still into a parish church. Where such a development took place, the alignments of the original Roman buildings might be preserved. In Gloucestershire the churches of Frocester (Gracie 1963), King's Stanley (unpublished), and Woodchester (RCHM 1976, plate 31) all stand on villa sites and use their alignments: there may be other examples to be found. In most such cases, the most interesting part of the site is under the church, rendering extensive excavation unlikely. However, at the now demolished church of St Peter, Frocester, an excavation (Gracie 1963) showed that in the Roman building under the church were several burials, orientated east-west, and sealed by dark earth containing grass-tempered pottery of the fifth to eighth centuries (Appendix 1). The Roman building must in its later life have been used as a cemetery. The church itself was also dated by a grass-tempered cooking pot, said at the time to be twelfth-century (Dunning 1963, 162–163; G. Dunning, C. Ireland, and E. Price pers. comm.).

The minster at Gloucester was founded with a grant from the Mercian king

Æthelred. Finberg (1957, 14–16) thought that the 'three hundred *tributarii*' mentioned in its charter as its endowment showed that the original Roman land tax was still in existence. While this might not be true, some aspects of the Roman administration would have been intact; it may be significant that all but one of Gloucester's Roman cemeteries were important sites (minster, palace, hundred moot) in the late Saxon town (Heighway 1980b). However, if administration functioned, the town was a shadow of its former self. The archaeological evidence suggests that the minster enclosure was laid out on Roman streets which were just visible, but over which the minster boundaries subsequently encroached. Roman buildings were pulled down and paths led across derelict sites. By this time all buildings must have been of timber although the walls and at least two of the gates (North and East) were still standing and in use (Heighway *et al*. 1983). Also still standing was a massive colonnade in the north part of the town. It was probably ruinous, but a new, non-Roman road used the columns to mark its course across the town. This Roman colonnade survived the medieval period, although then encased or covered by medieval buildings, and it is possible that the space between the columns served to mark out plots along the side of the new road (Heighway and Garrod 1980). There are as yet no archaeological levels of the seventh and eighth centuries, but in the ninth and tenth centuries most cultural objects were of wood, which is of course highly perishable, and the proportion of pottery used was very small. There was agriculture and stockading of animals in the city centre. Indeed, this should not surprise us, since control of animals in the streets was still a subject of concern to the City Fathers as late as the seventeenth and eighteenth centuries, and even at that time there was still plenty of open space (e.g. Friars' Orchard) within the town walls.

Another possible link with the Roman past is to be found at the church of St Mary de Lode. This may have been founded as a parish church for the minster lands of St Peter's; at any rate its parish seems to be the remainder of the parish of the Old Minster (Heighway 1980a). Excavations in 1978 and 1979 showed several churches pre-dating the Norman one: the earliest may originate in the fifth to eighth century. It was built on exactly the same alignment as the walls of an opulent Roman house. In the fifth century the site of the house was used as a burial chapel, which was also laid out on the Roman alignment (Bryant 1980).

In the eighth century, therefore, Roman Gloucester, in spite of the ruins which must have been visible, was no longer a reality. Nothing better demonstrates its end than the fact that the Roman street grid vanished almost entirely. The main north-south and east-west streets were retained, because the gates continued to be used, and the town was a through-way. There must always have been some traffic on these streets, or they would not have remained open, but the back streets were probably deserted. I cannot agree with Morris (1973, 227) that the 'three hundred *tributarii*' all lived in the town, since this figure surely included the town's territory as well.

More information is needed concerning the countryside in the later centuries of the Saxon period. Tangible evidence for Anglo-Saxon rural settlement comes from ecclesiastical sites in the form of architecture and sculpture, the bulk of the surviving material belonging to the period after 900. Michael Hare (pers. comm.) has recently com̧ ted the first stage of a survey of the Anglo-Saxon period. In fact, the survey has shown that the Taylors have listed nearly all the extant Anglo-Saxon churches in their gazetteer (Taylor 1975; Taylor 1978, appendix F). The only church not listed by the Taylors to which a firm Anglo-Saxon date can be attributed is St Peter's, Duntisbourne Abbots, where there are remains of long-and-short quoins at the west end. Detailed structural analysis, using the techniques described by Taylor, has already been carried out in Gloucestershire at Deerhurst (Rahtz 1976b; Taylor 1975, 193–211; Taylor 1977), and at St Oswald's, Gloucester (Heighway 1978 and 1980a), while a Saxon church has been excavated at Cirencester (Brown 1976). It is clear that many other Anglo-Saxon churches in the county would benefit from similar detailed study. For instance, no accurate plans or elevations have ever been published of Bibury, Coln Rogers, Daglingworth, or Duntisbourne Rouse, all well-known examples of Anglo-Saxon work.

Turning to Anglo-Saxon sculpture, the same survey has revealed that there is a considerable amount of unpublished or inadequately published sculpture in Gloucestershire. This is now being studied in more detail by Hare in conjunction with Richard Bryant, and they hope to publish the results as a gazetteer.

Other evidence for rural Saxon settlements might be expected from archaeology, yet there is only a single *Grubenhaus* (sunken floored hut) excavated at Bourton-on-the-Water (Dunning 1932), traces of Saxon settlement at Upton, in Blockley (Rahtz 1969 and 1976a), and the possible late Saxon hall at Tewkesbury (Hannan 1976). There may also have been a settlement at Eastington (Appendix 2), while an apparently ninth-century burial at Blockley (Birm-428: *Radiocarbon* 16, 299–300) and a possible sixth-century cemetery at Winchcombe (Saville forthcoming) indicate potential post-Roman settlements. Fowler (1977, 41–42) has already re-marked on the conspicuous lack of evidence from the sixth to the tenth century extracted from the work on the M5 motorway. As he comments, this may result from the fact that the motorway avoids existing settlements, where evidence for early Saxon settlement is most likely to be found. A survey of the archaeological potential of the larger of these settlements has recently been published (Leech 1981); yet even if the evidence has not been destroyed by subsequent intensive use of the sites, excavation is expensive and insufficient funds are available.

Other kinds of investigation may be more cost-effective; for instance, there is scope for detailed study of Anglo-Saxon charters. Grundy (1936 and 1937) has used these to plot the areas of Anglo-Saxon woodland (cf. Darby 1954, 30–31), and to map the trackways of the Saxon period (Grundy 1934a, 1934b and 1935). In the latter study the drawbacks are also clear. The coverage provided by the charters is uneven; for instance, the 'charter-less' space around Gloucester, where there must have been Saxon routeways in plenty, is all too apparent (Grundy 1934b, 250, pl.III). Hooke (1978) has also studied some of the charters and concluded that the Cotswolds, though predominantly woodland, were extensively cleared during the Saxon period, probably as the result of the increasing use of the land for sheep-pasture, especially on the major ecclesiastical estates. Finberg (1957, 13) has discussed the evidence for sheep-rearing and has shown that sheep-runs were a feature of the Cotswold economy as early as the eighth century. In the heyday of Offa of Mercia, that King's famous exports of woollen cloaks doubtless originated on the Cotswold sheep-runs. Apart from these great estates, agriculture presumably did not produce a surplus of the kind necessary to support large urban populations, though it is likely that it was at this period that the recovery of the towns was initiated.

The areas of Gloucestershire for which there is least evidence are, as several contributors to this volume have noted, the Forest of Dean and north-west Gloucestershire. Both historical and archaeological material are extremely sparse. Even the ecclesiastical material, which is found throughout most of Gloucestershire, is for these areas represented only by two pieces of sculpture from Newent (Kendrick 1938, plate 77; Zarnecki 1953). This is disappointing, since the area west of the Severn is likely, as suggested above, to have been Christianized very early as a result of Celtic influence. There was an eighth-century church at Tidenham and a seventh-century ecclesiastical establishment at Lancaut (Davies 1978). Recent examination of a stone from St Briavels shows it to be a Roman altar with what may be a debased fifth-century Christian inscription (currently on display in Gloucester Cathedral). By the time of Domesday Book, the Forest of Dean was still only sparsely populated (Darby 1954, 23).

## LATE SAXON GLOUCESTERSHIRE

After the reign of Offa, Mercian power waned and the kingdom came under the overlordship of Wessex. The English were constantly occupied with Danish invasions, but hostilities were concentrated to the east and in the Midlands; the Severn Valley remained unscathed. Danish ships were in the Bristol Channel in 845 but were driven off by the men of Somerset and Devon. In 874 the Danes, again from the east of the country, drove out King Burgred of Mercia and set up Ceolwulf as their 'puppet king'. However, the Danes reached Gloucestershire only in 877 when, worsted by King Alfred at Exeter, they harrassed western Mercia and appeared suddenly at Gloucester. Here they did not sack the town (this is a mis-reading of Ethelweard's Latin) but camped ('built booths') in the streets. This implies a fairly peaceful stay; at any rate their passing has left no trace. A single stirrup from near Gloucester is probably to be dated to a century or more later (Seaby and Woodfield 1980, 114, no. 24). Evidence of Danish occupation has not been found at Cirencester, where the Danes stayed before returning to East Anglia in 880 (Taylor 1893; Whitelock 1961).

By the tenth century, towns as we know them in the medieval period were emerging. It is probably not without significance that the principal town and *colonia* of Gloucester (McWhirr, this volume) became the shire town. Gloucester and Cirencester, even if nearly deserted, were not only 'central places' in 577, but were surely also the fortified centres described in charters of Offa, in which the requirement to contribute to the upkeep of fortresses constantly occurs (Stenton 1971, 289). Cirencester, with its governorship of the Seven Hundreds, must by the tenth century have been a substantial place, even though this is not yet apparent from its archaeology. There were also new, non-Roman centres. Bristol had a mint by 1050 and was occupied in the tenth century, according to finds of late Saxon buildings and pottery (Ponsford 1970); it may yet prove to have an equal importance with the shire-town of Gloucester, and to show the evidence of long-distance and continental trade which Gloucester almost certainly lacks. Also Bristol, like Cirencester, controlled a large area in the tenth century (Slater 1976, 82).

Both Gloucester and Winchcombe were shire-towns in the tenth century, and their administrative functions would have added to or created their mercantile significance. Winchcombe, with its late eighth-century minster, was a defended town which had been one of the chief royal centres of the sub-kingdom of the Hwicce. Its shire is supposed to have been created in the tenth or eleventh century (Finberg 1961, 228–235; Stenton 1971, 337), but the town was an important administrative centre long before that. The dismantlement of the shire under Æthelred II would have been a principal reason for the town's decline. The significance of Winchcombe always seems to have been administrative and ecclesiastical rather than commercial (Aldred and Hannan 1981; Bassett 1977).

Tewkesbury was a borough and market centre by 1086 (Moore 1982, f. 163b), although no archaeological or other evidence for its urban status in the late Saxon period has been found (Hannan 1981). Berkeley, an eighth-century minster and the centre of a large estate, had a market by 1086 (Moore 1982, f. 163a), as did Thornbury, now in north Avon (Moore 1982, f. 163d).

More is now known about tenth-century Gloucester. It had a royal palace which may have much earlier origins since the palace was placed on the site both of the first-century Roman fort and of a late Roman cemetery containing the mausoleum of a high-ranking person (Heighway 1980b; Hurst 1975). This may not be coincidence; it may represent the sort of administrative continuity from Roman times that has been shown to have occurred on the Continent (Böhner 1977). The royal palace at Gloucester has been partly excavated to reveal a hall-building similar to the tenth-century halls at Cheddar (Hurst 1975), but there is no dating evidence.

Gloucester not only claimed a royal palace, but may have had special significance for Mercian royalty in the late ninth and early tenth centuries. Although the Mercian rulers were now subject to Wessex, Earl Æthelred governed Mercia with some independence. His wife Æthelflaed was King Alfred's daughter and eldest child. Æthelred was older than his wife, perhaps considerably older, and in ill-health, thus from about 902, Æthelflaed governed alone. It was she who founded the New Minster of St Oswald and she who, it is thought, laid out the street plan of Gloucester based on similar military centres planned by Alfred in Wessex (Biddle and Hill 1971; Hurst 1972, 66–68; Wainwright 1975). Gloucester was well-placed as a principal city; it was well behind the 'front line' of the Danish wars, yet not too far from all parts of Mercia, and it still had a surviving Roman defence which could be utilized. It had a mint of Alfred, a royal palace, and a venerated Old Minster, St Peter's Abbey. To all this Æthelflaed introduced a new religious centre, the New Minster of St Oswald. This church was built partly of Roman stone quarried from the old town. It had a western apse in Carolingian style, and a wealth of sculpture the equal of anything in Britain. Most significant of all, it was provided with sacred relics, those of Æthelflaed's ancestor, St Oswald of Northumbria. The bones of the Saint were brought from Bardney, Lincolnshire, which in 909 was still Danish territory. The translation took place after a great raid by Æthelflaed's brother, Edward of Wessex. It seems a very special effort was made to ensure that the New Minster had fitting relics. The significance of Gloucester was finally demonstrated at the death of Æthelred and later of his wife, when both were buried in Gloucester, even though Æthelflaed died at Tamworth, many scores of miles away, and the traditional capital of Mercia in earlier times (Heighway 1978 and 1980a). A burial vault 8·5m square, added at the east end of St Oswald's church in the early tenth century, could represent the mausoleum of Æthelflaed and her husband.

Excavations in the centre of Gloucester show ninth-century buildings of wattle, cattle byres, manure heaps, and piles of domestic rubbish. Cloth was being made both on the old warp-weighted and the new horizontal looms. Leather objects, mostly shoes, were being manufactured. Furniture and utensils were all skilfully made of wood. What little pottery was used was brought in from elsewhere, although by the tenth century a potter was working in the town centre. Animals were stabled in the town, and the fodder brought in for them showed the remains of spelt, an old-fashioned strain of wheat which had not been used for centuries in other parts of the country. There was no sign in the eighth to tenth centuries of the quantities of pottery imported from the Continent to other ports such as Southampton. Gloucester was something of a backwater, a mixture of agricultural and manufacturing activities (Heighway et al. 1979), yet its activities were sufficiently diverse and profitable to support a town which, as has been shown, was of considerable significance for the rulers of Mercia at the beginning of the tenth century.

Some idea of the economy of the county in the tenth and eleventh centuries is provided by Domesday Book. By the late eleventh century there were 363 settlements in Gloucestershire (Darby 1954, 6), most of which are still in existence, and the map of these provides the most reasonable picture of the density of population at the time of the survey. By then much of the woodland had been cleared, although there appears to have been a broad belt of woodland along the edge of the Cotswolds from near Winchcombe in the north to Minchinhampton in the south. The Forest of Dean was probably densely wooded, despite omission of this woodland from Domesday Book (Darby 1954, 29–30). Most of the population would, of course, have been engaged in agriculture, but the contribution of other industries should not be forgotten. There were extensive fisheries on the Severn, and economic links with the salt manufacturers at Droitwich (Darby 1954, 37–38). There were large numbers of mills along the eastern valleys of the Cotswolds: some villages had three or more, and the Stroud valley had most of all. As far as can be ascertained, all the mills were for grinding corn, although Taylor (1889, 108) admits the possibility that some of the mills were forge-mills. Iron-working, after all, was an important industry. Although iron seems to have played little part in the economy of, for example, ninth-century Gloucester (Heighway *et al.* 1979, 204), by 1086 the town's render included 'thirty-six dickers of iron, and one hundred drawn iron rods for nails for the King's ships' (Moore 1982, f.162a). In addition, one of the Gloucester burgages, owned by the manor of Woodchester, paid as rent 'twenty nails' (ferra) (Moore 1982, f.170c). There was iron-working at Pucklechurch (Moore 1982, f. 165b), and surely also in the Forest of Dean where the iron is found and where mining and smelting must have taken place. Nevertheless, Gloucester seems to have been the most extensive manufacturer of iron artefacts, as indeed it remained for centuries to come.

A number of people in Gloucestershire would have been engaged in quarrying. It is quite clear that not all buildings were put together from Roman ruins, and the local oolite stone was a source for the many churches that were built in the late Saxon period. Some urban Roman buildings were, it is true, re-used for their stone (Heighway 1978, 108), but this type of source would have been quite insufficient for the many churches far from any such convenient supply of building material.

Another industry was the manufacture of pottery. The Severn Valley, having been almost aceramic, acquired a few potteries in the tenth century. Their number was almost trebled in the eleventh century and their output also increased (Vince 1981). At Gloucester there was a tenth-century pottery within the town (Vince 1979); in the eleventh century the industries were rurally based. Presumably the availability of fuel, raw materials, and space had become more important than proximity to the local market.

The rise of the few towns as administrative centres and markets could be said to be the theme of the eleventh century. Although the seeds of urban renewal were sown earlier, at any rate in the case of Gloucester, and in the case of Winchcombe even before then, the development of the towns as dominant centres is apparently an eleventh-century phenomenon; one which is marked by the separate inclusion, at the very head of Domesday Book, of the boroughs of Gloucester and Winchcombe.

## ACKNOWLEDGEMENTS

I am most grateful to all those who have helped with this paper: Michael Hare, for allowing me to quote from his survey of Anglo-Saxon churches, and for his other helpful comments; Dr. David Hill who made many constructive criticisms; and Cherry Goudge and Caroline Ireland for information about the pottery.

## APPENDIX 1: GRASS-TEMPERED POTTERY

*Alan G. Vince*

Pottery dating between the fifth and the eighth century has been found at fourteen sites in Gloucestershire. With the exception of two out of four urns from a cemetery at Burn Ground, Hampnett (Grimes 1960, B and D), the main tempering material is chaff. Despite the blandness of the fabric, sufficient differences exist in the character of the clay matrices to enable basic clay sources to be separated. For example, the presence or absence of fine quartz silt, white mica, and the identity of large solid inclusions can at least demonstrate that the pottery from Andoversford, St Oswald's Priory at Gloucester, and Frocester Court were made from different clay sources. However, there is little possibility of using petrological methods to show that wares from different sites come from the same source. Two of the Burn Ground, Hampnett, urns, on the other hand, contain in addition to some chaff temper, a quartz sand. Rare elements in this sand are fragments of a coarse-grained sandstone. Similar sandstone fragments are present in thin-sections of Saxon pottery from Hatton Rock, Warwickshire, Maidens Bower, Solihull, and Signet Field, Kidderminster. It would seem likely, therefore, that the two Burn Ground urns were made somewhere to the north of Hampnett. (Local sands contain mainly calcareous material derived from the Cotswolds.) Little new evidence for the dating or cultural associations of chaff-tempered pottery in the West of England has come to light since Fowler's summary in 1970. The most important new find is of three sherds of chaff-tempered pottery from Wycomb, Andoversford, two of which have typological features typical of pagan Saxon pottery (a footring, a feature also found at Bourton, together with a small lug, and the rim of a crudely-made cup or bowl). These sherds come from the lower filling of a ditch associated with unabraded late Roman pottery (Rawes 1980, 40). This is, however, not conclusive evidence that the wares are contemporary.

*A list of findspots of 'Dark Age' pottery in Gloucestershire*

Andoversford, Wycomb (Rawes 1980, 39, no. 119)
Bourton-on-the-Water (Dunning 1932)
Cirencester (Brown 1976)
Cirencester, amphitheatre (unpublished)
Cirencester, Grove Lane ring road (unpublished; J. Keely pers. comm.)
Dumbleton (P. Whitehead pers. comm.)
Eastington (Travell and Fowler 1971, 61)
Ewen (Reece 1974, 133)
Frocester Court, Roman villa (Fowler 1970)
Frocester, St Peter's Church (Dunning 1963)
Gloucester, excavations 1968–1973 (unpublished)
Gloucester, St Oswald's Priory (Vince 1982)
Lechlade (in Stroud Museum, unpublished; C. Ireland pers. comm.)

Upton (Rahtz 1969)
West Hill, Uley (unpublished)

*Findspots of decorated Saxon pottery in Gloucestershire*
Cirencester (Brown 1976)
Burn Ground, Hampnett (Grimes 1960)


APPENDIX 2: POSSIBLE SAXON OBJECTS FROM EASTINGTON, NEAR STROUD

*Caroline Ireland*

During the construction of the M5 motorway several sherds of chaff-tempered pottery were recovered from an area north of the Claypits in the parish of Eastington (*c*.SO 773060). It was noted that the sherds were found beneath a bank left from *c*.1920 gravel-workings (Travell and Fowler 1971). This very minimal evidence suggested the possibility of a post-Roman site in the area, although the general date range for this type of ware would place this anywhere between the fifth to eighth century (Fowler 1970).

The area given over to gravel-extraction during the 1920s and 1930s, centred on SO 771065, produced a large quantity of archaeological material, including Roman pottery and finds, several burials, and numerous settlement features typical of gravel terraces, but for which plans are unlikely to have been made in any detail. Observation of this area was carried out by C. Gardiner, who published some of the finds which are now in Stroud Museum (Gardiner 1932).

Included amongst the Roman artefacts was a bone pin-beater and a pair of ribs from a composite bone comb decorated with ring and dot (Fig. 2, 2–3; Gardiner 1932, plate 23b). While similar objects can be found on Roman sites, attention should be drawn to the many Saxon settlement sites where the pin-beater and comb are a common find, attesting to the importance of wool-production in the Anglo-Saxon economy. From Gardiner's notes and from the published descriptions, it is impossible to discover whether these items were associated with any particular feature. It would seem that the bulk of objects were collected over a period of time and that recording only encompassed the interesting group burial, and a general inventory of artefacts. It may be that the suggested post-Roman settlement lay in this area amongst the various ditches and pits uncovered by the gravel-workings.

A further item, also connected with weaving, is an annular loomweight of baked clay tempered with small limestone fragments (Fig. 2,1), consistent with the type current in the early to middle Saxon period (cf. Dunning 1932, plate 55). Its exact findspot is unknown, but it too may have come from this area, since almost all the finds deposited in Stroud Museum during this period from Eastington are likely to have been found as a result of the gravel-working.

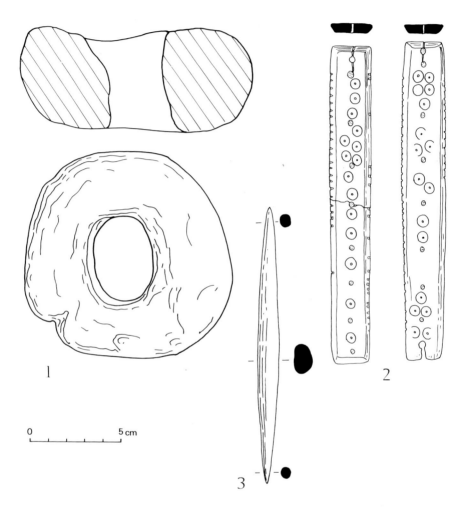

0 |___|___|___|___|___| 5 cm

*Figure 2*   Possible Saxon objects from Eastington, near Stroud.
1.   Annular baked clay loomweight of reddish sandy clay with limestone inclusions. The accession register simply notes 'from Eastington' (Stroud Museum 2798).
2.   Two bone strengthening ribs from a composite bone comb. The difference in spacing of the rivets and the dissimilar patterns may suggest two combs (Stroud Museum 2069).
3.   Bone pin-beater, length 145mm. The surfaces are smooth and polished (Stroud Museum 2069).
(Drawn by Caroline Ireland.)

It must be stressed that the association of these objects with each other and with the pottery found on the M5 site is purely hypothetical, and is in no way conclusive evidence for a settlement of Saxon date, although if the objects are of Saxon origin, there is good reason to suppose that any settlement features that may have been present were destroyed by gravel-extraction. Such evidence only serves to emphasize the paucity of information which survives about this multi-period site, which, to judge by the arbitrary finds that were recovered, would have richly repaid excavation.

*Acknowledgement*

I am very grateful to Lionel Walrond, curator of Stroud Museum, for allowing me to publish the items in this note.

REFERENCES

Aldred, D.H. and Hannan, A. 1981. Winchcombe. In R. Leech, *Historic towns in Gloucestershire: archaeology and planning*, 96–101. Bristol. (=CRAAGS Survey No. 3.)

Atkinson, D. 1957. The Cirencester word-square. *TBGAS* 76, 21–34.

Barker, P.A. 1975. Excavations on the site of the Baths Basilica at Wroxeter 1966–1974: an interim report. *Britannia* 6, 106–117.

Bassett, S. 1977. *The origins and development of Winchcombe and its district.* Unpublished MA thesis, University of Birmingham.

Biddle, M. and Hill, D.H. 1971. Late Saxon planned towns. *Antiq J* 51, 70–85.

Biek, L. 1979. A note on preservation. In C.M. Heighway *et al.*, Excavations at 1 Westgate Street, Gloucester. *Medieval Archaeol* 13, 205–210.

Böhner, K. 1977. Urban and rural settlement in the Frankish Kingdom. In M.W. Barley (ed.), *European Towns: their archaeology and early history*, 185–201. London.

Branigan, K. 1972. The end of Roman West. *TBGAS* 91, 117–128.

Brown, D. 1976. Archaeological evidence for the Anglo-Saxon period. In A. McWhirr (ed.), *Studies in the archaeology and history of Cirencester*, 19–45. Oxford. (=BAR Brit Ser 30.)

Brown, K. 1970. Note on Bishop's Cleeve Anglo-Saxon cemetery. In D.M. Wilson and J.G. Hurst (eds.), Medieval Britain in 1969. *Medieval Archaeol* 14, 156.

Bryant, R.M. 1980. Excavations at St Mary de Lode church, Gloucester, 1978–1979. *Glevensis* 14, 4–12.

Darby, H.C. 1954. Gloucestershire. In H.C. Darby and I.B. Terrett (eds.), *The Domesday geography of midland England*, 1–56. Cambridge.

Davies, W. 1978. *An early Welsh microcosm: studies in the Llandaff charters*. London.

Dunning, G.C. 1932. Bronze age settlements and a Saxon hut near Bourton-on-the-

Water, Gloucestershire. *Antiq J* 12, 279–293.

Dunning, G.C. 1963. Medieval pottery and finds. In H.S. Gracie, St Peter's Church, Frocester. *TBGAS* 82, 162–166.

Ellison, A. 1980. Natives, Romans and Christians on West Hill, Uley: an interim report on the excavation of a ritual complex of the first millennium AD. In W.J. Rodwell (ed.), *Temples, churches and religion: recent research in Roman Britain*, 305–328. Oxford. (=BAR Brit Ser 77.)

Finberg, H.P.R. 1955. Roman and Saxon Withington: a study in continuity. Leicester. (=Leicester University College Department of English Local History, Occasional Paper No. 8.)

Finberg, H.P.R. 1957. Some early Gloucestershire estates. In H.P.R. Finberg (ed.), *Gloucestershire studies*, 1–16. Leicester.

Finberg, H.P.R. 1961. *The early charters of the West Midlands*. Leicester.

Fowler, P.J. 1970. Note on some coarse potsherds from the Roman villa. In H.S. Gracie, Frocester Court Roman villa, Gloucestershire: first report 1961–1967. *TBGAS* 90, 50–52.

Fowler, P.J. 1977. Archaeology and the M5 motorway, Gloucestershire, 1969–1975: a summary and assessment. *TBGAS* 95, 40–46.

Frend, W.H.C. 1979. Ecclesia Britannica: prelude or dead end? *J Eccles Hist* 30, 129–144.

Gardiner, C.I. 1932. Recent discoveries in the Stroud valley. *PCNFC* 24, 163–180.

Gelling, M. 1978. *Signposts to the past: place-names and the history of England*. London.

Gracie, H.S. 1963. St Peter's Church, Frocester. *TBGAS* 82, 148–167.

Gracie, H.S. 1970. Frocester Court Roman villa, Gloucestershire: first report 1961–1967. *TBGAS* 90, 15–86.

Gracie, H.S. and Price, E.G. 1979. Frocester Court Roman villa, second report 1968–1977: the courtyard. *TBGAS* 97, 9–64.

Grimes, W.F. 1960. *Excavations on defence sites 1939–1945, 1: mainly neolithic-bronze age*. London. (=Ministry of Works Archaeological Reports No. 3.)

Grundy, G.B. 1934a. Ancient highways and trackways of Worcestershire and the middle Severn, part 1. *Archaeol J* 91, 66–96.

Grundy, G.B. 1934b. Ancient highways and trackways of Worcestershire and the middle Severn, part 2. *Archaeol J* 91, 241–268.

Grundy, G.B. 1935. Ancient highways and trackways of Worcestershire and the middle Severn, part 3. *Archaeol J* 92, 98–141.

Grundy, G.B. 1936. The ancient woodland of Gloucestershire. *TBGAS* 58, 65–155.

Grundy, G.B. 1937. The ancient woodland of Gloucestershire: additional notes. *TBGAS* 59, 205–209.

Hannan, A. 1976. Holm Castle, Tewkesbury. *Glevensis* 10, 10–11.

Hannan, A. 1981. Tewkesbury. In R. Leech, *Historic towns in Gloucestershire: archaeology and planning*, 90–95. Bristol. (=CRAAGS Survey No. 3.)

Hawkes, S.C. 1974. Some recent finds of late Roman buckles. *Britannia* 5, 386–393.

Hawkes, S.C. and Dunning, G.C. 1961. Soldiers and settlers in Britain, fourth to fifth century, with a catalogue of animal-ornamented buckles and related belt-fittings in Britain. *Medieval Archaeol* 5, 1–70.

Heighway, C.M. 1978. Excavations at Gloucester, fourth interim report: St Oswald's Priory, Gloucester 1975–1976. *Antiq J* 58, 103–132.

Heighway, C.M. 1980a. Excavations at Gloucester 1977–1978, fifth interim report: St Oswald's Priory. *Antiq J* 60, 207–226.

Heighway, C.M. 1980b. The cemeteries of Roman Gloucester. *TBGAS* 98, 57–72.

Heighway, C.M. and Garrod, A.P. 1980. Excavations at nos. 1 and 30 Westgate Street, Gloucester. *Britannia* 11, 73–114.

Heighway, C.M., Garrod, A.P., and Vince, A.G. 1979. Excavations at 1 Westgate Street, Gloucester. *Medieval Archaeol* 23, 159–213.

Heighway, C.M. *et al.* 1983. *The East and North Gates of Gloucester and associated sites: excavations 1974–1981*. Bristol. (=Western Archaeological Trust Excavation Report No. 4.)

Hills, C. 1978. The archaeology of Anglo-Saxon England in the pagan period. In P. Clemoes (ed.), *Anglo-Saxon England*, 8, 297 ff.

Hooke, D. 1978. Early Cotswold woodland. *J Hist Geogr* 4, 333–341.

Hurst, H. 1972. Excavations at Gloucester 1968–1971: first interim report. *Antiq J* 52, 24–69.

Hurst, H. 1975. Excavations at Gloucester, third interim report: Kingsholm 1966–1975. *Antiq J* 55, 267–294.

Hurst, H. 1976. Gloucester (Glevum): a colonia in the West Country. In K. Branigan and P.J. Fowler (eds.), *The Roman West Country: classical culture and celtic society*, 63–80. Newton Abbot.

Kendrick, T.D. 1938. *Anglo-Saxon art to AD 900*. London.

Leech, R. 1981. *Historic towns in Gloucestershire: archaeology and planning*. Bristol. (=CRAAGS Survey No. 3.)

Levison, W. 1946. *England and the Continent in the eighth century*. Oxford.

Meaney, A. 1964. *A gazetteer of early Anglo-Saxon burial sites*. London.

Moore, J.S. (ed. and trans.) 1982. *Domesday Book: 15: Gloucestershire*. Chichester.

Morris, J.R. 1973. *The age of Arthur: a history of the British Isles from 350 to 650*. London.

Morris, J.R. (ed.). 1978. *Gildas; 'The ruin of Britain' and other works*. London and Chichester.

Morris, R. and Roxan, J. 1980. Churches on Roman Buildings. In W.J. Rodwell (ed.), *Temples, churches and religion: recent research in Roman Britain*, 175–209. Oxford. (=BAR Brit Ser 77.)

Plummer, C. 1896. *Venerabilis Baedae opera historica*. Oxford.

Ponsford, M.W. 1970. Note on finds at Bristol. In D.M. Wilson and J.G. Hurst (eds.), Medieval Britain in 1969. *Medieval Archaeol* 14, 156.

Pretty, K. 1975. *The Welsh Border and the Severn and Avon Valleys in the fifth and sixth centuries AD: an archaeological survey*. Unpublished PhD thesis, University of Cambridge.

Rahtz, P.A. 1969. Upton, Gloucestershire, 1964–1968: second report. *TBGAS* 88, 74–126.

Rahtz, P.A. 1976a. Gazetteer of Anglo-Saxon domestic settlement sites. In D.M. Wilson (ed.), *The Archaeology of Anglo-Saxon England*, 405–452. London.

Rahtz, P.A. 1976b. *Excavations at St Mary's Church, Deerhurst, 1971–1973*. London. (=CBA Res Rep 15.)

Rawes, B. 1980. The Romano-British site at Wycomb, Andoversford, excavations 1969–1970. *TBGAS* 98, 11–55.

RCHM 1976. *Iron age and Romano-British monuments in the Gloucestershire Cotswolds*. London.

Reece, R. 1974. Early medieval quarries at Ewen, 1971–1972. *TBGAS* 93, 131–135.

Richmond, I.A. 1959. The Roman villa at Chedworth, 1958–59. *TBGAS* 78, 5–23.

Rodwell, W.J. and K.A. 1973. Excavations at Rivenhall church, Essex: an interim report. *Antiq J* 53, 219–231.

Saville, A. Forthcoming. Salvage recording of Roman, Saxon, medieval and post-medieval remains at North Street, Winchcombe.

Seaby, W.A. and Woodfield, P. 1980. Viking stirrups from England and their background. *Medieval Archaeol* 24, 87–122.

Slater, T. 1976. The town and its region in the Anglo-Saxon and medieval periods. In A. McWhirr (ed.), *Studies in the archaeology and history of Cirencester*, 81–108. Oxford. (=BAR Brit Ser 30.)

Stenton, F.M. 1971. *Anglo-Saxon England* (third edn). Oxford.

Taylor, C.S. 1889. *An analysis of the Domesday survey of Gloucestershire*. Bristol.

Taylor, C.S. 1891. Early Christianity in Gloucestershire. *TBGAS* 15, 120–138.

Taylor, C.S. 1893. The Danes in Gloucestershire. *TBGAS* 17, 68–95.

Taylor, C.S. 1957. The origin of the Mercian shires. In H.P.R. Finberg (ed.), *Gloucestershire Studies*, 17–51. Leicester.

Taylor, H.M. 1977. *Deerhurst studies, 1: the Anglo-Saxon fabric, 1971–1976*. (Privately printed.)

Taylor, H.M. 1978. *Anglo-Saxon architecture, vol. III*. Cambridge.

Taylor, H.M. and J. 1975. *Anglo-Saxon architecture, vols. I-II*. Cambridge.

Travell, M. and Fowler, P.J. 1971. Eastington, Site 1. In P.J. Fowler and C.V. Walthew (eds.), Archaeology and the M5 motorway, first report. *TBGAS* 90, 61.

Vince, A.G. 1979. The pottery. In C.M. Heighway *et al.*, Excavations at 1 Westgate Street, Gloucester, 1975. *Medieval Archaeol* 23, 170–181.

Vince, A.G. 1981. The medieval pottery industry in southern England: tenth to thirteenth centuries. In H. Howard and E.L. Morris (eds.), *Production and distribution: a ceramic viewpoint*, 309–322. Oxford. (=BAR Int Ser 120.)

Vince, A.G. 1982. Grass-tempered pottery. In C.M. Heighway and A. Parker, The Roman tilery at St Oswald's Priory, Gloucester. *Britannia* 13, 122–123.

Wacher, J. 1976. Late Roman developments. In A. McWhirr (ed.), *Studies in the archaeology and history of Cirencester*, 15–17. Oxford. (=BAR Brit Ser 30.)

Wainwright, F.T. 1975. Æthelflaed, Lady of the Mercians. In H.P.R. Finberg (ed.), *Scandinavian England*, 305–324. Chichester.

Wheeler, R.E.M. and T.V. 1932. *Report on the excavation of the prehistoric, Roman, and post-Roman site in Lydney Park, Gloucestershire*. London. (=Soc Antiq Res Rep 9.)

Whitelock, D. (ed.). 1961. *The Anglo-Saxon chronicle: a revised translation*. London.

Wilson, M. 1969. The Hwicce. *Trans Worcestershire Archaeol Soc* 2, 20–25.

Zarnecki, G. 1953. The Newent funerary tablet. *TBGAS* 72, 49–55.

**January 1984**

# Late Saxon and Medieval Pottery in Gloucestershire

## Alan G. Vince

### INTRODUCTION

There are over one hundred separate findspots of Saxon and medieval pottery in Gloucestershire (Fig. 1 and Appendix 2). Most are from sites along the Cotswold ridge and there are very few from any sites west of the Severn or on the eastern border of the county, on the dip-slope of the Cotswolds. Few collections consist of more than thirty sherds and even fewer are stratified; there are fewer than ten stratified, published collections in the county. Despite this lack of published data, a reliable relative chronology for most pottery types can be provided by excavations in Gloucester, where over a dozen major Saxon or medieval sites have been excavated. The results of these, and of numerous minor excavations, enable the sequence of fabrics and forms to be established with some precision.

Both the fabrics and the forms found in Saxon and medieval pottery varied considerably within the county, and even at the possible royal palace of Kingsholm (Hurst 1975), only a mile from the centre of Gloucester, different types of medieval pot are found. Luckily, however, there are similar intensively investigated cities to the south, west, and north of the county at Bristol (Ponsford 1980), Hereford (Vince forthcoming a), and Worcester (Morris 1980). Only in the east of the county is there any difficulty in providing a master chronology, and there are collections of medieval pottery from Cirencester whose publication should fill this gap (Ireland forthcoming; Vince 1982a).

The range of sites from which pottery has been recovered is quite narrow. Castles have been investigated at Upper Slaughter (O'Neil 1962–63), Lydney (Casey 1931), St Briavels (unpublished) and Holm Castle, Tewkesbury (Hannan 1976), but none of these sites can compare with the major royal and magnate residences. The Holm Castle collection, however, does include both the highest proportion of jugs to cooking vessels in the county and jug types from sources not otherwise represented. Two abbeys have been excavated, at Cirencester (Brown 1976; Ireland forthcoming) and Hailes (Musty forthcoming), but medieval levels at the latter site were deliberately not investigated. The pottery from Cirencester Abbey does, however, include several interesting and unusual types. Surprisingly, no manor houses and only a few moated sites have been investigated, at King's Stanley (unpublished), Leckhampton (Clift 1933), Prestbury Manor (O'Neil 1956), and Prestbury, Noverton Lane (unpublished). The majority of the findspots are from field-scatters or deserted farm sites, such as those at Ewen (Reece 1974a), Painswick (Green 1935), or Tarlton (Baddeley 1910; Dunning 1949). Collections are known from four towns: Cirencester, Gloucester, Tewkesbury, and Winchcombe. Apart from the size of the pottery collections there is little to distinguish urban from rural. All these factors suggest that the rather bland picture of Gloucestershire pottery obtained elsewhere is a function of the sites investigated rather than the intellectual or technical impoverishment of local potters.

Post-medieval pottery from Gloucestershire is extremely interesting but shows less regional variation than medieval pottery. The material from the East and North Gates of Gloucester provides a rich and detailed framework which can be applied over most of the county (Vince 1983a). The only geographical variation is in the proportion of red earthenwares to be found. The present survey therefore stops where the Gloucester post-medieval sequence starts, in the mid-sixteenth century.

Detailed discussion of the dating of Saxon and medieval pottery in the county is not included here and it must be admitted that there is considerable room for chronological refinement and adjustment. Nevertheless, both the basic sequence and its approximate dating are secure and will enable the general pattern of development in pottery use and production to be revealed.

The final sections of this survey are a catalogue of the pottery types identified within the county, arranged by fabric characteristics and date (Appendix 1), and a gazetteer of findspots (Appendix 2).

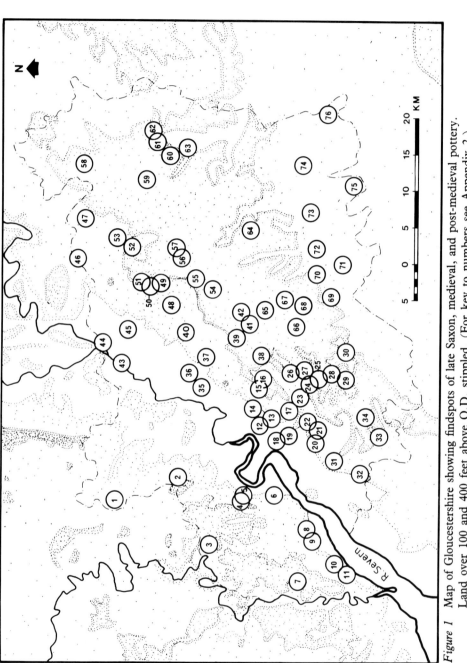

*Figure 1*  Map of Gloucestershire showing findspots of late Saxon, medieval, and post-medieval pottery. Land over 100 and 400 feet above O.D. stippled. (For key to numbers see Appendix 2.)

## POTTERY BEFORE THE TENTH CENTURY

Excavations in Gloucester and elsewhere in the county show that Romanized pottery industries survived into the early fifth century (Hassall and Rhodes 1974, horizon 14; Vince and Goudge 1980). Even the latest groups contain factory-made products from areas where fifth-century Germanic settlement can be demonstrated and there is thus little likelihood of any of these Romanized assemblages dating to as late as the sixth century (as has been suggested at Cadbury-Congresbury in Avon).

Handmade, low-fired, chaff-tempered pottery has been found associated with Roman pottery at Wycomb, near Andoversford, and at Barnsley Park villa pottery of this type was thought by the excavators to have been contemporary with the use of Romanized pottery, but occurred exclusively in excavations of the field system. This may indicate that Germanic settlers were living in huts situated at the edge of the fields.

Chaff-tempered pottery has been found at a surprising number of sites in Gloucestershire (Heighway this volume), and at two of these sites was definitely in a pagan Saxon context. At Burn Ground, Hampnett, Saxon cremation urns were inserted into a bronze age round barrow. At a site discovered by R. Reece on the line of the Cirencester ring road, a small occupation spread was found, including chaff-tempered and stamped sherds (the latter in a sandstone-tempered fabric, not chaff-tempered). Stamped vessels could date from the mid-Saxon period but are most likely evidence of sixth- or seventh-century Saxon occupation.

The remaining occurrences might be late fourth- to early fifth-century Germanic, fifth- to seventh-century pagan Saxon, or seventh- to ninth-century mid-Saxon, although there is no proof that any of the sherds are as late as the ninth century. A late ninth-century date is probable for chaff-tempered pottery from below the bank of the *burh* at Cricklade, just to the south of the Gloucestershire border, and an eighth- or ninth-century date is certain for a group of chaff-tempered sherds from Ramsbury, in the Wiltshire Vale of Pewsey (Haslam 1980).

Given this evidence that chaff-tempered pottery is widespread in the county and that some of it could be of mid-Saxon date, it is surprising that so little has been found in Gloucester, where the earliest Saxon occupation appears to be aceramic. At some sites in the city large pits or other traces of occupation have been found cutting through Roman levels and themselves cut by tenth-century or later features. All these sites lie along the main streets of the city and are tentatively dated by the author to the late ninth to early tenth centuries. Extensive excavations at St Oswald's Priory (Heighway 1978 and 1980), outside the Saxon *burh* at Gloucester, revealed the foundations of the early tenth-century church. Fragments of re-used cross-shaft testify to the presence of late ninth-century activity in the area as well and yet no sherds of pottery were found in the pre-church levels, except for two sherds of chaff-tempered pottery which may well pre-date the church by as much as four centuries (Vince 1982b).

This absence of pottery is a feature of the earliest Saxon occupation at Hereford, thought to extend from the eighth to the mid-tenth centuries (Victoria Street periods 1 to 5b and Berrington Street period 1 were all aceramic, Shoesmith 1982). However, the ceramic history of Herefordshire differs from Gloucestershire in that, as in Wales, no locally-produced pottery is known to date between the end of the Roman occupation and the twelfth century (Knight 1977). Pottery was similarly scarce or absent in Somerset until the middle of the tenth century (Rahtz 1974, 103–104).

## THE TENTH CENTURY

The pottery sequence in Gloucester starts in the late ninth or, more probably, early to mid-tenth century (Vince 1979). The earliest ware in regular use in the town was probably made within the walls, as shown by the discovery of a pit full of wasters from 1 Westgate Street in 1975. The central position of this pit, almost at the cross, shows that tenth-century Gloucester was quite different from its medieval successor. Urban industries which produced as much smoke, inconvenience, and fire-risk as pottery manufacture were invariably relegated to the suburbs or fringes of the town. Intra-mural pottery production of late Saxon date is known at Norwich and Thetford (both in a distinct potting quarter), at Chichester, and at Exeter. This Gloucester-made pottery, known as Gloucester TF41a (TF being short for the Gloucester City Excavation Unit Type Fabric), has only been found at five settlements outside of Gloucester: the possible royal palace at Kingsholm, an isolated pit or well on a gravel site at Frampton on Severn, and the *burhs* of Hereford, Winchcombe, and Worcester. Wares associated with Gloucester TF41a include a wheelthrown, red-firing ware, probably produced at Stafford, and previously known as 'Chester-type' ware because of the discovery of a late tenth-century hoard in a roller-stamped cooking pot of this ware found at Chester in 1950. Rare sherds of wheelthrown greyware of east midlands origin (so-called 'Thetford-type' wares) and two fossil-shell-tempered wares ('St Neots-type' ware and Oxford Fabric B) have also been found in association. Wheelthrown glazed wares from Stamford, the Winchester area, and an unidentified source ('Hereford-type' ware) appear to belong mainly to the very end of the tenth century and the early eleventh century.

It is quite clear from this list of tenth-century wares that pottery was being moved around the country over considerable distances, and there is no reason why it should be more common on urban sites than on rural ones. One would probably be able to recognize a tenth-century rural settlement by its pottery, and the almost complete absence of such sites is presumably a reflection of the difficulty of locating their presence archaeologically.

Both the size and number of rural settlements are likely to have been greater in the eleventh and twelfth centuries than before. Tenth-century settlements probably occupied the highest-quality farming land, underneath present-day villages, whereas the medieval farms and villages investigated archaeologically are in the main eleventh- to twelfth-century foundations.

## THE ELEVENTH CENTURY

At North Street, Winchcombe (Saville forthcoming) a small group of late Saxon pits was excavated. These probably date to the early eleventh century and are dated by the occurrence of Gloucester TF41a vessels and some of the late tenth- to early eleventh-century non-local wares. The most common, handmade, squat cooking pots are made in a limestone-tempered fabric (here termed Winchcombe-type ware). The earliest vessels appear to be straight-sided, club-rimmed pots of a type known from the work of Jope to be extremely common in the north Cotswolds (Jope and Threlfall 1959). There have been three previous excavations in Winchcombe (Aldred and Hannan 1981), none of which has produced evidence for earlier Saxon occupation.

Winchcombe-type cooking pots occur on numerous sites in the north Cotswolds, although no petrological comparison has yet taken place. There is no doubt that similar vessels were in use in the twelfth and early thirteenth centuries and it is not, therefore, possible to show whether any of the north Cotswold sites have pre-conquest occupation.

To the west of the Severn two sites outside the county, Chepstow and Hereford, show that pottery-making was not practised until the twelfth century. Pottery might have been in use in settlements in the Forest of Dean but would probably have been imported from the Vale of Gloucester, the source of the major eleventh- to twelfth-century ware used in Gloucester.

Gloucester TF41b is thought to have been produced at Haresfield, a small Domesday *vill* to the south of Gloucester. Three reasons for this attribution can be put forward. Firstly, potters are documented at Haresfield in Domesday Book, one of only three such records. This suggests that either they were recorded as a whim by the commissioner, or that pottery production made a significant contribution to the value of the *vill*. Secondly, late eleventh-century contexts at Gloucester, one of them coin-dated to the reign of William the Conqueror or later, consist almost wholly of vessels made in Gloucester TF41b. Thirdly, petrological analysis of this fabric indicates that the clay matrix was probably obtained from the Middle Lias and is highly micaceous and variable in colour. The tempering, however, is probably derived from the Great Oolite and consists of waterworn fragments. This description of the likely source agrees well with the geology of Haresfield. Furthermore, sampling of Quaternary, limestone-bearing sands from sites along the Severn Valley shows that such pure oolitic sands are not common, most having an admixture of rounded quartz derived from the north.

The distribution of Gloucester TF41b vessels confirms that the industry producing it was operating on a relatively large scale. Rare examples have been found east of the Cotswold scarp, but to the north (to Droitwich), to the west (to Hereford), and to the south (as far as Chepstow and Bristol and from there on to Dublin), the ware is found in much larger quantities. At Hereford, in particular, one late eleventh-century assemblage consists almost totally of Gloucester TF41b vessels.

The most common vessel type in Gloucester TF41b is the cooking pot. Spouted pitchers are also found, although most may be of twelfth-century date. One large fragment of a glazed tripod pitcher came from New Market Hall in Gloucester, and a few sherds of similar vessels are known.

At Frocester, where E. Price has systematically collected field scatters, Gloucester TF41b vessels are not the only potentially pre-conquest type present despite Frocester's proximity to Haresfield. The other wares represented also have handmade, limestone-tempered fabrics but have quartz sand inclusions as well. Other handmade cooking-pot wares are known from Wotton-under-Edge and at Hillesley, now in Avon. The Lower Severn Valley was therefore supplied by its own pottery industries, some of which may have started in the eleventh century.

Imports into the county are more rare in the late eleventh century than before, and the only definite examples are Stamford ware and handmade cooking pots from west Wiltshire (Bath Fabric A, which equals Gloucester TF48).

## THE TWELFTH CENTURY

In the Gloucester sequence the major differences between late eleventh- and early twelfth-century assemblages are the presence of Malvern Chase cooking pots, and occasional glazed tripod pitchers of Malvern Chase and Minety-type ware. In later twelfth-century groups the proportion of glazed wares increases, as does the proportion of Malvern Chase cooking pots. The only other new type is late twelfth-century Developed Stamford ware, which is much less common in Gloucester than the earlier glazed pitchers. Although Gloucester provides the only sequence in the county, several sites have produced twelfth-century groups. In the Forest of Dean these are dominated by Forest of Dean sandstone-tempered ware: at Awre (Dornier 1966), Littledean Camp (Scott-Garrett 1958), Lydney Castle (Casey 1931), and St Briavels Castle (unpublished excavations by P. Curnow). Littledean Camp also produced a Gloucester TF41b cooking pot, and Lydney produced a glazed pitcher probably made in the Ham Green area, to the west of Bristol.

In the Severn Vale the twelfth-century assemblages are more mixed – those to the north of Gloucester contain Worcester-type cooking pots as well as Malvern Chase and Gloucester TF41b vessels, for example Prestbury Manor (O'Neil 1956), Stoke Orchard (Spry 1971), and Winchcombe (Vince forthcoming b).

On the Gloucestershire Cotswolds there are few assemblages of any size, but the small groups which are found suggest that cooking pots in a limestone temper similar to Winchcombe-type ware and Gloucester TF41b were in use. The same is true of the west Oxfordshire region as reflected in the Ascott Doilly assemblage (Jope and Threlfall 1959) and the period III pottery at Upton (Rahtz 1969). At Cirencester in the twelfth century a different ware is found, Cirencester Fabric 202, with a wider range of forms, including rare open pots and glazed vessels (Vince 1982a). This evidence suggests that four or five potteries supplied the county with cooking pots, although only the Malvern Chase and Gloucester TF41b fabrics have been reliably characterized. Their distributions suggest that pottery was rarely traded beyond twenty miles from its source. Over and above this network of potteries supplying cooking vessels, three were also producing tripod pitchers: Malvern Chase, Minety, and the Bristol area (in a fabric similar to Ham Green ware – although from evidence at Chepstow it appears that this source only started production in the late twelfth century). These travelled much further, and both Minety-type and Malvern Chase pitchers are found on sites where the corresponding cooking pots are absent.

Not everything is as clear-cut as the analysis given above. There is at

Gloucester one distinctive locally-produced ware, TF43, which is only found
at Deerhurst (Rahtz 1976) and Gloucester, and is not very common at either
site. Nevertheless, the overall picture is of local production and distribution
with little long-distance trade.

## THE EARLY TO MID-THIRTEENTH CENTURY

At Gloucester all the twelfth-century wares continued to be used in the
thirteenth century, often with only slight typological differences. Gradually,
more and more wares from the Ham Green and Worcester kilns were used.
The Worcester-type jugs are very finely potted in comparison with local
twelfth-century glazed wares and Ham Green ware. In addition to wheelthrown, glazed, roller-stamped jugs (with white slip under the glaze at the
rim), this industry produced wheelthrown roller-stamped cooking pots and
slab-built rectangular or oval dripping dishes, all of them introductions to the
area. The Worcester potters were probably immigrants to this region, but so
far the parent industry is not known.

Alongside the eight common fabrics at Gloucester (from six different
centres), there are numerous wares represented by one or two vessels. Some
of these are recognizable as coming from the south, for example sherds of
scratch-marked cooking pots and coarse, sandy, tripod pitchers from south-
east Wiltshire. Other wares are at present unidentified. The overall picture is
of greatly increased pottery trade, and a proliferation of local wares.
Gradually, however, the number of local wares decreased, and it is suspected
that a number of local potteries disappeared during this century. Although
these were mainly producing cooking pots (e.g. Gloucester TF41b), glazed
ware types also declined. The Ham Green industry disappeared, to be
replaced by potteries in the suburbs of Bristol, as did the Worcester industry,
probably because of its proximity to that of Malvern Chase. It is possible to
point to numerous assemblages containing early thirteenth-century ceramics
because of the wide distribution of distinctive types, but there are no
associated early thirteenth-century groups from the county, excluding
Gloucester.

## THE LATE MEDIEVAL PERIOD

For later medieval groups the main problem is the absence of distinguishing
criteria by which to separate late thirteenth- from fourteenth- or even early
fifteenth-century pottery. This can be done at Gloucester only if large

contemporary assemblages are being compared, when the relative proportions of the different fabrics can be used to order the groups. Outside
Gloucester it is not possible to date any assemblage closely. This is
unfortunate since it is at this period that many sites were deserted and where
an accurate desertion date from pottery would amplify the documentary
evidence.

The two hundred years between *c*.1250 and *c*.1450 must have formed a
period of great stability for the pottery industry. At Gloucester, the major
fabrics are Malvern Chase and Minety-type ware, and these two wares are
common over much of the county. Exceptions to this pattern occur at sites in
the Forest of Dean, where fine, wheelmade wares, made from a silty,
red-firing, micaceous clay, are found instead; at sites in the north Cotswolds,
where a wheelthrown limestone-tempered ware (here termed 'North Cotswolds II') is found; and at sites in the Lower Severn Valley, where Bristol
Redcliffe products are common.

Glazed vessels from many sources were imported to the county from other
parts of England, principally Bristol, Herefordshire, Nuneaton, and the
Oxford area. Gloucester itself has produced vessels from further afield: a
single jug from south Wales (probably Glamorgan) and a few sherds of
Saintonge ware from south-west France, as well as a large number of
unidentified fabrics, many of which, by a process of elimination, must come
from the north and north-east. This large number of wares is partly due to
Gloucester's position on the River Severn; but also due to the large quantity
of late medieval pottery found in the town. In other words, these wares would
have formed a very small proportion of the pottery used in the town, and so
will not be represented in a small sample.

All the pottery used in Gloucestershire in the later middle ages was
wheelthrown and glazed, and most of the vessels used were jugs, although
glazed cooking pots were made at both Malvern Chase and Minety. There
appear to be significant regional variations in the use of ceramic cooking pots
in the late medieval period, perhaps because of the increased availability of
metal vessels. In some counties handmade pots identical to those of the
twelfth and thirteenth centuries were used. In others, as in Gloucestershire,
cooking pots of superior quality to their twelfth- and thirteenth-century
predecessors were used, while elsewhere ceramic cooking pots virtually
disappeared. This appears to be the case in some contexts at Gloucester, and
may be a reflection of the affluence of some Gloucester households in
comparison with their rural counterparts. Perhaps the most surprising aspect
of the late medieval pottery of the county is that none of it, at least in the Vale
and along the Cotswold escarpment, was being made in Gloucestershire,

despite the widespread availability of suitable clays and, in the Forest of Dean, timber for fuel.

The potting industry had obviously undergone a significant shift in structure in the thirteenth century. The industry had gravitated to a few areas, seemingly having few locational factors in common, with the exception of the local availability of clay, water, and timber. Some potteries were situated near major transport routes, for example Malvern Chase, and most were rural and on the edges of tracts of forest. In the West Country, Bristol stands out as the only urban-based industry, with potteries centred on the south bank of the Avon in the suburb of Redcliffe.

## THE LATE FIFTEENTH TO EARLY SIXTEENTH CENTURY

In Gloucester the main characteristics of late fifteenth- to early sixteenth-century assemblages are the presence of Malvern Chase wares and a decline in the quantity of Minety-type ware, together with the presence in small quantities of Surrey wares (Tudor Green ware and a coarser white ware) and imported wares, principally Raeren stoneware. There is much more variety in the forms found at this time, although the three main forms, bowls, jars (and cisterns), and jugs, dominate all the assemblages.

The Surrey wares present comprise thin-walled cups and jugs which were sometimes copied in Malvern Chase ware, but not in Minety-type ware. In the rest of the county the main features are that in the Forest of Dean the micaceous, silty wares were replaced by Malvern Chase wares, which were also more common in the Vale south of Gloucester than in the preceding period. On the Cotswolds around Cirencester, Minety-type ware was still abundant, and the distribution of Minety-type flanged bowls and cisterns shows how much more limited was the market for Minety-type ware during the Tudor period. No collections of this date are yet known from the north-west of the county, always an under-represented area. Pottery from Winchcombe shows that Malvern Chase wares were common in the Tudor period, but the abandonment of the Upton settlement robs us of any knowledge of such pottery in the north Cotswolds.

Tudor-period assemblages contain fewer fabrics than late medieval ones, partly because there were fewer production centres, but there are, for example, no Tudor Donyatt wares, nor Nuneaton wares from the county. On the other hand, the number and range of imported wares was much greater. First and foremost was Raeren stoneware, the earliest German stoneware to be found in the county, but also present were south-west French chafing dishes, white unglazed flasks (Hurst's Type 1: Hurst 1966), and tin-glazed wares from Spain and the south Netherlands.

These data would suggest that there were very few pottery-producing areas in southern England in the Tudor period, and that pottery trading was carried out over greater distances than in the preceding period. What is also clear is that there was a change in the marketing of some of these wares. The Tudor Green wares and Raeren stoneware occur with sufficient frequency to show that they were regularly traded for considerable distances overland.


## DISCUSSION

There were several major changes in pottery technology during the late Saxon and medieval periods. The earliest pottery used at Gloucester includes vessels thrown on the potter's wheel, and although glaze is not used on these pots, an early eleventh-century glazed ware was probably made in the region (Hereford-type ware). Daub fragments found at 1 Westgate Street, Gloucester, were probably part of a kiln superstructure (Vince 1979, 175).

Despite the probable use of a kiln, these early wares, and those of the later eleventh and twelfth centuries, were black-cored. This indicates a short-duration, low-temperature firing. Later twelfth- and thirteenth-century cooking pots usually have grey cores and grey or oxidized surfaces. Therefore the firing methods must have improved. From the thirteenth century onwards there is evidence of good control of firing since the colour and firing pattern of vessel types becomes standardized but varies from industry to industry, showing the personal preference of different groups of potters. Completely oxidized wares are typical of the late medieval period, and within this period there is a change in colour and hardness of Malvern Chase wares, which indicates a rise in firing temperature from $700 - 800°$ to $1000 - 1100°$ centigrade (as judged by comparison with a test series refired in standard conditions). The local use of the wheel disappeared with Gloucester TF41a and did not re-appear on locally-made ceramics until the early thirteenth century, with Worcester-type ware. The technique was not universally adopted until the end of the century. Glaze, too, fell out of use locally until the early twelfth century (with one or two rare exceptions in Gloucester TF41b).

These twelfth-century glazes were often immature and sparse. Ham Green and Worcester-type ware glazes were of better quality, while the use of colouring agents in glaze, either iron or copper, was a late medieval introduction. It has been shown that Minety-type glazes often contain a high tin content, although not sufficient to opacify the glaze (Jope in Dunning 1949, 31).

Turning from the pottery itself to its place of manufacture, it is now clear that much late Saxon pottery was produced commercially, and that its first appearance in Gloucestershire post-dates the foundation of the *burhs* of Alfred and Edward in the late ninth and early tenth centuries. The Gloucester industry was urban-based, but by the early eleventh century Winchcombe-type ware was being produced. We do not know the location of the production site(s) of this ware, but it is clearly related in style to Gloucester TF41b, which was probably rurally-produced at Haresfield. The location of production sites for these eleventh- to thirteenth-century cooking pot wares must be the next task for understanding the pottery industry. From the late eleventh to the sixteenth century there was a continuous decrease in the number of production sites in the area. Reasons for this nucleation may include an improvement in transport and, as we have seen, increased efficiency in production. On the other hand, the industries which fell by the wayside were often situated in good marketing locations, for example Bristol and Worcester. It appears that pottery-making was relegated to the less agriculturally productive areas, such as Malvern Chase and the Forest of Braydon (Minety-type ware).

To conclude, until the late thirteenth century most pottery used in Gloucestershire was probably made within the county, either at rural sites such as Haresfield, or in the suburbs of towns such as Gloucester, where Stevenson (1893, 159 and 171) records two references to potters in the west and north suburbs of the town during the early thirteenth century. Place-name evidence, although often capable of many interpretations, can form a starting-point for research, for example Crockmede at Brockworth (Smith 1964, 119) and Pottersbury at Wotton-under-Edge (Smith 1964, 261). Whilst the search for production sites, and hopefully the examination of such sites by survey and excavation, is logically the next step in this study, there is still much basic groundwork to be done. There are no large medieval pottery assemblages in either east Gloucestershire or west Oxfordshire, while our knowledge of the main part of this period in most areas of the county is based on unstratified or poorly stratified material.

## ACKNOWLEDGEMENTS

I would like to thank the staff at the various museums containing Gloucester-shire pottery who have allowed me to study material in their care. I am also extremely grateful to the numerous archaeologists, both professional and amateur, who have shown me material from their excavations or other fieldwork. In particular I wish to acknowledge my debt to Henry Hurst and Dr David Peacock, without whose help and encouragement I would never have started work on the pottery of Gloucestershire.

## APPENDIX 1: CATALOGUE OF POTTERY TYPES

In this catalogue wares are listed under their principal inclusions and, within this, are ordered as far as possible chronologically. In many cases the divisions between fabrics have been determined by thin-section, but not all wares are petrologically distinctive, and therefore some fabric groups may come from more than one source. These groups are noted. Full fabric descriptions, including hardness, Munsell colour, and size-range of inclusions can be found in the reports on Gloucester Eastgate (Vince 1983a), and North Street, Winchcombe (Vince forthcoming b). The description given here includes only those details needed to distinguish wares with the same inclusion types. Further documentation on the sites and findspots mentioned in this article can be found in the author's unpublished PhD thesis (1983b) together with a full bibliography (see also Vince 1977a, 293–295).

### 1.  Shell-tempered wares

Two sites have produced handmade black vessels tempered with coarse, probably fossil, shell fragments: Gloucester TF45 (Vince 1979) and Upton medieval village fabric Q (Rahtz 1969). Coarse shell-tempered wares are extremely rare in the west of England although shell-bearing clays occur in the Cotswolds, and later prehistoric pottery in the area was sometimes made in such a fabric. In view of the scarcity of this pottery and its presence in quantity at Oxford (Durham 1977; fabrics B, C and H) it is likely to have been imported to the area. No examples of fine wheelthrown shell-tempered wares, such as St Neots-type ware (Durham 1977; fabric R) and St Neots-type jugs, have been found in the county, although isolated finds have been recorded from Hereford (one cooking pot and two jug sherds), Saltford, Avon (jug sherds), and Worcester (cooking pots).

### 2.  Chalk- and flint-tempered wares

Gloucester TF47

Late Saxon. A black, handmade ware tempered with flint and chalk fragments in a fine-textured matrix. Four cooking-pot sherds are known, one is a complete profile (Vince 1979, fig. 7, 58). Three other sherds from Gloucester from medieval levels contain flint temper and quartz sand. They cannot so far be grouped with each other nor with any ware seen outside the county.

## Bath Fabric A (Gloucester TF48)

Late Saxon to 14th century. A variable ware containing flint, chert, chalk, or polished, rounded quartz grains in a matrix with a high quartz silt and moderate white mica content. Cooking pots are known from four sites in the county, including a complete profile from Gloucester in a late 11th-century context and fragments of several cooking pots from 11th-century quarries at Ewen (Reece 1974a). This ware is characteristic of pottery made in west Wiltshire using the Gault clay, for example Nash Hill, Lacock, cooking pots, and probably Crockerton medieval cooking pots. The ware produced by the Westbury potters recorded in Domesday Book should be of this type.

## East Wiltshire Flint-Tempered Ware

13th to late 14th or early 15th century. A distinctive ware tempered with rounded quartz sand, flint, and chalk fragments. One cooking-pot base comes from Cirencester. Distribution evidence suggests that this ware was produced in the Kennet Valley. A settlement known as Crockerstrope is recorded on the northern bounds of the Forest of Savernake from 1257 (Cardigan 1949). This community is almost certain to have been producing ware of this fabric since virtually no other fabric is found in local collections.

## 3. Limestone-tempered wares

Limestone tempering is extremely common in Gloucestershire pottery. Virtually all of the limestone is derived from the Cotswold ridge and contains ooliths, calcite, and fossils. Contrary to popular belief the limestone is usually not crushed rock but more or less rounded sand- and gravel-sized fragments. Such material occurs in the Quaternary gravel-deposits that flank the Cotswolds to the west in the Severn Valley and to the east on the dip-slope of the Cotswolds and the headwaters of the Thames. The clays themselves are weathered Jurassic clays, such as the Lower Lias or the Oxford Clay, or more recent deposits formed by reworking these clays.

## Gloucester TF41a

9th or 10th century to early 11th century. Three cooking-pot forms are found (i) handmade with an everted rim and a thickened neck, (ii) wheelthrown with a cylindrical rim slightly everted at the tip, (iii) wheelthrown with a lid-seated rim. None of the bases have a sharp carination. Probably in this fabric from 1 Westgate Street, Gloucester are (iv) straight-sided club-rimmed vessels probably of early 11th-century date. This fabric is found at Gloucester (several sites), Hereford (Vince forthcoming a; fabric D1), Winchcombe, and Worcester (Morris 1978; fabrics 46 and 48).

## Gloucester TF41b

11th to 13th century. All the vessels are handmade. They comprise cooking pots with

(i) everted rims, (ii) club rims, and (iii) flat-topped everted rims, all with curved walls and sagging bases. Spouted pitchers occur in a higher-fired version of this ware with a red external surface. Two glazed pitchers are known, both from Gloucester (Hassall and Rhodes 1974). This fabric is found in Droitwich, Fladbury, Hereford (fabric D2), Pershore, and Worcester, all in the county of Hereford and Worcester, Bristol (Mary Le Port Street), Chepstow, and Dublin (Christchurch Place). Within Gloucestershire there is great difficulty in identifying this ware because of the large number of limestone-tempered wares and the fact that in most surface collections the temper is leached out and the surfaces of the sherds abraded. Positive identifications have been made at Frocester, Littledean Camp, Stoke Orchard, Upton medieval village, and Winchcombe.

Winchcombe-type

11th to ?13th century. This ware contains fewer oolitic limestone fragments than Gloucester TF41b and more quartz. Superficially the wares are similar except that the inclusions in Gloucester TF41b are better sorted in grain size. The most common form is the straight-sided cooking pot (Jope and Threlfall 1959) with a clubbed rim. Other forms are thickened, everted-rimmed vessels with curved walls and, less frequently, unglazed pitchers, globular pitchers with cylindrical rims (one with stamping on the shoulder), and a lamp. No detailed thin-section comparisons have been made between the Winchcombe ware and other limestone-tempered wares on the Cotswolds (except those described here) and the limestone-tempered wares from Upton medieval village (fabrics A, G, and P) are visually very similar in fabrics and forms.

Cirencester-type

C.11th century to 13th century. Forms in this ware comprise globular handmade cooking pots, turntable finished, with rolled-out rims, large pans, 'bee-hive bases', glazed cooking pots and pitchers, a rectangular dish and a wheelthrown jug. A ?late 12th-century context at St Johns Hospital, Cirencester (Vince 1982a) produced cooking-pot sherds, two glazed pitcher sherds and one body sherd of a large pan or curfew. The presence of a wheelthrown vessel and a rectangular dish suggests that the ware was still being produced in the early 13th century. This ware forms the major constituent of assemblages associated with the construction of Cirencester Abbey (probably early 12th century) and quarry pits at Ewen (possibly 11th century).

Minety-type Ware (Gloucester TF44)

12th to 16th century. Since the publication of kiln waste from Minety by Musty in 1973, thin-section analysis has shown that wares in an identical fabric (here termed Minety-type ware because of the possibility of other Braydon Forest kilns) have a long ancestry and wide distribution in Gloucestershire, Wiltshire, and beyond. At Gloucester the stratification enabled a form sequence to be established starting in the 12th century and continuing up to the late 15th century. Finds from closer to Minety suggest that the ware was still produced (but not traded to Gloucester) in the early 16th century.

Early 12th century: tripod pitchers with a globular body, straight rim, D-sectioned tubular spout and two rod handles. Decoration of wide, thumbed strips and combing.

Later 12th century: tripod pitchers with flaring rims, complex plaited handles (made usually of three strips of clay) and O-sectioned tubular spouts. Decoration of triangular-sectioned applied strips over combed wavy lines. This form is present at Bristol Castle by *c*.1125 (Ponsford 1980).

Early 13th century: tripod pitchers as in the 12th century but with pulled spouts and strap handles. Some vessels at this time have thumbed bases instead of feet. 'Selsley Common' cooking pots – handmade with combed decoration and a glaze wash on the inside of the rim.

Late medieval: all vessels are wheelthrown. Small jugs, baluster jugs (rare), cooking pots (often mistaken for Selsley Common-type but always wheelthrown and usually not decorated), large cooking pots or storage jars, curfews (only seen at Cirencester Abbey), oval dishes, handled pans, ridge tiles, and finials.

Tudor: cistern lids, flanged bowls, jugs (see Musty 1973), and ridge tiles.

Lyveden Ware

14th century. One jug, from Holm Castle, Tewkesbury.

Carboniferous limestone-tempered Ware

12th century. One stamped lid and a cooking-pot sherd with an applied, thumbed strip, from Gloucester, TF56. This fabric is paralleled at Bristol and Chepstow in the 12th century but the forms are unknown there.

### 4.  *Quartz sand-tempered wares*

A useful division of the sandy wares found in Gloucestershire can be made on the basis of the iron content of the clay. Those with little or no iron appear white, very pale brown, or light grey, depending on firing. Those with a moderate iron content appear yellow, pink, or light brown, whilst those with a high iron content appear red, brown, or grey. A black colour, however, is independent of iron content and is caused solely by carbon from organic matter in the clay not being removed during firing.

*White Wares*

Stamford Wares (Gloucester TF51)

10th to 13th century. Only two sites in Gloucestershire have produced Stamford wares; Gloucester and Winchcombe. Both have produced cooking pots and glazed pitchers and the pitchers include examples typical of the full production period with glazes of Kilmurry types 1, 3, and 4 (Kilmurry 1980). Most sherds, however, come from late 11th-or 12th-century glazed pitchers.

Normandy Gritty Ware (Gloucester TF128)

12th to 13th century. The rim and handle of an unglazed pitcher were found in a 13th-century context at Gloucester.

Nuneaton Ware (Gloucester TF102)

Late 13th to 15th century. Sherds of green-glazed sand-tempered jugs with a fine white body have been found at Gloucester, Upton medieval village, and Winchcombe, in small quantities.

Saintonge Ware (Gloucester TF81)

Late 13th to 15th century. Sherds of green-glazed jugs have been found at Gloucester and Holm Castle, Tewkesbury, while polychrome ware is represented by a single sherd from Gloucester only.

Surrey White Wares (Gloucester TF65)

Lobed cups and jugs of 'Tudor Green' ware have been found at six sites in Gloucestershire: Cirencester Abbey, Ewen, Frocester Court Roman villa, Hailes Abbey, Winchcombe (1963 excavation), and various excavations in Gloucester. Only at Gloucester could the relative frequency of the ware be calculated and here the ware appears to be a small but regular part of late 15th- and early 16th-century assemblages. There are two fabrics present, distinguished by the presence or absence of rounded, red quartz grains and a pinkish tinge to the coarser fabric, but there is no proven difference in date. Both were probably products of the Farnborough Hill kilns or unfound kilns in the same area (Holling 1977).

Forest of Dean Sandstone-Tempered Wares (Gloucester TF49)

12th to 13th century. A handmade ware, tempered with coarse quartz and sandstone sand. The most common vessel form is the inturned-rimmed, cylindrical cooking pot, although handmade jugs have been found at Bledisloe Tump, Awre (Dornier 1966). The ware is virtually confined to the Forest of Dean and the lower Wye Valley, but a few vessels have been found in Gloucester and at sites in the Severn Valley on the eastern side of the river.

*Low Iron-Content Wares*

South-East Wiltshire Wares (Gloucester TF101 and TF109)

11th to 14th century. Pottery made in a fine, white-firing clay and tempered with a coarse quartz sand was being made around Salisbury from the late 11th century onwards. The cooking pots were usually fired black and are characteristically coarsely wiped on the outside ('scratch-marked'). Glazed tripod pitchers in the same fabric were also produced, probably from the beginning of the industry. During the 13th century these were replaced by finer, wheelthrown glazed wares, some of which, together with coarse cooking pots, were produced at Laverstock (Musty *et al.* 1969). These kilns were over forty miles from Gloucestershire and their products are rare. At present only the cooking pots and tripod pitchers have been recognized, at Gloucester.

### Ham Green Ware and Bristol Redcliffe Ware (Gloucester TF53 and TF92)

13th to 15th century. Glazed, handmade jugs from the Ham Green kilns and wheelthrown jugs from the Bristol kilns have been found on a number of sites in Gloucestershire, mainly in the Severn Valley but also on sites on the Cotswolds and in the Forest of Dean. There is a noticeable decline in the frequency of Bristol jugs compared to Ham Green jugs at Gloucester and this is probably true of all sites in the county.

### Gloucester TF99

Late 13th to early 15th century? This wheelthrown, white ware is very similar to Bristol Redcliffe ware but includes vessels with a very different typology, e.g. baluster jugs with rod handles. It has only been recognized at Gloucester and Hereford but is of minor numerical importance at both towns.

### Oxford Late Medieval Ware (Gloucester TF83)

Mid-13th to early 15th century. Wheelthrown jugs of this fabric, often decorated with rouletted strips, are common to the east of the Cotswold ridge but are rare in the Severn Valley, although examples have been found at the major towns of Gloucester, Hereford, and Worcester.

### Gloucester TF79

This is a sparsely-glazed, untempered, or sparsely sand-tempered ware found so far only in Gloucester in late medieval to Tudor contexts. Although it is uncommon a local source seems probable. If so, this would in fact be the only late medieval pottery made within the county. The distribution within Gloucester fluctuated from site to site, suggesting that the ware had a short life, possibly in the 15th century.

### Spanish Lustrewares (Hurst 1977)

A complete jug of Andalusian Lustreware was said to have been found at Moor Wood, Bagendon (Corinium Museum G93 A.140). This find may be a modern import. Three sherds from Valencian Lustreware vessels (Gloucester TF129) have been found at Gloucester. A base from a flanged bowl comes from a 15th-century pit group at New Market Hall, and the other two sherds were unstratified from the Quay Wall and St Mary's Street.

### South Netherlands 'Altar Vases' (Gloucester TF130)

Fragments of blue-painted tin-glazed vases, provisionally identified as south Netherlands 'Altar Vases', have been found at two sites in Gloucester (St Mary's Street and 13–17 Berkeley Street) and at Hailes Abbey. They should date from *c.*1500.

*High Iron-Content Wares*

Late Saxon Import

A wheelthrown, reduced, sandy cooking pot was the only vessel securely stratified in ?9th-century levels at 1 Westgate Street, Gloucester (Vince 1979, no. 68).

Malvern Chase Wares (Gloucester TF40 and TF52)

There is little to add to my 1977 paper on Malvern Chase wares regarding their date range and distribution in Gloucestershire (Vince 1977a). Kiln waste from the production of bulbous jugs of 14th-century type has, however, been found at Gilberts End, Hanley Swan, and an area of 16th- or 17th-century kilns has been located about half a mile to the north.

Worcester-type Wares (Gloucester TF90 and TF91)

Sand-tempered, handmade cooking pots, probably of Worcester origin, are found in 12th- and early 13th-century contexts in the Severn Valley north of Gloucester and at Upton medieval village, but are rare at Gloucester and are not found in other parts of the county. Wheelthrown jugs, also from Worcester, with characteristic roller-stamping have a wider distribution, especially in the Severn Valley, but these types, too, are absent from the Cotswolds, with the exception of Upton medieval village.

Herefordshire Fine Micaceous Wares (Gloucester TF54)

Micaceous, oxidized glazed-wares with few visible inclusions were made in various areas of the Welsh Marches, utilizing the Devonian 'Marl' (a micaceous, silty clay containing calcareous nodules) or boulder clays derived therefrom. Wheelthrown jugs with a copper-green glaze and, sometimes, applied decoration in white or red clays are found at Gloucester in late medieval contexts and are common on sites in the Forest of Dean. They are not found elsewhere in the county.

'Cistercian Wares' (Gloucester TF60)

Black-glazed cups in a red, often overfired, earthenware are first found in the county in the 16th century, probably at the time of, or before, the dissolution. Waste from the production of such cups has been found with saggars at Falfield, Avon (Bennett *et al.* 1974, 123), in the Severn Valley.

*5. Stonewares*

Raeren Stoneware (Gloucester TF68)

Drinking mugs in a grey- or brown-washed, saltglazed stoneware are found at Cirencester Abbey, Gloucester, and Hailes Abbey, and are all probably of mid-16th-century date.

Cologne Stoneware (Gloucester TF68)

Grey stoneware mugs with applied, moulded decoration have been found only at Gloucester. No examples of Siegburg or Langerwehe stoneware have yet been found in the county.

## APPENDIX 2: FINDSPOTS OF LATE SAXON, MEDIEVAL, AND POST-MEDIEVAL POTTERY IN GLOUCESTERSHIRE AS PLOTTED ON FIG. 1.

| Location | Parish | Date of pottery | Collection | Publication |
|---|---|---|---|---|
| 1. Haind Park Wood | Dymock | Early 17thC kiln site | GCM | — |
| 2. Newent Glasshouse, etc. | Newent | Late 17th – early 18thC kiln sites | GCM | Vince 1977b |
| 3. Warfield Farm | Ruardean | Late 16thC storage jar | Priv. coll. | — |
| 4. Littledean Camp | Littledean | 12thC | GCM | Scott-Garrett 1958 |
| 5. Littledean Road | Newnham | 17th – 18thC | GCM | — |
| 6. Bledisloe Tump | Awre | 12th – 14thC | GCM | Dornier 1966 |
| 7. St Briavels Castle | St Briavels | Late 12thC – post-med | DOE/Excavated by P. Curnoe | — |
| 8. Whitecross Manor | Lydney | 13thC – post-med | Excavated by R. Wilson | — |
| 9. (a) site unknown, probably town | Lydney | Late med – post-med | BM | — |
| (b) Lyndey Castle | Lydney | 12thC | BM; Lydney Park | Casey 1931 |
| 10. Brookend | Woolaston | 12thC | | Scott-Garrett 1958 |
| 11. Stroat Kiln | Tidenham | Early 17thC kiln site | GCM; NMW; Priv. coll. | — |
| 12. Parkend Lodge Farm | Moreton Valance | 17th/18thC Spanish olive jar | GCM | Hunter 1961 |
| 13. (a) Green Farm | Standish | 12th – 13thC | SM | Aston and Spry 1971 |
| (b) Manor Farm | Standish | 12th – 13thC | ? | Fowler et al. 1976, 50 |
| 14. (a) NW of Pool Farm | Haresfield | Med and post-med | GCM | Fowler and Green 1971 |
| (b) S of Summerhouse Farm | Haresfield | Med and post-med | GCM | — |
| 15. Harescombe | Harescombe | Med | GCM | — |
| 16. Edge | Painswick | Med | SM | — |
| 17. Brickyard | Stonehouse | Med | SM | — |
| 18. (a) Frampton on Severn | Frampton on Severn | Possible late Saxon | Excavated by A.P. Garrod | — |
| (b) Frampton Court | Frampton on Severn | 13thC | GCM | — |
| 19. Site 2 | Eastington | Post-med | — | Travell 1971 |
| 20. (a) Cam | Cam | Post-med | Priv. coll. | — |

| Site | Place | Period | Collection | Reference |
|---|---|---|---|---|
| (b) Cam House | Cam | Med | SM | — |
| (c) Waterend Farm | Cam | Med | BCM; SM | Bennett 1976a |
| 21. Coaley | Coaley | Med | GCM | — |
| 22. Various sites | Frocester | 11th/12thC to post-med | GCM; Priv. coll.; SM | Dunning 1963 |
| 23. Churchyard | King's Stanley | Med | SM | — |
| 24. (a) Light Pill | Stroud | Med | SM | — |
| (b) Selsley Common | King's Stanley | 13thC | SM | Dunning 1949 |
| 25. Roman villa | Woodchester | Med | SM | — |
| 26. Stroud | Stroud | Med | SM | — |
| 27. Spillmans Court | Rodborough | Med | SM | — |
| 28. Nailsworth | Nailsworth | Med | SM | — |
| 29. — | Nailsworth | Med | GCM | — |
| 30. Avening church | Avening | Med | CM | — |
| 31. (a) Clingre Farm | Stinchcombe | Med | BCM | Bennett 1976b |
| (b) — | Stinchcombe | Med | Priv. coll. | — |
| 32. Woodford | Alkington | Post-med | Priv. coll. | — |
| 33. Wotton-under-Edge | Wotton-under-Edge | Post-med | Priv. coll. | — |
| 34. Symonds Hall Farm | Wotton-under-Edge | Med | GCM | — |
| 35. City centre: various sites | Gloucester | Late Saxon – post-med | GCM | Vince 1983; etc. |
| 36. Longlevens | Gloucester | Med | GCM | — |
| 37. (a) Barnwood | Gloucester | Med | GCM | — |
| (b) Hucclecote villa | Gloucester | Med | GCM | — |
| 38. (a) Cockshoot Manor | Painswick | Med | GCM | — |
| (b) Upper Holcombe Farm | Painswick | Med | GCM | Green 1935 |
| 39. — | Cranham | Med ridge tile; 19thC kiln sites | CAGM | — |
| 40. Chandlers Farm | Badgeworth | 13thC | GCM | — |
| 41. Manless Town | Brimpsfield | Med | Excavated by G. Harding | Medieval Archaeol 8, 284 |
| 42. — | Brimpsfield | Med | Excavated by G. Harding | Medieval Archaeol 6/7, 339 |

| No. / Site | Place | Period | Repository | Reference |
|---|---|---|---|---|
| 43. Church and village | Deerhurst | Med and post-med | ? | Rahtz 1976 |
| 44. (a) 45–48 Church Street | Tewkesbury | Med | ? | — |
| (b) Holm Castle | Tewkesbury | 12th – 14thC | ? | Hannan 1976 |
| (c) Sabrina Cinema | Tewkesbury | Med | ? | Hannan 1974 |
| 45. Manor Farm | Stoke Orchard | 12th – 13thC | CAGM | Spry 1971 |
| 46. Littleton | Dumbleton | Med | ? | — |
| 47. Stone Cot | Stanton | Post-med | Priv. coll. | Saville 1975, 8 |
| 48. Highbury Lane | Cheltenham | 13thC and post-med | CAGM | — |
| 49. Noverton Lane | Prestbury | Med | CAGM | — |
| 50. Prestbury Manor | Prestbury | Med | AM; CAGM | Jope and Hodges 1956 |
| 51. Cleeve Hill | Southam | Med | CAGM | — |
| 52. (a) Abbey Grounds | Winchcombe | Late Saxon – post-med | DOE/Excavated by B. Davison | — |
| (b) Abbey Grounds | Winchcombe | Late Saxon – post-med | DOE/Excavated by J. Hinchliffe | — |
| (c) Abbey Grounds | Winchcombe | Med | DOE/Excavated by A. Musty | — |
| (d) North Street | Winchcombe | Late Saxon – post-med | CAGM | Vince forthcoming b |
| 53. (a) Site of ?castle | Stanway | 13thC | Priv. coll. | — |
| (b) Hailes Abbey | Stanway | 13thC – post-med | DOE/Excavated by P. Brown | Musty forthcoming |
| 54. Upper Coberley | Coberley | Med | GCM | — |
| 55. Upper Field | Dowdeswell | Med | GCM | — |
| 56. Whittington Court | Whittington | Late Saxon – med | AM | Jope 1952 |
| 57. Old Sennington | Sevenhampton | Med | ? | — |
| 58. Upton DMV | Blockley | Late Saxon – 14thC | BirmCM | Hilton and Rahtz 1966; Rahtz 1969 |
| 59. Chalk Hill | Temple Guiting | Med | ? | Baldwyn and O'Neil 1958 |
| 60. Castle Mound | Upper Slaughter | 12thC | CM | O'Neil 1962/63 |
| 61. Lower Swell churchyard | Swell | Med | CM | — |
| 62. — | Stow-on-the-Wold | Med | CM | — |

| No. | Site | Parish | Period | Collection | Reference |
|---|---|---|---|---|---|
| 63. (a) | — | Bourton-on-the-Water | Med | GCM | Dunning 1932 |
| (b) | Bow House | Bourton-on-the-Water | Med | SM | — |
| 64. (a) | Old Farm | Chedworth | Med | GCM | — |
| (b) | Various sites | Chedworth | Med | CM | — |
| 65. (a) | — | Miserden | Med | SM | — |
| (b) | Miserden Castle | Miserden | Med ridge tile | ? | Dunning 1979, fig. 71 |
| 66. | Bournes Green | Bisley-with-Lypiatt | Med | SM | — |
| 67. | — | Edgeworth | Med | SM | — |
| 68. | — | Sapperton | Med | ? | *Medieval Archaeol* 8, 271 |
| 69. | Hullasey | Rodmarton | Med | BM; CM; GCM | Baddeley 1910; Dunning 1949 |
| 70. | Trewsbury | Coates | 12thC | Priv. coll. | — |
| 71. | Ewen | Kemble | 11thC – post-med | ? | Reece 1974a |
| 72. (a) | Abbey | Cirencester | 12thC – post-med | CM | Hurst 1968, fig. 2, 8; Wacher 1964; Vince 1982a |
| (b) | Various sites | Cirencester | 12thC – post-med | BM; CM; SM | — |
| 73. | — | Ampney Crucis | Med | GCM | — |
| 74. | Quenington Court | Quenington | Med | CM | Reece 1974b |
| 75. | — | Down Ampney | Med | GCM | — |
| 76. | — | Lechlade | Med | SM | — |

Note: the following abbreviations are used in this appendix

| | | | |
|---|---|---|---|
| AM | Ashmolean Museum, Oxford | GCM | Gloucester City Museum |
| BCM | Bristol City Museum | Med | unspecified medieval pottery |
| BirmCM | Birmingham City Museum | NMW | National Museum of Wales, Cardiff |
| BM | British Museum, London | Post-med | unspecified post-medieval pottery |
| CAGM | Cheltenham Art Gallery and Museums | Priv. coll. | private collection (contact the author for further information) |
| CM | Corinium Museum, Cirencester | SM | Stroud District (Cowle) Museum |
| DOE | Department of the Environment, Fortress House, London | | |

REFERENCES

Aldred, D.H. and Hannan, A. 1981. Winchcombe. In R. Leech, *Historic towns in Gloucestershire: archaeology and planning*, 96–101. Bristol. (=CRAAGS Survey No. 3.)

Aston, P. and Spry, N. 1971. Standish, Green Farm. In P.J. Fowler and C.V. Walthew (eds.), Archaeology and the M5 Motorway: first report. *TBGAS* 90, 54–57.

Baddeley, W. St C. 1910. The Manor and site of Hullasey, Gloucestershire. *TBGAS* 33, 338–354.

Baldwin, R.C. and O'Neil, H.E. 1958. A medieval site at Chalk Hill, Temple Guiting, Gloucestershire, 1957. *TBGAS* 77, 61–65.

Bennett, J. 1976a. Cam, Waterend Farm. In P.J. Fowler *et al.* (eds.), Archaeology and the M5 Motorway: fourth report. *TBGAS* 94, 50.

Bennett, J. 1976b. Stinchcombe, Clingre Farm. In P.J. Fowler *et al.* (eds.), Archaeology and the M5 Motorway: fourth report. *TBGAS* 94, 50–51.

Bennett, J., Ponsford, M.W., and Solley, W. 1974. Falfield, Heneage Court. In P.J. Fowler and J. Bennett (eds.), Archaeology and the M5 Motorway: third report. *TBGAS* 93, 123–126.

Brown, D. 1976. Archaeological evidence for the Anglo-Saxon period. In A. McWhirr (ed.), *Studies in the archaeology and history of Cirencester*, 19–45. Oxford. (=BAR Brit Ser 30.)

Cardigan, Earl. 1949. *The warders of Savernake Forest*. London.

Casey, D.A. 1931. Lydney Castle. *Antiq J* 11, 240–262.

Clift, J.G.N. 1933. Leckhampton Moat. *TBGAS* 55, 235–248.

Dornier, A. 1966. Bledisloe excavations, 1964. *TBGAS* 85, 65–67.

Dunning, G.C. 1932. Bronze age settlements and a Saxon hut near Bourton-on-the-Water, Gloucestershire. *Antiq J* 12, 279–293.

Dunning, G.C. 1949. Report on the medieval pottery from Selsley Common, near Stroud. *TBGAS* 68, 30–44.

Dunning, G.C. 1963. Medieval pottery and finds. In H.S. Gracie, St Peter's Church, Frocester. *TBGAS* 82, 162–166.

Dunning, G.C. 1979. Head of a horse and rider roof-finial. In B.W. Cunliffe (ed.), *Excavations in Bath 1950–1975*, 149–153. Bristol. (=CRAAGS Excavation Monograph No. 1.)

Durham, B. 1977. Archaeological investigations in St Aldgates, Oxford. *Oxoniensia* 42, 83–203.

Fowler, P.J., Bennett, J., and Hill, V.S. (eds.). 1976. Archaeology and the M5 Motorway: fourth report. *TBGAS* 94, 47–91.

Fowler, P.J. and Green, H.S. 1971. Haresfield, Pool Farm. In P.J. Fowler and C.V. Walthew (eds.), Archaeology and the M5 Motorway: first report. *TBGAS* 90,

Green, C. 1935. Upper Holcombe, Painswick. *PCNFC* 25, 303.

Hannan, A. 1974. Sabrina Cinema site, Oldbury Road. *Glevensis* 8, 7.

Hannan, A. 1976. Holm Castle, Tewkesbury. *Glevensis* 10, 10–11.

Haslam, J. 1980. A middle Saxon iron smelting site at Ramsbury, Wiltshire. *Medieval Archaeol* 24, 1–68.

Hassall, M. and Rhodes, J. 1974. Excavations at the New Market Hall, Gloucester, 1966–67. *TBGAS* 93, 15–100.

Heighway, C.M. 1978. Excavations at Gloucester, fourth interim report: St Oswald's Priory, Gloucester 1975–1976. *Antiq J* 58, 103–132.

Heighway, C.M. 1980. Excavations at Gloucester 1977–1978, fifth interim report: St Oswald's Priory. *Antiq J* 60, 207–226.

Hilton, R.H. and Rahtz, P.A. 1966. Upton, Gloucestershire, 1959–64. *TBGAS* 85, 70–146.

Holling, F.W. 1971. A preliminary note on the pottery industry of the Hampshire-Surrey borders. *Surrey Archaeol Coll* 68, 57–89.

Hunter, A.G. 1961. 17th – 18th century amphora from Moreton Valance. *TBGAS* 80, 180–181.

Hurst, H. 1975. Excavations at Gloucester, third interim report: Kingsholm 1966–1975. *Antiq J* 55, 267–294.

Hurst, J.G. 1966. Imported flasks. In C.V. Bellamy, Kirkstall Abbey excavations 1960–64. *Pub Thoresby Soc* 51, 54–59.

Hurst, J.G. 1968. Near Eastern and Mediterranean medieval pottery found in north-west Europe. *Archaeol Ludensia* 3, 195–204.

Hurst, J.G. 1977. Spanish pottery imported into medieval Britain. *Medieval Archaeol* 21, 68–105.

Ireland, C. Forthcoming. The medieval and post-medieval pottery from Cirencester Abbey.

Jope, E.M. 1952. Medieval pottery from Whittington Court. *TBGAS* 71, 61–76.

Jope, E.M. and Hodges, H.W.M. 1956. The medieval pottery. In H.E.O'Neil, Prestbury Moat, a manor house of the Bishops of Hereford in Gloucestershire. *TBGAS* 75, 25–34.

Jope, E.M. and Threlfall, R.I. 1959. The twelfth-century castle at Ascott Doilly, Oxfordshire. *Antiq J* 39, 219–273.

Kilmurry, K. 1980. *The pottery industry of Stamford, Lincolnshire, AD 850–1250.* Oxford. (=BAR Brit Ser 84.)

Knight, J.K. 1977. Pottery production in Wales during the Anglo-Norman Conquest. In P.J. Davey (ed.), *Medieval pottery from excavations in the north-west*, 113–114. Liverpool. (Institute of External Studies, University of Liverpool.)

Morris, E.L. 1978. Late Saxon pottery from Worcester. *Trans Worcestershire Archaeol Soc* 6, 75–81.

Morris, E.L. 1980. Medieval and post-medieval pottery in Worcester – a type series. *Trans Worcestershire Archaeol Soc* 7, 221–254.

Musty, A. Forthcoming. Excavations at Hailes Abbey, Gloucestershire.

Musty, J. 1973. A preliminary account of a medieval pottery industry at Minety, north Wiltshire. *Wiltshire Archaeol Mag* 68, 79–88.

Musty, J., Algar, D.J., and Ewence, P.F. 1969. The medieval pottery kilns at Laverstock, near Salisbury, Wiltshire. *Archaeologia* 102, 84–150.

O'Neil, H.E. 1956. Prestbury Moat, a manor house of the Bishops of Hereford in Gloucestershire. *TBGAS* 75, 5–34.

O'Neil, H.E. 1962/63. The Norman motte at Upper Slaughter, Gloucestershire. *PCNFC* 34, 32–36.

Ponsford, M. 1980. *Bristol Castle: archaeology and history of a royal fortress.* Unpublished M.Litt. thesis, University of Bristol.

Rahtz, P.A. 1969. Upton, Gloucestershire, 1964–1968: second report. *TBGAS* 88, 74–126.

Rahtz, P.A. 1974. Pottery in Somerset, AD 400–1066. In V.I. Evison *et al.* (eds.), *Medieval pottery from excavations*, 95–126. London.

Rahtz, P.A. 1976. *Excavations at St Mary's Church, Deerhurst, 1971–1973.* London. (=CBA Res Rep 15.)

Reece, R. 1974a. Early medieval quarries at Ewen, 1971–1972. *TBGAS* 93, 131–135.

Reece, R. 1974b. The Knights Hospitaller at Quenington. *TBGAS* 93, 136–141.

Saville, A. 1975. *Pre-Regency Cheltenham: an archaeological survey.* Cheltenham.

Saville, A. Forthcoming. Salvage recording of Roman, Saxon, medieval, and post-medieval remains at North Street, Winchcombe.

Scott-Garrett, C. 1958. Littledean Camp. *TBGAS* 77, 48–60.

Shoesmith, R. 1982. *Hereford City Excavations, Vol. 2: excavations on or close to the defences.* London. (=CBA Res Rep 46.)

Smith, A.H. 1964. *The place-names of Gloucestershire, part II.* Cambridge.

Spry, N. 1971. Stoke Orchard, Manor Farm. In P.J. Fowler and C.V. Walthew (eds.), Archaeology and the M5 Motorway: first report. *TBGAS* 90, 34–42.

Stevenson, W.H. (ed.). 1893. *Calendar of the records of the Corporation of Gloucester.* Gloucester.

Travell, M. 1971. Eastington, site 2. In P.J. Fowler and C.V. Walthew (eds.), Archaeology and the M5 Motorway: first report. *TBGAS* 90, 61.

Vince, A. 1977a. The medieval and post-medieval ceramic industry of the Malvern region: the study of a ware and its distribution. In D.P.S. Peacock (ed.), *Pottery and early commerce: characterization and trade in Roman and later ceramics*, 257–305. London.

Vince, A. 1977b. *Newent Glasshouse: a late 16th and 17th century Glasshouse and late 17th and 18th century pottery.* Bristol. (=CRAAGS Occasional Papers No. 2.)

Vince, A.G. 1979. The pottery. In C.M. Heighway *et al.*, Excavations at 1 Westgate Street, Gloucester, 1975. *Medieval Archaeol* 23, 170–181.

Vince, A.G. 1982a. Post-Roman pottery. In R.H. Leech and A.D. McWhirr, Excavations at St John's Hospital, Cirencester, 1971 and 1976. *TBGAS* 100, 202–207.

Vince, A.G. 1982b. Grass-tempered pottery. In C.M. Heighway and A. Parker, The Roman tilery at St Oswald's Priory, Gloucester. *Britannia* 13, 122-123.

Vince, A.G. 1983a. The medieval and post-medieval pottery. In C. Heighway, *The East and North Gates of Gloucester*, 125–161. Bristol. (=Western Archaeological Trust Excavation Monograph No. 4.)

Vince, A.G. 1983b. *The medieval ceramic industry of the Severn Valley.* Unpublished PhD thesis, University of Southampton.

Vince, A.G. Forthcoming a. The ceramic finds. In R. Shoesmith, *Excavations in Hereford, Vol 3.* (=CBA Res Rep.)

Vince, A.G. Forthcoming b. The pottery. In A. Saville, Salvage recording of Roman, Saxon, medieval, and post-medieval remains at North Street, Winchcombe.

Vince, A.G. and Goudge, C.E. 1980. The Roman pottery from 1 Westgate Street. In C.M. Heighway and A.P. Garrod, Excavations at Nos. 1 and 30 Westgate Street, Gloucester: the Roman levels. *Britannia* 11, 73–114.

Wacher, J.S. 1964. Cirencester 1963: fourth interim report. *Antiq J* 44, 9–19.

**April 1984**

# The Study of Deserted Villages in Gloucestershire

## Mick Aston and Linda Viner

Before 1954, few people thought that such things as deserted villages of the medieval period even existed. In Gloucestershire only a handful of sites had been examined: W St Clair Baddeley excavated medieval buildings, including a possible chapel and manor house, at Hullasey before 1910 (Baddeley 1910) and Mrs O'Neil excavated a medieval building at Sennington in 1936 (Beresford and Hurst 1971). If other sites were known, they were not discussed and published.

In 1954, Beresford wrote the now classic work on *The Lost Villages of England*, which for the first time established that the landscape formerly had far more settlements than appear on the modern map. For Gloucestershire he listed twelve or thirteen sites, located mainly from medieval records. The formation of the Deserted Medieval Village Research Group (now the Medieval Village Research Group) stimulated further research and by 1971, when *Deserted Medieval Villages* (Beresford and Hurst 1971) was published, 67 (former Gloucestershire) sites had been accepted on the list (of which Lark Stoke is now in Warwickshire and Oldbury in Avon). During the 1960s other excavations took place at Brimpsfield (by Harding in 1961), Manless Town (by Harding in 1962; Beresford and Hurst 1971), and Upton (Hilton and Rahtz 1966; Rahtz 1969).

Since 1971 no major research has been undertaken on deserted village sites in the county. However, recognition of new sites has continued steadily over the years as they have been identified from fieldwork, aerial photographs, and

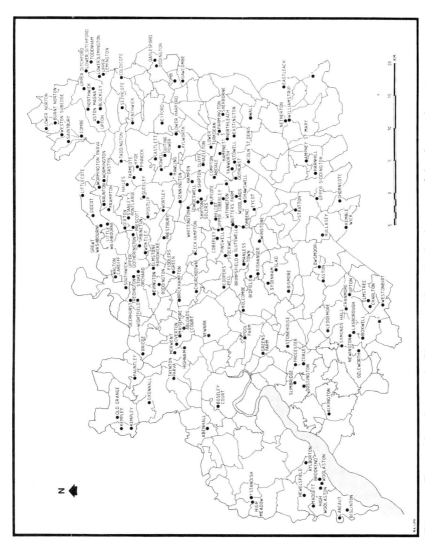

*Figure 1* Deserted settlements in Gloucestershire: distribution map of sites known in 1984.

*Figure 2*  Farmington: aerial photograph of shrunken village earthworks (ANI73 taken on 23rd March 1966, Cambridge University Collection, copyright reserved).

documentary research. These sites were, and still are being, added to the Sites and Monuments Record maintained by Bernard and Barbara Rawes under the auspices of the Gloucester and District Archaeological Research Group. By the time Saville published his *Archaeological Sites in the Avon and Gloucestershire Cotswolds* in 1980, 39 sites were listed for the Cotswold region of the modern county alone. There is no doubt that many more sites remain

*Figure 3*    Hawling: aerial photograph of shrunken village earthworks (AIK7 taken on
5th February 1964, Cambridge University Collection, copyright reserved).

to be discovered. Information from all known sources in 1981 was gathered
into a gazetteer by the present authors (Aston and Viner 1981). This
gazetteer, including doubtful and suspect possibilities, listed some 168 sites
(revised to 195 in early 1984). The varying number of sites emphasizes the
difficulty of how we define what are deserted villages, what we expect them to
look like in the field, and how they can be recognized from early documents
(Fig. 1).

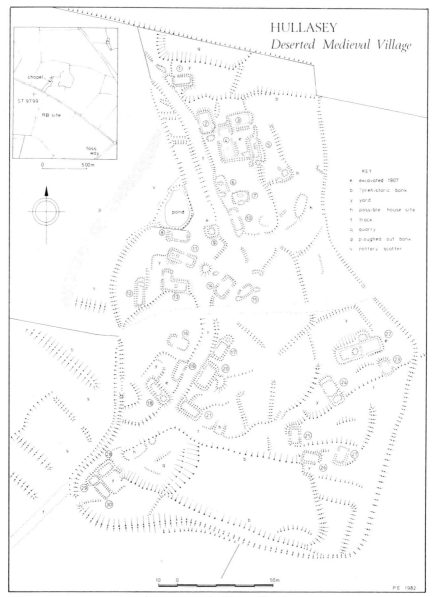

*Figure 4* Hullasey: plan of the deserted village. (Courtesy Peter Ellis and Western Archaeological Trust.)

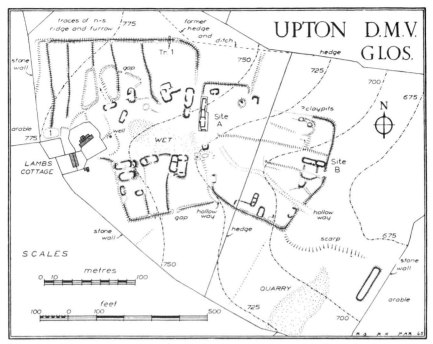

*Figure 5* Upton: plan of the deserted village. (Courtesy Philip Rahtz.)

## WHAT IS A DESERTED VILLAGE?

When the Deserted Medieval Village Research Group began its work, it was primarily concerned with identifying large nucleated settlements, like most of the villages with which we are familiar today, that had formerly existed but which were now totally, or almost totally, abandoned. Usually, earthworks remaining on their sites distinguished them from other archaeological remains. Strictly speaking, to be classified as a deserted medieval village, such former village sites should have had a church in the past, or at least a chapel, and they should have been abandoned by the end of the Middle Ages, if not before.

Such sites are rare – there do not seem to be any in Gloucestershire. Much more common is the deserted, or practically deserted, hamlet where, as far as we know, there was at the most only a chapel, indicating the settlement's subsidiary status to the main settlement, with the parish church elsewhere. Very many of the Gloucestershire examples fall into this category – the Ditchfords and Upton in Blockley, Hullasey in Coates, the site at Chapel

Hayes in Didmarton, and Lower Norton in Weston Subedge – and at each of them the characteristic earthworks of such sites can be seen.

Even more common than deserted medieval settlements are those places which were either abandoned or shifted in more recent centuries, or where substantial shrinkage or movement has taken place but the settlement remains as a modern village. Gloucestershire is particularly rich in the former, since with the creation of large emparked estates, mostly on the Cotswolds and particularly in the eighteenth and nineteenth centuries, villages were often demolished or removed when landscaping took place. This partly explains why medieval churches (or their former sites) stand isolated next to large country houses in the middle of parks like Sezincote (church demolished), Sherborne, Sudeley, Toddington, and Westonbirt. Often no earthworks remain to indicate the former village sites, the church is frequently rebuilt in eighteenth- or nineteenth-century style, and a village may still remain in the parish as an estate village (or 'closed village'), as at Badminton (in Avon), Sherborne, and Westonbirt.

As for shrunken villages, there are few settlements in any county that do not display some abandoned house or farm sites. However, substantially shrunken or shifted settlements, often still with either a church, public house, post office and/or shops and so on, are quite common. In Gloucestershire the best examples are Farmington (Fig. 2), Hampnett, Hawling (Fig. 3), Shipton Solers, and Whittington.

At the lower end of the scale, there are many places which were probably never more than a grouping of several farmsteads. Often, all that remains today may be a single farm, but earthworks or documentary references may suggest other, earlier, abandoned farms and cottages. Sometimes this may be no more than a single farm on different sites at different times. Lowesmoor, in Cherington, where only a single farm remains, probably has two or three other farmstead sites nearby, as are indicated by earthworks and buried foundations. Many of the suggested sites in the west of the county, which so far have received little attention, may well fall into this category.

In many parts of Gloucestershire the medieval settlement pattern probably consisted not of villages or hamlets, but of single farmsteads, isolated in their own fields. Such places were frequently moated, especially in the Vale on clayey sites; examples include Bengrove Farm (Sandhurst), several sites in Quedgeley, and the newly identified site of Breckness Court, near Coleford in the Forest of Dean, where impressive earthworks remain of a moated manor and fishponds. Elsewhere, many other examples probably remain to be identified, such as the excavated medieval farm sites at Temple Guiting examined by O'Neil in 1937 and 1957 (Baldwyn and O'Neil 1958).

It can thus be seen that to concentrate solely on the identification of deserted medieval villages is to ignore many other facets of the early settlement pattern. We need to include the complete range, from surviving but shrunken villages, through hamlets of various sizes, down to farmsteads, and to be concerned with changes at all dates, from late Saxon times through to the present day.

## WHAT DO DESERTED SETTLEMENTS LOOK LIKE?

If we examine a well-preserved deserted village site such as Hullasey in Coates (Fig. 4) or Upton in Blockley (Fig. 5), certain characteristic features can usually be seen. House sites generally only remain where foundations were of stone, and they indicate longhouses (with cattle at one end and people at the other), as in the excavated example at Upton. Other buildings were probably barns, cottages, outbuildings, and so on. Such buildings stood in yards, which remain as platforms or enclosures, frequently with larger enclosures adjacent, which were formerly paddocks and/or gardens. The farmsteads would have faced onto roads, now in the form of hollow-ways, or onto open areas which were formerly greens. A prominent bank or ditch often separated the crofts of the village from the surrounding fields, which can sometimes be identified from ridge-and-furrow earthworks. Other features which can occasionally be seen are manor house sites, church sites, fishponds, moats, and earthen castle remains (as at Newington Bagpath). For example, at Weston Subedge there is a deserted manor site, with a moat and fishponds, while at nearby Lower Norton deserted village (Fig. 6) there are a moat, an abandoned dry fishpond, and extensive areas of ridge-and-furrow. This site lies in the Vale on clay. Generally in this area of the county no clear house sites are visible; they were probably built of timber, turf, and clay. However, the earthworks of such sites may be very impressive, as at Upper and Lower Ditchford (Beresford and St Joseph 1979), with platforms for the farmsteads, hollow-ways for lanes and boundaries, boundary banks, and ridge-and-furrow earthworks being very clear on the ground and on aerial photographs (Figs. 7 and 8).

The majority of sites, however, have only very indeterminate earthworks, which are frequently difficult or impossible to interpret, although aerial photographs may help. Such sites include Coberley, Lemington, and Shaws-well. Elsewhere, as has already been stated, nothing remains to show that a village site formerly existed.

*Figure 6*   Lower Norton: aerial photograph of deserted village earthworks (PN51 taken on 13th April 1955, Crown copyright).

## WHEN AND WHY WERE THE SITES DESERTED?

If no trace remains on the ground, how do we know a village site existed, and is it possible to find out when and why the settlement disappeared? Fortunately for the study of Gloucestershire we have the recent research of Dyer (1980 and 1982) and an unusual late fifteenth-century list of 'lost places'. At first sight, the Black Death (1348–1349), other plagues, and the

*Figure 7*  Upper Ditchford: aerial photograph of deserted village earthworks
(AWO71 taken on 27th January 1969, Cambridge University Collection,
copyright reserved).

numerous wars of the Middle Ages seem ideal explanations for the disappear-
ance of villages, but as we shall see, the situation was more complicated.
Local legends may also be misleading. The local interpretation of the name
'Manless Town' in Brimpsfield is that all the men failed to return or were
killed, but its earlier, more reasonable, name was Haywick (Rawes and
Gander 1978).

*Figure 8*   Lower Ditchford: aerial photograph of deserted village earthworks (also
known as Middle Ditchford) (LT80 taken on 3rd May 1953, Crown
copyright).

Domesday Book lists a handful of places which cannot be confidently
identified; these may represent Saxon settlements abandoned after the
Norman period (Moore 1982). Although there were two Royal Forests in
Gloucestershire (Dean and Kingswood) and three Cistercian abbeys (Flaxley,
Hailes, and Kingswood), their creation does not seem to have occasioned any
settlement removal as it did elsewhere (in the New Forest, for example, and

at the Cistercian abbeys of Combe and Stoneleigh, Warwickshire, and Revesby, Lincolnshire).

In the 1490s, John Rous, a chantry priest at Guys Cliffe outside Warwick, compiled a list of 58 places where there were abandoned churches, and by implication deserted villages. Most of these are in Warwickshire, but he includes Sezincote and possibly 'Norton' and Upper and Middle Ditchford in Gloucestershire. These and other places are assumed to have been abandoned in the economic change from arable farming to pasture for the rearing of sheep and cattle, frequently accompanied by the eviction of villagers. Thus at Middle Ditchford 'arable cultivation ceased abruptly in the 1480s, as if there had been some sudden enclosure or eviction' (Dyer 1982, 26). However, the best example is Didcot, where thirty villagers were evicted by the Abbot of Tewkesbury in 1491 (Beresford 1954).

Although Beresford emphasized the late fifteenth century as the main period for village desertion, Dyer has suggested that a number of places were in decline even before the Black Death, and also that, especially on the Cotswolds, the late fourteenth century (the decades immediately after the Black Death) was in fact a very important period for desertion. In the early fourteenth century at Aylworth and Harford 'many tenants left their holdings and left them vacant and uncultivated' and at Littleton in Aston Blank 'seven parishioners . . . abandoned their holdings and left the parish' (Dyer 1982, 22). After the Black Death, in the 1370s and 1380s, other places declined, including Bidfield, Hilcot, Lasborough, Ledgemore, Upton, and Wontley. Some of these settlements may have been on marginal sites, while over-cultivation, together with lack of livestock and hence the essential manure, may have led to soil depletion. The common field system, widespread on the Cotswolds, was also difficult to operate when many villagers had died in the plagues. This may, in part, help to explain the differences in incidence and distribution of places deserted in the county.

Although we have already noted the impact that the large house and its emparked ground may have had on some settlements, the example of Sezincote shows that such estates could in some cases be laid out on sites which were already abandoned and laid down to pasture. There, depopulation and enclosure occurred in 1638, the church was in ruins by 1751, and the benefice was formally amalgamated with Longborough. Thus, slow decline and several contributory factors may be involved in the disappearance of some settlements. At Whittington there is still a small village and, at some distance away, a medieval church and manor house, built by 1566, on an earlier moated site. Earthworks nearby show that either the village was once larger in extent or that it has shifted northwards (Fig. 9). It is also a

*Figure 9*  Whittington: aerial photograph of shifted or shrunken village earthworks
(CCF49 taken on 18th May 1977, Cambridge University Collection,
copyright reserved).

possibility that the deserted area was cleared to provide a more open vista for
the large house. The picture is further complicated by the existence of a
Roman villa (and Roman village?) under the village earthworks, perhaps
indicating a much older or more continuous use of the site than has
previously been suspected. At High Meadow in Staunton, a map of the
Forest of Dean in 1608 shows a small linear village. Earthworks now mark
the site next to the ruins of a late medieval manor house. However, the site
may have been removed when a large house was built in the eighteenth

century further up the valley. This, too, has now gone and earthworks show its site and adjacent gardens.

The decline and disappearance of most of the deserted and shrunken settlements in Gloucestershire is likely to have been a long and gradual process. It is only by detailed examination of all the records for particular places that such decline can be seen clearly. For most sites this has not yet been done.


## FUTURE RESEARCH

In other counties the study of deserted villages has led to a re-examination and reappraisal of how and when the surviving villages, hamlets, and farmsteads came into being. It has always been assumed that the contemporary pattern and types of settlement are the norm, and that there has been little change. It can now be seen that there has been a lot of desertion and shrinkage, and research elsewhere is suggesting that change is more common than stability in the English landscape, and that 'everything is older than we think' (Hoskins 1955, 12).

This latter point is shown by Manless Town, Whittington, and other places which have produced evidence of Roman settlement on the same site. It cannot be assumed that there has been complete continuity of settlement, but this is perhaps likely in view of the suggestions of Finberg (1955) for Withington and the recent work of Wool (1982) on Gloucestershire generally. Possibly more common is the association of medieval earthworks with earlier features. At Hawling and Hullasey it looks very likely that the village closes are linked to a pre-existing pattern of probably prehistoric or Roman field or land boundaries. This has been noted elsewhere, in particular at Hound Tor on Dartmoor (Beresford 1979) and at Wharram Percy in Yorkshire (Hurst 1979).

In addition, research elsewhere in the country, particularly in the East Midlands and the northern counties, is suggesting that nucleated villages are relative newcomers to the landscape, perhaps in late Saxon or early medieval times (Taylor 1983). Furthermore, the earlier pattern seems often to be one of dispersed farmsteads and hamlets. A probable local example which demonstrates this is Frocester, where the research of Eddie Price (pers. comm.) suggests a number of small settlements in use until the twelfth century at the latest, when not only were they abandoned, but their sites were overploughed with ridge-and-furrow (Fig. 10). It is likely that the present village of Frocester (which is now itself shrunken) was created at that time,

# Frocester    MEDIEVAL SETTLEMENT

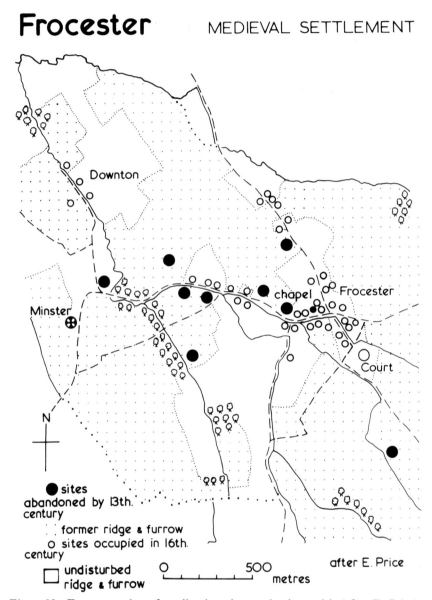

*Figure 10*  Frocester: plan of medieval settlement in the parish (after E. Price).

*Figure 11*   Hampnett: aerial photograph of shrunken village with central green
(BWC064 taken on 18th November 1975, Cambridge University Collection, copyright reserved).

together with the new fields – but how common is this generally in the
county?

This creation of new villages can be recognized principally from the study
of village plans and forms. Very regular plans, frequently associated with
village greens, have been shown in Durham and Yorkshire to be the result of
deliberate planning and village creation. The study of village plans in
Gloucestershire has hardly begun, but preliminary analysis of some aerial

photographs suggests great regularity around village greens at, for example, Caudle Green and Hampnett (Fig. 11), while Taylor suggests that the Cotswold village of Lower Slaughter has undergone drastic changes in the past, since '. . . the seemingly ageless stone-built cottages that edge the stream are actually built on an earlier green, though . . . when the encroachment took place is not known' (1983, 152).

We must be aware of such alterations, the flexibility of settlements in the Gloucestershire landscape, and the possibility of great changes in the past. The study of deserted villages is, therefore, only the first stage in our understanding of when and why the surviving villages have their present appearance, which we find so attractive, and this might enable us to conserve them more effectively in future.

## ACKNOWLEDGEMENTS

It is a pleasure to acknowledge the help of Eddie Price for Fig. 10 and Carinne Allinson for typing an unintelligible manuscript. Fig. 5 is reproduced by permission of Professor Philip Rahtz, and Fig. 4 by permission of Peter Ellis and Western Archaeological Trust. Figs. 2, 3, 7, 9 and 11 are from the Cambridge University Collection, with copyright reserved as appropriate. Figs. 6 and 8 are Crown Copyright.

## REFERENCES

Aston, M. and Viner, L. 1981. Gloucestershire deserted villages. *Glevensis* 15, 22–29.

Baddeley, W.St C. 1910. The Manor and site of Hullasey, Gloucestershire. *TBGAS* 33, 338–354.

Baldwyn, R.C. and O'Neil, H.E. 1958. A medieval site at Chalk Hill, Temple Guiting, Gloucestershire, 1957. *TBGAS* 77, 61–65.

Beresford, G. 1979. Three deserted medieval settlements on Dartmoor: a report on the late E. Marie Minter's excavations. *Medieval Archaeol* 23, 98–158.

Beresford, M.W. 1954. *The lost villages of England*. London.

Beresford, M.W. and Hurst, J.G. (eds.). 1971. *Deserted Medieval Villages*. London.

Beresford, M.W. and St Joseph, J.K.S. 1979. *Medieval England: an aerial survey*. Cambridge. (2nd edn.)

Dyer, C. 1980. *Lords and peasants in a changing society*. Cambridge.

Dyer, C. 1982. Deserted medieval villages in the West Midlands. *Economic History Review* 35(1), 19–34.

Finberg, H.P.R. 1955. *Roman and Saxon Withington: a study in continuity*. Leicester.

(=Leicester University College Department of English Local History, Occasional Paper No. 8.)

Hilton, R.H. and Rahtz, P.A. 1966. Upton, Gloucestershire, 1959–1964. *TBGAS* 85, 70–146.

Hoskins, W.G. 1955. *The making of the English landscape.* London.

Hurst, J.G. (ed.). 1979. *Wharram: a study of settlement on the Yorkshire Wolds, Vol. 1.* London. (=Society for Medieval Archaeology Monograph Series No. 8.)

Moore, J.S. (ed. and trans.) 1982. *Domesday Book: 15: Gloucestershire.* Chichester.

Rahtz, P.A. 1969. Upton, Gloucestershire, 1964–1968: second report. *TBGAS* 88, 74–126.

Rawes, B. and Gander, E.D. 1978. An ancient quarry at Manless Town in the parish of Brimpsfield. *TBGAS* 96, 79–82.

Saville, A. 1980. *Archaeological sites in the Avon and Gloucestershire Cotswolds: an extensive survey of a rural archaeological resource with special reference to plough damage.* Bristol. (=CRAAGS Survey No. 5.)

Taylor, C. 1983. *Village and farmstead: a history of rural settlement in England.* London.

Wool, S.T. 1982. *Fundus and Manerium: a study of continuity and survival in Gloucestershire from Roman to medieval times.* Unpublished PhD thesis, University of Bristol.

**March 1984**

# Medieval Urban Archaeology in Gloucestershire

## Roger Leech

INTRODUCTION

In recent decades there has been an increased interest in the medieval towns of Gloucestershire. Their origins and early history have been summarized by Finberg (1957). The detailed histories of Fairford, King's Stanley, Lechlade, Minchinhampton, Moreton-in-Marsh, Newnham, Painswick, Stow-on-the-Wold, Stroud, and Tetbury have been studied by the *Victoria County History*. The urban topography and growth of Gloucester have been studied from several viewpoints (Heighway 1974; Lobel 1969). Archaeological research has also been concentrated in Gloucester (Heighway *et al.* 1979 and 1983; Hurst 1972, 1974 and 1975), though excavations have taken place in Tewkesbury, while the archaeological recording of buildings has been more widely undertaken.

A more informed data-base for archaeological research has been provided by devoting resources in the first instance to identifying the locations of medieval towns. For most, the surviving plan of streets and property boundaries, rarely recorded in detail before the seventeenth or eighteenth centuries, is the most readily available evidence for its medieval topography. Together with documentary evidence, these have now been used with probably varying degrees of success to define the land-use of each former medieval town (Heighway 1974; Leech 1981; Saville 1975).

There have been important developments in the wider study of medieval urbanism. Archaeologists have become increasingly aware that expensive urban excavations must be more carefully directed towards answering particular problems. At the same time, sampling methods, now widely used in rural contexts, may be difficult to implement in a complex urban situation where past human activity has a non-random distribution (cf. Freke 1978, 87). The need to formulate post-depositional models for each successive phase, of what are invariably multi-period sites, adds further to the complexities of urban excavation. Moreover, by virtue of their occupation to the present day, many former medieval towns, and particularly the most successful, present a continuing sequence of opportunities for archaeological excavation in advance of redevelopment, far greater in number than current resources or research needs will permit or require to be investigated.

In this paper, therefore, a review of the current state of knowledge of medieval urbanism in Gloucestershire is followed by an attempt to define more closely the particular problems which archaeological research is best able to answer.

## LATE SAXON URBANIZATION (Fig. 1)

By 1086 there were boroughs at Gloucester, Tewkesbury, and Winchcombe, and markets at Berkeley and Cirencester. Berkeley, Gloucester, and Winchcombe were also the sites of late Saxon mints. Cirencester and Gloucester were on the sites of earlier Roman towns, but extensive excavations have produced no evidence for continuity of urban life. All five were closely associated with monastic foundations and may have originated as market centres outside their gates. Gloucester and Winchcombe were also significant royal centres, the former with an important royal palace nearby at Kingsholm, the latter possibly one of the chief royal centres of the sub-kingdom of the Hwicce.

Only at Gloucester has there been sufficiently detailed archaeological work to be able to discuss the physical appearance of the town. The Saxon and medieval street plan has been shown to be not directly related to the Roman one, although some surviving Roman buildings may have stood until the early tenth century. However, the date of the new street plan, on historical evidence possibly laid out by Æthelflaed, is still to be confirmed by archaeological evidence. More important, perhaps, has been the evidence from artefacts, metal-working residues, and floral and faunal remains for the economy and subsistence of mid- to late Saxon times. This has indicated that there was little long-distance trade at Gloucester, in contrast to ports such as Hamwih (now Southampton). Analysis of plant remains has shown that spelt

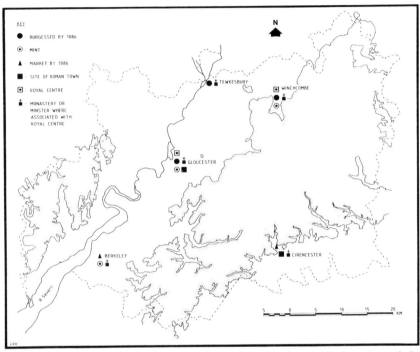

*Figure 1*   Gloucestershire: late Saxon urbanization. Land over 400 feet above O.D. stippled.

continued to be cultivated in the late Saxon period, as in Roman times, in contrast to sites in south-eastern England, such as Hamwih and Winchester, where it had been replaced by free-threshing cereals (Heighway *et al.* 1979).

At Winchcombe, archaeological research has been focussed on the Saxon burh defences (Aldred and Hannan 1981). Excavation of the rampart at Back Lane has revealed evidence for a timber palisade, whilst on the east the defences possibly enclosed a far greater area than has been appreciated hitherto (Bassett 1977). More recent salvage recording at a site on North Street demonstrated the presence of eleventh-century pits but located no structures (Saville forthcoming).

In the other Saxon towns, archaeological excavation has taken place only at Cirencester and Tewkesbury. However, the scope of the work at Tewkesbury was very limited, whilst at Cirencester research has been concentrated upon the Saxon abbey church. In these towns, and at Berkeley, even the location of the Saxon urban centre is probably uncertain, for all have street plans typical of those towns founded after the Norman conquest.

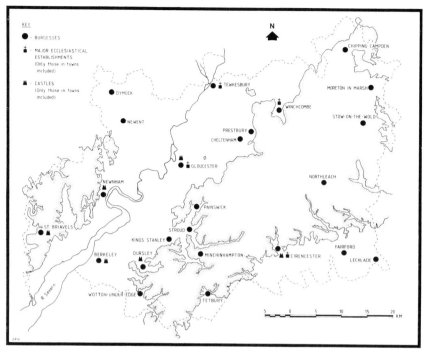

*Figure 2*   Gloucestershire: urbanization in the twelfth and thirteenth centuries. Land over 400 feet above O.D. stippled.

## URBANIZATION IN THE TWELFTH AND THIRTEENTH CENTURIES (Fig. 2)

Seventeen new boroughs emerged in Gloucestershire in the prosperous twelfth and thirteenth centuries, the greatest number being founded between 1200 and 1250 (Finberg 1957; Leech 1981). The deliberate foundation of new towns can be seen most clearly in those with regular street plans. These plans usually comprise a single wide street, often narrowing at the ends for toll bars, with long, narrow burgage plots on each side, approached also from the rear by back lanes; for instance at Cheltenham, Chipping Campden, Moreton-in-Marsh, Newnham, Northleach, and Wotton-under-Edge, where in each the town was probably added to an existing settlement centred around a church and manor house (Fig. 3). In other towns, for example Dursley, Painswick, and Tetbury, the earliest recorded street plan indicates a rather more complex development, still associated with an earlier settlement.

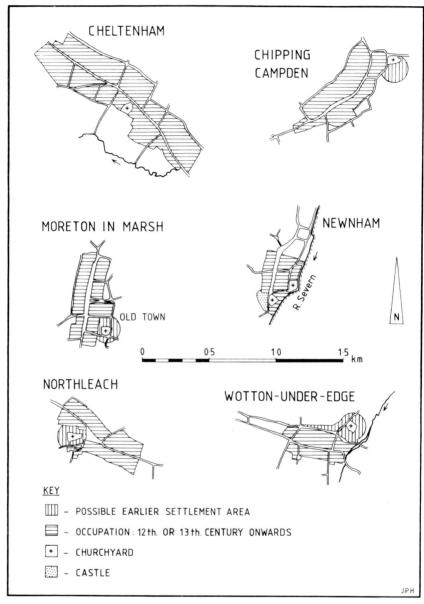

*Figure 3*  New towns (and new towns added to existing settlements) of the twelfth or
thirteenth centuries in Gloucestershire.

Archaeological research has been through excavation and the survey of surviving medieval structures. Excavation has been confined to Gloucester and Tewkesbury. Survey of surviving buildings, only rarely pre-fifteenth century in date, has been carried out in most of the towns but only of isolated, threatened examples.

Ideally, one might pursue a thematic approach within which the changes of the twelfth and thirteenth centuries might be analysed. Sampling would enable comparison based on logical analyses to be made between different situations within one town or between towns. This is not yet possible, for only the excavations at 1 Westgate Street and the East and North Gates in Gloucester have been published fully (Heighway *et al.* 1979 and 1983). Interim reports for the other excavations at Gloucester and Tewkesbury do not refer in detail to the assemblages. Such analyses might also refer to the assemblages from excavations in Bristol since 1965, but again only interim reports are available.

Several aspects to changes in the twelfth and thirteenth centuries would merit such a thematic approach. Archaeological research is clearly able to provide much data about demographic trends only rarely available through documentary sources. In Gloucester, excavations at 13–17 Berkeley Street have shown that by the later thirteenth century relatively dense development was already occurring, individual tenement plots being only *c*.20 feet wide by *c*.100 feet in length. Buildings at the rear of these plots were predominantly of two storeys; although there is as yet no evidence for their function, they could prove to be detached kitchens. In contrast, 82–84 Northgate Street (Moss and Spry 1975) still occupied a plot *c*.45 feet wide some 150 years later; this part of Gloucester was thus less densely populated, possibly with superior houses. Both these sites have failed to provide evidence for the earliest street-frontage buildings; this makes difficult an estimate of the total population of each plot. Indeed, such evidence may only be forthcoming in the less prosperous and less densely-populated towns, where it has not been destroyed by later development and cellar construction. However, such data can be obtained from sources other than plans of buildings. At 1 Westgate Street the plant remains included cereal fragments, orchard crops, and economic plants such as flax. The increased quantity of orchard crops from the later pits on the site might indicate a larger amount of domestic faecal remains, and thus an increased population in the eleventh and twelfth centuries.

The evidence from the excavations at Gloucester also provides a basis for examining residential differentiation. It seems likely that the streets around 13–17 Berkeley Street – Brodesmythstrete, Vicus Fabricorum, and Gorelane

– were a relatively poor neighbourhood with small, cramped houses, in contrast to Westgate Street, where undercrofts of twelfth-century date still survive on much larger plots at 74–76 and at the Fleece Inn (NMR records).

Whereas the data for demographic trends will be supplemented by information from the documentary sources, the data for subsistence, technology, and trade generally cannot be obtained other than by excavation. At the same time, it is this evidence which is not yet easily sampled to form a basis for logical analysis and comparison. At present, only a piecemeal approach is possible.

Analysis of the restricted medieval faunal assemblage from 1 Westgate Street indicated that sheep, cattle, and pig were all kept for their meat rather than for other purposes. This might well indicate a distinctive urban subsistence. Certainly in the surrounding countryside one might expect to find sheep over-wintered for several years for their wool, cattle being kept to a considerable age for plough teams, and pigs kept for breeding; but as yet no quantified comparisons can be made.

Again, technological data for the twelfth and thirteenth centuries have come principally from Gloucester. Excavation has provided evidence for changes in weaving technology, the warp-weighted loom first being introduced in the tenth century. The late Saxon phases have also provided data for glass smelting. There are also data for changes in building technology. At Eastgate Street, from at least the ninth century onwards, buildings were of timber construction with timber posts set in postholes. At Westgate Street, buildings of similar construction, or with the timber uprights set into sill beams, were being constructed from the sixteenth century.

From the early twelfth century onwards, buildings in Gloucester were of stone. This transition is dated rather earlier at Gloucester than at Lower Brook Street, Winchester, where stone houses first appeared in the early thirteenth century (Biddle 1972). Since information is not yet available from other towns in the county, the real significance of this cannot be assessed.


## THE FOURTEENTH AND FIFTEENTH CENTURIES

The traditional view that the fourteenth and fifteenth centuries were a period of economic decline has now been challenged on several points. One, particularly relevant to this study, emerges from a recent reassessment of late medieval Gloucester (Langton 1977). Mapping the documentary evidence available from rentals, it was possible to argue that 'the crowding, new building and accumulation of and investment in real estate by the laity and the church' indicated a vigorous rather than a declining economy. Notably, this study declined to make use of any archaeological evidence from Gloucester, and discussion of the plan-forms and construction of medieval houses was based on documentary sources both from Gloucester and elsewhere, including Warrington.

However, considerable archaeological evidence is now available to indicate degrees of population density, although little of it can yet be used to provide data for growth or decline, chronologically or between individual towns. Such evidence is obtainable particularly from the study of buildings in several towns. In Wotton-under-Edge, 3 and 5 Bradley Street were possibly of fifteenth-century date (Leech 1981, 102–103). Each was built at right angles to the street, occupying a relatively narrow plot 24 feet wide, and probably represented a single dwelling unit, consisting of a shop (with chambers over) on the street frontage and with the hall and solar behind. In Tewkesbury, the twenty-four cottages built by the Abbot of Tewkesbury in the mid-fifteenth century show an even greater density of housing and must represent the lower end of the housing scale (Platt 1978, fig. 108).

In Gloucester, evidence from the study of standing buildings helps to answer some of the questions unanswerable in detail from the documentary evidence. Study of 64–68 Westgate Street indicates the density of housing in the central area of the city (Dodd, Lawrence and Moss 1976; NMR records). On the street frontage were three separate tenement-units, each consisting of a shop at ground floor level with one room on each floor above. At the rear, a range at right angles to the street provided a further two units, each with six rooms. The total accommodation on this 44-feet-wide plot was thus five dwelling units, each of six rooms and attics.


## SOME CONCLUSIONS

It is thus possible to identify some of the problems which archaeological research might answer and the ways in which they might be tackled. Population density and the social structure of towns could be studied more closely if, for the twelfth and thirteenth centuries, more extensive excavation of uncellared street-frontage sites had occurred. However, especially in the larger towns, these will exist in only a few places. For later periods extensive study of standing buildings, often related to study of documentary sources, will provide much information; indeed, for Tewkesbury a large amount of data is already available (records by S.R. Jones in the NMR; records by the former Tewkesbury Archaeological Centre), but requires synthesis.

The relative growth of different towns requires further research. For towns such as Chipping Campden and Northleach, where many of the tenement plots apparently are not subdivided, it would be of particular interest to know if their plans in fact devolved from a more intensely subdivided landscape of the thirteenth century.

For the above, and for questions concerning trade, subsistence, and technology, it is clear that research must be directed to a number of towns and other medieval settlements, preferably as a co-ordinated project with shared sampling strategies. At a preliminary stage in the formulation of research models, synthesis of the data from excavations already undertaken in the two major regional centres of Bristol and Gloucester over the last twenty years must surely be essential.

The archaeological study of medieval towns in Gloucestershire has been fairly typical of that in many other areas. Research has focussed largely on the more important towns, with often almost no attention at all having been paid to the many smaller market centres founded in considerable numbers in the twelfth and thirteenth centuries. There is now a need to integrate the results obtained from the examination of pottery fabric types and building plans with a broader, regional synthesis and analysis of Gloucestershire medieval towns, so that the study of wider problems of urbanization can begin.

## REFERENCES

Aldred, D.H. and Hannan, A. 1981. Winchcombe. In R. Leech, *Historic towns in Gloucestershire: archaeology and planning*, 96–101. Bristol. (=CRAAGS Survey No. 3.)

Bassett, S. 1977. *The origins and development of Winchcombe and its district.* Unpublished MA thesis, University of Birmingham.

Biddle, M. 1972. Excavations at Winchester, 1970: ninth interim report. *Antiq J* 52(1), 93–131.

Dodd, A., Lawrence, A., and Moss, P. 1976. 66 Westgate Street. *Glevensis* 10, 9–10.

Finberg, H.P.R. 1957. The genesis of the Gloucestershire towns. In H.P.R. Finberg (ed.), *Gloucestershire Studies*, 52–88. Leicester.

Freke, D. 1978. Medieval urban archaeology in Sussex. In P.L. Drewett (ed.), *Archaeology in Sussex to AD1500*, 87–92. London. (=CBA Res Rep 29.)

Heighway, C.M. 1974. *Archaeology in Gloucester: a policy for city and district.* Gloucester. (Gloucester District Council.)

Heighway, C.M., Garrod, A.P., and Vince, A.G. 1979. Excavations at 1 Westgate Street, Gloucester. *Medieval Archaeol* 23, 159–213.

Heighway, C.M. *et al.* 1983. *The East and North Gates of Gloucester and associated sites:*

*excavations 1974–1981*. Bristol. (=Western Archaeological Trust Excavation Monograph No. 4.)

Hurst, H. 1972. Excavations at Gloucester, 1968–1971: first interim report. *Antiq J* 52, 24–69.

Hurst, H. 1974. Excavations at Gloucester 1971–1973: second interim report. *Antiq J* 54, 8–52.

Hurst, H. 1975. Excavations at Gloucester, third interim report: Kingsholm 1966–1975. *Antiq J* 55, 267–294.

Langton, J. 1977. Late medieval Gloucester: some data from a rental of 1455. *Trans Inst Brit Geogr* 2, 259–277.

Leech, R. 1981. *Historic towns in Gloucestershire: archaeology and planning*. Bristol. (=CRAAGS Survey No. 3.)

Lobell, M.D. (ed.) 1969. *Historic towns. Vol 1*. Oxford.

Moss, P. and Spry, N. 1975. Disappearing Gloucester 2: 84 Northgate Street. *Glevensis* 9, 24–25.

Platt, C. 1978. *Medieval England: a social history and archaeology from the Conquest to AD1600*. London.

Saville, A. 1975. *Pre-Regency Cheltenham: an archaeological survey*. Cheltenham.

Saville, A. Forthcoming. Salvage recording of Roman, Saxon, medieval, and post-medieval remains at North Street, Winchcombe.

**March 1984**

# The Medieval Houses of Rural Gloucestershire

## Lionel F.J. Walrond

### INTRODUCTION

The 'house' has evolved over many centuries, admittedly with a few periods of regression, and a convenient date must be selected for the close of the medieval period. The writer has chosen *c*.1540, a time when changes in chantry and monastic practices were revolutionizing everyday life. Standards of living were similarly soon to change, and these would in themselves constitute the start of a new architectural era.

The medieval houses of the county show an enormous variety in their building materials, style, size, and social importance. One factor was the difference in the available resources in each of the geographical regions – Cotswold, Northavon, the Severn Vale, and the Forest of Dean. Whereas the lesser yeoman was dependent upon the products of his own land, the wealthy could afford to buy and transport better and more fashionable materials, and theirs are the more likely buildings to be standing today. The survival rate for medieval houses is far from consistent. Their total absence in some villages is as remarkable as their frequency in others.

In the preparation of this essay it has been possible to consider about one hundred and fifty rural houses, the majority of which have only been recognized as of medieval origin in the last twenty-five years. The writer has examined most of these houses in person, but a few have been included on the basis of published work or unpublished communications. Only those houses that contain medieval material, however fragmentary, in their fabric have been included. The presence of early pottery, irregularities of ground plan, or documentary references, is not in itself sufficient evidence. Urban buildings are omitted because of their considerable difference in function, layout, site limitation, and concern with both fashions and building regulations. Many of the larger villages in the county began as market towns and so retain some urban characteristics.

## THE EARLY PERIOD

It is almost inconceivable that we should expect to find complete houses surviving from the early medieval period. Nevertheless, a considerable amount of one survives at Horton Court in Northavon, there is a Norman undercroft at Bury Court, Redmarley D'Abitot, near Dymock, and an ornate Norman arch is preserved at Southrop Manor near Lechlade. Otherwise most of our knowledge of twelfth- to fourteenth-century houses must be gleaned from excavations. Compared with some counties Gloucestershire is not rich in early sites, and only a few of these have been competently excavated, but the full social range is covered, from the peasant crofts at Upton, near Blockley, through a mixed settlement at Hullasey, near Tarlton, to the moated manorial site at Prestbury. Although in some houses timber might have been used on a limited scale, the excavated examples appear to have been predominantly of stone. It is noticeable that the homes of manorial status used carefully-laid dressed blocks, but the peasants used, and repeatedly reused, small undressed rubble in walls that needed to be rebuilt every decade or so. This element of diminishing permanence within the social hierarchy explains why very early work has survived only in the houses of manorial status or those of the clergy. Some allowance must, however, be made for wilful demolition, repeated restorations, and accidental fires.

## SURVIVING BUILDINGS

To appreciate our medieval heritage we must look more closely at the standing houses, which, by the nature of their building materials, cannot be totally representative of their period. Elsewhere in southern England medieval houses were usually timber-framed, but the local evidence is not so consistent. Certainly on the Cotswolds and near the escarpment, the surviving medieval houses seem to have been predominantly of stone and the same may prevail in the western half of Northavon and in the Forest of Dean, though much more research is needed in the area west of the River Severn.

The stone-walled manor houses of the fourteenth and early fifteenth century were not only better built than their precursors, they were more logically arranged and better proportioned. The open hall was the principal room at every social level. In fact, any structural evidence for an open hall is in itself sufficient to imply a medieval date, though the converse does not apply. Ashleworth Manor (or Vicarage), built c.1460, was of two storeys from the start. Starsmead Farmhouse, Haresfield, c.1500, had original ceilings over the hall and service areas, but was open above the passage and unheated parlour. Rodford Hill Farm, Westerleigh (now demolished), must have been one of the last of the medieval hall houses. Built around 1550, it had a chimney in the front wall between superb tall windows. Not until a later date was a floor inserted, probably to make accommodation for servants. The arch-braced roof of this house could have implied an earlier date, but the open hall incorporated datable features with no evidence for a major rebuild. The owner was clearly seeking to retain the principal features of medieval formalism.

*The Cotswolds*

Building timber was available on the Cotswolds in the fifteenth century. Not only do we see its use in the churches, but some houses, as at Alderton Manor and Brockworth Court, were partially timber-framed. Icomb Place and Little Sodbury Manor were among the many with roofs comprising arch-braced collars and wind braces that were attractive as well as functional. Buckland Rectory (1466–1483) was finer than most, with a hammer-beam roof spanning its two-bay hall. Arlington Row at Bibury, however, shows plainly that good building timber was either scarce or costly. Restoration work in 1971 uncovered earlier trusses surviving from a stone-walled medieval house. One of these was a cruck in which the blade was made from three separate timbers scarfed together. It may well have been the weakening of these joints that prompted a virtual rebuild in the seventeenth century resulting in a row of units rather than a single house. The original low building at Arlington Row appeared to be of seven bays with smoke-blackened trusses (Mercer 1975, 157–158; and details recorded by the present writer which were covered or lost before the RCHM survey was made).

One factor in the preservation of the houses along the Cotswold escarpment is that their wealthy owners in the ensuing centuries chose not to demolish and rebuild, but to add new wings, as at Daneway House, Sapperton, or to update, as at Leckhampton Court. Later still we find these enlarged houses being restored by architects of repute. No fewer than three have since been adapted for use as schools.

## The Severn Vale

In direct contrast to the houses of the Cotswold escarpment are those of the Severn Vale, and it is in this area that most research has been undertaken in the past quarter-century. These houses are essentially timber-framed, often cruck-built, and are frequently too low at the eaves to permit the division of the open hall without personal discomfort to the occupier. The same pattern of upper-class manorial and ecclesiastical housing is present, but there are in addition an enormous number of houses that must have belonged to yeoman farmers, whose holdings could be as small as forty acres. Frampton on Severn contains no fewer than fifteen houses we may regard as medieval and this number could well be increased by further research. Ashleworth and Sandhurst are also very productive, though the latter village may contain the remnants of one or more deserted or shrunken hamlets by way of explanation. Most of these houses appear to date from the fifteenth or sixteenth century.

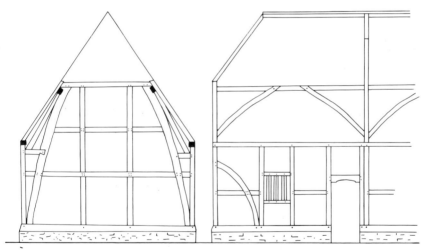

*Figure 1*   Stylized gable and side wall of a 'Gloucestershire' cruck to show spur ties, packing-pieces, a downward brace, and a double stud.

Of the seventy or more cruck houses known, a very high proportion have so many characteristics in common that they virtually constitute a 'Gloucestershire cruck' form (Fig. 1), extending north into Worcestershire, but differing from those seen in other nearby counties. The house, usually of three or four bays, has at least one half-hipped gable end and is timber-framed throughout. Tie beams are rare, being replaced by spur ties which are dovetailed onto the cruck face. The outer end of the spur tie is mortised into the wall stud, which usually rests on the sill beam but can be notched onto the back of the cruck. The upper end of the stud supports the wall plate, with the ends of the common rafters sitting in shallow notches on the upper surface. Below the rafter lies a second, shorter packing-piece, its end resting on the outer end of the spur tie. There are also large, downward, tension or foot braces, usually running from the corner posts, but which can occur at any point in the side walls. That these were looked upon as decorative as well as functional is apparent in the small barn at Tump Farm, Tirley, where their similarity to the half-hipped gable cruck is clearly no accident.

Another feature present both here and in south Worcestershire is the use of the double wall-stud. This seems to occur only once in any house, and usually about a bay from the end of a side wall. It is clearly not the product of alterations and is more likely to be a feature of the process of erection. One assumes that the rearing of the first gable cruck in any house was the most difficult. Since there was no tall support to which it could be roped, the two side walls would be built to give it stability. Subsequent trusses could be steadied by the continuation of one wall and the use of a few ropes. The remaining wall would be completed last, and the use of the extra wall-stud would remove the need to open out the existing framing to fit the final mortises.

Seen from within, the yeoman's cruck house must have been very different from its wealthy, stone-built counterpart. The hall was often small, and effect was achieved by the impressive size of its timbers contrasting with lime-washed wattle-and-daub panels. Corse Court, near Ashleworth, was probably the most impressive. Here the dais panel, between a pair of doorways, consisted of a row of closed arches. The central cruck-truss was arch-braced to a cambered collar, above which a cusped king-post divided a pair of foiled, decorative openings. Most hall roofs had wind braces.

There were other ways of building a timber-framed house. Simple box-framing exists but is harder to date. Sometimes the principal wall-posts project inwards, without jowls, and are stopped short to take a roof principal 'bird's-mouthed' over the upper end, as at Tanhouse Farm, Frampton on Severn. At the former Swan Inn, Whitminster, and Sutgrove Cottage, Stroud Road, Gloucester, the roof levels have been raised, leaving an apparently meaningless truncated post. Manor Farm Cottage, Frampton on Severn, has an alien form of framing, probably due to influences from Warwickshire. In the same village several medieval houses have jettied ends. This could be a mark of sophistication, but there is a folk memory that this feature allowed grain or meal to be lowered to a cart beneath. Tudor House, Leonard Stanley, had at the rear an industrial range of c.1500 with jettied side walls, the lower part being close-studded whilst the floor above had square framing. This style quickly gave way to the use of close studding in the upper floor, sometimes jettied, with stone below, as at Brockworth Court (1539) or Manor Farm, Frampton on Severn (1525–1550). In the latter, and at Field Court, Quedgeley, we find very small ogee braces in the corners of the framing. In the post-medieval period these braces multiply and develop into one form of 'Midland pattern framing' to be found in the centre of Gloucester.

There is one other feature which, though important, is rarely seen except when the houses are being altered. The sides of the wattle-filled wall panels have a groove into which the ends of the split hazel wands were driven. The fact that the junction of the daub finish no longer had a straight contact with the surface of the post may well have reduced seasonal draughts and penetrating moisture. This practice appears to have been in use on either side of our terminal date of 1540 (Fig. 2).

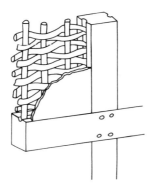

*Figure 2*    Detail of timber framing to show the grooved vertical timbers, sixteenth-century.

## Northavon

Both timber-framing and stone-construction have been noted in the Forest of Dean but the number of known survivals is too small to allow one to generalize; a lot more work is called for in that area. In the south of the former county, now Northavon, the Severn Vale traditions can be identified at Wood Lane Cottage, Horton, but elsewhere all surviving examples point to a tradition of stone-building. Ostbridge Manor Farm and Green Farm, both at Olveston, retain their wind-braced roofs. Two undisputed medieval houses at Rodford Hill, Westerleigh, have been demolished and there is a remarkable sixteenth-century long-house preserved among the outbuildings of Castle Farm, Marshfield.

## HOUSE PLANS

The houses under consideration range from those of the extremely poor to those of the most wealthy. The function of the house may differ within the social classes and we must remember that the early medieval period saw the integration of the house as we understand it, replacing the random siting of rooms built piecemeal to meet a succession of circumstances.

The simplest house-form possible survives as a part of Madams End Farm at Hardwicke. Although apparently consisting of one room, it is probable that the arrangement of the contents provided two distinct functional areas, one for living and the other for storage and sleeping. This is precisely what one finds in the 'one and a half bay' house, as at Ashleworth and Upton St Leonards, or very slightly larger in Maisemore and Redmarley D'Abitot, where the division of the roof is often into unequal portions governed by the position of the partition between the two rooms. In every instance the hearth was at the gable end with the main entrance alongside. There was often a second entrance into the inner room, which traditionally was occupied in many cases by the mule or pony, which presumably shared the family's sleeping-quarters. This end of the house usually had a loft. At Manor Farm Cottage, Frampton on Severn, the inner room was itself divided to give a buttery and a sleeping chamber. This pairing of room functions occurs in other plan-forms and continues until the late seventeenth century. Another unusual variation on the arrangement of rooms in a small house occurs in The Thatched Cottage, Arlebrook, Standish, dating from the close of our period. The main end is of two storeys, whilst the inferior end is of three. This gives a five-roomed house, but no two rooms are on the same level.

An entirely different plan-form comprised those houses where the entrance led into a passage with a doorway on the opposite side of the house. This arrangement was used by the wealthier yeomen and at manorial level. On one side of the passage was the hall, separated by a partial division called a spere truss, as at Cains Cottage, Longhope, or in the simpler, smaller house with no structural division at all. Beyond the hall was an undercroft with a solar or parlour above, as at Ashleworth Court. The undercroft gradually developed into a parlour and the upper room into a bedchamber. The service rooms were usually sited on the opposite side of the passage.

In some houses the service area remained socially the lower end, while elsewhere several traditions evolved. The undercroft beyond the hall became a buttery and/or bedchamber, whilst a number of superior functions were placed in the service end. At Alkerton Farm, Eastington, the cross-wing below the former passage contains a pair of solar bedchambers, beneath which are a cider cellar and a parlour. Similar arrangements were noted at the now demolished Crown Inn, King's Stanley, where there was no partition between the passage and the hall. On the other side of the entry, the service area and the parlour stood side by side. But this dated from the early sixteenth century and there were bedrooms over all the rooms, with working attics above them. Food was probably still being prepared in a detached kitchen as hitherto.

There are also a number of houses which do not conform. These are usually found to have had a special function, or combined several purposes under one roof. The oldest part of Frocester Court, late fifteenth-century, was just a large hall above a heated undercroft. This, no doubt, was the court room of the Abbots of Gloucester, used on the periodic visits to that part of their estates. More complex is the plan of Over Court, Bisley, with what appears to be an entire suite of rooms for the visiting earl and his entourage, and a second hall area as the home of the 'farmer' or steward. Field Place, Quedgeley, has upstairs rooms which occupy the greater part of the six-bay, three-storey, sixteenth-century cross-wing. This property appears not to have belonged to some absentee landlord, but we cannot rule out the survival of its use for some form of manorial court or seasonal ceremony. At Icomb Place the gatehouse, hall, parlour, chapel, and all subsidiary buildings were compacted to form a close unit around two very small courtyards.

Medieval oriels took the form of a small structural projection opening out from the upper end of the hall and adjoining the solar range. They occur at Ashleworth Court and Over Court, Bisley, both being houses of greater than average importance. Oriels might house a stairway to the solar, or even an oratory or chapel. Porches were another affectation, probably more common than we imagine. Until relatively recent times they existed at Wanswell Court, Hamfallow, and Tudor House, Leonard Stanley, but a fine example survives at Little Sodbury Manor.

## MISCELLANEOUS DETAIL

Thus far we have dealt with the basic elements of the medieval house in Gloucestershire. Internal and external detail is important, if only to give a more vivid image of the period. Until about 1800 roofs were thatched in all but those important houses where the owners deliberately tried to break from tradition. Frocester Court had stone slates all of which were eight and a half inches in length. The grading of slate sizes appears to have been a later innovation. Excavations on a number of sites have produced a few stone tiles and a few ridge tiles but, in the opinion of the writer, the proportions are normally insufficient to indicate either a stone- or clay-tiled roof. Contrary to common belief, thatched roofs could have had glazed ceramic crestings, often with ornamental ventilators and finials. The quality of the straw would not have permitted wide eaves in the current Devon tradition, and the lower edge may well have run out onto a couple of courses of stone tiles along the tops of the walls.

Smoke from the open hearths might sometimes have been dispersed through these ceramic ventilators, but louvres would have been more common. Corse Court retains a cluster of sticks, between the central hall truss and the chimney of c.1600, which are the sole remains of a wattle chimney, no doubt originally clay-covered. In Frampton on Severn the pattern of smoke-staining on The Old Cruck House indicates the presence of some sort of vent at the gable end immediately under the half hip of the roof.

These hearths would have been laid on the floor, with perhaps a low wall or reredos to reflect the heat. Sometimes, however, the fire was against a wall, the smoke being received into a projecting hood, as at St Briavels Castle, or there was a wide stone fireplace with period decoration or mouldings as at Plusterwine Farm, Alvington, near Lydney. These needed chimneys, and a discrepancy in the solar jetty-framing at Alkerton Farm, Eastington, may well have been due to the former presence of such a low chimney or louvre. The hearth beneath would have been moved when the central chimney was built c.1600. Chimney caps have survived in relatively large numbers and occur at St Briavels Castle (thirteenth-century), with later examples from Bibury, Longhope, and beside the Broadwell in Dursley.

Windows in the stone buildings frequently included tracery. Those with a transom, as at Ashleworth Court, would have been glazed in the upper part with horn or glass. The lower part may have been unglazed and there is evidence for wooden shutters that could be closed from the inside. In the timber-framed buildings the windows were less elaborate. However, Denfurlong Farm, Frampton on Severn, once had a delightful oriel window in which the edge-rolls of the wooden mullions were carried up to join the roll around the lintel beam. That the function of a window was to let in light rather than to exploit a pretty view was shown in a house in Cooks Lane, Redmarley D'Abitot, where the hall windows were sited quite high in the walls (Fig. 3). A working range of c.1500 at Tudor House, Leonard Stanley, had no windows at all on the ground floor. We may assume that some of the gaps in the close studding were left open, and were protected by hanging cloths if the weather made work unpleasant.

The wealthy homes would have had garderobes, visible still as shallow

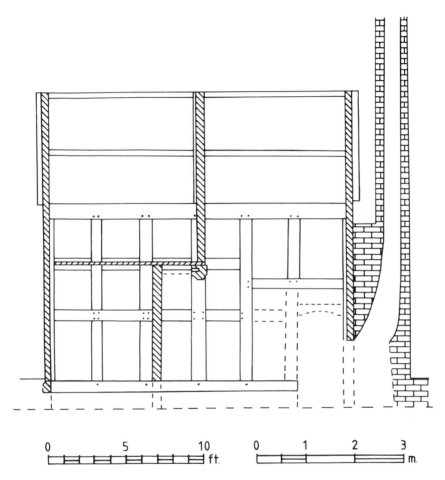

*Figure 3*  Small house at Cooks Lane, Redmarley D'Abitot, destroyed by fire in
September 1983. Section to show the two room layout with sleeping
chamber above, internal jetty over the seat, and a pair of windows above
the (conjectured) original doorway. The brick chimney is a later rebuild.

projections on the outside of the house. They survive at Buckland rectory,
Standish Vicarage, Alkerton Farm, Eastington, and Ostbridge Manor Farm,
Olveston. Washing facilities have rarely survived, but a stone basin and drain
remain in the hall at Icomb Place.

Inside these open halls there is evidence for a high seat facing the fire and
fixed to the wall of the inner room. In at least three instances, the

above-mentioned house at Redmarley D'Abitot (Fig. 3), Packers Cottage, Quedgeley, and Wood Lane Cottage, Horton, the effect would have been heightened by the jettying of the upper room over the seat to form a structural cove.

At the close of the medieval period, when ceilings were becoming more frequent, the supporting timbers became the subject of interest. The principal beams were given a very wide chamfer, often slightly hollowed, and the very simplest of stops where the chamfer met the wall. By contrast the secondary ceiling joists, often laid flat rather than square or upright, had chamfers and ornate stops. Of these stops, the pyramid type declined in popularity around 1550.

Paint as a means of decoration did not become popular for another fifty years. Nevertheless, a type of orange-brown paint was used extensively through much of the sixteenth century. It occurs throughout the county on ceiling beams, fireplace lintels, and exposed roof members where its presence might perhaps have served as a fungicide on the inadequately seasoned timbers. A similar paint was used long before to decorate the roof members of Britannia Cottage, King's Stanley. Here in the first floor solar, stylized flowers, comprising six painted discs, lay between parallel bands. Decoration may have existed elsewhere, but has vanished under layers of lime, emulsion paint, and creosote.

## ACKNOWLEDGMENT

The writer acknowledges the kind co-operation received from the owners and occupiers of houses, medieval and later, during his researches. It must be stressed that the mention of any building in this paper in no way implies rights of access or entry by the general public.

SOURCES USED IN THE COMPILATION OF THIS ARTICLE

Alcock, N.W. *et al.* 1981. *Cruck construction: an introduction and catalogue.* London. (=CBA Res Rep 42.)

Hall, L.J. 1983. *The rural houses of north Avon and south Gloucestershire, 1400–1720.* Bristol. (=City of Bristol Museum and Art Gallery Monograph No. 6.)

Mercer, E. 1975. *English vernacular houses: a study of traditional farmhouses and cottages.* London, RCHM (E).

RCHM. 1963. *Monuments threatened or destroyed: a select list, 1956–1962.* London.

Wood, M. 1965. *The English medieval house.* London.

**February 1984**

# PART SIX:

# GLOUCESTERSHIRE IN THE INDUSTRIAL AGE

# Industrial Archaeology in Gloucestershire

## David Viner

## INTRODUCTION

It seems fitting that this volume should be concluded with a contribution, however brief, on the latest addition to the Gloucestershire archaeologists' repertoire, the discipline of industrial archaeology. Unlike their more 'classical' colleagues, industrial archaeologists usually have far greater resources of surviving documentation at their disposal for these comparatively modern periods of study. In this sense at least, the study of industrial remains has been a valuable part of local historical research for many years. The phrase 'industrial archaeology' dates back only to the mid-1950s (Rix 1967, 5), and Gloucestershire can claim one of the first county industrial archaeology societies, the Gloucestershire Society for Industrial Archaeology (GSIA), formed in 1964 and now with a membership of over 250. The primary aim of GSIA is to stimulate interest in, to record, to study, and, where appropriate, to preserve items of industrial archaeological importance in the county. The involvement with preservation implies a difference of approach from that of most 'conventional' archaeological societies, and the close links with neighbouring county industrial archaeology societies is, and has always been, a most welcome and mutually beneficial aspect of its activities.

First impressions of the county hardly suggest a strong industrial element – Gloucestershire is after all one of the primary agricultural areas of southern England. But the Forest of Dean has a long tradition of industrial exploitation, probably two thousand years old, and the surviving industrial architecture of the valleys centred upon the manufacturing town of Stroud reminds us of that area's once important role in the processing and manufacture of woollen cloth.

This survey must be restricted to an appreciation of only the more important, surviving, industrial remains, with reference to studies already undertaken, and to an assessment of the current level of industrial archaeological activity within the county. A more general view can be obtained from the many recent surveys available (e.g. Buchanan 1980; Hudson 1968).


EXTRACTIVE INDUSTRY

The student must begin with those areas rich in mineral deposits and particularly the Forest of Dean, an area which even today retains strong characteristics of its own. Iron ore was extracted in antiquity by surface exploitation, which now leaves its mark in the so-called 'scowles'. Two small horizontal adits or mines discovered in association with the important Romano-British site at Lydney Park (Wheeler 1932) give a clue to what must have been a far greater exploitation of iron ore and other mineral deposits in the Forest during the Roman period than has so far been substantiated. Further work at the associated settlement at *Ariconium* (Weston under Penyard), just outside the county in Hereford and Worcester, should prove fruitful in this respect (Hart 1971, 1–3), but meanwhile there is little solid evidence for the Romano-British presence in the Forest other than the Lydney site and the interesting road system (Margary 1967, 327–333). Of particular note in the latter case is the preserved section of an eight-foot wide cobbled and kerbed road, the so-called Dean Road, at Blackpool Bridge (SO 652087), which must have been an important link in the network between *Ariconium*, the mining areas of the Forest, and the Severn estuary at Lydney.

Hart's major study of the Forest of Dean (1971) details the evolution of iron production in the region with the introduction of the charcoal blast-furnace early in the seventeenth century and an increased demand for ore. Most of the major developments of the industry, however, belong to the nineteenth century, when the development of coke blast-furnaces and the use of steam power, together with improved transport systems, allowed the extraction of over four million tons of iron ore during that century. Inevitably, larger and more sophisticated workings obliterated earlier evidence and many of these similarly have been eradicated in the clearance programmes of recent years. But sufficient remains to encourage the industrial archaeologist (e.g. Bick 1980a; Newman 1982). Indeed, the industrial remains in the Forest provide a core of evidence not yet sufficiently well recorded in the face of destruction from forestry, tourism, and new industrial developments.

The principal surviving remains of the processing of iron include the furnace tower at Guns Mill (SO 675159), which formed one of the earliest fieldwork projects of the GSIA (Cave 1974; Harris 1974), and, from the coke blast-furnace period, the substantial remains at Whitecliffe near Coleford (SO 568103). This structure dates from 1799–1802 and is associated with David Mushet, of the famous family of ironmasters, who was a partner in experiments at Whitecliffe on coke as a fuel (Standing 1980 and 1981). These trials quickly proved unsuccessful but the association with Mushet, plus the considerable remains, encouraged a small group in 1978 to form a trust seeking to acquire the site, and with the support of the Department of the Environment, under whose auspices the furnace has been scheduled as an ancient monument, to finance its repair and restoration and ensure public access. The project has been the subject of a public appeal for £50,000 and serves to indicate clearly the preservation role with which the work of many industrial archaeologists is inevitably associated.

The Mushet family's achievements in laying the foundations for the production methods of modern steel-making are perhaps more closely associated with the site at Darkhill (SO 590087), where the furnace remains were during 1977 the subject of a Manpower Services Commission scheme, designed to aid the preservation of the structure and to undertake an archaeological excavation of the site, one of the first systematic excavations to be undertaken on an industrial monument in Gloucestershire.

The well-established rights to free-mining of those born within the Hundred of St Briavels were claimed as early as 1244 and applied to the winning of coal as well as iron. By the seventeenth century, pits were being sunk as deeply as the water level allowed. By 1841, with the use of more efficient steam pumps, 69 pits were at work and in the following fifteen years this number rose dramatically to a peak of 221. In this century the history of the Forest of Dean coalfield has been typical of many of the smaller colliery areas, with a steady contraction of the industry. By 1965 all the large collieries had closed, leaving only the independent free-miners working small operations in primitive conditions scattered throughout the Forest. Although the evidence of the larger mines has been virtually obliterated, the small workings can still be found, as at Bicslade (SO 599105).

In the county as a whole the main extractive industry has always been the winning of stone. The Cotswold range of hills is well-known for its high quality limestone used as a building material since prehistoric times and quarried extensively until the present day. The colour of the stone varies

*Figure 1*  Westington stone quarry and mine near Chipping Campden, photographed
c.1895 by the celebrated Oxford photographer H.W. Taunt.
(Photo: Corinium Museum, Cirencester; courtesy Oxfordshire County
Libraries.)

from a delicate creamy-grey in the region around Bath, a pale buff over most
of the Cotswolds, to a rich orange-brown in the north and east of the area.
The quarry remains are everywhere to be found, frequently small and now
overgrown, and often used exclusively for one project, being re-opened at
intervals when repairs to buildings and new developments create demand.
Several larger quarries are still working but mostly producing roadstone or
the raw materials for reconstituted stone substitutes. Examples are Upper
Coscombe near Stanway (SP 079302), Westington (Fig. 1) above Chipping
Campden (SP 139368), and at Naunton/Temple Guiting (SP 1225).

Of the abandoned sites the best known and most extensively studied is
Leckhampton (SO 9418), where research has unravelled the complicated
history of the extensive area of workings (Bick 1971). Much of Leckhampton
Hill is now a public open space, which makes this site perhaps the most
accessible and certainly one of the most fascinating industrial archaeological
areas in the county. By the mid-nineteenth century, quarrying had extended

along the western and northern faces of the hill and the famous Devil's Chimney (SO 947184) was probably no more than a remnant left by quarrymen during the working of this face of the hill about 1800. The development of Regency Cheltenham stimulated activity in the quarries and the surviving remains from this period can be traced amongst the evidence from the last great period of activity from 1921–1926, when new access routes were constructed together with lime-kilns, etc. The historic photographs of this final phase, gathered by Bick from various private collections, serve as a reminder of the significance of such contemporary material in the recording of a site. Ephemeral at the time, it is often the hardest category of material to gather into the record.

Stone was mined as well as quarried and, although the honeycomb nature of underground horizontal shafts or adits is probably best preserved in the limestone workings near Bath in Avon (Perkins, Brooks and Pearce 1979), considerable remains do survive in the county near Minchinhampton at Balls Green (SO 864995 and 867995) and at Burleigh (SO 862015 and 867017). Stone from the former was used in the Houses of Parliament and from the latter is still used for repair work at Gloucester Cathedral.

Only a limited amount of work continues to be devoted to the extraction and preparation of freestone, the best quality building stone, and the processes perhaps can be seen better in the Forest of Dean, where the Pennant Sandstone quarried at Bicshead (SO 597107) is used for a wide variety of purposes. The associated stone-cutting works at Bicslade (SO 607099) offers an insight into the nature of such establishments, with its simple, covered working area, basic office provision, and a fascinating variety of cutting equipment including a number of horizontal saws. 'Bicshead Blue' stone and 'Barnhill Grey' from an associated quarry have been used in recent years at Berkeley nuclear power station, the University College of Wales buildings at Aberystwyth, and in the service station at Aust on the M4 motorway.

Every industry has its curiosity and the overgrown quarry at Tally Ho, south of Guiting Power in the Cotswolds (SP 094232), certainly hides a fascinating story. Here the Stone Pipe Company dug stone to make water-pipes and installed pipe-drilling machinery driven by a Boulton and Watt rotative engine. The Company managed to obtain a monopoly for the supply of pipes to a water-supply project for the City of Manchester, despite the considerable transport difficulties and the low strength of the limestone as a raw material for such a purpose. The fraud was perpetrated for some time until the inability of the stone pipes to withstand the required water pressure was revealed and the Company went into liquidation. Discarded stone cores and pipe remains can be traced re-used in the walls around the site.

## POWER SUPPLY

The second main theme of an industrial archaeologist's research must be the use of various power sources, both natural and manufactured. Water-power was generally more reliable and plentiful than wind-power and most parishes possessed or shared a water-powered corn-mill. Many survive, albeit converted to prosperous country homes, and the revival of interest in traditional milling methods and production has encouraged the preservation *in situ* of original equipment. The restoration of Kilcott Mill (ST 786894) near Hillesley, just outside the county boundary in north Avon, has recently been described (Medlam 1977–8), and the country life museum developed at Arlington Mill, Bibury (SP 114068) incorporates original equipment plus a waterwheel brought from North Cerney mill.

Corn-milling by water-power was often accompanied by brewing as an associated activity, and the recording of the remaining brewery buildings has occupied the attentions of many enthusiasts in the face of progressive centralization and redevelopment programmes by the major breweries. Much the same can be said for surviving maltings. Public reaction against some of the products of modern processing has given a lifeline to many smaller operations and Gloucestershire can boast the Donnington Brewery, near Stow-on-the-Wold (SP 174272), which continues to supply its dozen or so public houses in the vicinity in much the same pattern as was previously commonplace. Originally a corn mill, Donnington has been a brewery since 1865 and a family business since 1827. Two water-wheels supplied all the power until 1959 but have since been supplemented by a diesel engine. Of the larger breweries the demolition of the former Stroud Brewery buildings in Cheapside, Stroud, following closure in 1967, robbed that town of a potential site for preservation and continues to present an unsightly and under-used open space.

Postlip upper mill near Winchcombe (SP 009271) was another corn-mill subsequently developed for the manufacture of paper, in which capacity it still functions producing filter and blotting papers. Steam-power was available at Postlip from 1870–1950 but the millpond still supplies up to 80,000 gallons an hour for the plant. The history of paper-making in the region has been the subject of three studies in recent years (Harris 1976; Harris and Angel 1975; Shorter 1952). Although out of use since 1860, the buildings at Sudeley Mill (SP 027281) in the same area are still recognizable as a paper-mill with a drying loft.

*Figure 2*  The 19th-century buildings at Ebley Mill, near Stroud.
(Photo: D. Viner.)

*Figure 3*  Stanley Mill, near Stonehouse, rebuilt in brick in 1812–1813, is one of the earliest fireproof textile mills in Britain. (Photo: Peckham's Studios, Stroud; courtesy National Monuments Record.)

Probably the most impressive industrial architecture in Gloucestershire can be seen in the river valleys of the Frome, centred upon Stroud, and of the Ewelme and Little Avon to the south. Here the production of woollen cloth from the fleeces of Cotswold sheep became increasingly mechanized and sophisticated, and has been well studied by Walrond and others and set into a wider context by Ponting (Mann 1971; Ponting 1971; Tann 1967; Walrond 1967 and 1973). The industrial archaeologist's challenge is to unravel the palimpsest of surviving evidence and to record adequately the major features of the industry. Apart from the work of those mentioned, it has to be said that relatively little has been recorded in detail. The great majority of the mill buildings of the district belong to the phase of rebuilding and renewal in the first quarter of the nineteenth century, and offer an excellent opportunity to study the growth and development of an industry within a geographically well-defined area. Two hundred mills close to Stroud were producing cloth in 1820 and five are still in use today. Some architecturally fine buildings have been demolished in recent years, notably Wallbridge Mill in Stroud in 1964, but splendid examples remain and particular reference should be made to Dunkirk Mill (SO 845005), near Nailsworth, which is really a group of four buildings in line, each with a datestone, ranging from 1798 to 1855. Four of the five Dunkirk Mill waterwheels were in working order until 1940, and three survive. Of the mills still used for cloth production, Cam (ST 754999), Lodgemore (SO 844050), and Longfords at Nailsworth (ST 867993) belong to the same company producing fine cloth for military and industrial use, including the famous scarlet of the Guards.

Between Stroud and Stonehouse are two other important survivors producing a range of woollen products. Ebley Mill (SO 825045) is 'perhaps the finest example of a stone-built mill in the county' (Awdry 1983, 24) and belongs to the rebuilding phase already mentioned (Fig. 2). Its crowning feature, however, is a later nineteenth-century addition, a tower-block designed by the architect G.F. Bodley, whose work also includes a home for mill-owner Sir Samuel Stephens Marling on the hill above at Selsley and the adjacent village church, with a tower similar to that of the mill, which complements it in the architecture of the valley (Verey 1970, 389–390). At Stanley Mill (SO 813043), Gloucestershire has one of the earliest fireproof textile-mills dating from a rebuilding in 1812–1813 (Fig. 3). The building is in brick and the important feature is the cast-iron frame with double columns down the centre of each floor, supporting cast-iron arches (Fig. 4). It is also notable as a sizeable building, reflecting the importance of its proprietor as a clothier of influence (Moir 1971).

There are many other mill buildings listed by Tann (1967) and worthy of

*Figure 4*   The interior of Stanley Mill showing the cast-iron frame with a central
double column.
(Photo: courtesy National Monuments Record; Crown copyright reserved.)

comment. Several, for example St Mary's Mill at Chalford (SO 886023), have
experienced a variety of uses; St Mary's being formerly a cloth-mill, briefly
used for paper-manufacture from 1846–51, then for thirty years a flock-mill,
and for most of this century used as one of only two factories still producing
walking sticks and umbrella-stems. A recent fire illustrates the difficulty of
maintaining such buildings as legislation continues to become less flexible,
and it is the steady diminution of the stock of industrial buildings in the face
of a variety of pressures which produces a real need for a programme of
detailed recording. The GSIA survey of a dyehouse at Brimscombe before its
demolition well illustrates the nature of this daunting task (Pountney and

Beddow 1976). Similarly, smaller structures present no less significant a challenge (Crawford 1982; Haine 1981 and 1982).

## COMMUNICATION

Transport historians and industrial archaeologists have much in common and the volume of published material on the history of communications continues to grow apace (Cox *et al*. 1973). Popular interest in canals and railways, and particularly in their preservation and re-use, has never been greater and thereby much of value has been rescued from destruction.

Predictably there is rather less interest in the system of communication by road and its development, perhaps because road transport remains a commonplace of everyday life. Survivors from prehistoric and Roman routes apart, the greatest improvements belong to the eighteenth and nineteenth centuries when turnpikes were established to develop and maintain lines of communication. The first turnpike act in the county concerned the route from Gloucester to the top of Birdlip Hill in 1697/8 and in the subsequent 150 years a network of such roads was established across the county. Individual routes with surviving documentation form excellent recording projects, working from the archives in the County Record Office to the surviving remains on the same route today. GSIA members have thus examined the Northgate Turnpike at Gloucester (Spry 1971), the routes from Gloucester to Cheltenham and Tewkesbury (Bayes and Roberts 1971), and more recently the early histories of the Bibury and Nailsworth Turnpike Trusts (Cox 1979; Crawford 1977–8). The examination of the Northgate Turnpike included some archaeological excavations.

The combination of archival research and field work is best seen in two studies in the mid-1960s by Cox (1964 and 1967), in which the author set out to record, in the area around Stroud, the surviving remains, and by implication the level of destruction, of the two most obvious features of turnpike roads: milestones and tollhouses. The individual nature of the groups of milestones was noted and no fewer than twenty-four tollhouses recorded as extant. These include the fine example in neo-Gothic style at Butterrow, Rodborough (SO 856042), an octagonal building with the typical three-sided frontage to the road and also notable as still in possession of its tollboard listing the variety of charges for passing the gate. A few other good examples survive elsewhere in the county as at Oxenton (SO 952313), on the A435 Cheltenham to Evesham road, but studies by the present writer in Hampshire and Dorset (Viner 1969 and 1982a) show clearly the loss-rate of

*Figure 5* Thomas Telford's Mythe Bridge at Tewkesbury, constructed in 1823–1826 with a single span in cast iron. (Photo: Staffordshire County Council; courtesy National Monuments Record.)

*Figure 6*  The 18th-century Halfpenny Bridge across the Thames at Lechlade.
(Photo: courtesy National Monuments Record; Crown copyright reserved.)

these small buildings, constructed by their very nature at points where road improvements now demand their removal. Two general assessments of the problem have also been published (Cox and Surry 1965; Viner 1982b).

The county also possesses a fine group of bridges which should not go unnoticed. At Over, near Gloucester (SO 816196), Thomas Telford's 1831 road bridge has survived the remodelling of the modern road system around it and should now be preserved. Telford's slightly earlier Mythe Bridge at Tewkesbury (SO 889337), remains largely unaltered despite some strengthening earlier this century (Fig. 5). At Tewkesbury and at Lechlade, King John's Bridge (SO 894332) and St John's Bridge (SU 223990) both have medieval origins, but Halfpenny Bridge at Lechlade (SU 213993) is an eighteenth-century structure with a notable symmetry and an attractive tollhouse added later (Fig. 6).

Transport by water has made a major contribution to Gloucestershire history. The county is effectively bisected by the River Severn and trade across the river has been almost as significant as trade along its length. Long-abandoned crossing points can still be detected on the western side at Newnham and at Purton, although perhaps more interesting is the tiny port at Bullo Pill (SO 691099), little more than a tidal creek used for boat-building until 1800 but developed thereafter as a port for coal from the Forest of Dean and in use from 1814 to 1926. Although now increasingly overgrown, remains of three deep-water wharves with coal-chutes and the entrance lock-chamber can be seen. Better preserved is the canal and harbour area at Lydney (SO 652013–635018), which developed over the course of a century as the main port for the Forest. Still in occasional use, the surviving remains offer a rare opportunity for sympathetic restoration as part of recreational development.

The desire to link the manufacturing centre of Stroud with the River Severn led to the construction of a canal, promoted by the clothiers of the valleys, to bring in coal more cheaply than by road. The Stroudwater Canal was opened in 1779 with thirteen locks in the eight miles up to Stroud from the Severn at Framilode (SO 751105). It was designed and built as a broad canal able to accommodate the characteristic broad-bottomed vessel of the river, the trow, with its length of 72 feet and beam of $15\frac{1}{2}$ feet. The history of the Stroudwater has been studied in depth by Handford in recent years (1979); meanwhile it remains in the ownership of its original promoters and must offer a good opportunity for restoration in the future.

Further east from Stroud, and chronologically next in line, the Thames and Severn Canal was promoted as the first main east-west link between the two major rivers of southern Britain. From the eastern reaches of the valley of the Frome above Brimscombe and Chalford, the line of the canal was driven by tunnel through the Cotswold scarp to join the headwaters of the Thames near Cirencester. Opened in 1789, its chequered history has also been documented in depth (Household 1983) in a study rightly regarded as a classic of its kind. Now derelict, the Thames and Severn provides considerable industrial archaeological interest, and the entire western section from Stroud to the summit at Daneway basin (SO 938035) can be explored by towpath as a public right of way (Handford and Viner 1984). The crowning glory, however, remains the Sapperton tunnel, 3817 yards long and constructed over a period of five years. Portals at either entrance compensate for

*Figure 7* The classical or eastern portal of the Sapperton Tunnel on the Thames and Severn Canal at Coates, built in 1783–1789 and restored in 1976–1977. (Photo: Chris Bowler, Cirencester.)

*Figure 8* Gloucester docks, photographed in September 1972. In the foreground the Llanthony warehouse built c.1870 was one of the latest of the dock's larger warehouses. The groups beyond date to thirty or forty years earlier. (Photo: courtesy National Monuments Record; Crown copyright reserved.)

much unsophisticated canal architecture elsewhere; at Daneway (SO 944033) the design is gothic although much vandalized, while at Coates (SO 965006) a classical façade was constructed (Fig. 7). This too had been the victim of decay and destruction prior to an imaginative and successful restoration undertaken by the Stroudwater, Thames and Severn Canal Trust (Viner 1979). Elsewhere, much of the route of the canal has been appropriated for new uses, as emphasized in a case study of the 1¼-mile-long branch to Cirencester (Viner 1976).

The difficulties of navigation on the winding part of the Severn south of Gloucester stimulated the construction of a canal to bypass this section of the river. Originally intended to enter the river at Berkeley Pill, the Gloucester and Sharpness Canal opened in 1827 but was shortened to Sharpness (SO 668022), thus creating a company town at the junction. The biggest in England at the time of its construction, the canal remains in use today and its towpath can be followed throughout. The 'level crossing' with the route of the Stroudwater at Saul Junction (SO 758094) is a major feature of a canal which, other than its distinctive bridge-keepers' cottages, has most to offer the industrial archaeologist at either end of its length. At Sharpness some features of the docks have been studied (Preece 1977), and equally of interest is the dock company's own housing development (Isherwood 1976). At the northern end of the canal is the port of Gloucester, an entrepôt for traffic up the Severn and as such a point for transhipment. Of all the industrial archaeological remains in Gloucestershire, the enclosed docks in the city provide arguably the county's most pressing problem (Fig. 8). The chief characteristic is the grouping of multi-storey brick warehouses dating from the period 1826–1873 and reflecting the growth in the corn trade at this time. The buildings are functional but constructed with a distinct sense of proportion and the homogeneity of the group remains, despite the passage of time and their increasing redundancy as warehouses. Original plans of many of the buildings have been preserved (Conway-Jones 1977–8; Stimpson 1980).

The development of railways as a means of transport in the county should be studied first in the Forest of Dean, where horse tramroads were built during the period 1798–1835 as little more than feeders into the waterway system (e.g. Clissold and Standing 1980). Most were subsequently converted to steam railways and the region boasted a mass of railway lines providing a transport system for the industries of Dean. A few tramroads survived as plateways and their remains can still be seen, as for example on the Bicslade Tramroad (SO 608100). The pattern of the railways of the Forest has been well-examined (Paar 1965 and 1973). Elsewhere, the development of the

*Figure 9* The terminus station at Cirencester Town, constructed in 1841 and closed shortly after this photograph was taken in 1964. The building was used as a bus station until recently and is now (1984) used as a printing works. (Photo: Chris Bowler, Cirencester.)

network must be traced through the growth of the Great Western Railway and its main rival, the Midland, together with the history of their respective precursors (Maggs 1969). Chronologically the Great Western's expansion north-westwards from Swindon brought the influence of Brunel into the county at an early date, with a Brunel-inspired terminus station at Cirencester in 1841 (SP 021018), which survives less well (Fig. 9) than the better-preserved Stroud station (SO 850052). The later development at Kemble Junction in 1882 has many of the characteristics of earlier days and survives in use substantially intact.

In the north of the county, influence from the Midland was strong, the two rivals clashing almost head-on at Gloucester, where the respective station layouts and working arrangements perpetuated the animosity well into the present century. Gloucester station has been almost totally rebuilt, but the station at Cheltenham Lansdown (SO 932220), although deprived of its pillared portico, preserves much of S.W. Daukes's original design of 1840. Between Gloucester and Cheltenham the history of the line and its development from a tramroad serving the limestone quarries on Leckhampton Hill has been documented by Bick (1968), while elsewhere in the county the popular interest in railway history is also reflected in a growing body of published material. In the north-west the history of railways between Gloucester, Newent, and Ledbury is inextricably bound up with the ill-fated Hereford and Gloucester Canal, which was completed only in 1845 and proved too late to be viable, closing in 1881 for part of its route to be used as a railway (Bick 1979a). In eastern Gloucestershire the Oxford, Worcester and Wolverhampton Railway (Jenkins and Quayle 1977) skirted the Cotswolds leaving this upland central region to be permeated by late interlopers, invariably small and impoverished companies subsequently absorbed by the Great Western Railway. The latter had a branch-line character in the county, owing not a little to these erstwhile independent routes (Jenkins 1975; Maggs 1980; Sands 1959).

## HOUSING, PRISONS, AND AGRICULTURE

Beyond the more obvious classifications of extractive industries, power supply, and communications, there is much to which industrial archaeologists may legitimately turn their attention. One of the more significant of the many recent general studies of the subject (Butt and Donnachie 1979, 226) defines a whole area of 'social archaeology', under which classification may be examined the effects of manufacturing or commercial development upon

*Figure 10*   The cell-blocks, work-rooms, and exercise yard at the Northleach house of correction, opened in 1791. These buildings were demolished in 1936. (Photo: courtesy Butt Studio, Bourton-on-the-Water.)

social conditions, in particular housing. Isherwood's study (1976) has already been noted, to which may be added the examination of an improved dwelling company's influence upon a small area of late-Victorian development at Watermoor in Cirencester (Slater 1976), and to a lesser extent the peculiarities of specific-purpose canal and railway housing provision for lengthmen, crossing-keepers, etc. (Awdry 1983, 29–30). Two groups of railway housing deserve mention. Cookson Terrace at Lydney (SO 635018) incorporated varied house styles into a single terrace and was constructed by the Severn and Wye Railway for its employees in 1858. Across the county at Kemble (ST 985977) the GWR built for its employees a row of semi-detached houses overlooking the station.

Social conditions of a particular nature may be examined in the development of the prison system in the county. A leading pioneer of late eighteenth-century prison reform was a native of Gloucestershire; Sir George Onesiphorus Paul was a mill-owner and philanthropist who, for the first time, separated prisoners into groups by age and sex and introduced new types of prison buildings. His work to the designs of William Blackburn can best be seen at Littledean (SO 674137), where the substantially complete building remains in police use; at Gloucester prison, which continues in use as the county gaol; and to a lesser, but more accessible, extent at Northleach prison (SP 109149), where the façade and plan (Fig. 10) are preserved and recently have been presented as a feature of the Cotswold Countryside Collection museum of rural life (Harwood 1982; Whiting 1975 and 1979).

In recent years the work of agricultural historians has also begun to find a home in the literature of industrial archaeology. Standard histories of local businesses may encompass the range of products intended for the agricultural market and such firms may command markets of a national and international scale. One excellent Gloucestershire example is R.A. Lister & Co. of Dursley (Evans 1979). The process of mechanization in agriculture can be studied through the products of a specialized manufacturer serving a local market, as for example Kells of Gloucester and Ross (Davies 1981), or through the involvement of many of the county's major landowners in one of the current 'improvements' of the time (Miller 1981). The general context of such developments can be examined in the one general assessment of this subject (Harvey 1980).

## CONCLUSION

It remains to assess the contribution of industrial archaeology to studies in the history of Gloucestershire. As a discipline it still remains loose in its definitions; it might be argued, for example, that the study of housing development is rather more legitimately the province of vernacular architecture, although it is surely more significant that the techniques and approaches to the material remains should be as sophisticated and catholic as possible. The contribution of the Gloucestershire Society for Industrial Archaeology has been considerable during the twenty years since its formation, particularly in view of its relatively small membership. The bibliography reveals the extent of the Society's activities, although it is clear that much research remains of an archival nature, in the school of the local historian, and is not necessarily concerned with the surviving material remains. The latter represent the greatest challenges to the discipline of industrial archaeology; as a branch of a wider study of material remains, its practitioners must come to terms with the classification of the evidence and its detailed recording. To this end the Society's production of a gazetteer of sites in the county (Awdry 1983), first published in 1973, was a major achievement in the face of financial difficulties and such co-operative ventures must remain the keystone to fieldwork activity. In neighbouring Wiltshire, the second edition of a similar gazetteer has assumed a more substantial format (Corfield 1978). Nor is the process untimely; in the ten years since the first publication of the Gloucestershire gazetteer, at least half a dozen of the buildings or significant remains listed therein have been demolished or destroyed. A modest contribution against such odds has been the installation of plaques recording sites of industrial archaeological significance; thus at Newent (SO 722263) in 1968 the site of the former canal and railway routes was recorded on the line of the new bypass.

The process of recording remains the critical factor; often it can be incomplete (Chatwin 1976), or fraught with problems of sheer scale, as at Gloucester docks. The use of surviving original records can form the basis for a detailed on-site survey but should not become merely a substitute for it, although in certain circumstances it remains a valuable contribution, as at Fairford and Tetbury, where most railway buildings have already disappeared (Karau 1977). The use of other forms of surviving documentation has already been mentioned (see also Bick 1979b; Crawford 1981); the photographic record has much to contribute (Bick 1980b) and is particularly useful in transport studies (e.g. Bartholomew 1982; Russell 1977; Viner 1975 and 1981). The discipline of the subject is also well-suited to the particular enthusiasms of the individual and valuable contributions can result, for example Chatwin's excellent study of the ornamental ironwork of Cheltenham (1975).

In the process of conservation of historic buildings, the industrial archaeologist is already much-involved. The preservation of buildings frequently implies some form of rehabilitation to a new use with consequent loss of original evidence, which must be documented prior to change. There remains a clear need for a policy of preservation of a select number of major industrial archaeological monuments in the county, to which end a number of projects-cum-appeals have already appeared in print (e.g. Parr 1977–8; Standing and Coates 1979). The excavation of industrial archaeological sites regrettably remains relatively unsophisticated, and must play a secondary role in the immediate future to the above-ground survey of threatened and significant material remains. The publication of results and documentation is no less significant to the industrial archaeologist than to his 'classical' colleagues, and it must be concluded that the steady improvement in both the quality and the range of published material in the discipline, although at times painfully slow to develop generally in Britain, is now beginning to reveal just how great is the wealth of material remains in Gloucestershire to be documented, recorded, and, where appropriate, preserved for the benefit of future generations.

## ACKNOWLEDGEMENTS

The author wishes to thank Revd. W.V. Awdry and Miss Amina Chatwin, respectively President and former Secretary of the Gloucestershire Society for Industrial Archaeology, for kindly reading the first draft of this paper and commenting upon it. Other members of GSIA added useful information, but all outstanding errors must remain the responsibility of the author.

## REFERENCES

Awdry, W. (ed.). 1983. *Industrial Archaeology in Gloucestershire*. (3rd rev edn.) Dursley.

Bartholomew, D. 1982. *Midland & South Western Junction Railway*. Berkshire.

Bayes, J.F. and Roberts, J. 1971. Turnpike Roads from Gloucester to Cheltenham and Tewkesbury. *GSIAJ* 1971, 74–84.

Bick, D.E. 1968. *The Gloucester and Cheltenham Railway*. Lingfield.

Bick, D.E. 1971. *Old Leckhampton*. Cheltenham.

Bick, D.E. 1979a. *The Hereford & Gloucester Canal*. Newent.

Bick, D.E. 1979b. Records of the Newent Coalfield. *GSIAJ* 1979, 1–8.

Bick, D.E. 1980a. Remnants of the Newent Furnace. *GSIAJ* 1980, 29–37.

Bick, D.E. 1980b. *The Old Industries of Dean*. Newent.

Buchanan, C.A. and R.A. 1980. *The Batsford Guide to the Industrial Archaeology of Central Southern England*. London.

Butt, J. and Donnachie, I. 1979. *Industrial Archaeology in the British Isles*. London.

Cave, B.V. 1974. Mill sites on the Longhope-Flaxley and Westbury Streams. *GSIAJ* 1974, 8–31.

Chatwin, A. 1975. *Cheltenham's Ornamental Ironwork*. Cheltenham.

Chatwin, A. 1976. Hampen Flax Mill. *GSIAJ* 1976, 17–25.

Clissold, G. and Standing, I. 1980. Mr. Teague's Railway. *GSIAJ* 1980, 51–60.

Conway-Jones, A.H. 1977–8. The Warehouses at Gloucester Docks. *GSIAJ* 1977–8, 13–19.

Corfield, M.C. (ed.). 1978. *A Guide to the Industrial Archaeology of Wiltshire*. Trowbridge.

Cox, C. 1964. Milestones of the Stroud District. *TBGAS* 83, 119–142.

Cox, C. 1967. Turnpike Houses of the Stroud District. *TBGAS* 86, 118–150.

Cox, C. 1979. Building the Nailsworth Turnpike. *GSIAJ* 1979, 21–38.

Cox, C., Hadfield, C. and Bick, D.E. 1973. Transport. In C. and A.M. Hadfield (eds.), *The Cotswolds: a new study*, 139–177. Newton Abbot.

Cox, C. and Surry, N. 1965. The Archaeology of Turnpike Roads. *Industrial Archaeol* 2, 33–40.

Crawford, N. 1977–8. The Bibury Turnpike Trust. *GSIAJ* 1977–8, 1–12.

Crawford, G.N. 1981. The Gloucester & Berkeley Manuscripts in the Telford Collection. *GSIAJ* 1981, 9–29.

Crawford, G.N. 1982. The Woodchester Roundhouse. *GSIAJ* 1982, 41–43.

Davies, S. 1981. Kells of Gloucester and Ross: agricultural implement makers. *TBGAS* 99, 157–166.

Evans, D.E. 1979. *Lister's: the first hundred years*. Gloucester.

Haine, C. 1981. Wool-Drying Stoves along the Painswick Stream. *GSIAJ* 1981, 30–31.

Haine, C. 1982. Cloth Mills along the Painswick Stream. *GSIAJ* 1982, 17–34.

Handford, M.A. 1979. *The Stroudwater Canal*. Gloucester.

Handford, M. and Viner, D.J. 1984. *Stroudwater & Thames and Severn Canals Towpath Guide*. Gloucester.

Harris, F.J.T. 1974. Guns Mill as a Paper Mill. *GSIAJ* 1974, 32–40.

Harris, F.J.T. and Angel, J.L. 1975. History of papermaking in and near Winchcombe. *GSIAJ* 1975, 9–65.

Harris, F.J.T. 1976. Paper and Board Mills in or near Gloucestershire. *TBGAS* 94, 124–135.

Hart, C. 1971. *The Industrial History of Dean*. Newton Abbot.

Harvey, N. 1980. *The Industrial Archaeology of Farming in England and Wales*. London.

Harwood, A.R. 1982. The Northleach House of Correction. *GSAIJ* 1982, 2–6.

Household, H. 1983. *The Thames & Severn Canal*. (2nd rev edn.) Gloucester.

Hudson, K. 1968. *The Industrial Archaeology of Southern England*. (2nd rev edn.) Newton Abbot.

Isherwood, A.J. 1976. Dock Company Housing, Sharpness, Gloucestershire. *GSIAJ* 1976, 30–50.

Jenkins, S.C. 1975. *The Witney & East Gloucestershire Railway*. Blandford.

Jenkins, S.C. and Quayle, H.I. 1977. *The Oxford, Worcester & Wolverhampton Railway*. Blandford.

Karau, P. 1977. *Great Western Branch Line Termini. Vol. 1*. Oxford.

Maggs, C.G. 1969. *The Bristol & Gloucester Railway*. Lingfield.

Maggs, C.G. 1980. *The Midland & South Western Junction Railway*. Newton Abbot.

Mann, J. de L. 1971. *The Cloth Industry in the West of England from 1640 to 1880*. Oxford.

Margary, I.D. 1967. *Roman Roads in Britain*. London.

Medlam, W.G. 1977–8. Kilcott Mill. *GSIAJ* 1977–8, 20–24.

Miller, C. 1981. The Gloucestershire Steam Plough Company 1860–2. *TBGAS* 99, 141–156.

Moir, E. 1971. Marling & Evans, King's Stanley and Ebley Mills, Gloucestershire. *Textile History* 2(1), 28–56.

Newman, R. 1982. The Origins of the Cinderford Coke Iron Furnace. *GSIAJ* 1982, 12–16.

Paar, H.W. 1965. *The Great Western Railway in Dean*. Dawlish.

Paar, H.W. 1973. *The Severn & Wye Railway*. (2nd rev edn.) Newton Abbot.

Paar, H.W. 1977–8. The Redbrook Tramroad incline in the Wye Valley. *GSIAJ* 1977–8, 30–33.

Perkins, J.W., Brooks, A.T. and Pearce, A.E. McR. 1979. *Bath Stone: a quarry history*. Cardiff and Bath.

Ponting, K.G. 1971. *The Woollen Industry of South West England*. Bath.

Pountney, M. and Beddow, G. 1976. Dyehouse at Brimscombe Mill. *GSIAJ* 1976, 7–12.

Preece, G.P.J. 1977. Railway and Canal Coal-Drops at Sharpness Docks. *Industrial Archaeol Rev* 11(1), 78–84.

Rix, M. 1967. *Industrial Archaeology*. London. (=Historical Association No. G65.)

Russell, J.H. 1977. *The Banbury and Cheltenham Railway 1887–1962*. Oxford.

Sands, T.B. 1959. *The Midland & South Western Junction Railway*. Lingfield.

Shorter, A.H. 1952. Paper Mills in Gloucestershire. *TBGAS* 71, 145–161.

Slater, T.R. 1976. The Cirencester improved Dwellings Company 1880–1914. In A.D. McWhirr (ed.), *Studies in the archaeology and history of Cirencester*, 171–197. Oxford. (=BAR Brit Ser 30.)

Spry, N. 1971. The Northgate Turnpike. *GSIAJ* 1971, 1–58.

Standing, I.J. 1980. The Whitecliff Iron works in the Forest of Dean, part one 1798–1808. *GSIAJ* 1980, 18–28.

Standing, I.J. 1981. 'Dear Mushet' – a history of the Whitecliff Ironworks, part two, 1808–10. *GSIAJ* 1981, 32–71.

Standing, I. and Coates, S. 1979. Historical Sites of Industrial Importance on Forestry Commission Land in Dean. *GSIAJ* 1979, 16–20.

Stimpson, M. 1980. *The history of Gloucester Docks and its associated canals and railways.* London.

Tann, J. 1967. *Gloucestershire Woollen Mills.* Newton Abbot.

Verey, D.C.W. 1970. *Gloucestershire: The Cotswolds.* Harmondsworth.

Viner, D.J. 1969. The Industrial Archaeology of Hampshire Roads: a survey. *Proc Hampshire Fld Club Archaeol Soc* 26, 155–172.

Viner, D.J. 1975. *The Thames & Severn Canal: a survey from historical photographs.* Nelson, Lancs.

Viner, D.J. 1976. The Thames & Severn Canal in Cirencester. In A.D. McWhirr (ed.), *Studies in the archaeology and history of Cirencester*, 126–144. Oxford. (=BAR Brit Ser 30.)

Viner, D.J. 1979. On the threshold of Darkness: canal tunnel restoration in Gloucestershire. *Country Life* 18 January 1979, 162–163.

Viner, D.J. 1981. *Transport in the Cotswolds from old photographs.* Nelson, Lancs.

Viner, D.J. 1982a. The Wimborne & Puddletown Turnpike Trust (1841–78) and the toll-house at Athelhampton. *Proc Dorset Natur Hist Archaeol Soc* 104, 25–32.

Viner, D.J. 1982b. The turnpike toll-house. *Period Home* August/September 1982, 5–12.

Walrond, L.F.J. 1967. Industrial Archaeology in the Stroud Area. *TBGAS* 86, 173–182.

Walrond, L.F.J. 1973. Wool, Woolmen and Weavers. In C. and A.M. Hadfield (eds.), *The Cotswolds: a new study*, 178–203. Newton Abbot.

Wheeler, R.E.M. and T.V. 1932. *Report on the excavations of the Prehistoric, Roman and Post-Roman site in Lydney Park, Glos.* Oxford.

Whiting, J.R.S. 1975. *Prison Reform in Gloucestershire 1776–1820.* London and Chichester.

Whiting, J.R.S. 1979. *A House of Correction.* Gloucester.

**January 1984**

# INDEX OF PLACES

## Compiled by Alan Saville

All the places listed are in the modern county of Gloucestershire unless another county is specified. This index also provides a concordance with the parish names for each Gloucestershire location mentioned. References to illustrations within the text are given in bold type.

Ablington Camp, Bibury
hillfort 165
Adlestrop
long barrow 81
Alderton
Alderton Manor 306
Alkington
post-medieval pottery 269
Alvington
Plusterwine Farm 312
Amberley Camp, Minchinhampton
iron age pottery 158
Ampney Crucis
medieval pottery 271
Ampney St Peter
Roman villa(?) 195, 206
see also Ranbury Ring
Ancaster, Lincolnshire
Mrs O'Neil at 33
Andoversford
mesolithic finds 76; Saxon pottery 240, 251
Ariconium
see Weston under Penyard
Arlebrook, Standish
The Thatched Cottage 310
Arlingham
Hock Cliff section 51, 52
Ascott Doilly, Oxfordshire
medieval pottery 255
Ascott-under-Wychwood, Oxfordshire
long barrow 83, 96
Ashleworth
Ashleworth Court 310–312; Ashleworth Manor 306; medieval houses 307, 310
Ashville, Abingdon, Oxfordshire
iron age & Roman site 206
Aust, Avon
bronze figurine 161; service station 321
Avening
medieval pottery 269; mesolithic finds 71, 76
Awre
bronze age axe 115; medieval pottery 255
see also Bledisloe Tump
Aylworth, Naunton
medieval settlement 287

Badgeworth
medieval pottery 269
see also Crickley Hill
Badminton, Avon
medieval settlement 282

Bagendon
Mrs Clifford at 19, **21**, 22–24, 141; currency bars 161; iron age coins 161; iron age pottery 159; iron age site 140, 148, 149, 160, 165, 182; medieval pottery 266; mesolithic finds 71, 76
Balls Green, Minchinhampton
limestone mine 321
Bardney, Lincolnshire
Saxon relics 237
Barnsley Park, Barnsley
iron age pottery 154; mesolithic finds 71, 76; Roman villa 209; Saxon pottery 251
Barnwood, Gloucester
beaker find 115; iron age pottery 154, 158–160; limestone cone 163; medieval pottery 269; mesolithic finds 72, **73**, 76; neolithic evidence 81, 91, 100, **101**; palaeolithic finds 61, 62, 66, 67, 75
Barton, Cirencester
Saxon cemetery **230**
Barton Court Farm, Abingdon, Oxfordshire
iron age & Roman site 206
Bath, Avon
limestone mine 321; Saxon capture of 229; Saxon minster 232
Batsford
see Dorn
Beachley, Tidenham
beaker burial 115
Beckbury, Temple Guiting
hillfort 145, 165; iron age pottery **155**, 158, 172
Beckford, Hereford and Worcester
bronze arrowhead 123; iron age pottery 156; iron age site 150, 151
Belas Knap, Sudeley
iron age pottery 158; long barrow 81, 87, **89**, 92, **94**, 95
Bengrove Farm, Sandhurst
medieval settlement 282
Berkeley
power station 321; Saxon minster & town 237, 295, 296, **296**, **297**
Bevan's Quarry, Temple Guiting
bronze age barrow & finds 121, 122, 136, 137
Beverstone
see Chavenage
Bevington Camp, Ham and Stone
hillfort 143, 165
Bibury
Arlington Mill 322; Arlington Row 306; bronze age dagger 117; medieval chimney caps 312;

Saxon cemetery **230**; Saxon Church 234
see also Ablington Camp; Saltway Barn
Bicshead, West Dean
  stone quarry 321
Bicslade, West Dean
  coalmine 319; stoneworks 321; tramroad 333
Bidfield, Miserden
  medieval settlement 287
Birdlip, Cowley
  iron age burial 160, 162; iron age pottery **153**, 158, 169; mesolithic finds 76; turnpike road 327; see also The Peak Camp
Bishops Cleeve
  iron age pottery 158; sand deposits 53; Saxon cemetery **230**, 231
  see also Wontley
Bisley-with-Lypiatt
  Avenis long barrow 92; bronze age axe 115, 116; medieval pottery 271; mesolithic finds 76; Overcourt 311
  see also Bournes Green; Daneway
Blacklains, Brimpsfield
  mesolithic finds 76
Blackpool Bridge, West Dean
  Dean Road 318
Blaisdon
  see Flaxley; Guns Mill; Welshbury
Bledisloe Tump, Awre
  medieval pottery 265, 268
Blockley
  Saxon burial 234; Saxon cemetery **230**
  see also Lower Ditchford; Upper Ditchford; Upton
Bournes Green, Bisley-with-Lypiatt
  mesolithic finds 76
Bourton-on-the-Water
  beaker find 115; bronze age finds 123; iron age pottery 158; medieval pottery 271; neolithic evidence 81, 100, **101**, 103; ring-ditch 137, 138; Roman settlement 183, 218, **218**, 219; Saxon hut 234; Saxon pottery 240
  see also Salmonsbury; Santhill Gravel Pit
Bown Hill, Woodchester
  long barrow 92, 95
Brackenbury Ditches, North Nibley
  bronze age saw 123; hillfort 143, 165
Brand Green, Pauntley
  quartzite tool 64
Breckness Court, Coleford
  medieval settlement 282
Bredon Hill, Hereford and Worcester
  currency bars 161; hillfort 143; iron age pottery 156
Brimpsfield
  medieval pottery 269; medieval settlement 276; mesolithic finds 76; West Tump long barrow **94**, 104
  see also Blacklains; Caudle Green; Manless Town
Brimscombe, Thrupp
  dyehouse 326
Bristol, Avon

medieval pottery 254, 256, 258, 260, 263, 264, 266; medieval town 299, 302; Saxon settlement 236
Broadwell
  Saxon cemetery **230**
Brockworth
  Brockworth Court 306, 309; dyke 149, 165; palaeolithic find 62, 75
  see also Crockmede
Bubb's Hill, Elkstone
  mesolithic finds 76
Buckland
  Buckland Rectory 306, 313
  see also Burhill
Bullo Pill, Newnham
  port 330
The Bulwarks, Haresfield
  hillfort 165
Burhill, Buckland
  hillfort 154, 165; iron age pottery **155**, 158, 170
Burleigh, Minchinhampton
  limestone mine 321
Burn Ground, Hampnett
  bronze age barrows 132, 135; bronze age pottery 118; long barrow 82, **89**, 91, 92, 97, 99, 104; Saxon cemetery **230**; Saxon pottery 240, 241, 251
Butterrow, Rodborough
  tollhouse 327

Cadbury-Congresbury, Avon
  6thC pottery 251
Cam
  mill 325; neolithic evidence 82, 101, **101**, 102, 104; post-medieval pottery 268, 269
Camp, Miserden
  mesolithic finds 76
Caudle Green, Brimpsfield
  medieval settlement 292
Cerney Wick, South Cerney
  palaeolithic find 62
Chalford
  St Mary's Mill 326
Chalk Hill, Temple Guiting
  medieval pottery 270
Charlton Abbots
  palaeolithic find 66, 75
Charlton Kings
  dyke 164
  see also Sandy Lane
Chastleton, Oxfordshire
  hillfort 145
Chavenage, Beverstone/Horsley
  mesolithic finds 76; Saxon cemetery **230**
Cheddar, Somerset
  Saxon hall 237
Chedworth
  Christianity at 231; medieval pottery 271; Roman villa 221; round barrows 135, 137
Cheltenham
  brickworks 52; ironwork 338; Lansdown station

335; medieval/post-medieval pottery 270; medieval town 297, **297, 298**; sand deposits 53
see also Charlton Kings
Chepstow, Gwent
medieval pottery 254, 255, 263, 264; Saxon occupation 253
Cherington
barrows 132; medieval settlement 282; mesolithic finds 69, 76
see also Troublehouse Covert
Chester, Cheshire
Saxon pottery 252
Chichester, West Sussex
Saxon pottery 252
Chipping Campden
bronze age axe 123, **123**; medieval town 297, **297, 298**, 302
see also Westington
Churcham
bronze age(?) enclosure 146
Churchdown
iron age pottery **155**, 158, 172
Cirencester
Abbey 249; bronze age spearhead 123; canal 333; the Danes at 236; iron age pottery 158, 159; medieval pottery 248, 255, 262, 263, 265, 267, 271; medieval town **297**; post-medieval pottery 271; railway station **334**, 335; Roman town 148, 212–217, **214**, 228; Saxon capture of 229; Saxon church 234; Saxon pottery 240, 251; Saxon town 295, 296, **296**; Watermoor 337; word-square 231
see also Barton; Corinium
Claydon Pike, Fairford/Lechlade
iron age pottery 157, 158; iron age site 140, 150, 151, 162, 193, 195, 197, 198, **198**, 199, **200**, 203, 206; Roman site 193, 195, 197, 199, **201**, 202, 208, 209
Cleeve Cloud, Southam
hillfort 145, 165; iron age pottery 154, **155**, 170
Cleeve Common, Southam
earthwork 149, 165
Cleeve Hill, Southam
bronze age axe 116; bronze age knife 123; limestone 54; medieval pottery 270; ringworks 149
Climperwell, Cranham
mesolithic finds 76
Coaley
medieval pottery 268
Coates
Sapperton tunnel **331**, 333
see also Hullasey; Trewsbury
Coberley
Dry Heathfield round barrow 134; medieval earthworks 283; medieval pottery 270
see also Crickley Hill
Coleford
see Breckness Court; Whitecliffe
Colesbourne
bronze age dagger 117
see also Norbury Camp

Coln Rogers, Coln St Dennis
Saxon church 234
Coln St Aldwyns
see Dean Camp
Coln St Dennis
Colnpen long barrow 95
see also Coln Rogers
Combe, Warwickshire
Abbey 287
Condicote
henge monument 82, 83, 85, **101**, 104, 118, 133, 146; pit alignment 149
Copse Hill, Upper Slaughter
iron age pottery 151, 158
Corinium
Roman town 207, **214**, 215, **216**, 217
Corse
Corse Court 308
Cow Common, Swell
bronze age finds 119; long barrow 86, **87**, 93, 101; mesolithic finds 72, 75
Cowley
mesolithic finds 76
see also Shab Hill
Cranham
medieval/post-medieval pottery 269; mesolithic finds 76
see also Climperwell; Ebworth; High Brotheridge
Cricklade, Wiltshire
Saxon pottery 251
Crickley Hill, Badgeworth/Coberley
beaker finds 115; iron age burial 160; iron age pottery 152; iron age site 140, 141, 143–145, 151, 164, 165; neolithic evidence 82, 87, 89, **89**, **90**, 91–93, 99, 105, 146
Crockmede, Brockworth
place-name 160
Croft Ambrey, Hereford and Worcester
iron age pottery 156
Cromhall, Avon
bronze age axe-hammer 117
Cutsdean
bronze age adze 117; possible henge 104

Daglingworth
Saxon church 234
Dane's Camp, Bredon Hill, Hereford and Worcester
iron age pottery 156
Daneway, Bisley/Sapperton
Daneway House 306; Sapperton Tunnel 330, 333
Darkhill, West Dean
furnace 319
Dean Camp, Coln St Aldwyns
hillfort 165
Deerhurst
medieval/post-medieval pottery 256, 270; Saxon church 234
Didcot, Dumbleton
medieval settlement 287
Didmarton
medieval settlement 282

The Ditches, North Cerney
  currency bars 161; hillfort 143, 145, 146, 165
Donnington
  brewery 322
Dorn, Batsford
  Roman settlement 218, **218**, 219
Dowdeswell
  The Castles hillfort 165; medieval pottery 270
Down Ampney
  bronze age hoard 121; medieval pottery 271;
  neolithic causewayed enclosure **89**, **90**, 91
Driffield
  Roman villa 195, 206
Droitwich, Hereford and Worcester
  iron age salt production 156; medieval pottery 254,
  263; Saxon salt production 238
Drybrook
  quarry 51
Dublin, Ireland
  medieval pottery 254, 263
Dumbleton
  iron age pottery **153**, 158, 169; medieval pottery
  270; Saxon pottery 240
  see also Didcot
Duntisbourne Abbots
  iron age pottery 159; mesolithic finds 76; Saxon
  church 234
Duntisbourne Rouse
  Saxon Church 234
  see also Pinbury
Dursley
  medieval chimney caps 312; medieval town 297,
  **297**
Dymock
  medieval town 297; mesolithic finds 74; post-
  medieval pottery 268; Roman settlement 218,
  **218**, 219, 220

Eastington
  Alkerton Farm 310, 312, 313; flint artefacts 67;
  iron age pottery 150, 158; mesolithic finds 76;
  post-medieval pottery 268; Saxon finds 241,
  **242**, 243; Saxon pottery 240; Saxon settlement
  234, 241, 243
Eastleach
  neolithic causewayed enclosure **89**, **90**, 91
Ebrington
  Saxon cemetery **230**
  see also Hidcote Bartrim
Ebworth, Cranham
  iron age pottery 154
Edge, Painswick
  medieval pottery 268
Edgeworth
  medieval pottery 271
  see also Juniper Hill
Elkstone
  flint artefact 64; round barrow **138**
  see also Bubb's Hill
English Bicknor
  see Symonds Yat

Ewen, Kemble
  medieval/post-medieval pottery 271; medieval
  pottery 249, 262, 265; Roman settlement 196;
  Saxon pottery 240
Exeter, Devon
  Saxon pottery 252
Eyeford Hill, Upper Slaughter
  long barrow 92, 93, 98, 100, 115

Fairford
  medieval town 294, **297**; palaeolithic find 62, 75;
  Saxon cemetery **230**
  see also Claydon Pike
Falfield, Avon
  medieval pottery 267
Farmington
  bronze age pottery 118; medieval settlement **278**,
  282
Farnborough, Hampshire  –
  medieval kilns 265
Fladbury, Hereford and Worcester
  medieval pottery 263
Flaxley, Blaisdon
  Abbey 286
Foxcote Manor, Withington
  iron age finds 150, 154, 158
Framilode, Fretherne with Saul
  canal 330
Frampton on Severn
  bronze age barrows 134; Denfurlong Farm 312;
  iron age pottery 158; Manor Farm Cottage
  308–310; medieval houses 307; medieval
  pottery 268; The Old Cruck House 312; quarry
  52; Saxon pottery 252, 268; Tanhouse Farm
  308
Fretherne with Saul
  see Framilode; Saul Junction
Frilford, Oxfordshire
  Saxon settlement 210
Frocester
  medieval pottery 254, 263, 269; medieval settlement 289, **290**; post-medieval pottery 269; St
  Peter's church/Roman site 232; Saxon pottery
  240
  see also Frocester Court; Nympsfield long barrow;
  Soldier's Grave
Frocester Court, Frocester
  iron age pottery 150, 158, 159; medieval fields 228;
  medieval house 311; medieval pottery 265;
  mesolithic finds 71, 76; Mrs O'Neil at **36**;
  Roman villa 227; Saxon pottery 240

Glevum
  Roman town 212, 215, 217
Gloucester
  Berkeley St 213, 266, 299; Crypt G.S. site iron age
  pottery 154, 158, 169; the Danes at 236; docks
  332, 333, 338; Eastgate St 300; Fleece Inn 300;
  Friars' Orchard, iron age pottery **153**, 158, 169;
  medieval pottery 249, 253–257, 259–267, 269;
  medieval town 294, **297**, 299–302; New Market

Hall 266; Northgate St 299; Northgate Turnpike 327; Over Bridge 329; post-medieval pottery 269; prison 337; Quay St 266; railways 335; Roman cemeteries 233, 237; Roman town 212, 213, 215–217, **216**, 227–229, 233; royal palace 237; Mrs O'Neil at 36; Saintbridge site neolithic evidence 102; St Mary de Lode church 233; St Mary's St 266; St Oswald's Priory 234, 237, 238, 251; St Peter's Abbey 237; Saxon capture of 229; Saxon minster 229, 232; Saxon pottery 251, 252, 259, 269; Saxon town 225, 229, 233, 236–239, 295, 296, **296**; Squire's Gate site neolithic evidence 100; Sutgrove Cottage 308; Telephone Exchange site neolithic evidence 88, **89**, 100, **101**; Telephone Exchange site Roman building 213; Westgate St 252, 259, 262, 267, 299–301
see also Barnwood; Glevum; Hucclecote villa; Kingsholm; Longlevens; Robinswood Hill
Gotherington
see Nottingham Hill
Great Lemhill, Lechlade
Great Lemhill Farm Roman site 196
Great Rissington
pit alignment 149
Great Witcombe
Mrs Clifford at 24; palaeolithic find 62, 75; Roman villa 19
Guiting Power
iron age pottery 152, 156; iron age site 150, 157; Tally Ho quarry 321
see also Wood House
Guns Mill, Blaisdon
furnace tower 319
Gwernvale, Powys
long barrow 96, 99

Hailes, Stanway
Abbey 249, 286; medieval pottery 265–267, 270
Ham and Stone
see Bevington Camp
Hamfallow
Wanswell Court 311
Ham Green, Avon
medieval pottery 255, 256, 266
Hampen, Shipton
flint artefact 72; mesolithic finds 76
Hampnett
barrows 132, 137; medieval settlement 282, **291**, 292
see also Burn Ground
Hamwih, Hampshire
Saxon Southampton 295, 296
Hanborough, Oxfordshire
iron age site 159
Hanley Swan, Hereford and Worcester
medieval pottery 267
Harcombe, Syde
mesolithic finds 71, 76
Hardwicke
Madams End Farm 310

Harescombe
medieval pottery 268
Haresfield
bronze age find 119; medieval/post-medieval pottery 268; medieval pottery 253, 254, 260; Starsmead Farmhouse 306
see also The Bulwarks; Ring Hill
Harford, Naunton
medieval settlement 287
Hawling
bronze age axe 115, **116**; bronze age(?) enclosure 146; bronze age pottery 121; medieval settlement **279**, 282, 289
Hazleton
long barrow 82, 86, **89**, **94**, 95, 96; mesolithic finds 69, 71, 74, 76
see also Salperton
Hereford, Hereford and Worcester
medieval pottery 254, 261–263, 266; Saxon occupation 252, 253
Hetty Pegler's Tump, Uley
long barrow **89**, 92, **94**
Hidcote Bartrim, Ebrington
Saxon cemetery **230**
High Brotheridge, Cranham
hillfort 164, 165
Hilcot, Withington
medieval settlement 287
Hillesley, Avon
Kilcott Mill 322; medieval pottery 254
Hinton
See Purton; Sharpness
Holm Castle, Tewkesbury
iron age date 164; medieval castle 249; medieval pottery 249, 264, 265
Horsley
see Ledgemore
Horton, Avon
Horton Court 305; Wood Lane Cottage 309, 314
Hound Tor, Dartmoor, Devon
settlement 289
Hucclecote (villa site), Gloucester
bronze age adze 117; bronze age settlement 121; iron age pottery 158; medieval pottery 269; Roman villa 19
Hullasey, Coates/Rodmarton
medieval pottery 249, 271; medieval settlement 276, **280**, 281, 283, 289, 305
Hull Plantations, Longborough
bronze age cemetery 131

Icomb
earthwork 149, 164, 165; Icomb Place 306, 311, 313; neolithic causewayed enclosure **89**, **90**, 91
Ireley Farm, Stanway
iron age pottery **155**, 157, 158, 171; iron age site 154, 160
Isles of Scilly, Cornwall
Mrs O'Neil at 33
Ivy Lodge, King's Stanley
beaker find 115; bronze age barrow 135

Juniper Hill, Edgeworth
dyke 149, 165

Kemble
railway housing 337; railway station 335; Saxon cemetery **230**
see also Ewen
Kempsford
bronze age spearhead 123; Saxon cemetery **230**
see also Whelford
King Arthur's Cave, Hereford and Worcester
palaeolithic finds 67
King's Beeches, Southam
iron age pottery, **153**, 154, 156, 157, 168; iron age site 150, 167, 168
Kingscote
mesolithic finds 76; Roman site 183, 185, 218, **218**, 219, 220
see also Newington Bagpath
Kingsholm, Gloucester
medieval pottery 248; royal palace 295; Saxon pottery 252
King's Stanley
Britannia cottage 314; church & Roman building 232; Crown Inn 311; dyke 149, 165; iron age pottery 158; medieval pottery 269; medieval town 294, **297**; moated site 249; Stanley mill **324**, 325, **326**
see also Ivy Lodge; Selsley
Kingswood
Abbey 286

Lancaut, Tidenham
Saxon site 235
see also Spital Mead
Langford Downs, Oxfordshire
iron age & Roman site 196
Lasborough, Westonbirt with Lasborough
medieval settlement 287
Lark Stoke, Warwickshire
medieval settlement 276
Laverstock, Wiltshire
medieval pottery 266
Leaze Farm, Lechlade
Roman settlement 208, 209
Lechlade
Halfpenny Bridge **329**, 330; iron age pottery 154; medieval pottery 271; medieval town 294, **297**; neolithic cursus **89**, 99; palaeolithic find 62, 75; Roman settlement 218, **218**; ring-ditches 131; St John's Bridge 329; Saxon pottery 240; Saxon settlement 210
see also Claydon Pike; Great Lemhill; Leaze Farm; The Loders; Roughground Farm; Thornhill Farm
Leckhampton
beaker find 115; Devil's Chimney 321; hillfort 143–145, 154, 165; iron age pottery 152, 157; Leckhampton Court 306; moated site 249; round barrow 160; Saxon cemetery **230**; stone quarry 320, 321, 335; tramroad 335

Ledgemore, Horsley
medieval settlement 287
Lemington, Todenham
medieval earthworks 283
Leonard Stanley
mesolithic finds 71, 76; Tudor House 308, 311, 312
Linch Hill Corner, Oxfordshire
neolithic burial 103
Littledean
medieval pottery 255, 263, 268; prison 337
Little Rissington
mammoth tusk 61
Little Sodbury, Avon
Little Sodbury Manor 306, 311
The Loders, Lechlade
neolithic evidence 101, 102
Longborough
see Hull Plantations
Longhope
Cains cottage 310; Hobbs' Quarries 50; medieval chimney caps 312
Longlevens, Gloucester
medieval pottery 269; palaeolithic find 62, **63**, 75
Long Newnton
mesolithic finds 69, 76
Longridge, Painswick
mesolithic finds 76
Lower Ditchford, Blockley
medieval settlement 281, 283, **286**, 287
Lower Norton, Weston Subedge
medieval settlement 282, 283, **284**
Lower Slaughter
bronze age pottery 117; medieval settlement 292; Roman settlement 218, **218**, 220; Saxon cemetery **230**
Lydney
Cookson Terrace 337; harbour 330; hillfort 143–145, 159, 165; iron age pottery 156, 157; iron bowl 162; medieval castle 249; medieval/post-medieval pottery 268; medieval pottery 255; Roman iron mine 318; Roman temple 221, 228
see also Whitecross Manor
Lyneham, Oxfordshire
hillfort 145

Maiden Castle, Dorset
neolithic barrow 105
Maisemore
medieval houses 310
Maiseyhampton
see Meysey Hampton
Malvern, Hereford and Worcester
currency bars 161
Malvern Chase, Hereford and Worcester
medieval pottery 257, 258, 260, 267
Manless Town, Brimpsfield
medieval pottery 269; medieval settlement 276, 285, 289
Marshfield, Avon
Castle Farm 309

Meon Hill, Warwickshire
 currency bars 161
Meysey Hampton, Maiseyhampton
 palaeolithic find 62, **65**, 75
Middle Ditchford, Blockley
 see Lower Ditchford
Midsummer Hill, Hereford and Worcester
 iron age pottery 156
Millhampost, Stanway
 iron age pottery 158, 171
Minchinhampton
 iron age site 148, 149, 165; medieval town 294, **297**
 see also Amberley Camp; Balls Green; Burleigh
Minety, Wiltshire
 medieval pottery 257, 260, 263
Miserden
 medieval pottery 271; mesolithic finds 271
 see also Bidfield; Camp; Whiteway
Moreton-in-Marsh
 bronze age spearhead 121; medieval town 294, 297, **297**, **298**
Moreton Valance
 post-medieval pottery 268
Mount Farm, Dorchester, Oxfordshire
 iron age & Roman site 206

Nailsworth
 Dunkirk Mill 325; Longfords Mill 325; medieval pottery 269
Naunton
 mesolithic finds 69, **70**, 75; stone quarry 320
 see also Aylworth; Harford
Newent
 bronze age palstave 119; medieval town **297**; post-medieval pottery 268; Saxon sculpture 235
Newington Bagpath, Kingscote
 castle 283
Newnham
 medieval town 294, 297, **297**, **298**; post-medieval pottery 268; Severn crossing 330
 see also Bullo Pill
Norbury Camp, Colesbourne
 hillfort 165
Norbury Camp, Northleach with Eastington
 hillfort 143, 145, 147, 160, 165
North Cerney
 round barrow **136**
 see also The Ditches
Northleach
 crop-marks 149, 150; medieval town 297, **297**, **298**, 302; prison **336**, 337
 see also Norbury Camp
North Leigh, Oxfordshire
 Mrs O'Neil at 37; Roman settlement 207
North Nibley
 bronze age spearhead 121
 see also Brackenbury Ditches
Norton
 see Wainlode
Norwich, Norfolk
 Saxon pottery 252

Notgrove
 round barrow 132; long barrow 19, **20**, 81, 84, 86, **89**, 92, **94**, 96, 98–100
Nottingham Hill, Gotherington
 bronze age hoard 123, 124; hillfort 143, 145–147, 165
Noverton Lane, Prestbury
 medieval pottery 270; moated site 249
Nympsfield long barrow, Frocester
 2, 19, 81, 83, 84, **89**, 92, **94**, 95, 98, 99, 104

Oddington
 bronze age axes 115, 116, **118**; Saxon cemetery **230**
Oldbury, Avon
 medieval settlement 276
Olveston
 Green Farm 309; Ostbridge Manor Farm 309, 313
Oxenton
 iron age pottery **153**, 154, 156, 157, 167; iron age site 150, 157, 166; tollhouse 327
Oxford, Oxfordshire
 medieval pottery 261

Painswick
 medieval pottery 249, 269; medieval town 294, 297, **297**; mesolithic finds 76; Painswick Beacon hillfort 165
 see also Edge; Longridge
Park Street, Hertfordshire
 Roman villa 33
Pauntley
 see Brand Green
The Peak Camp, Cowley
 neolithic causewayed enclosure 82, **89**, **90**, 91, 92, 98, 99, 146
Pen-y-Wyrlod, Powys
 long barrow 96
Pershore, Hereford and Worcester
 medieval pottery 263
Pinbury, Duntisbourne Rouse
 hillfort 165
Poles Wood, Swell
 East long barrow 92; South long barrow 92, 100
Poole Keynes
 palaeolithic find 62, 75
Postlip, Winchcombe
 mill 322
Pottersbury, Wotton-under-Edge
 place-name 260
Prestbury
 beaker find 115; medieval town **297**
 see also Noverton Lane; Prestbury Manor
Prestbury Manor, Prestbury
 medieval pottery 255, 270; moated site 249, 305; Mrs O'Neil at 34
Puckham, Sevenhampton
 mesolithic finds 69, **70**, 75
Pucklechurch, Avon
 Saxon iron-working 239
Purton, Hinton
 Severn crossing 330

Quedgeley
  Field Court 309; Field Place 311; medieval settlement 282; Packers Cottage 314
Quenington
  medieval pottery 271

Ramsbury, Wiltshire
  Saxon pottery 251
Ranbury Ring, Ampney St Peter
  hillfort 143, 165
Randwick
  dyke 149, 165; long barrow 92, **94**, 104
Redmarley D'Abitot
  Bury Court 305; medieval house 310, 312, **313**,
  314
Rendcomb
  see Shawswell
Revesby, Lincolnshire
  Abbey 287
Ring Hill, Haresfield
  discounted hillfort 164
Robinswood Hill, Gloucester
  brick-clay 52; iron age pottery 154
Rodborough
  bronze age axe 116; bronze bands 162; iron age
  pottery 159; medieval pottery 269
  see also Butterrow
Rodmarton
  long barrow 19, 81, 84, **89**, 99
  see also Hullasey
Roel, Sudeley
  hillfort 146, 165
Roughground Farm, Lechlade
  iron age site 150, 203; Mrs Jones at 35; neolithic
  evidence 101–103, 203; Roman site 195–197,
  203, **204**, 205, 206, 209
Ruardean
  16thC pottery 268
Ruspidge
  see Soudley Camp

St Briavels
  bronze age battle-axe 117; medieval castle 249,
  312; medieval pottery 255, 268; medieval town
  **297**; Roman altar 235
Saintbury
  bronze age barrow 132
Sale's Lot, Withington
  long barrow 82, 84, 86, 87, **89**, 92, 100, 135
Salisbury, Wiltshire
  medieval pottery 265
Salmonsbury, Bourton-on-the-Water
  currency bars 161; iron age enclosure 143–148,
  151, 157, 160, 165; iron age pottery 154, 156,
  157, 159; limestone pyramid 163; neolithic
  evidence 81, 100, **101**; Mrs O'Neil at 31, **32**,
  141; Saxon cemetery **230**
Salperton, Hazleton
  mesolithic finds 76
Saltford, Avon
  medieval pottery 261

Saltway Barn, Bibury
  long barrow 82
Sandhurst
  medieval houses 307
  see also Bengrove Farm
Sandy Lane, Charlton Kings
  bronze age site 121; iron age site 154
Santhill Gravel Pit, Bourton-on-the-Water
  palaeolithic find 64, 75
Sapperton
  medieval pottery 271; tunnel 330
Saul Junction, Fretherne with Saul
  canals 333
Selsley, King's Stanley
  church 325
Sennington, Sevenhampton
  medieval settlement 276
Sevenhampton
  medieval pottery 270; mesolithic finds 69, 70, 72,
  75
  see also Puckham; Sennington; Soundborough
Sezincote
  bronze age barrows **131**, 132; medieval settlement
  282, 287
Shab Hill, Cowley
  mesolithic finds 76
Shakenoak villa, Oxfordshire
  Roman villa 196
Sharpness, Hinton
  canal and docks 333
Shawswell, Rendcomb
  medieval earthworks 283
Shenberrow, Stanton
  hillfort 143–145, 147, 165; iron age pottery 152,
  154
Sherborne
  medieval settlement 282
Shipton
  see Hampen; Shipton Solers
Shipton Solers, Shipton
  medieval settlement 282
Shirehampton, Avon
  palaeolithic finds 64
Shurdington
  sand-pit 53
Siddington
  iron age pottery 154
Snail Down, Wiltshire
  bronze age cemetery 135
Snowshill
  bronze age barrows 132; bronze age finds 113, 116,
  117
Soldier's Grave, Frocester
  round barrow **101**, 103, 134–136
Soldiers' Grave, Tidenham
  bronze age barrow 117, 133
Soudley Camp, Ruspidge
  hillfort 165
Soundborough, Sevenhampton
  mesolithic finds 76
Southam

see Cleeve Cloud; Cleeve Common; Cleeve Hill; King's Beeches; Stables Quarry
Southampton, Hampshire
    Saxon town 238
    see also Hamwih
South Cerney
    bronze age finds 119, 121; palaeolithic finds 62, 75
    see also Cerney Wick
Southrop
    Southrop Manor 305
Spital Mead, Lancaut, Tidenham
    hillfort 165
Stables Quarry, Southam
    iron age pottery **153**, 156, 168
Stamford, Lincolnshire
    Saxon pottery 252
Standish
    medieval pottery 268; Standish Vicarage 313
    see also Arlebrook
Stanton
    post-medieval pottery 270
    see also Shenberrow
Stanway
    medieval pottery 270
    see also Hailes; Ireley Farm; Millhampost; Upper Coscombe
Staunton
    bronze age axe 116; medieval settlement 288
Stinchcombe
    medieval pottery 269
Stoke Orchard
    medieval pottery 255, 263, 270
Stonehouse
    brick-works 52; medieval pottery 268
Stoneleigh, Warwickshire
    Abbey 287
Stow-on-the-Wold
    medieval pottery 270; medieval town 294, **297**
Stroud
    Cheapside brewery 322; Ebley Mill **323**, 325; Lodgemore Mill 325; medieval pottery 269; medieval town 294, **297**; mesolithic finds 76; Wallbridge Mill 325
Sudeley
    bronze age finds 122; medieval settlement 282; mill 322;
    see also Belas Knap; Roel
Swell
    bronze age barrows 132, 133, 135, 137; bronze age dagger 117; bronze age pottery 121, 122; medieval pottery 270; mesolithic finds 72, 75; Royce collection from 72, 81; Saxon cemeteries **230**
    see also Cow Common; Poles Wood
Syde
    mesolithic finds 71, 76
Symond's Hall Farm, Wotton-under-Edge
    medieval pottery 269; mesolithic finds 76
Symonds Yat, English Bicknor
    cave site(?) 67; hillfort 165
Syreford, Whittington

iron age pottery 151, **153**, 158, 169; mesolithic finds 69, **70**, 71, 75

Temple Guiting
    Four Barrow Field round barrows 132; medieval farms 282; pit alignment 149; stone quarry 320;
    see also Bevan's Quarry; Chalk Hill
Tetbury
    medieval town 294, 297, **297**
Tewkesbury
    bronze age palstave 119; bronze jug 161; iron age pottery 158; King John's Bridge 329; medieval pottery 270;medieval town 294, **297**, 299, 301; Mythe Bridge **328**, 329; neolithic evidence 101, **101**, 103; Saxon hall 234; Saxon town 237, 295, 296, **296**
    see also Holm Castle; Windmill Hill
Thetford, Norfolk
    Saxon pottery 252
Thornbury, Avon
    Saxon town 237
Thornhill Farm, Lechlade
    Roman settlement 208, 209
Thrupp
    see Brimscombe
Tidenham
    bronze age palstave 119; flint artefacts 74; post-medieval pottery 268; Saxon church 235
    see also Beachley; Lancaut; Soldiers' Tump; Spital Mead
Tirley
    see Tump Farm
Toddington
    medieval settlement 282
Todenham
    see Lemington
Tog Hill, Avon
    mesolithic finds 69
Tormarton, Avon
    bronze age finds 121
Towbury Hill, Twyning
    hillfort 143, 165
Trewsbury, Coates
    hillfort 165; medieval pottery 271
Troublehouse Covert, Cherington
    mesolithic finds 76
Tump Farm, Tirley
    medieval barn 308
Twyning
    palaeolithic finds 66; quarry 52
    see also Towbury Hill

Uley
    bronze age barrow 132; Romano-celtic temple 162, 221, 228; Saxon pottery 241
    see also Hetty Pegler's tump; Uley Bury
Uley Bury, Uley
    currency bars 161; hillfort 143–145, 147, 148, 157, 159, 164, 165; iron age pottery 152, 157; neolithic evidence 91

Upper Coscombe, Stanway
  stone quarry 320
Upper Ditchford, Blockley
  medieval settlement 281, 283, **285**, 287
Upper Slaughter
  medieval castle 249; medieval pottery 270
  see also Copse Hill; Eyeford Hill
Upton, Blockley
  medieval pottery 255, 261, 263, 265, 267, 270;
    medieval settlement 258, 276, 281, **281**, 283,
    287, 305; Saxon pottery 241, 270; Saxon settle-
    ment 234
Upton St Leonards
  medieval houses 310

Wainlode, Norton
  river section 51
Warrington, Cheshire
  medieval town 301
Watling Street, Canon's Park, London
  Roman road 33
Wayland's Smithy, Oxfordshire
  long barrow 96
Welshbury, Blaisdon
  hillfort 165
Westbury-on-Severn
  Garden Cliff section 51
Westbury-on-Trym, Avon
  bronze age hoard 116
West Dean
  see Bicshead; Bicslade; Blackpool Bridge; Dar-
    khill
Westerleigh, Avon
  Rodford Hill Farm 306, 309
Westington, Chipping Campden
  stone quarry 320, **320**
Westonbirt with Lasborough
  medieval settlement 282; mesolithic finds 76
  see also Lasborough
Weston Subedge
  bronze age axe 121; medieval manor 283
  see also Lower Norton
Weston under Penyard, Hereford and Worcester
  Ariconium Roman settlement 318
Wharram Percy, Yorkshire
  medieval settlement 289
Whelford, Kempsford
  crop-marks 195
Whitecliffe, Coleford
  blast-furnace 319
Whitecross Manor, Lydney
  medieval/post-medieval pottery 268
Whiteway, Miserden
  mesolithic finds 76

Whitminster
  Swan Inn 308
Whittington
  bronze age axe 116; medieval settlement 282, 287,
    **288**, 289; Saxon & medieval pottery 270
  see also Syreford; Wycomb
Willersey
  hillfort 143, 165; iron age pottery 158; long barrow
    92
Winchcombe
  medieval pottery 253, 255, 258, 262–265; mediev-
    al/post–medieval pottery 270; medieval town
    **297**; Saxon (?) cemetery 234; Saxon minster
    232; Saxon pottery 252, 253, 270; Saxon town
    225, 236, 237, 295, 296, **296**
  see also Postlip
Winchester, Hampshire
  medieval town 300; Saxon pottery 252; Saxon
    town 296
Windmill Hill, Tewkesbury
  bronze age settlement 121
Windrush
  Windrush Camp hillfort 145, 165
Withington
  Roman & Saxon settlement 186, 187, 227, 289;
    Saxon cemetery **230**
  see also Foxcote Manor; Hilcot; Sale's Lot
Wolvercote, Oxfordshire
  palaeolithic findspot 62
Wontley, Bishops Cleeve
  medieval settlement 287
Woodchester
  church & Roman Building 232; medieval pottery
    269
  see also Bown Hill
Wood House, Guiting Power
  iron age pottery **155**, 156, 170; iron age site 150,
    160
Woolaston
  medieval pottery 268
Worcester, Hereford and Worcester
  medieval diocese 225; medieval pottery 256, 260–
    263, 266; Saxon bishopric 232; Saxon pottery
    252
Wotton-under-Edge
  medieval pottery 254; medieval town 297, **297**,
    **298**, 301; mesolithic finds 76; post-medieval
    pottery 269
  see also Pottersbury; Symond's Hall Farm
Wyck Rissington
  bronze age barrow **133**
Wycomb, Whittington
  iron age pottery 159; Roman settlement 218, **218**,
    219–221; Saxon pottery 251